CASE CLOSED

VOLUME 5

Gosho Aoyama

Case Briefing:

Subject: Jimmy Kudo a.k.a. Conan Edogawa
Occupation: High School Student/Detective
Special Skills: Analytical thinking and deductive reasoning, Soccer
Equipment: Bow Tie Voice Transmitter, Super Sneakers, Homing Glasses, Stretchy Suspenders

The subject is hot on the trail of a pair of suspicious men in black when he is attacked from behind and administered a strange substance which physically transforms him into a first grader. When the subject confides in the eccentric inventor Dr. Agasa, they decide to keep the subject's true identity a secret for the safety of everyone around him. Assuming the new identity of first-grader Conan Edogawa, the subject continues to assist the police force on their most baffling cases. The only problem is that most crime-solving professionals won't take a little kid's advice!

Table of Contents

CONFIDEN

CASE CLOSED

Volume 5
Shonen Sunday Edition

Story and Art by GOSHO AOYAMA

MEITANTEI CONAN Vol. 5
by Gosho AOYAMA
© 1994 Gosho AOYAMA
All rights reserved.
Original Japanese edition published by SHOGAKUKAN.
English translation rights in the United States of America, Canada, the United Kingdom,
Ireland, Australia and New Zealand arranged with SHOGAKUKAN.

English Adaptation
Naoko Amemiya

Translation
Joe Yamazaki

Touch-up & Lettering
Walden Wong

Cover Design
Veronica Casson

Interior Graphics & Layout Design
Andrea Rice

Editor
Andy Nakatani

Printed in Canada

Published by VIZ Media, LLC
P.O. Box 77010
San Francisco, CA 94107

10 9 8 7 6
First printing, April 2005
Sixth printing, August 2019

PARENTAL ADVISORY
CASE CLOSED is rated T+ for Older Teen
and is recommended for ages 16 and up.
This volume contains realistic and graphic
violence.

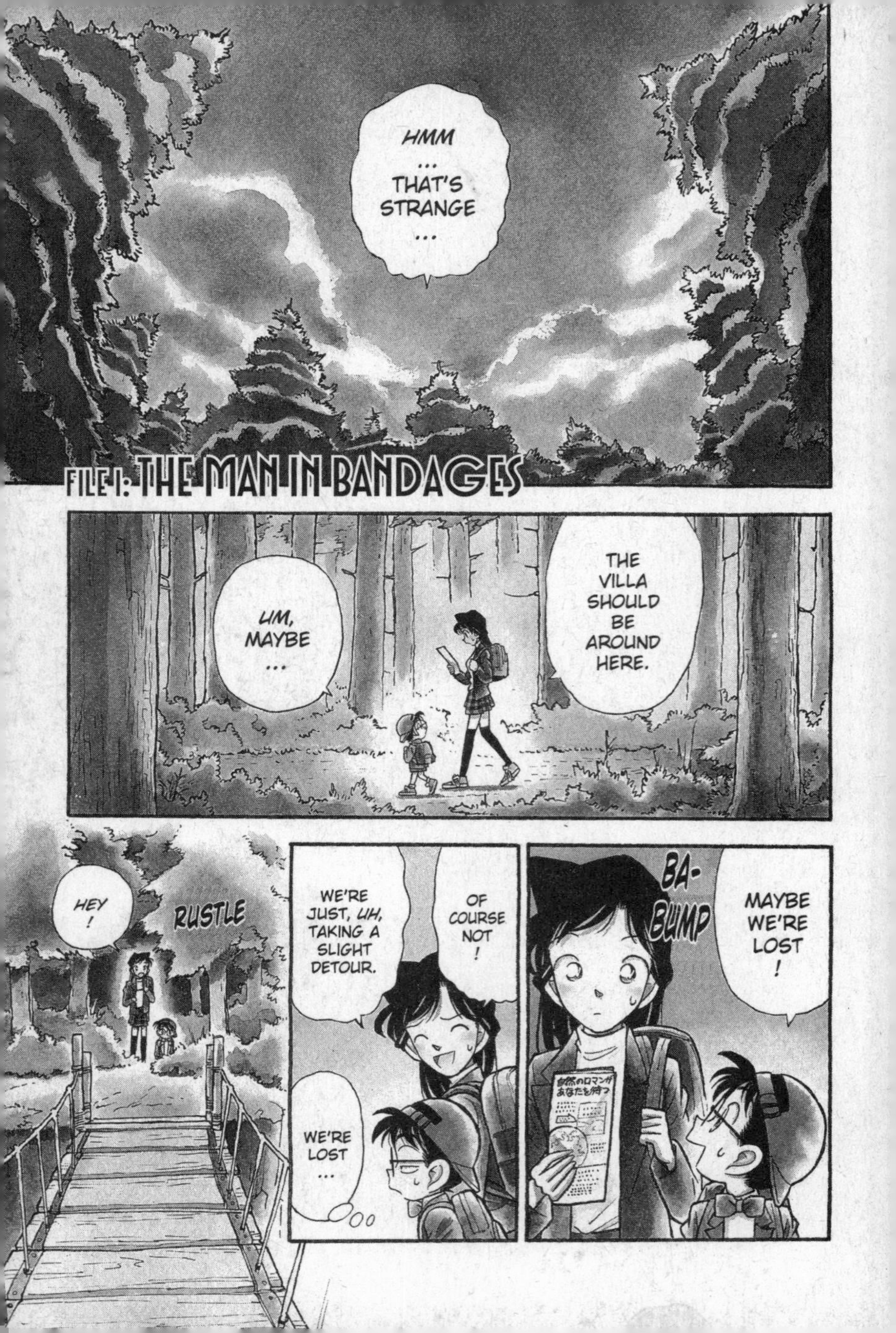
HMM ... THAT'S STRANGE ...
FILE 1: THE MAN IN BANDAGES
THE VILLA SHOULD BE AROUND HERE.
UM, MAYBE ...
BA-BUMP
MAYBE WE'RE LOST !
自然のロマンがあなたを待つ
OF COURSE NOT !
WE'RE JUST, UH, TAKING A SLIGHT DETOUR.
WE'RE LOST ...
HEY !
RUSTLE

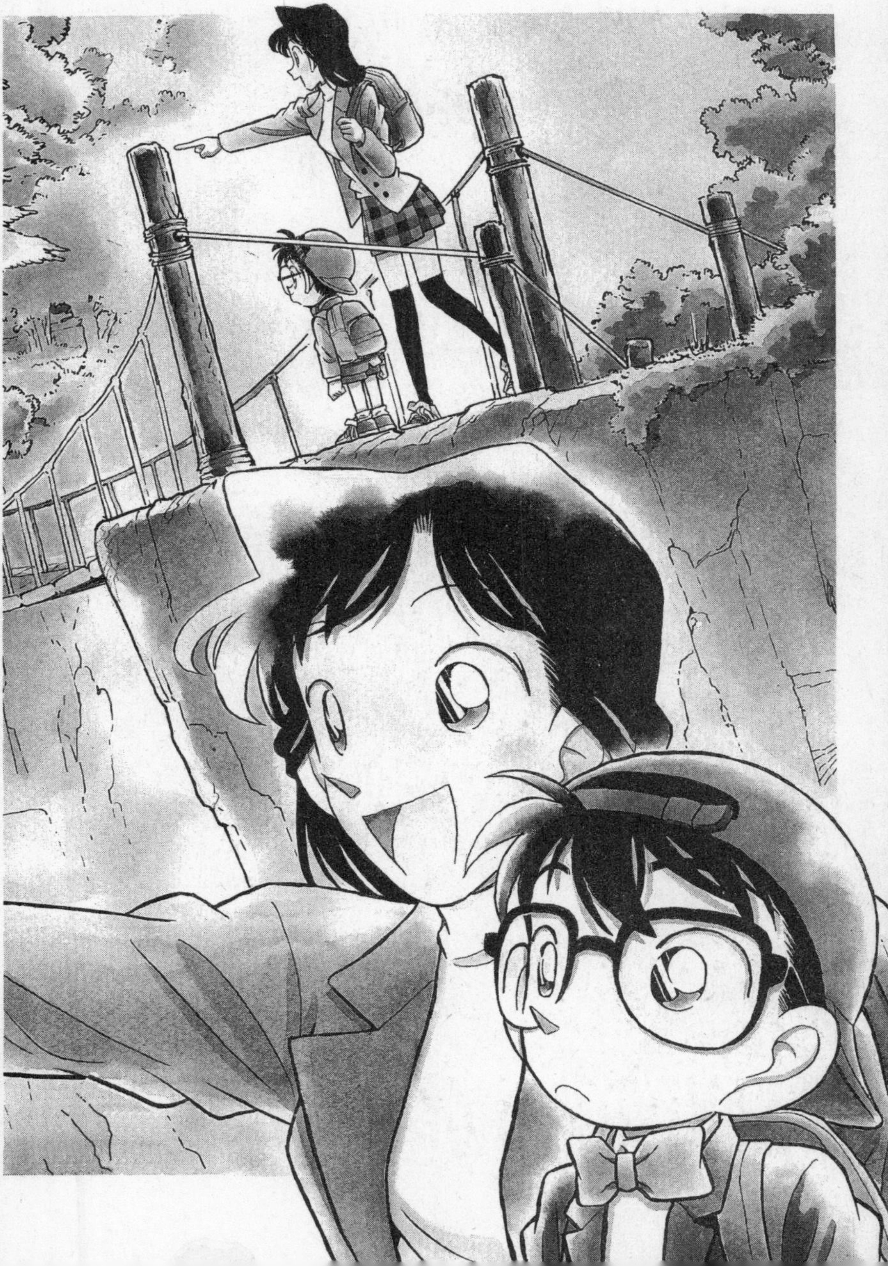

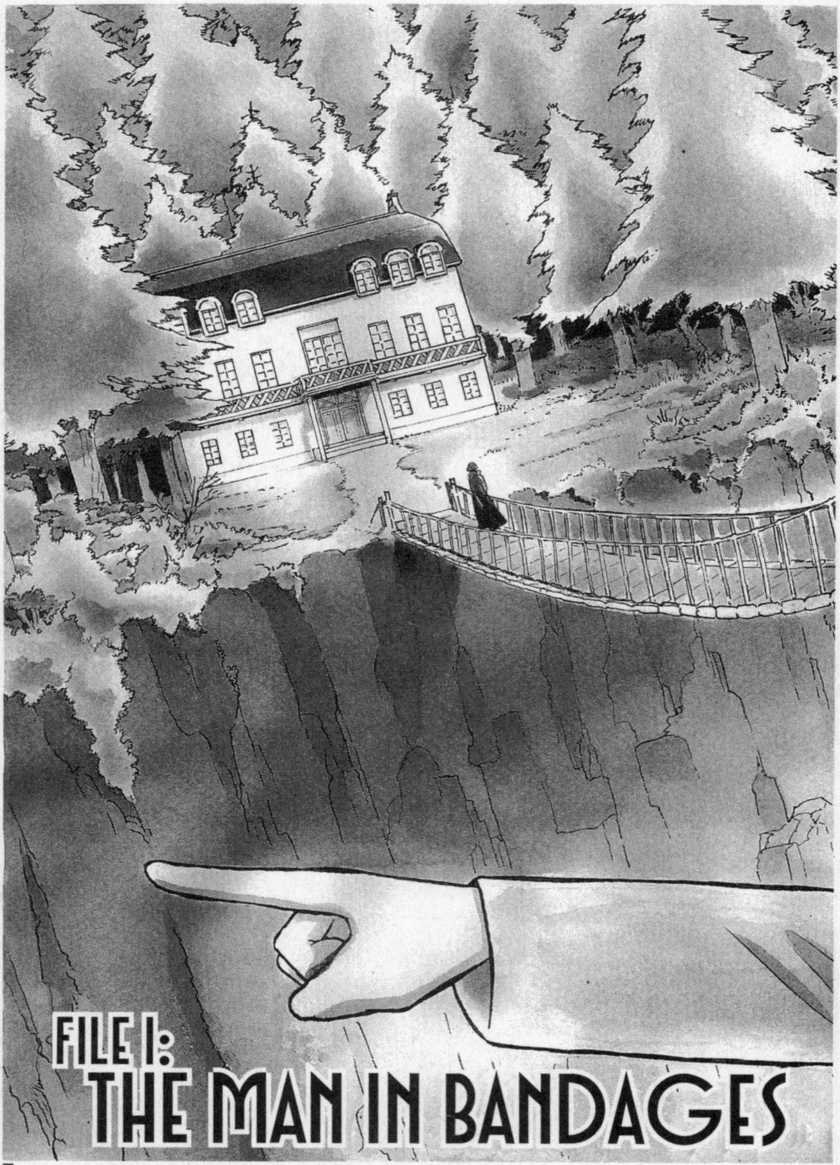
FILE 1:
THE MAN IN BANDAGES

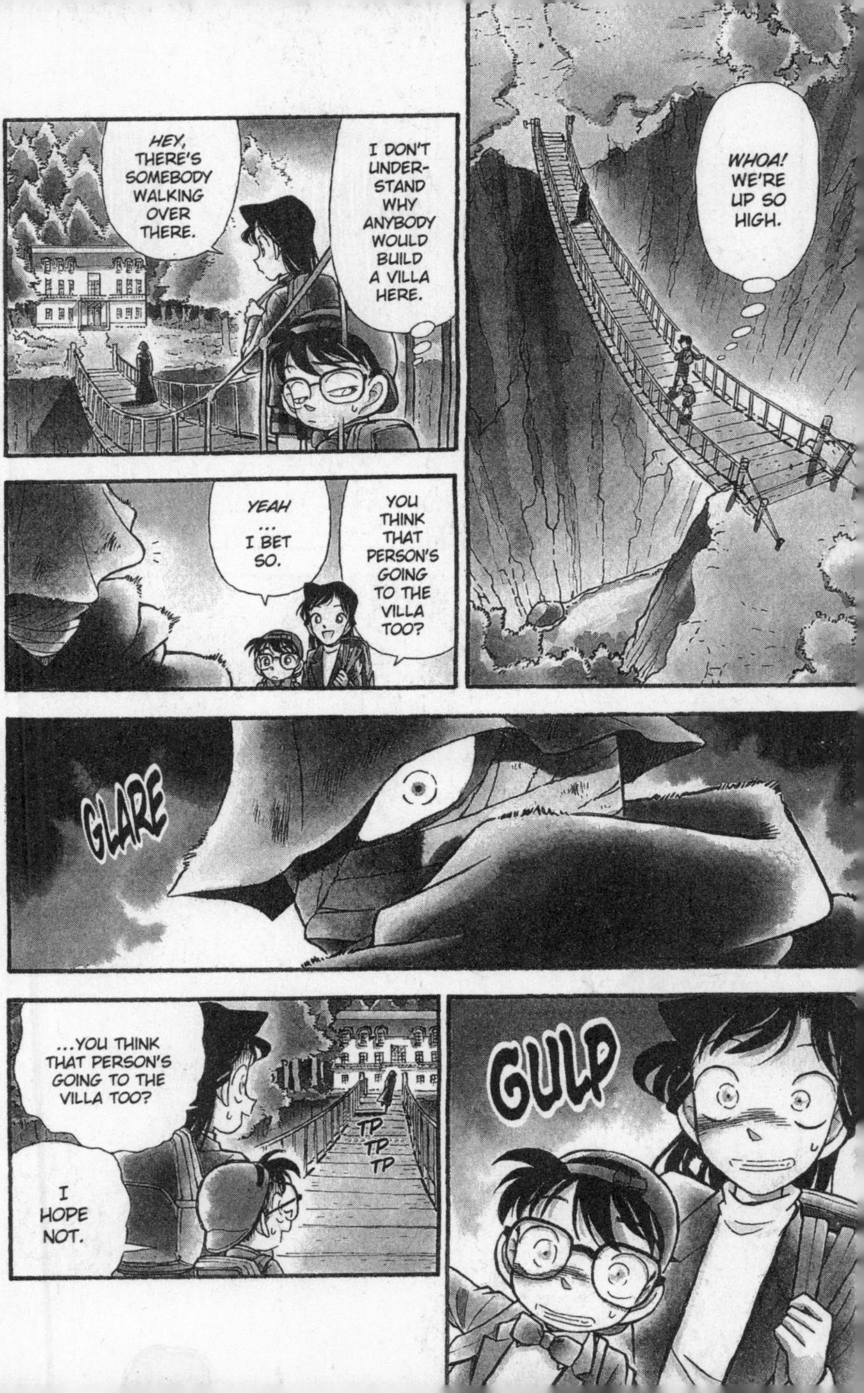
WHOA! WE'RE UP SO HIGH.
I DON'T UNDER-STAND WHY ANYBODY WOULD BUILD A VILLA HERE.
HEY, THERE'S SOMEBODY WALKING OVER THERE.
YOU THINK THAT PERSON'S GOING TO THE VILLA TOO?
YEAH ... I BET SO.
GLARE
GULP
...YOU THINK THAT PERSON'S GOING TO THE VILLA TOO?
TP TP TP
I HOPE NOT.

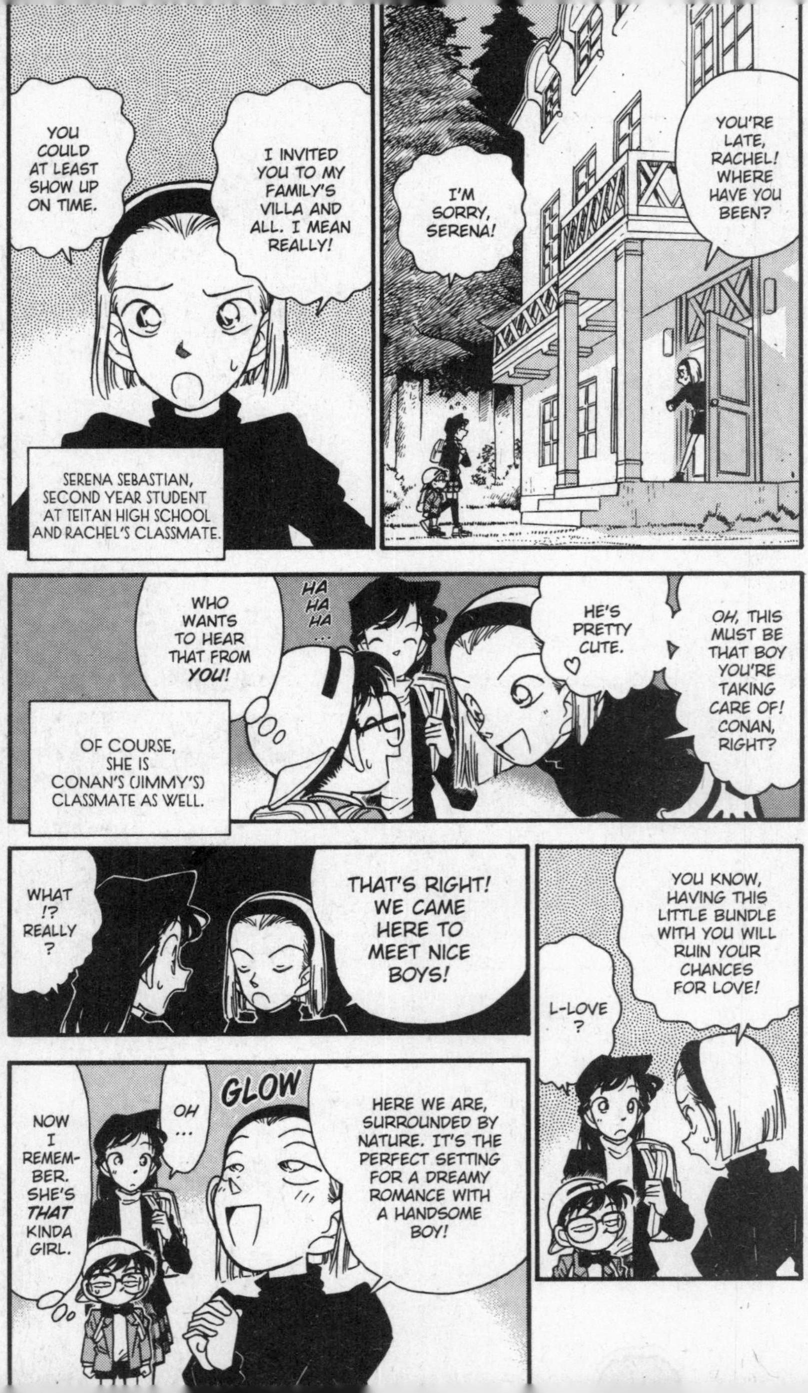
YOU'RE LATE, RACHEL! WHERE HAVE YOU BEEN?
I'M SORRY, SERENA!
I INVITED YOU TO MY FAMILY'S VILLA AND ALL. I MEAN REALLY!
YOU COULD AT LEAST SHOW UP ON TIME.
SERENA SEBASTIAN, SECOND YEAR STUDENT AT TEITAN HIGH SCHOOL AND RACHEL'S CLASSMATE.
OH, THIS MUST BE THAT BOY YOU'RE TAKING CARE OF! CONAN, RIGHT?
HE'S PRETTY CUTE.
HA HA HA ...
WHO WANTS TO HEAR THAT FROM *YOU*!
OF COURSE, SHE IS CONAN'S (JIMMY'S) CLASSMATE AS WELL.
YOU KNOW, HAVING THIS LITTLE BUNDLE WITH YOU WILL RUIN YOUR CHANCES FOR LOVE!
L-LOVE?
THAT'S RIGHT! WE CAME HERE TO MEET NICE BOYS!
WHAT!? REALLY?
HERE WE ARE, SURROUNDED BY NATURE. IT'S THE PERFECT SETTING FOR A DREAMY ROMANCE WITH A HANDSOME BOY!
GLOW
OH ...
NOW I REMEMBER. SHE'S *THAT* KINDA GIRL.

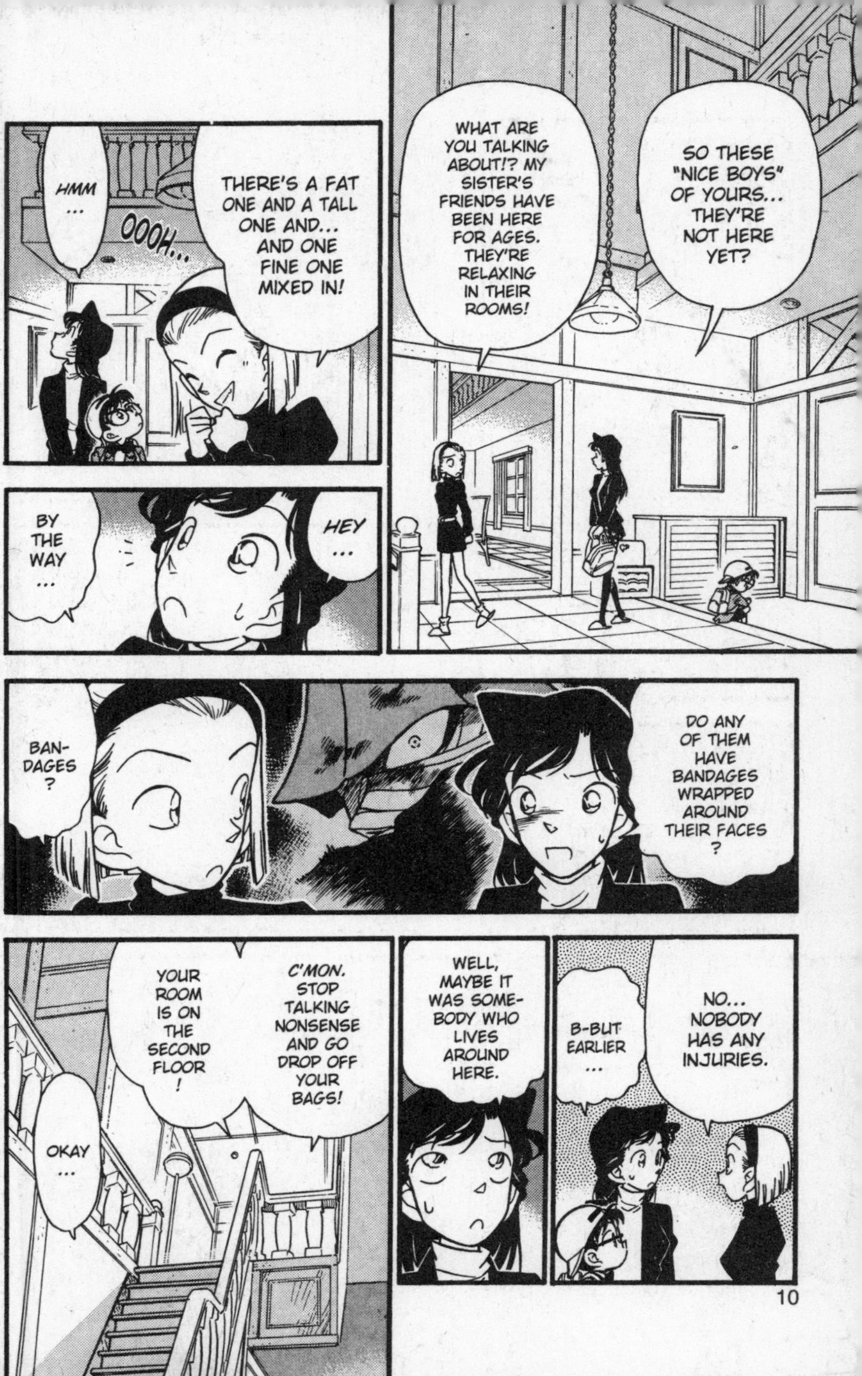
SO THESE "NICE BOYS" OF YOURS... THEY'RE NOT HERE YET?
WHAT ARE YOU TALKING ABOUT!? MY SISTER'S FRIENDS HAVE BEEN HERE FOR AGES. THEY'RE RELAXING IN THEIR ROOMS!
THERE'S A FAT ONE AND A TALL ONE AND... AND ONE FINE ONE MIXED IN!
OOOH...
HMM...
HEY...
BY THE WAY...
DO ANY OF THEM HAVE BANDAGES WRAPPED AROUND THEIR FACES?
BAN-DAGES?
NO... NOBODY HAS ANY INJURIES.
B-BUT EARLIER...
WELL, MAYBE IT WAS SOME-BODY WHO LIVES AROUND HERE.
C'MON. STOP TALKING NONSENSE AND GO DROP OFF YOUR BAGS!
YOUR ROOM IS ON THE SECOND FLOOR!
OKAY...

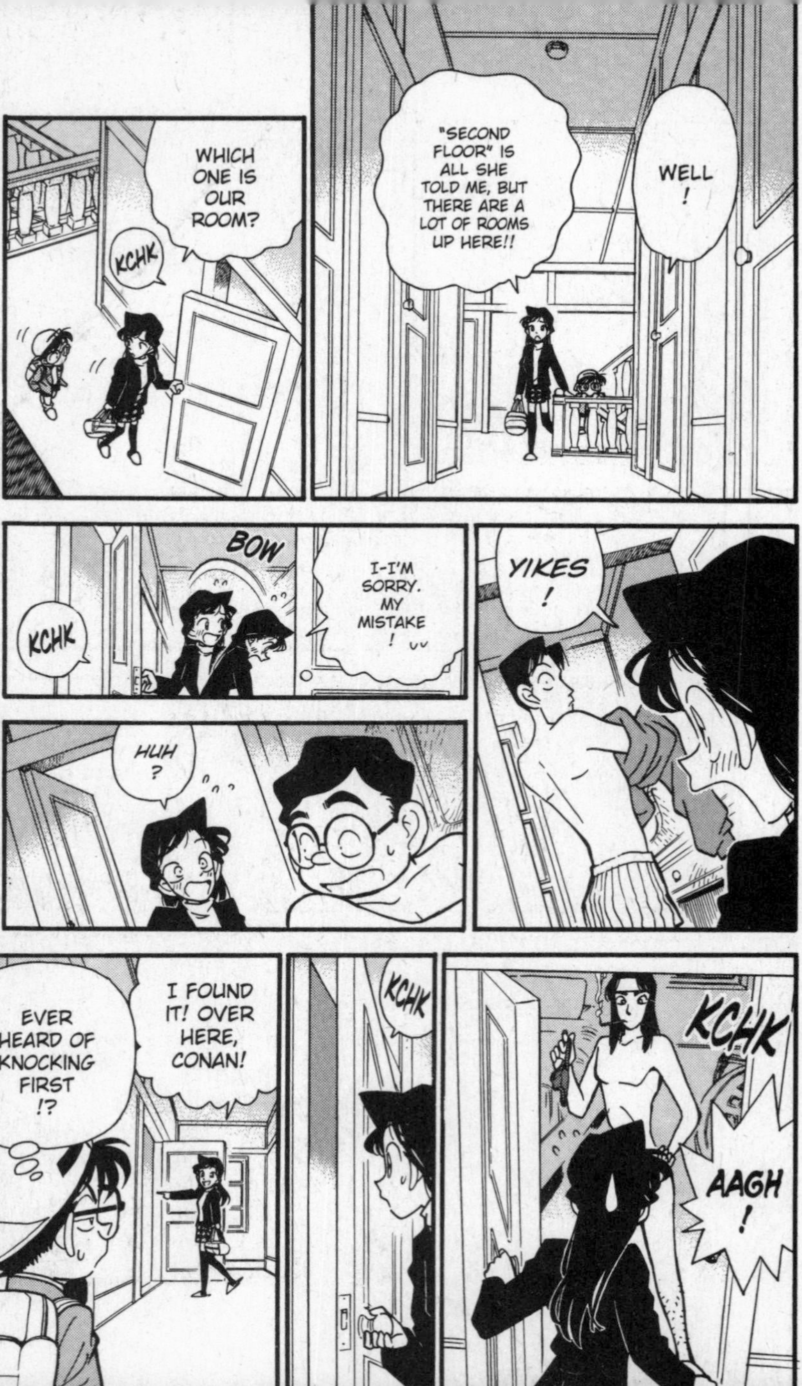
WELL!
"SECOND FLOOR" IS ALL SHE TOLD ME, BUT THERE ARE A LOT OF ROOMS UP HERE!!
WHICH ONE IS OUR ROOM?
KCHK
YIKES!
I-I'M SORRY. MY MISTAKE!
BOW
KCHK
HUH?
KCHK
AAGH!
KCHK
I FOUND IT! OVER HERE, CONAN!
EVER HEARD OF KNOCKING FIRST!?

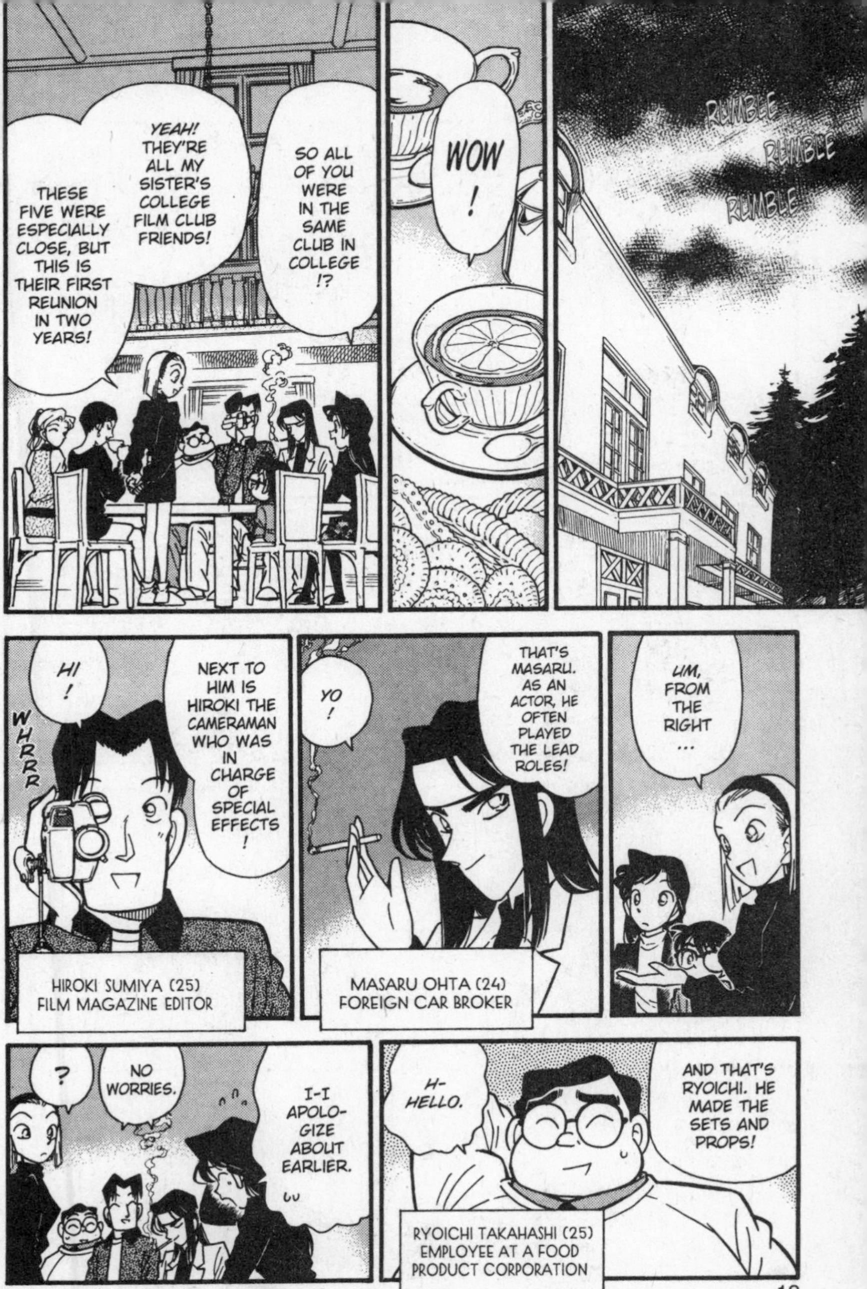
RUMBLE
RUMBLE
RUMBLE
WOW!
SO ALL OF YOU WERE IN THE SAME CLUB IN COLLEGE!?
YEAH! THEY'RE ALL MY SISTER'S COLLEGE FILM CLUB FRIENDS!
THESE FIVE WERE ESPECIALLY CLOSE, BUT THIS IS THEIR FIRST REUNION IN TWO YEARS!
UM, FROM THE RIGHT...
THAT'S MASARU. AS AN ACTOR, HE OFTEN PLAYED THE LEAD ROLES!
YO!
MASARU OHTA (24) FOREIGN CAR BROKER
NEXT TO HIM IS HIROKI THE CAMERAMAN WHO WAS IN CHARGE OF SPECIAL EFFECTS!
HI!
WHRRR
HIROKI SUMIYA (25) FILM MAGAZINE EDITOR
AND THAT'S RYOICHI. HE MADE THE SETS AND PROPS!
H-HELLO.
RYOICHI TAKAHASHI (25) EMPLOYEE AT A FOOD PRODUCT CORPORATION
I-I APOLOGIZE ABOUT EARLIER.
NO WORRIES.
?

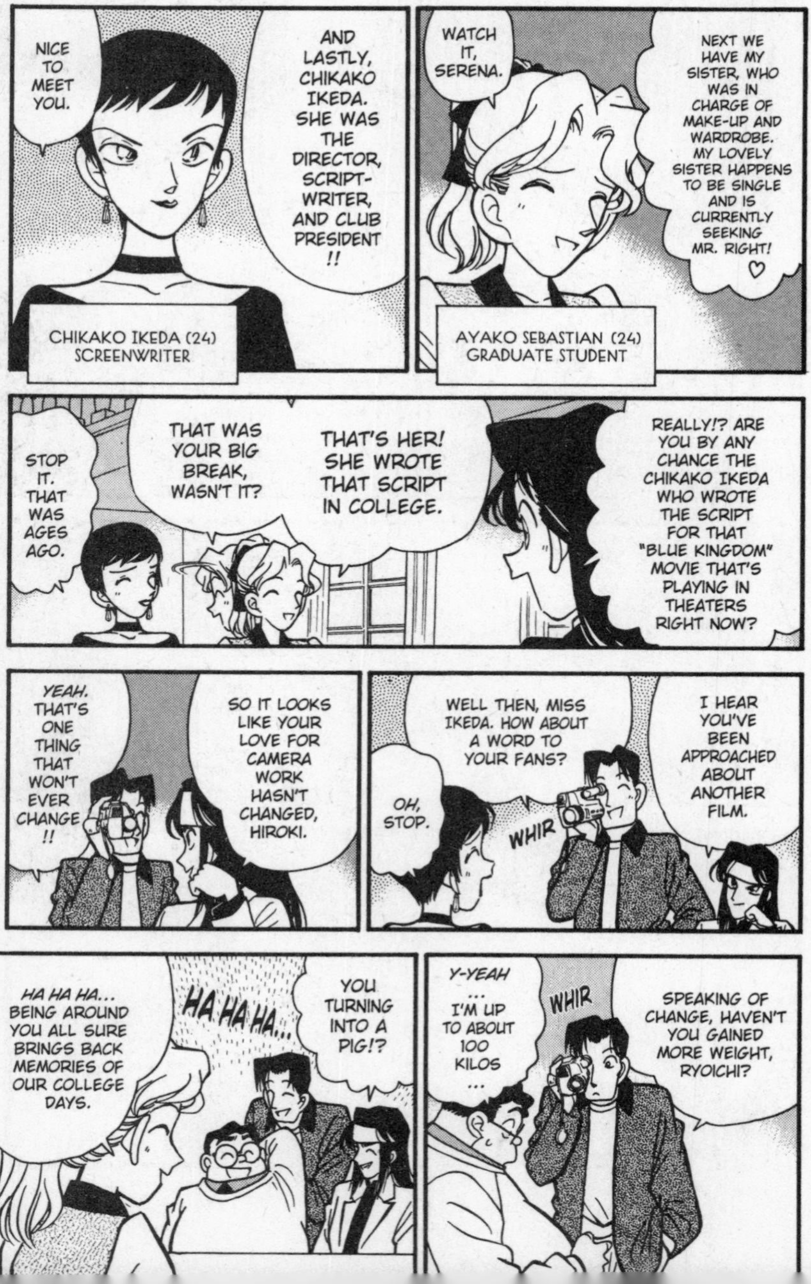

NEXT WE HAVE MY SISTER, WHO WAS IN CHARGE OF MAKE-UP AND WARDROBE. MY LOVELY SISTER HAPPENS TO BE SINGLE AND IS CURRENTLY SEEKING MR. RIGHT! ♡
WATCH IT, SERENA.
AYAKO SEBASTIAN (24) GRADUATE STUDENT
AND LASTLY, CHIKAKO IKEDA. SHE WAS THE DIRECTOR, SCRIPT-WRITER, AND CLUB PRESIDENT !!
NICE TO MEET YOU.
CHIKAKO IKEDA (24) SCREENWRITER
REALLY!? ARE YOU BY ANY CHANCE THE CHIKAKO IKEDA WHO WROTE THE SCRIPT FOR THAT "BLUE KINGDOM" MOVIE THAT'S PLAYING IN THEATERS RIGHT NOW?
THAT'S HER! SHE WROTE THAT SCRIPT IN COLLEGE.
THAT WAS YOUR BIG BREAK, WASN'T IT?
STOP IT. THAT WAS AGES AGO.
I HEAR YOU'VE BEEN APPROACHED ABOUT ANOTHER FILM.
WELL THEN, MISS IKEDA. HOW ABOUT A WORD TO YOUR FANS?
WHIR
OH, STOP.
SO IT LOOKS LIKE YOUR LOVE FOR CAMERA WORK HASN'T CHANGED, HIROKI.
YEAH. THAT'S ONE THING THAT WON'T EVER CHANGE !!
SPEAKING OF CHANGE, HAVEN'T YOU GAINED MORE WEIGHT, RYOICHI?
WHIR
Y-YEAH ... I'M UP TO ABOUT 100 KILOS ...
YOU TURNING INTO A PIG!?
HA HA HA...
HA HA HA... BEING AROUND YOU ALL SURE BRINGS BACK MEMORIES OF OUR COLLEGE DAYS.

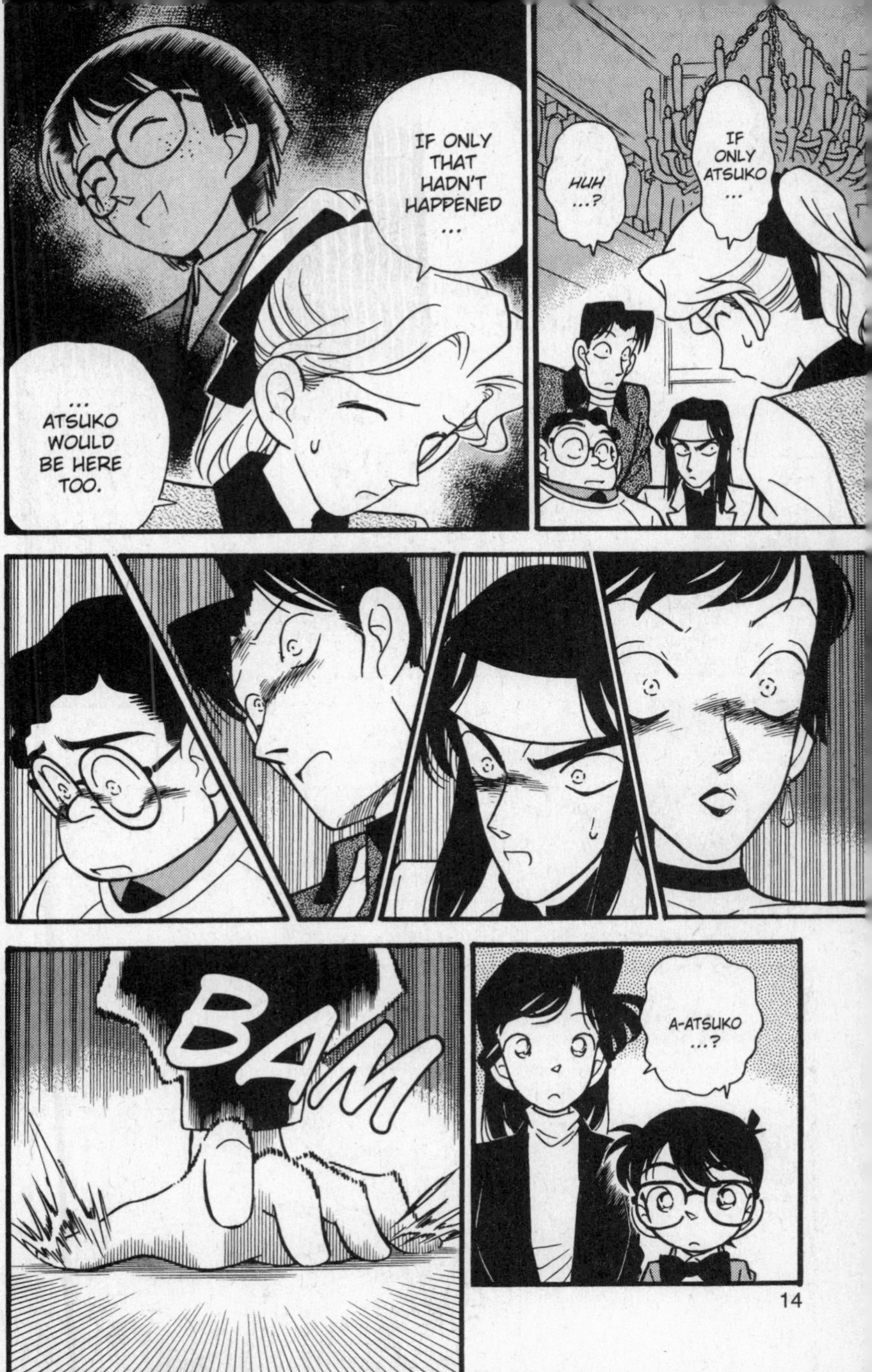
IF ONLY ATSUKO ...
HUH ...?
IF ONLY THAT HADN'T HAPPENED ...
... ATSUKO WOULD BE HERE TOO.
A-ATSUKO ...?
BAM

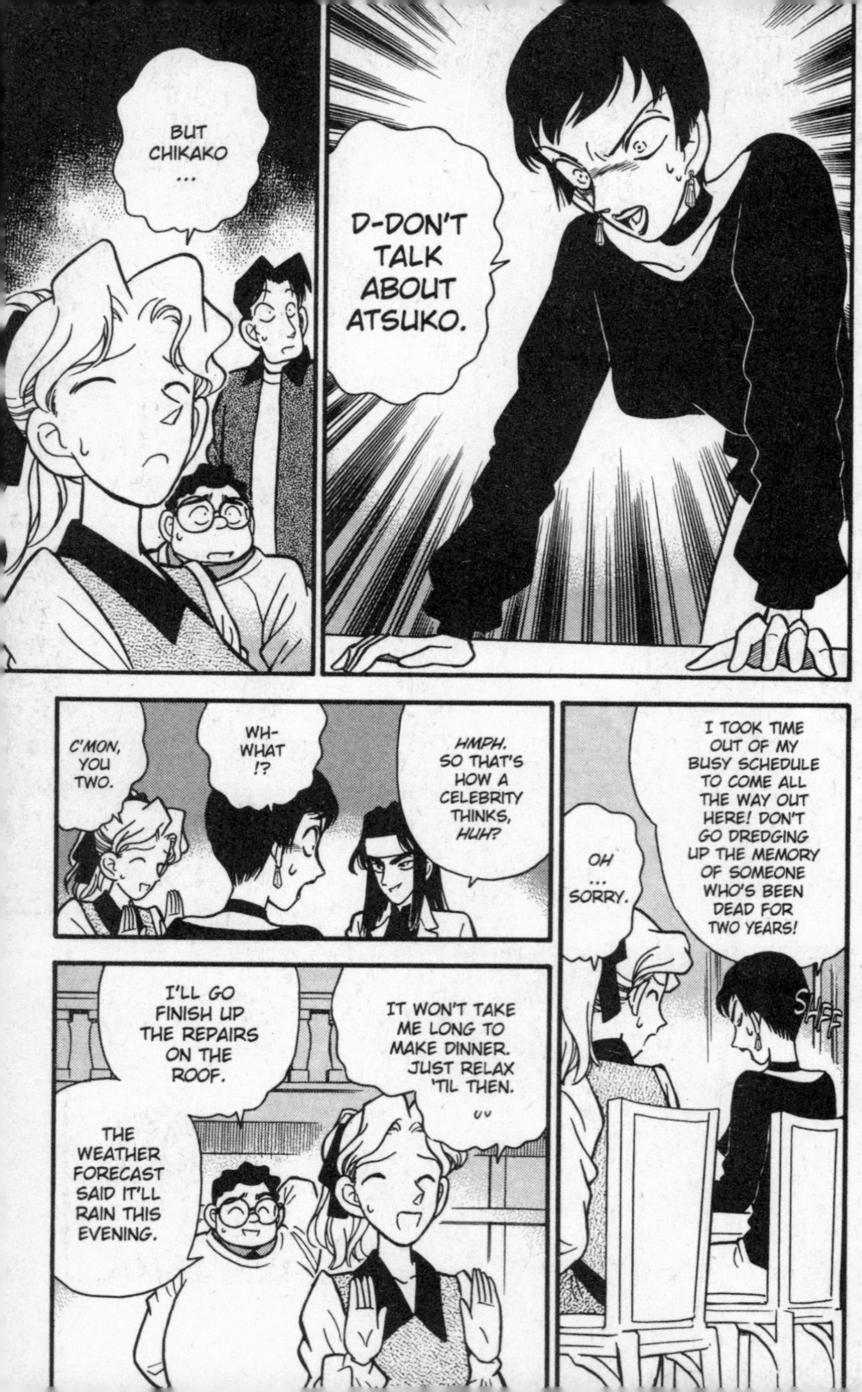
D-DON'T TALK ABOUT ATSUKO.
BUT CHIKAKO ...
I TOOK TIME OUT OF MY BUSY SCHEDULE TO COME ALL THE WAY OUT HERE! DON'T GO DREDGING UP THE MEMORY OF SOMEONE WHO'S BEEN DEAD FOR TWO YEARS!
OH ... SORRY.
SHFF
HMPH. SO THAT'S HOW A CELEBRITY THINKS, HUH?
WH-WHAT !?
C'MON, YOU TWO.
IT WON'T TAKE ME LONG TO MAKE DINNER. JUST RELAX 'TIL THEN.
I'LL GO FINISH UP THE REPAIRS ON THE ROOF.
THE WEATHER FORECAST SAID IT'LL RAIN THIS EVENING.

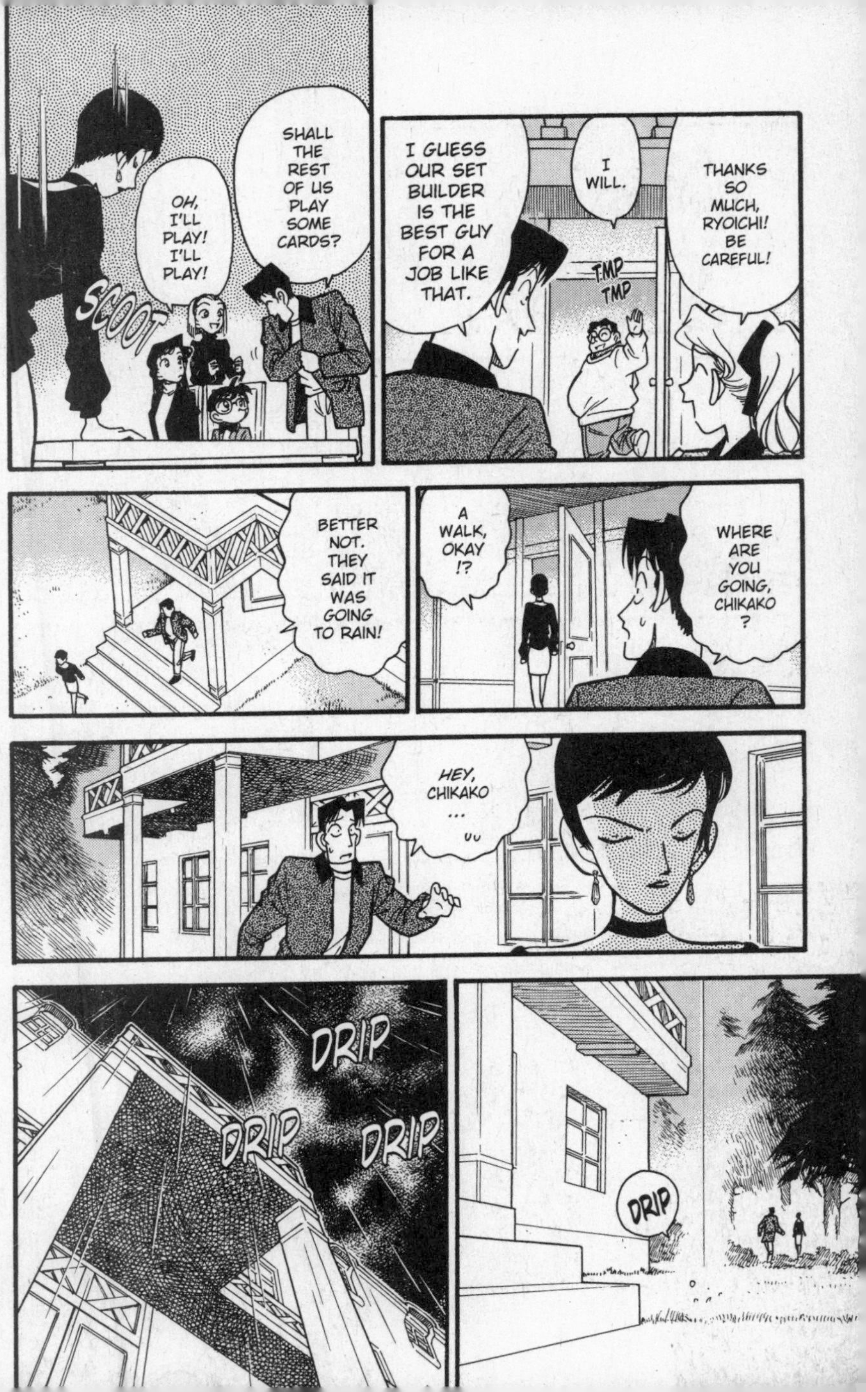
THANKS SO MUCH, RYOICHI! BE CAREFUL!
I WILL.
TMP TMP
I GUESS OUR SET BUILDER IS THE BEST GUY FOR A JOB LIKE THAT.
SHALL THE REST OF US PLAY SOME CARDS?
OH, I'LL PLAY! I'LL PLAY!
SCOOT
WHERE ARE YOU GOING, CHIKAKO?
A WALK, OKAY!?
BETTER NOT. THEY SAID IT WAS GOING TO RAIN!
HEY, CHIKAKO ...
DRIP
DRIP
DRIP
DRIP

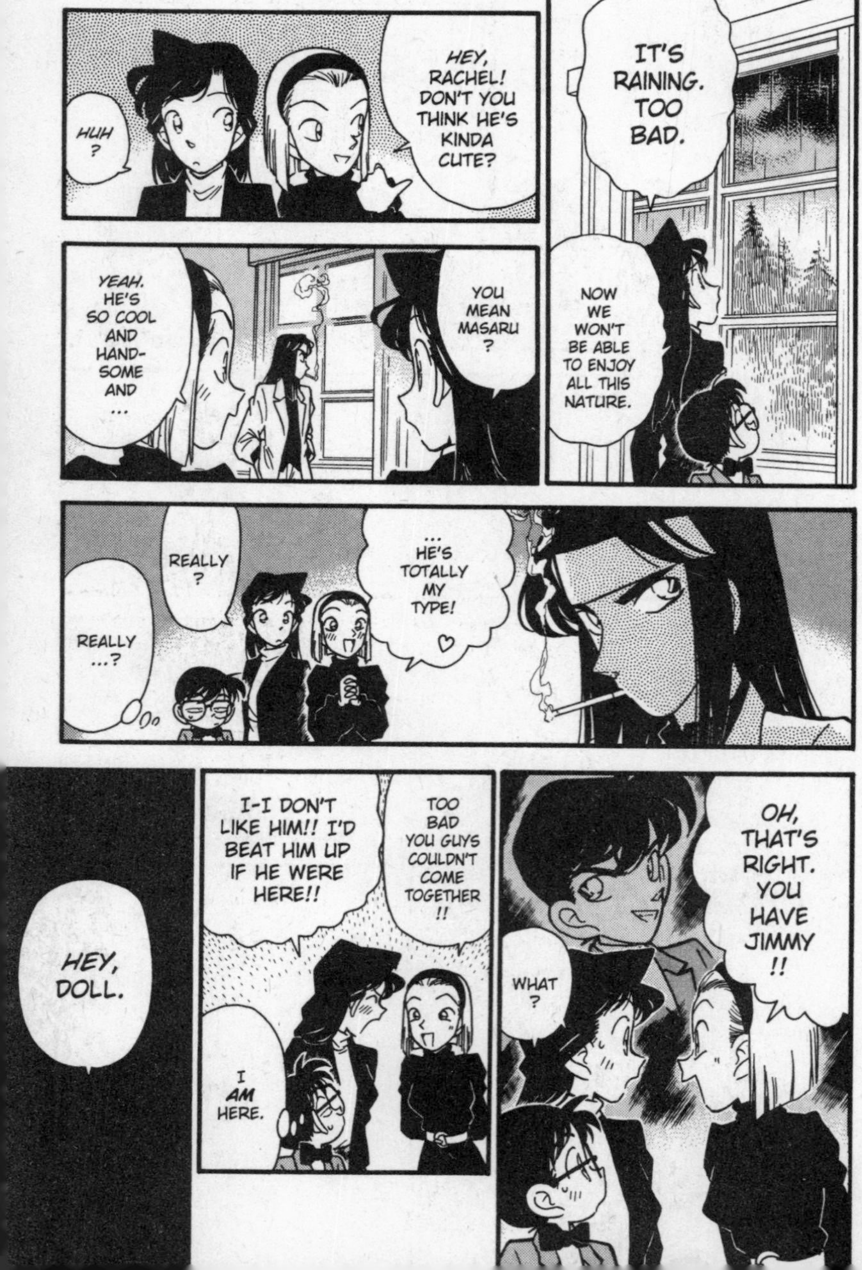
IT'S RAINING. TOO BAD.
NOW WE WON'T BE ABLE TO ENJOY ALL THIS NATURE.
HEY, RACHEL! DON'T YOU THINK HE'S KINDA CUTE?
HUH?
YOU MEAN MASARU?
YEAH. HE'S SO COOL AND HAND-SOME AND ...
... HE'S TOTALLY MY TYPE! ♥
REALLY?
REALLY ...?
OH, THAT'S RIGHT. YOU HAVE JIMMY!!
WHAT?
TOO BAD YOU GUYS COULDN'T COME TOGETHER!!
I-I DON'T LIKE HIM!! I'D BEAT HIM UP IF HE WERE HERE!!
I AM HERE.
HEY, DOLL.

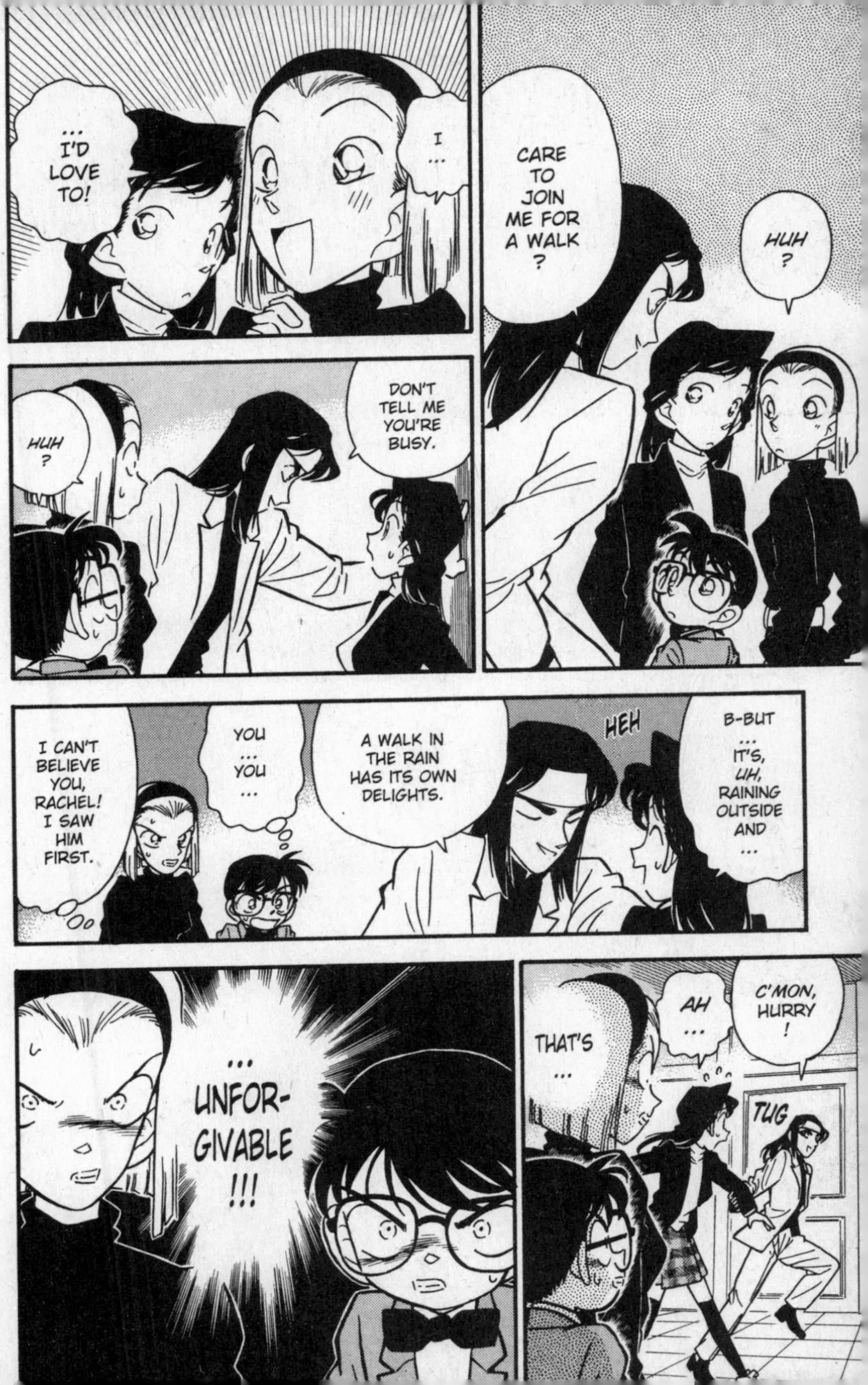
CARE TO JOIN ME FOR A WALK ?
HUH ?
I ...
... I'D LOVE TO!
DON'T TELL ME YOU'RE BUSY.
HUH ?
B-BUT ... IT'S, UH, RAINING OUTSIDE AND ...
HEH
A WALK IN THE RAIN HAS ITS OWN DELIGHTS.
YOU ... YOU ...
I CAN'T BELIEVE YOU, RACHEL! I SAW HIM FIRST.
C'MON, HURRY!
AH ...
TUG
THAT'S ...
... UNFORGIVABLE!!!

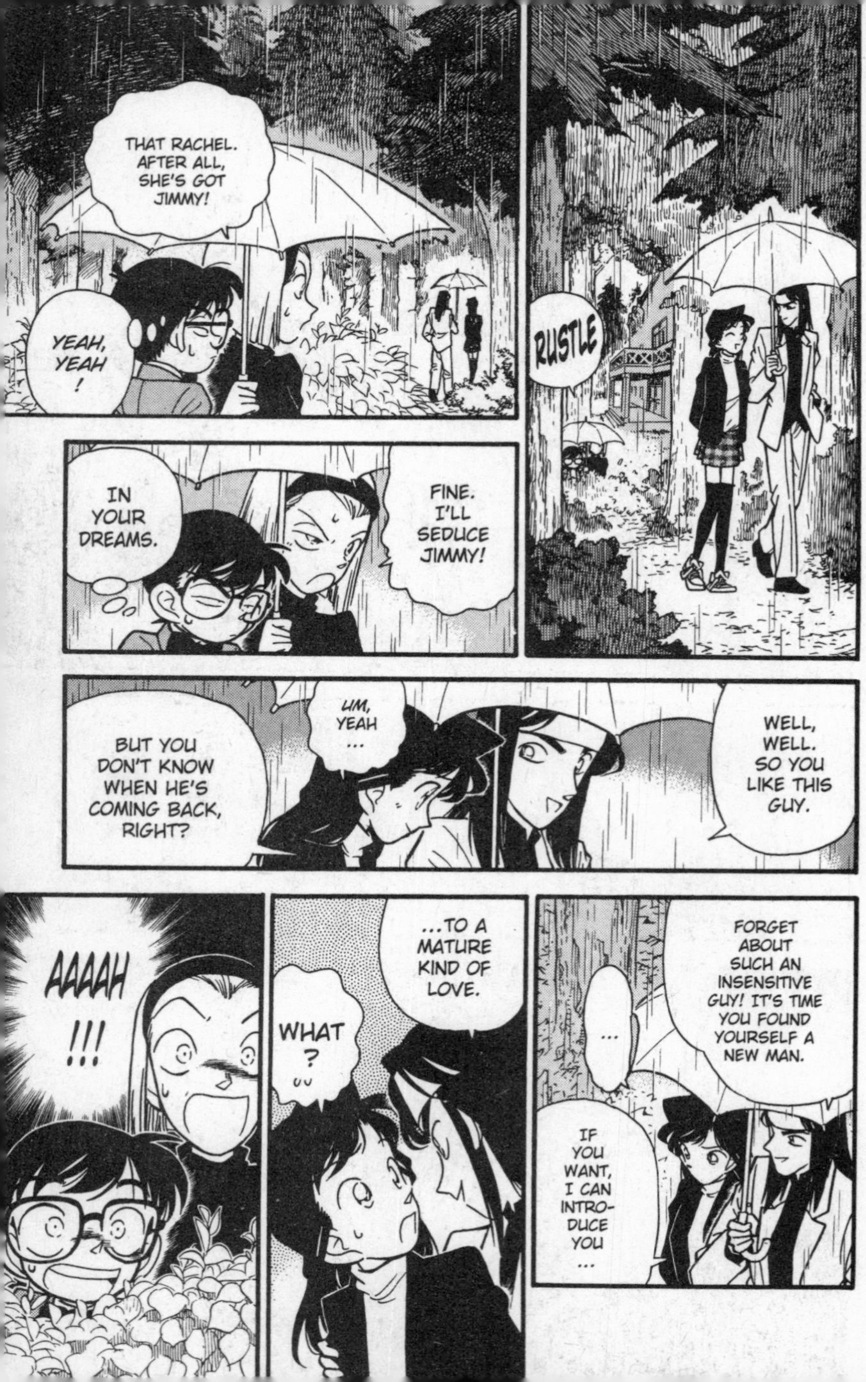
RUSTLE
THAT RACHEL. AFTER ALL, SHE'S GOT JIMMY!
YEAH, YEAH!
FINE. I'LL SEDUCE JIMMY!
IN YOUR DREAMS.
WELL, WELL. SO YOU LIKE THIS GUY.
UM, YEAH ...
BUT YOU DON'T KNOW WHEN HE'S COMING BACK, RIGHT?
FORGET ABOUT SUCH AN INSENSITIVE GUY! IT'S TIME YOU FOUND YOURSELF A NEW MAN.
...
IF YOU WANT, I CAN INTRO-DUCE YOU ...
...TO A MATURE KIND OF LOVE.
WHAT?
AAAAH!!!

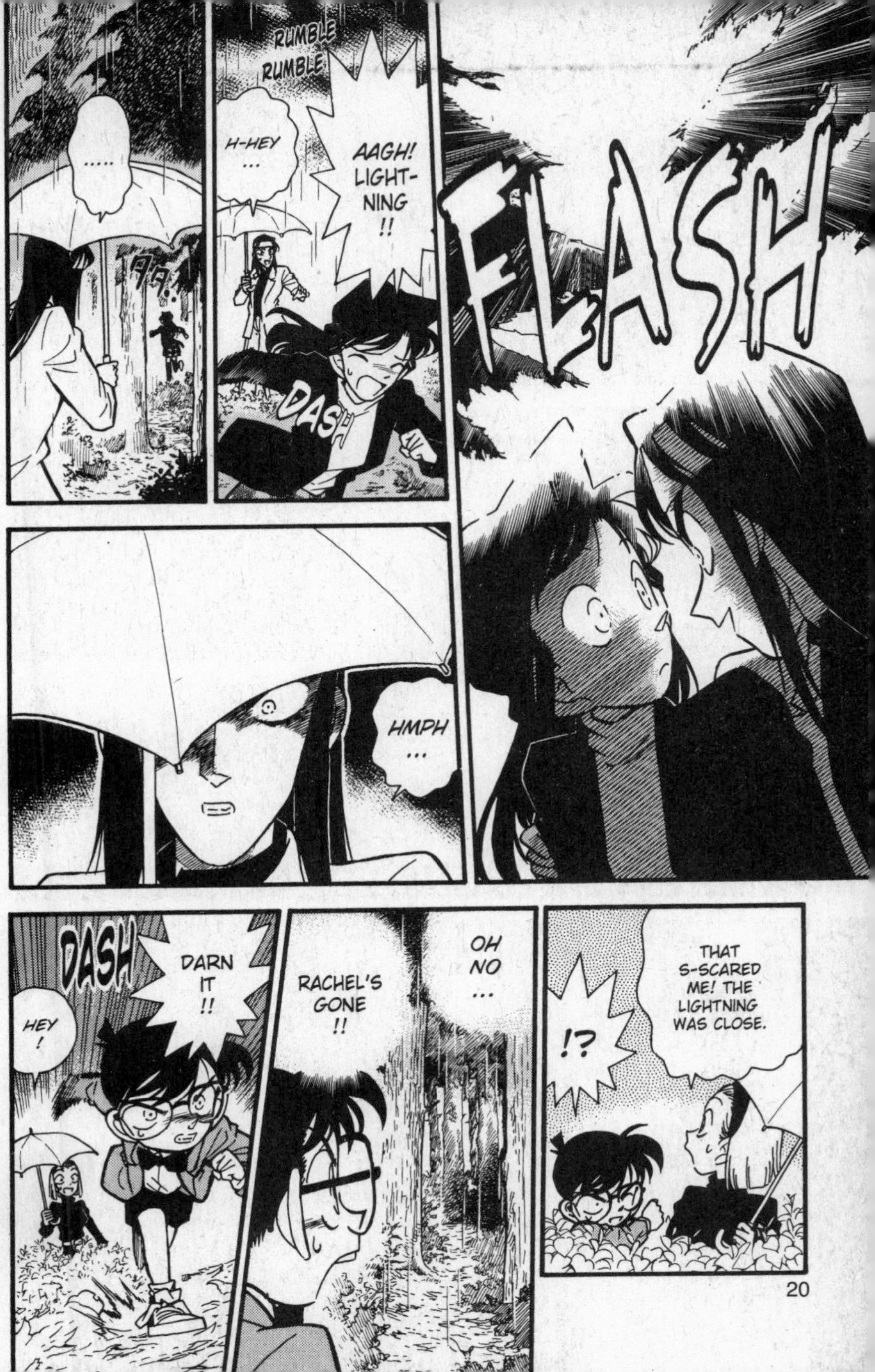
FLASH
RUMBLE
RUMBLE
AAGH! LIGHTNING!!
H-HEY ...
DASH
......
HMPH ...
THAT S-SCARED ME! THE LIGHTNING WAS CLOSE.
!?
OH NO ...
RACHEL'S GONE !!
DARN IT !!
DASH
HEY !

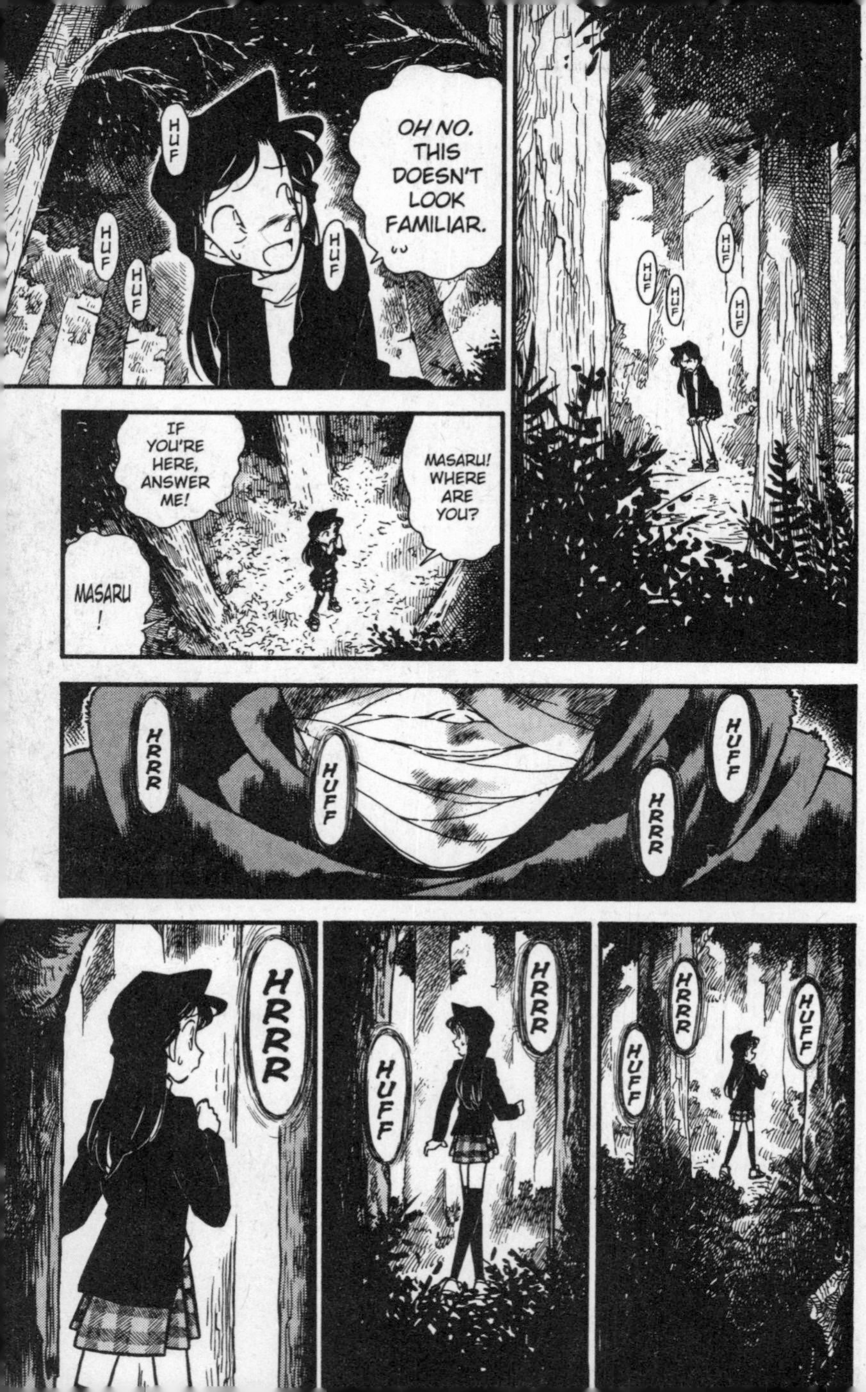
HUF
HUF
HUF
HUF
OH NO. THIS DOESN'T LOOK FAMILIAR.
HUF
HUF
HUF
HUF
MASARU! WHERE ARE YOU?
IF YOU'RE HERE, ANSWER ME!
MASARU!
HUFF
HRRR
HUFF
HRRR
HUFF
HRRR
HUFF
HRRR
HUFF
HRRR

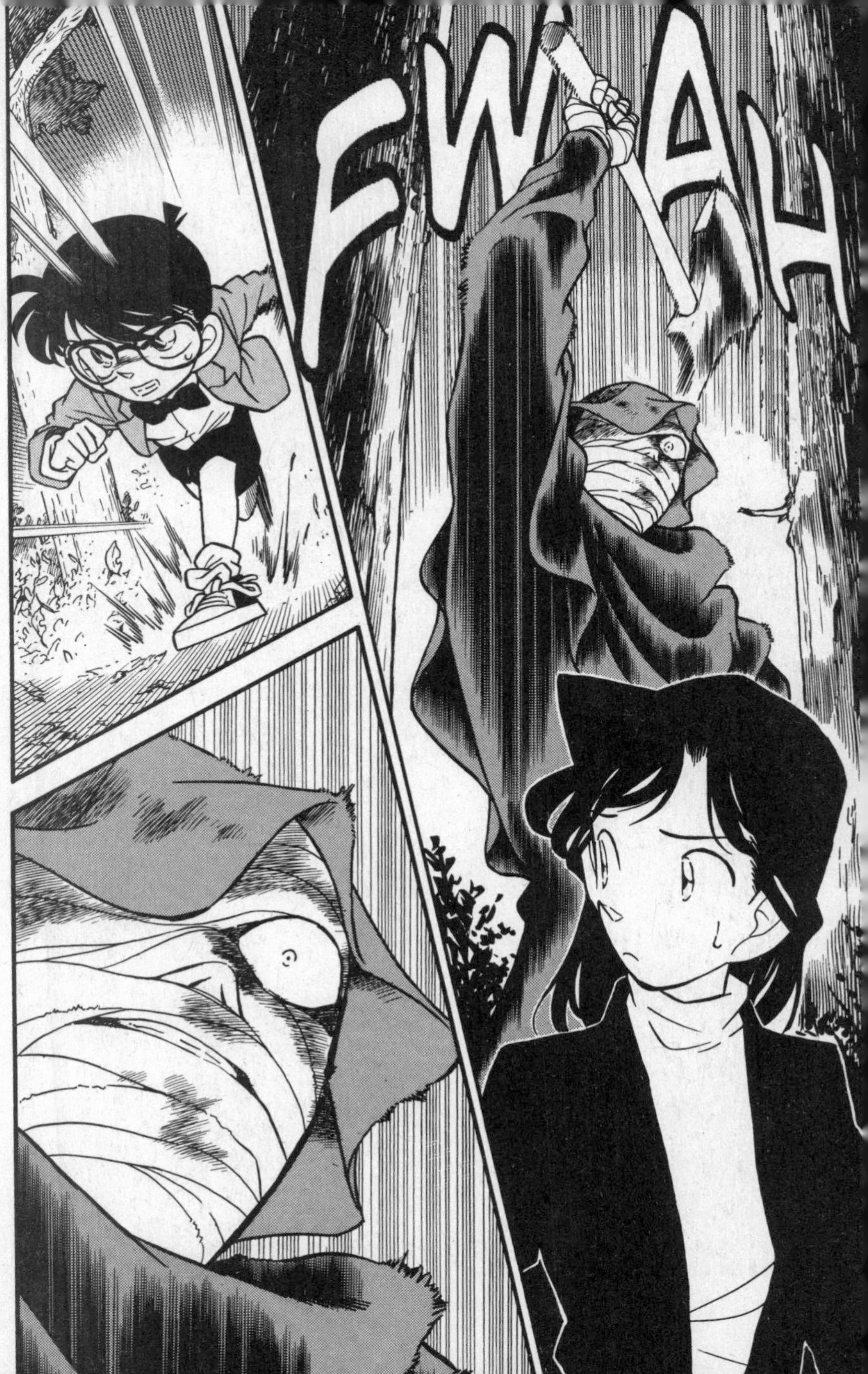
FWAAH

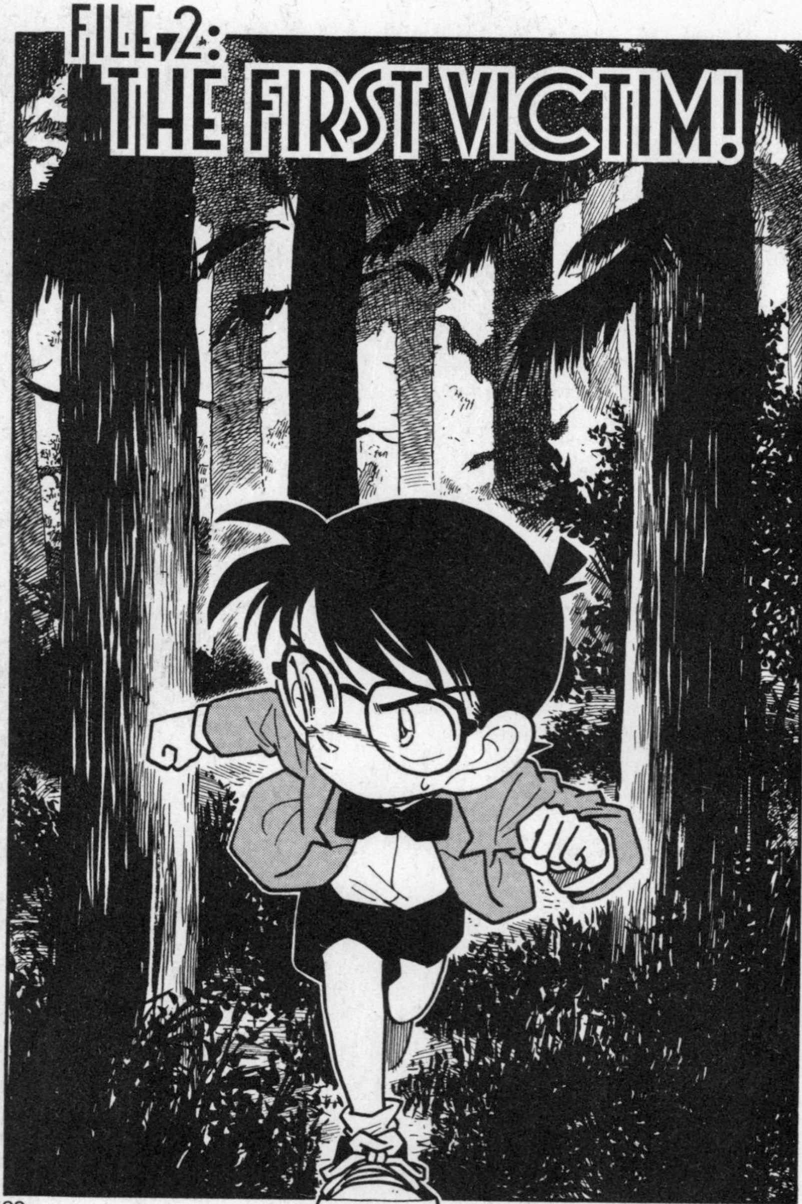
FILE 2:
THE FIRST VICTIM!

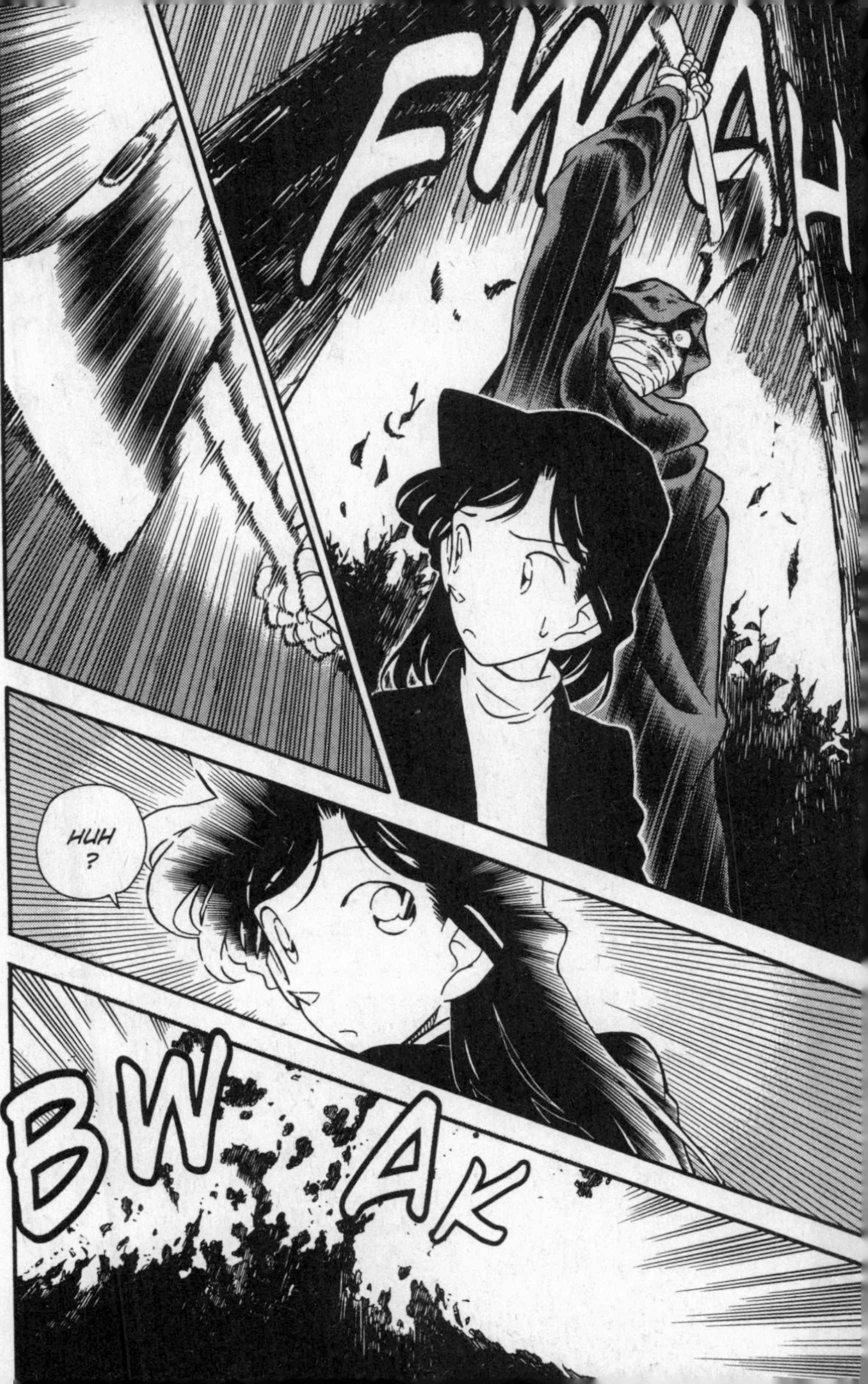
SWISH
HUH ?
BWAK

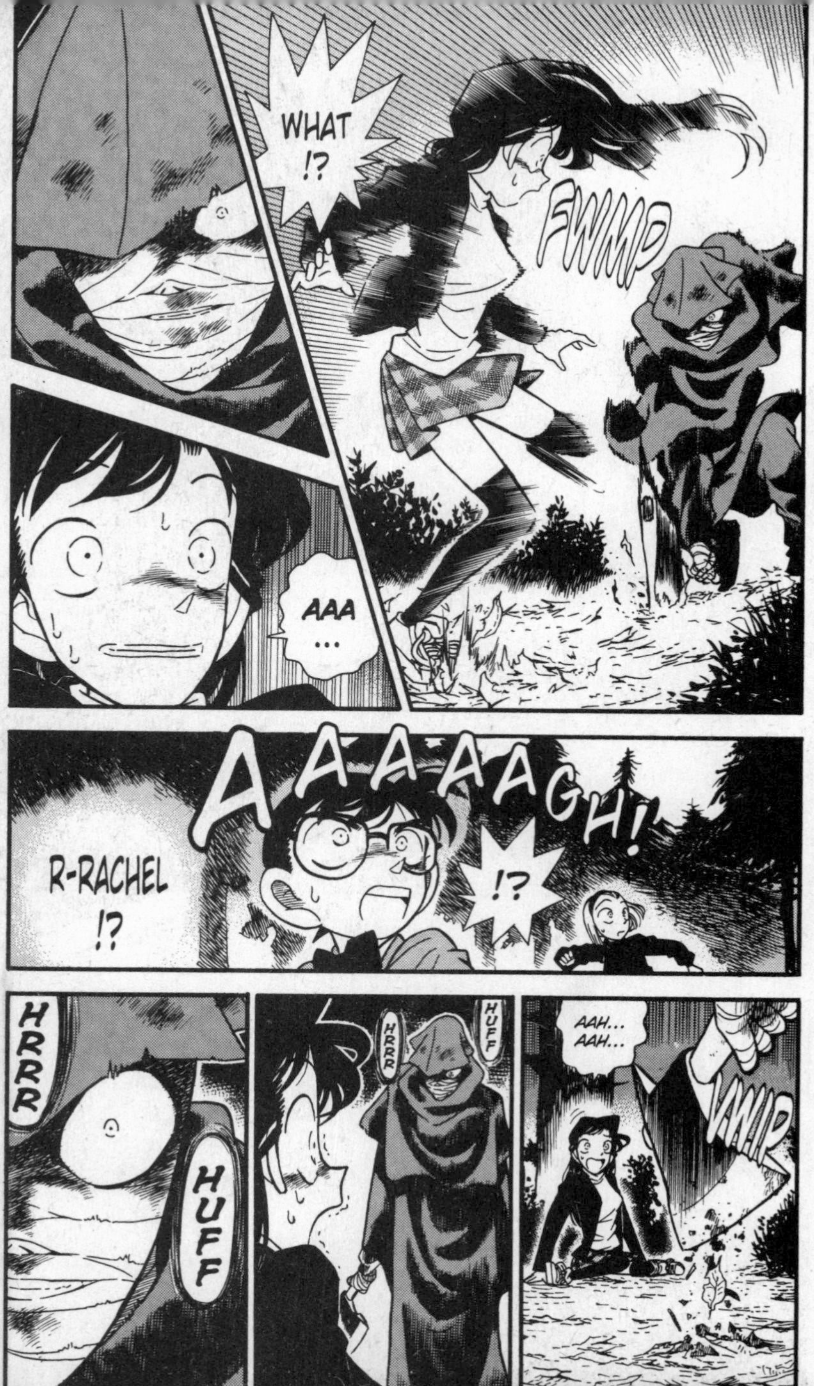
WHAT !?
FWIMP
AAA ...
AAAAAGH!
!?
R-RACHEL !?
AAH... AAH...
VWIP
HUFF
HRRR
HRRR
HUFF

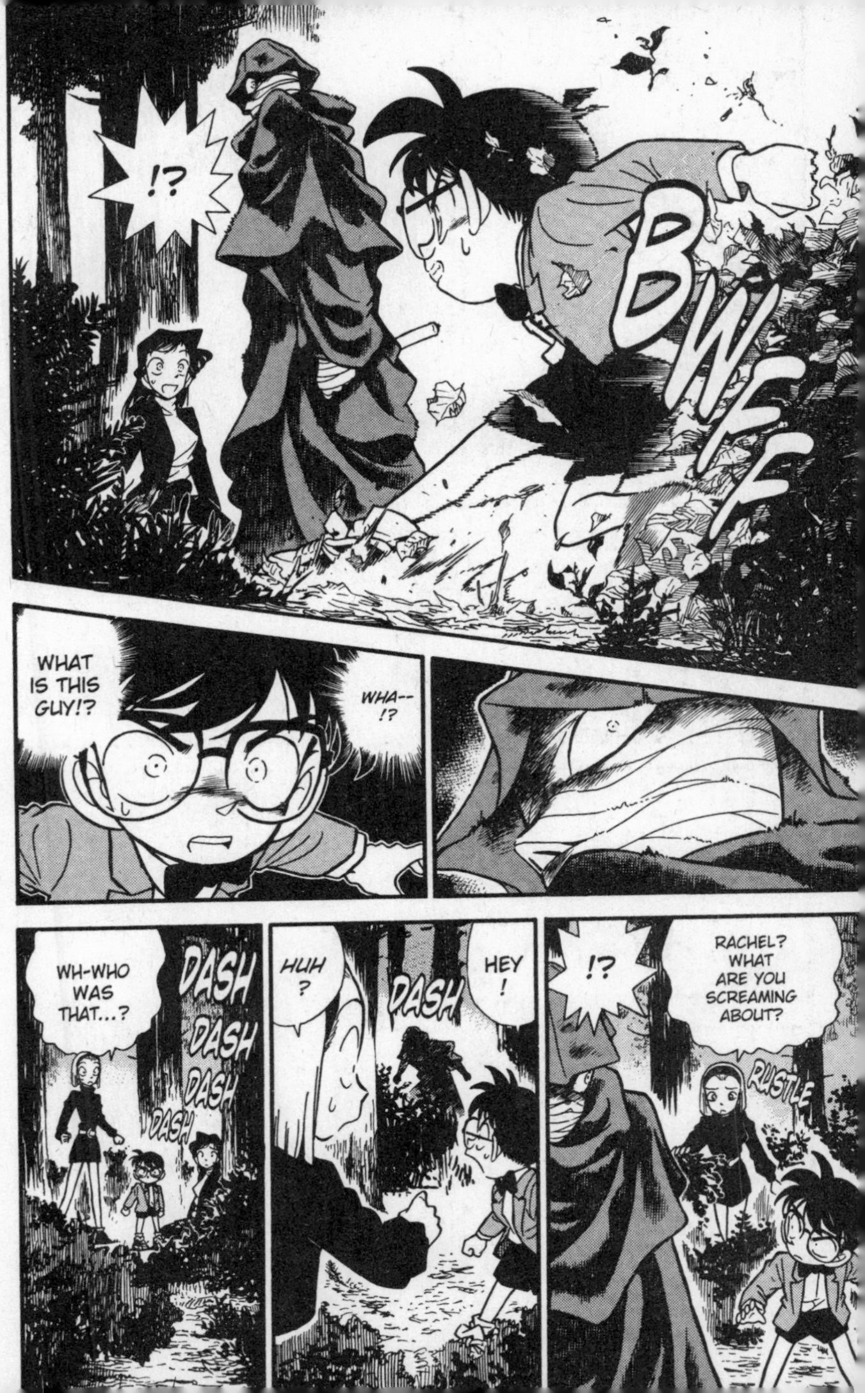
BWFF
!?
WHA-- !?
WHAT IS THIS GUY!?
RACHEL? WHAT ARE YOU SCREAMING ABOUT?
RUSTLE
!?
HEY!
DASH
HUH?
DASH DASH DASH DASH
WH-WHO WAS THAT...?

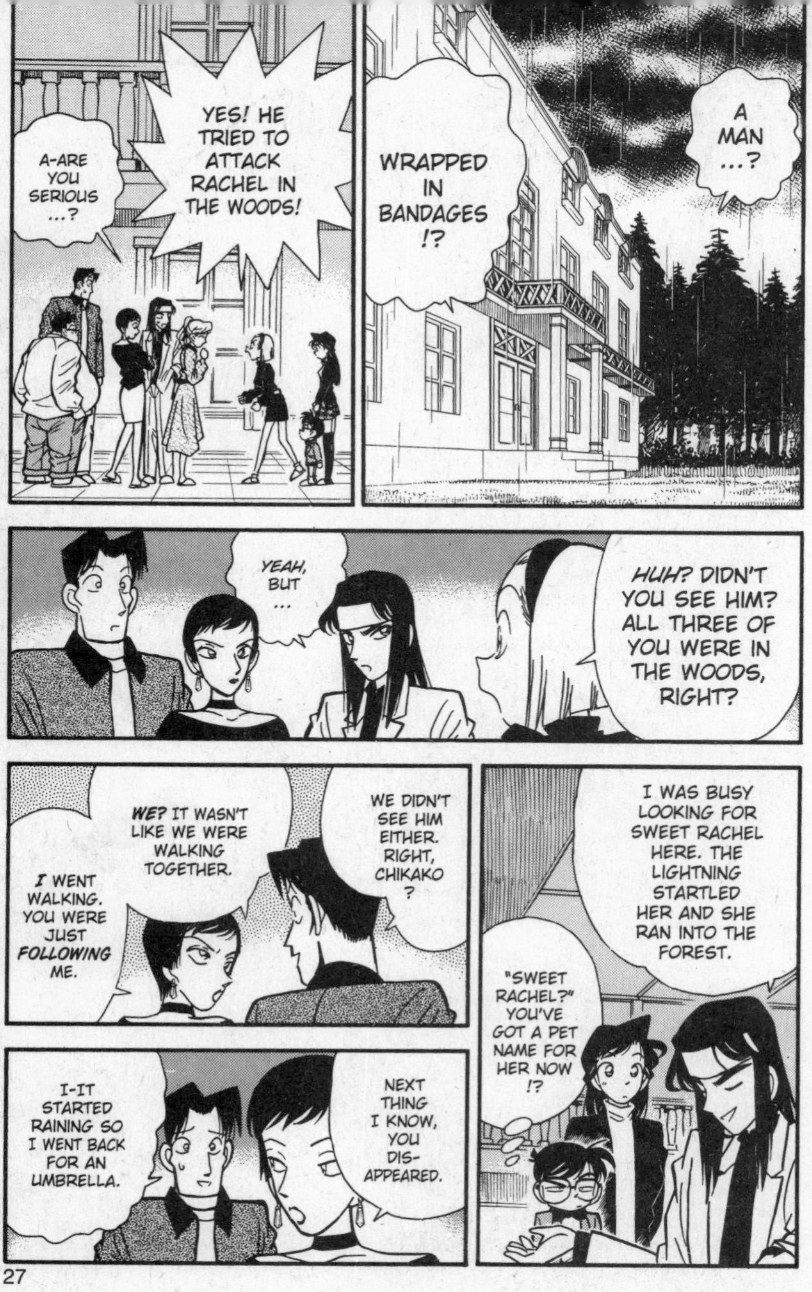
A MAN ...?
WRAPPED IN BANDAGES !?
YES! HE TRIED TO ATTACK RACHEL IN THE WOODS!
A-ARE YOU SERIOUS ...?
HUH? DIDN'T YOU SEE HIM? ALL THREE OF YOU WERE IN THE WOODS, RIGHT?
YEAH, BUT ...
I WAS BUSY LOOKING FOR SWEET RACHEL HERE. THE LIGHTNING STARTLED HER AND SHE RAN INTO THE FOREST.
"SWEET RACHEL?" YOU'VE GOT A PET NAME FOR HER NOW !?
WE DIDN'T SEE HIM EITHER. RIGHT, CHIKAKO ?
WE? IT WASN'T LIKE WE WERE WALKING TOGETHER.
I WENT WALKING. YOU WERE JUST FOLLOWING ME.
NEXT THING I KNOW, YOU DIS-APPEARED.
I-IT STARTED RAINING SO I WENT BACK FOR AN UMBRELLA.

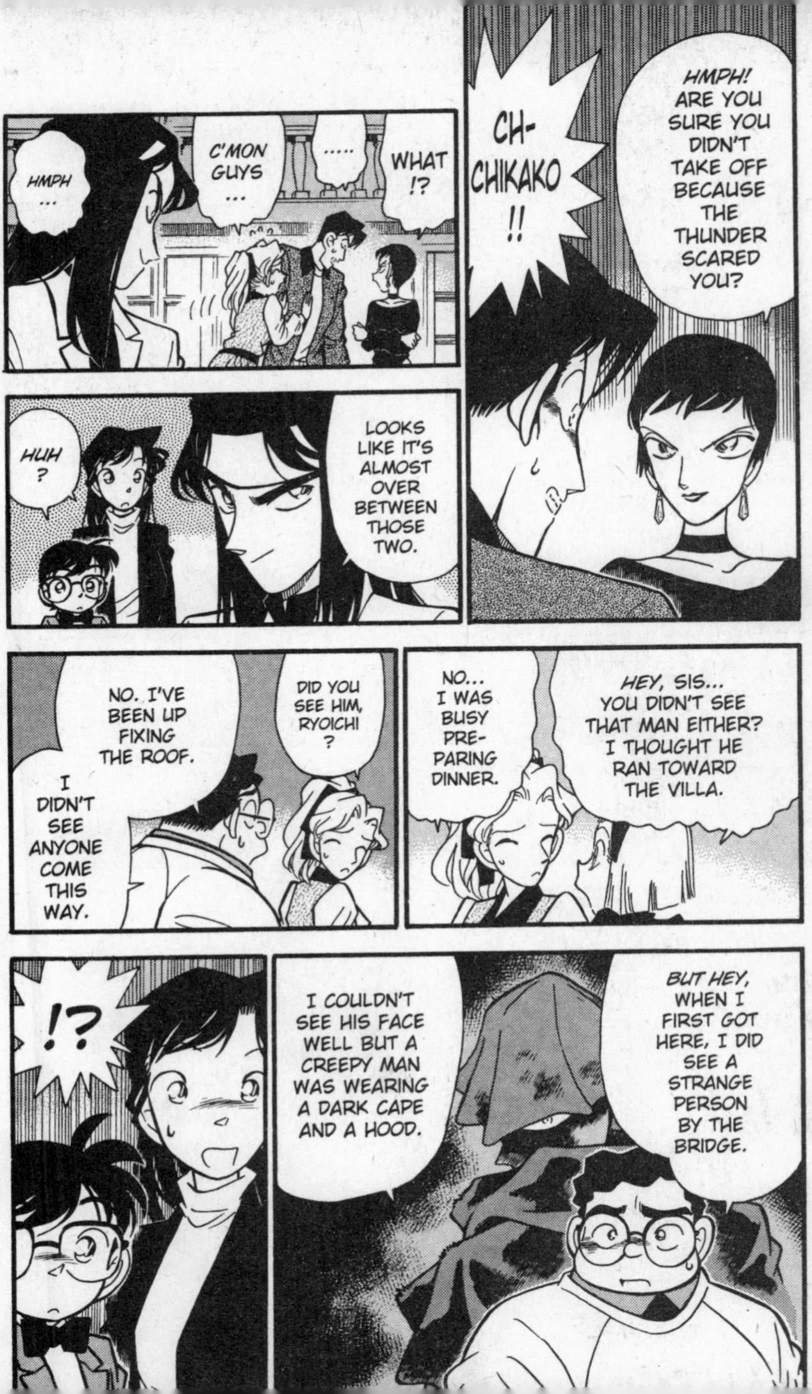
HMPH! ARE YOU SURE YOU DIDN'T TAKE OFF BECAUSE THE THUNDER SCARED YOU?
CH-CHIKAKO !!
WHAT !?
.....
C'MON GUYS ...
HMPH ...
LOOKS LIKE IT'S ALMOST OVER BETWEEN THOSE TWO.
HUH ?
HEY, SIS... YOU DIDN'T SEE THAT MAN EITHER? I THOUGHT HE RAN TOWARD THE VILLA.
NO... I WAS BUSY PRE-PARING DINNER.
DID YOU SEE HIM, RYOICHI ?
NO. I'VE BEEN UP FIXING THE ROOF.
I DIDN'T SEE ANYONE COME THIS WAY.
BUT HEY, WHEN I FIRST GOT HERE, I DID SEE A STRANGE PERSON BY THE BRIDGE.
I COULDN'T SEE HIS FACE WELL BUT A CREEPY MAN WAS WEARING A DARK CAPE AND A HOOD.
!?

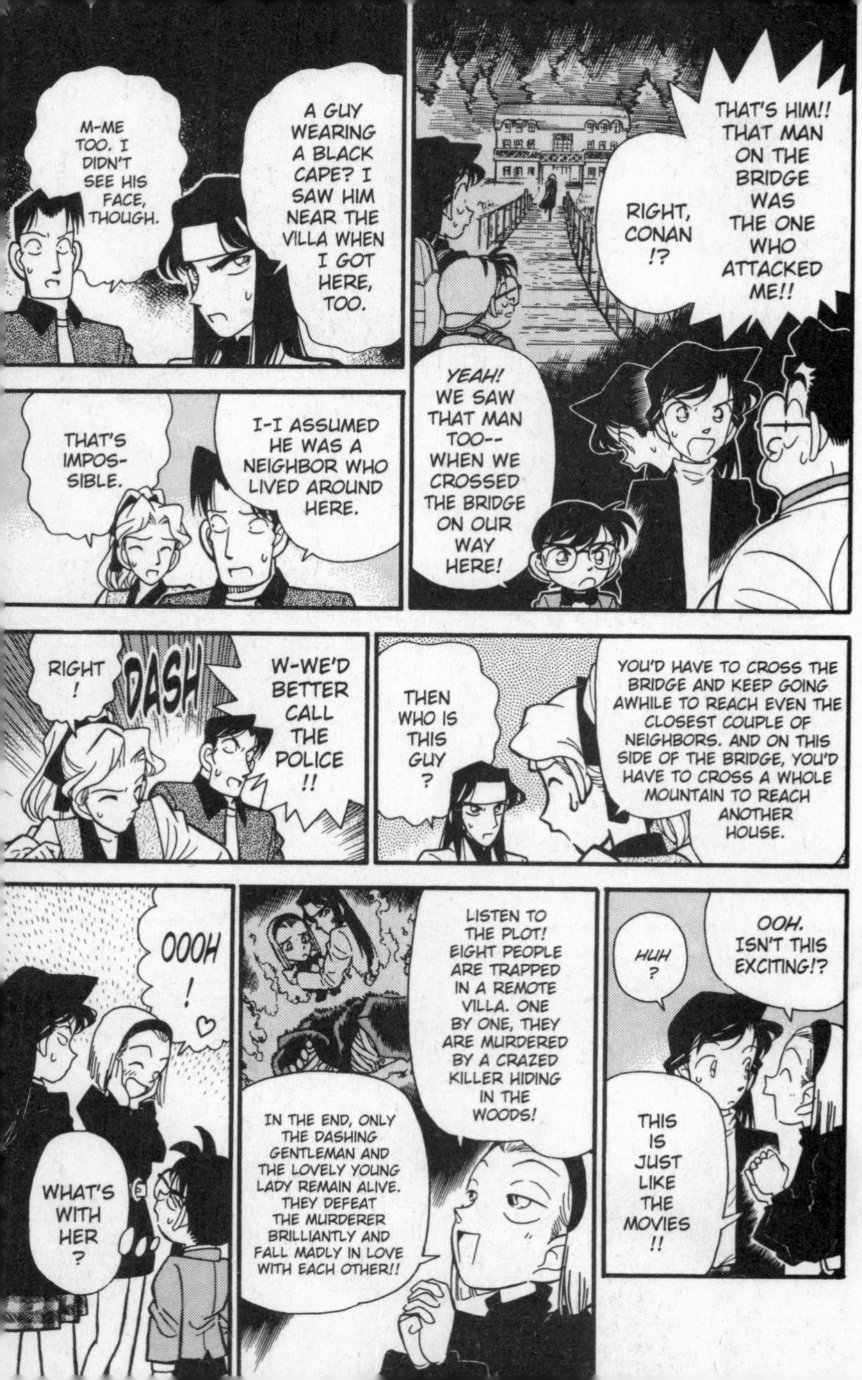
THAT'S HIM!! THAT MAN ON THE BRIDGE WAS THE ONE WHO ATTACKED ME!!
RIGHT, CONAN !?
YEAH! WE SAW THAT MAN TOO-- WHEN WE CROSSED THE BRIDGE ON OUR WAY HERE!
A GUY WEARING A BLACK CAPE? I SAW HIM NEAR THE VILLA WHEN I GOT HERE, TOO.
M-ME TOO. I DIDN'T SEE HIS FACE, THOUGH.
I-I ASSUMED HE WAS A NEIGHBOR WHO LIVED AROUND HERE.
THAT'S IMPOSSIBLE.
YOU'D HAVE TO CROSS THE BRIDGE AND KEEP GOING AWHILE TO REACH EVEN THE CLOSEST COUPLE OF NEIGHBORS. AND ON THIS SIDE OF THE BRIDGE, YOU'D HAVE TO CROSS A WHOLE MOUNTAIN TO REACH ANOTHER HOUSE.
THEN WHO IS THIS GUY ?
W-WE'D BETTER CALL THE POLICE !!
DASH
RIGHT !
OOH. ISN'T THIS EXCITING!?
HUH ?
THIS IS JUST LIKE THE MOVIES !!
LISTEN TO THE PLOT! EIGHT PEOPLE ARE TRAPPED IN A REMOTE VILLA. ONE BY ONE, THEY ARE MURDERED BY A CRAZED KILLER HIDING IN THE WOODS!
IN THE END, ONLY THE DASHING GENTLEMAN AND THE LOVELY YOUNG LADY REMAIN ALIVE. THEY DEFEAT THE MURDERER BRILLIANTLY AND FALL MADLY IN LOVE WITH EACH OTHER!!
OOOH !
WHAT'S WITH HER ?

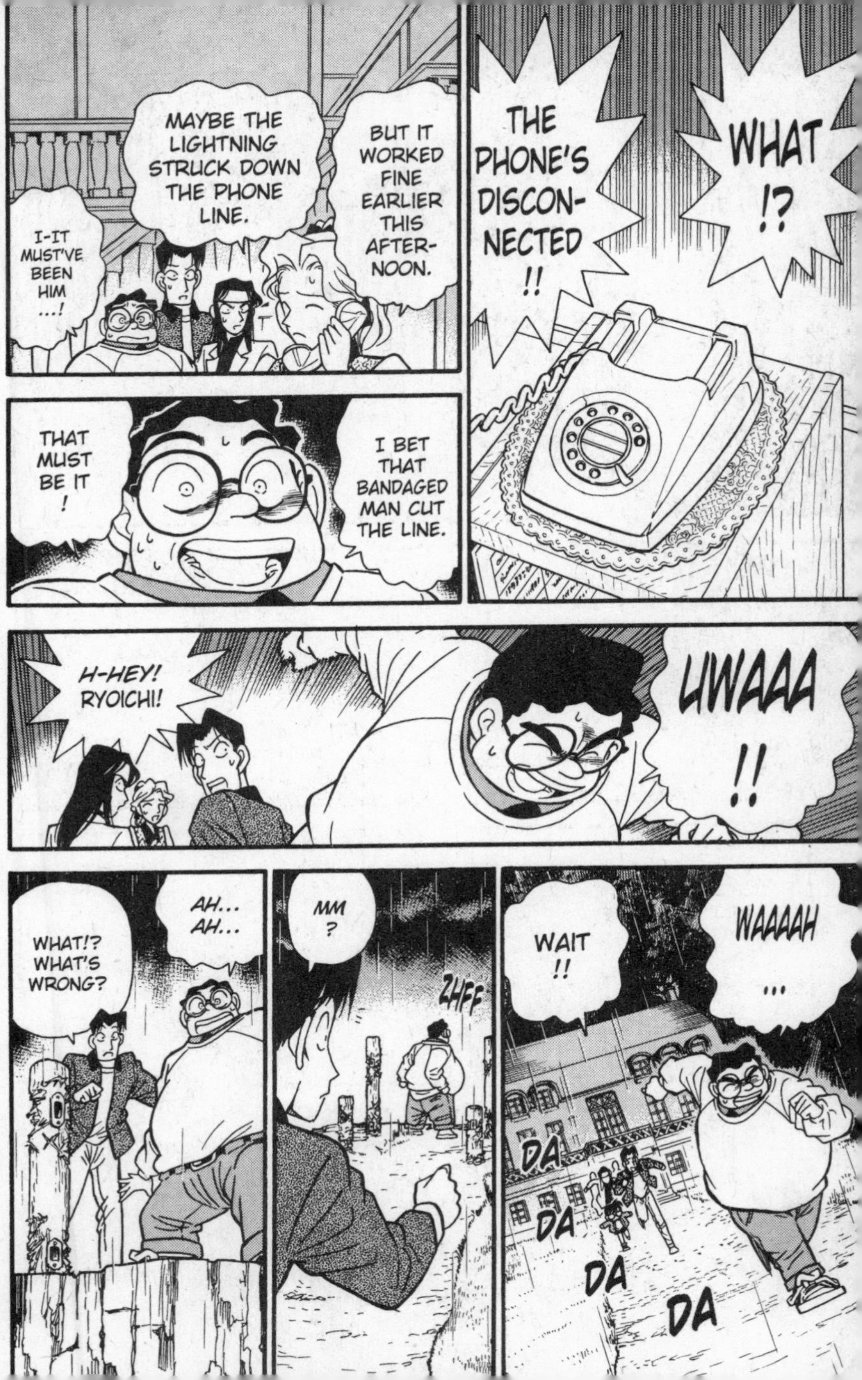
WHAT!?
THE PHONE'S DISCONNECTED!!
BUT IT WORKED FINE EARLIER THIS AFTERNOON.
MAYBE THE LIGHTNING STRUCK DOWN THE PHONE LINE.
I-IT MUST'VE BEEN HIM...!
I BET THAT BANDAGED MAN CUT THE LINE.
THAT MUST BE IT!
UWAAA!!
H-HEY! RYOICHI!
WAAAAH...
WAIT!!
DA
DA
DA
DA
ZHFF
MM?
AH... AH...
WHAT!? WHAT'S WRONG?

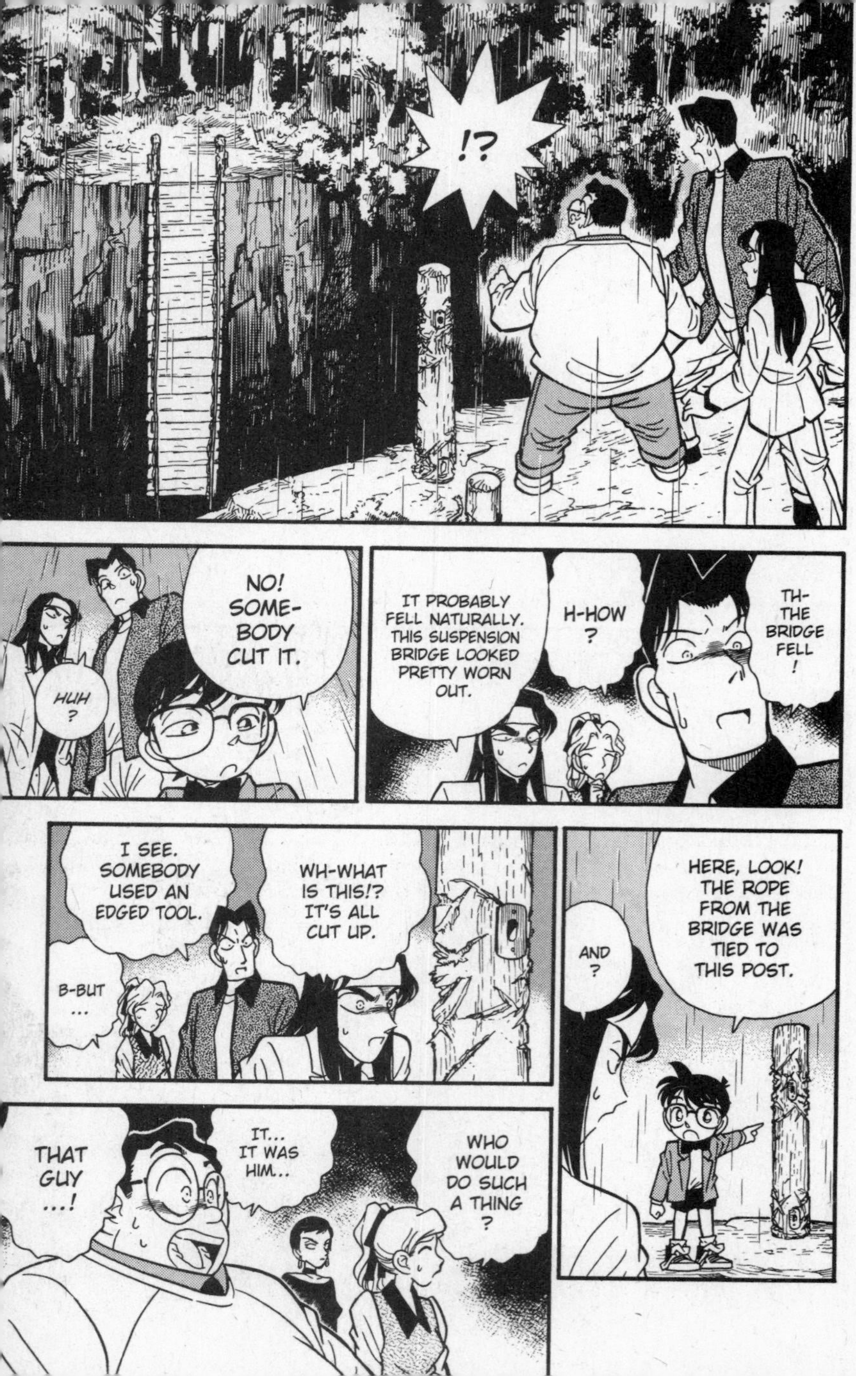
!?
TH-THE BRIDGE FELL!
H-HOW?
IT PROBABLY FELL NATURALLY. THIS SUSPENSION BRIDGE LOOKED PRETTY WORN OUT.
NO! SOMEBODY CUT IT.
HUH?
HERE, LOOK! THE ROPE FROM THE BRIDGE WAS TIED TO THIS POST.
AND?
WH-WHAT IS THIS!? IT'S ALL CUT UP.
I SEE. SOMEBODY USED AN EDGED TOOL.
B-BUT ...
WHO WOULD DO SUCH A THING?
IT... IT WAS HIM..
THAT GUY ...!

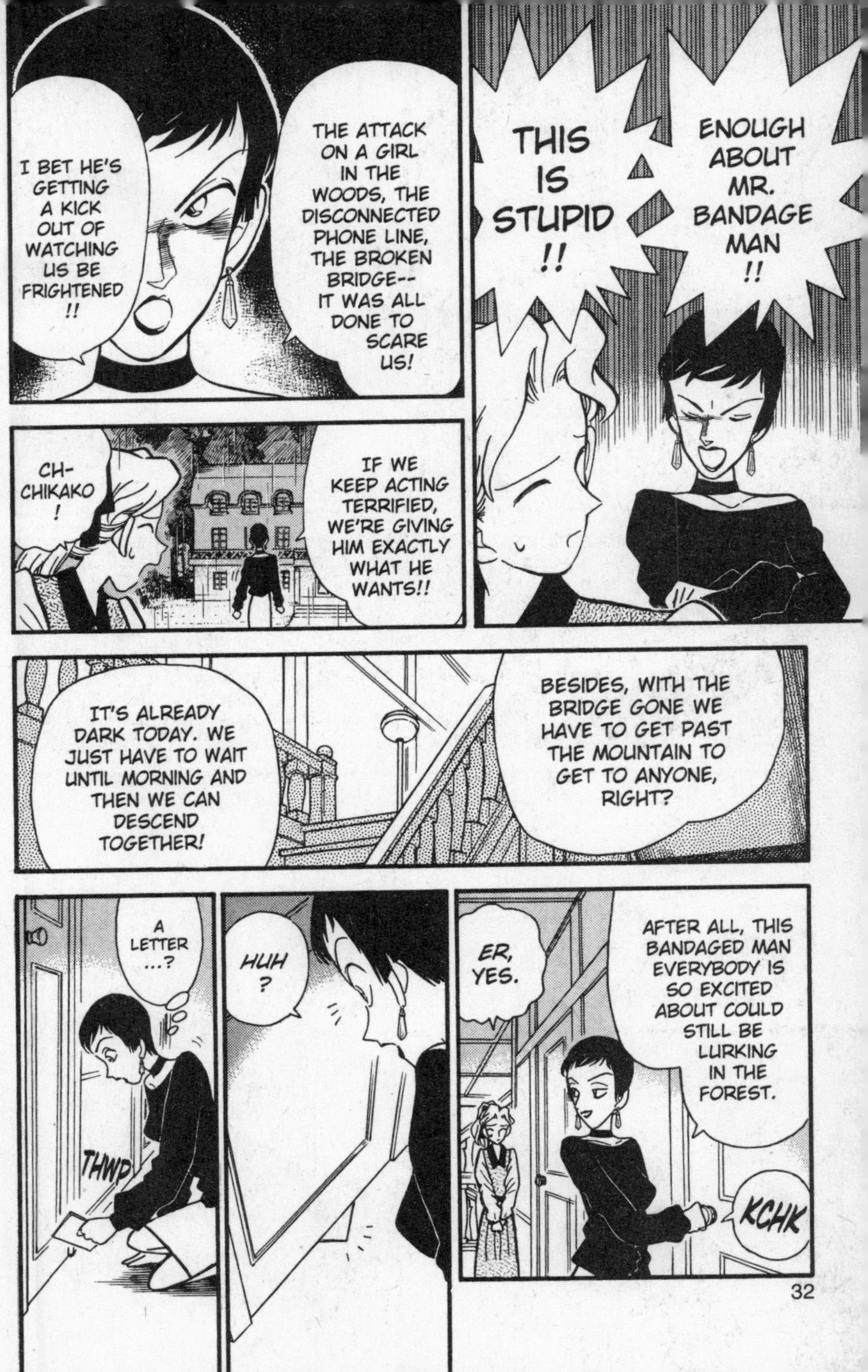
ENOUGH ABOUT MR. BANDAGE MAN !!
THIS IS STUPID !!
THE ATTACK ON A GIRL IN THE WOODS, THE DISCONNECTED PHONE LINE, THE BROKEN BRIDGE-- IT WAS ALL DONE TO SCARE US!
I BET HE'S GETTING A KICK OUT OF WATCHING US BE FRIGHTENED !!
IF WE KEEP ACTING TERRIFIED, WE'RE GIVING HIM EXACTLY WHAT HE WANTS!!
CH-CHIKAKO !
BESIDES, WITH THE BRIDGE GONE WE HAVE TO GET PAST THE MOUNTAIN TO GET TO ANYONE, RIGHT?
IT'S ALREADY DARK TODAY. WE JUST HAVE TO WAIT UNTIL MORNING AND THEN WE CAN DESCEND TOGETHER!
AFTER ALL, THIS BANDAGED MAN EVERYBODY IS SO EXCITED ABOUT COULD STILL BE LURKING IN THE FOREST.
ER, YES.
KCHK
HUH ?
A LETTER ...?
THWP

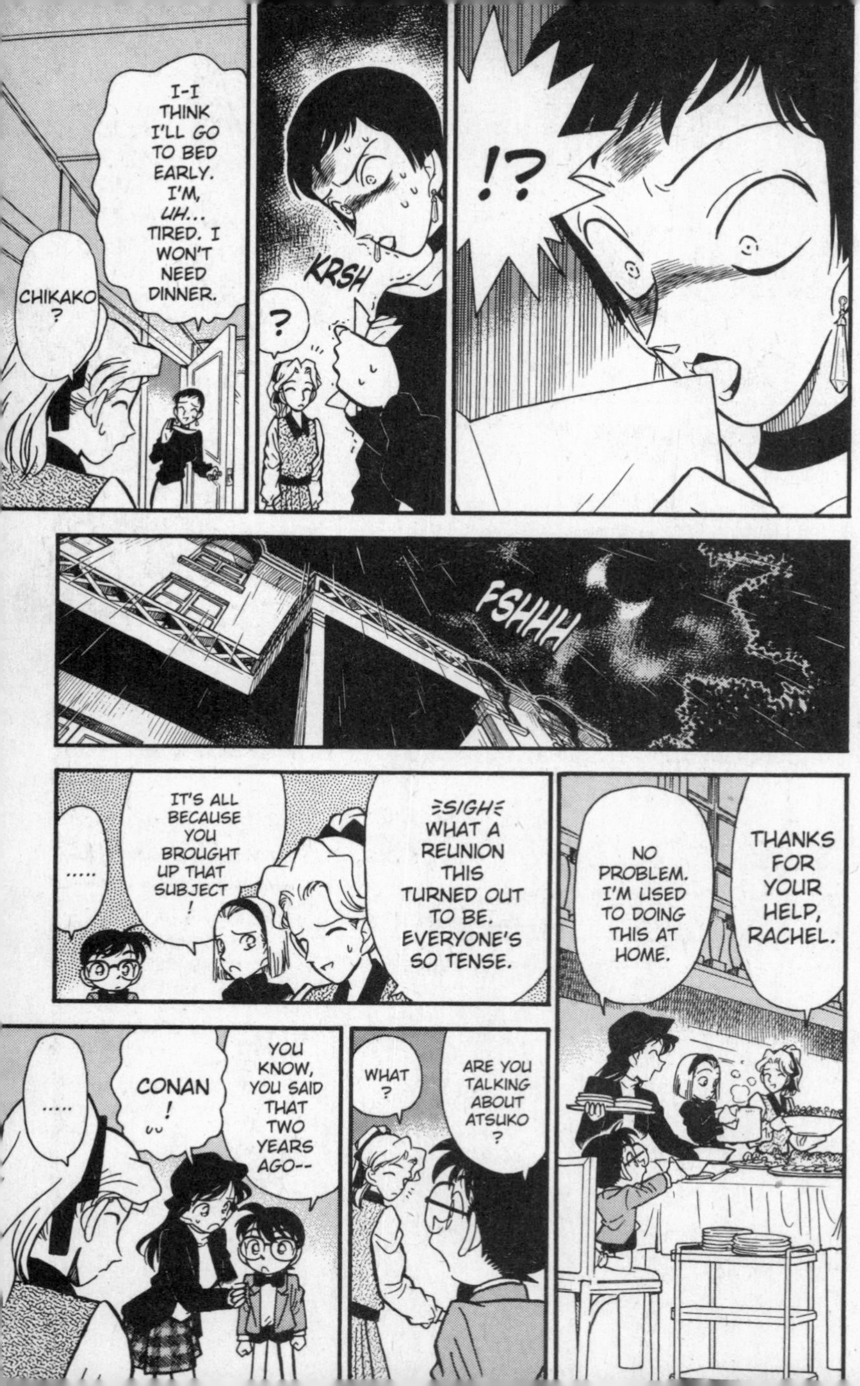
!?
KRSH
?
I-I THINK I'LL GO TO BED EARLY. I'M, *UH...* TIRED. I WON'T NEED DINNER.
CHIKAKO ?
FSHHH
THANKS FOR YOUR HELP, RACHEL.
NO PROBLEM. I'M USED TO DOING THIS AT HOME.
≷SIGH≶ WHAT A REUNION THIS TURNED OUT TO BE. EVERYONE'S SO TENSE.
IT'S ALL BECAUSE YOU BROUGHT UP THAT SUBJECT !
.....
ARE YOU TALKING ABOUT ATSUKO ?
WHAT ?
YOU KNOW, YOU SAID THAT TWO YEARS AGO--
CONAN !
.....

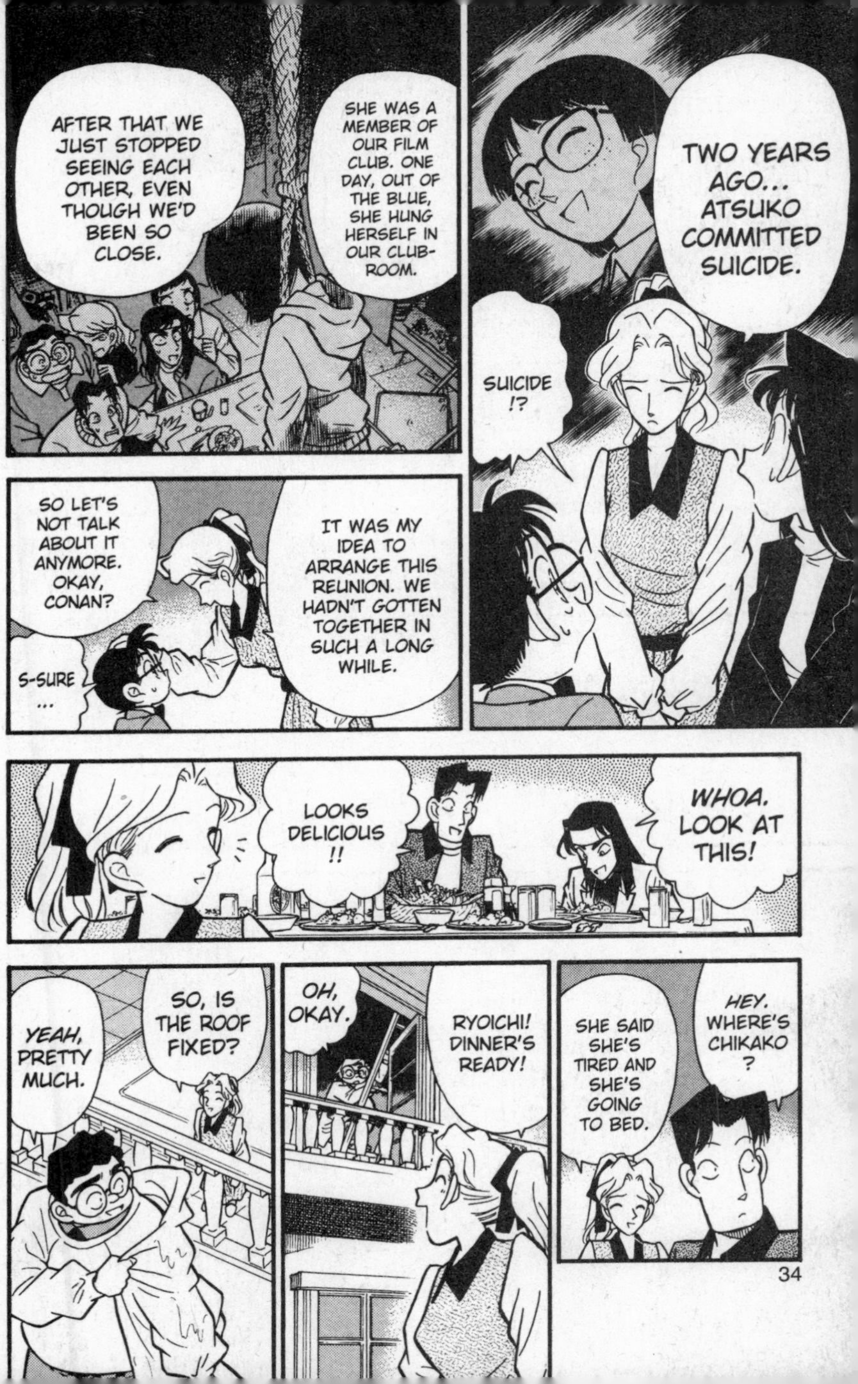

TWO YEARS AGO... ATSUKO COMMITTED SUICIDE.
SUICIDE !?
SHE WAS A MEMBER OF OUR FILM CLUB. ONE DAY, OUT OF THE BLUE, SHE HUNG HERSELF IN OUR CLUB-ROOM.
AFTER THAT WE JUST STOPPED SEEING EACH OTHER, EVEN THOUGH WE'D BEEN SO CLOSE.
IT WAS MY IDEA TO ARRANGE THIS REUNION. WE HADN'T GOTTEN TOGETHER IN SUCH A LONG WHILE.
SO LET'S NOT TALK ABOUT IT ANYMORE. OKAY, CONAN?
S-SURE ...
WHOA. LOOK AT THIS!
LOOKS DELICIOUS !!
HEY. WHERE'S CHIKAKO ?
SHE SAID SHE'S TIRED AND SHE'S GOING TO BED.
RYOICHI! DINNER'S READY!
OH, OKAY.
SO, IS THE ROOF FIXED?
YEAH, PRETTY MUCH.

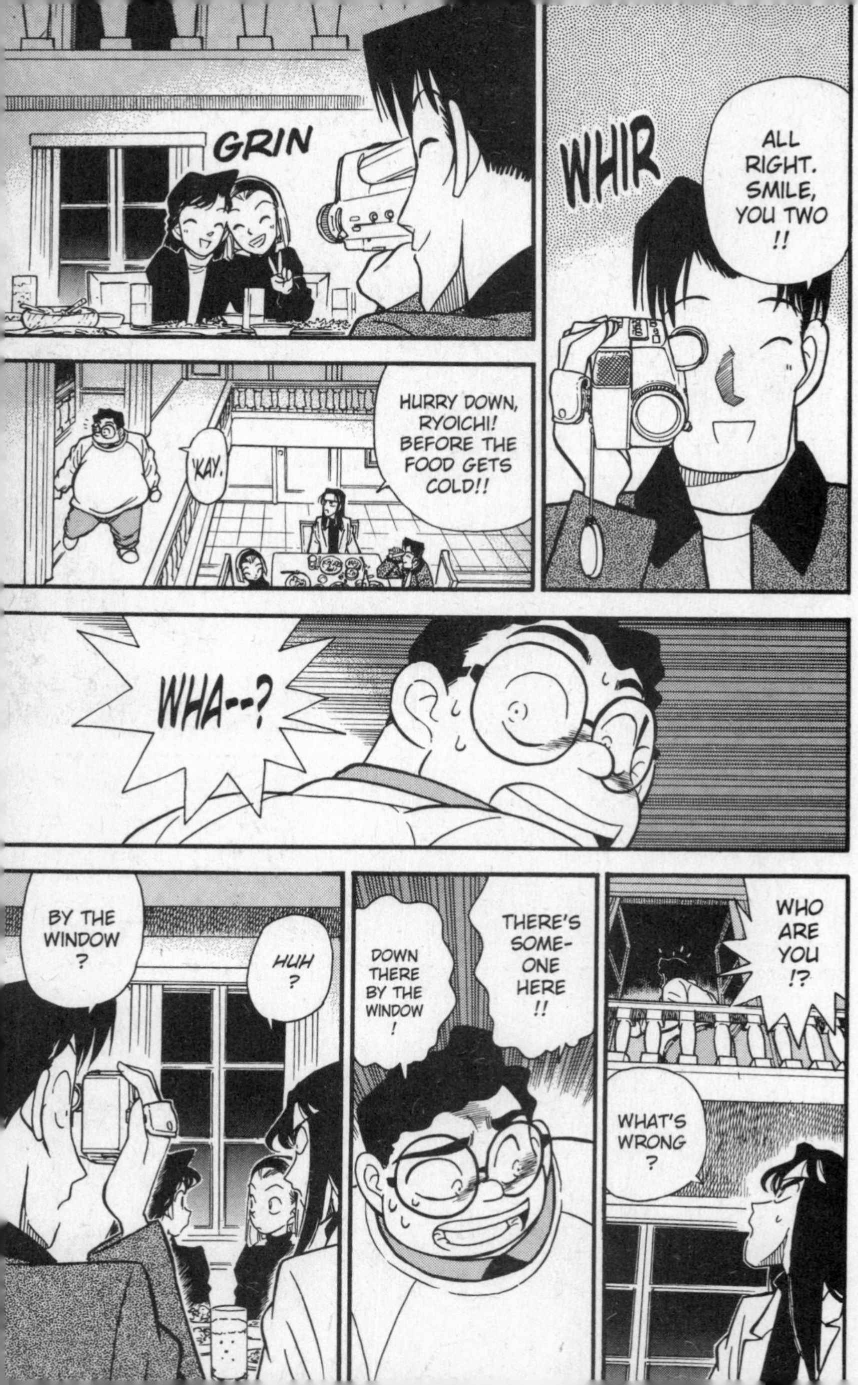
WHIR
ALL RIGHT. SMILE, YOU TWO!!
GRIN
HURRY DOWN, RYOICHI! BEFORE THE FOOD GETS COLD!!
'KAY.
WHA--?
WHO ARE YOU!?
WHAT'S WRONG?
THERE'S SOME-ONE HERE!!
DOWN THERE BY THE WINDOW!
HUH?
BY THE WINDOW?

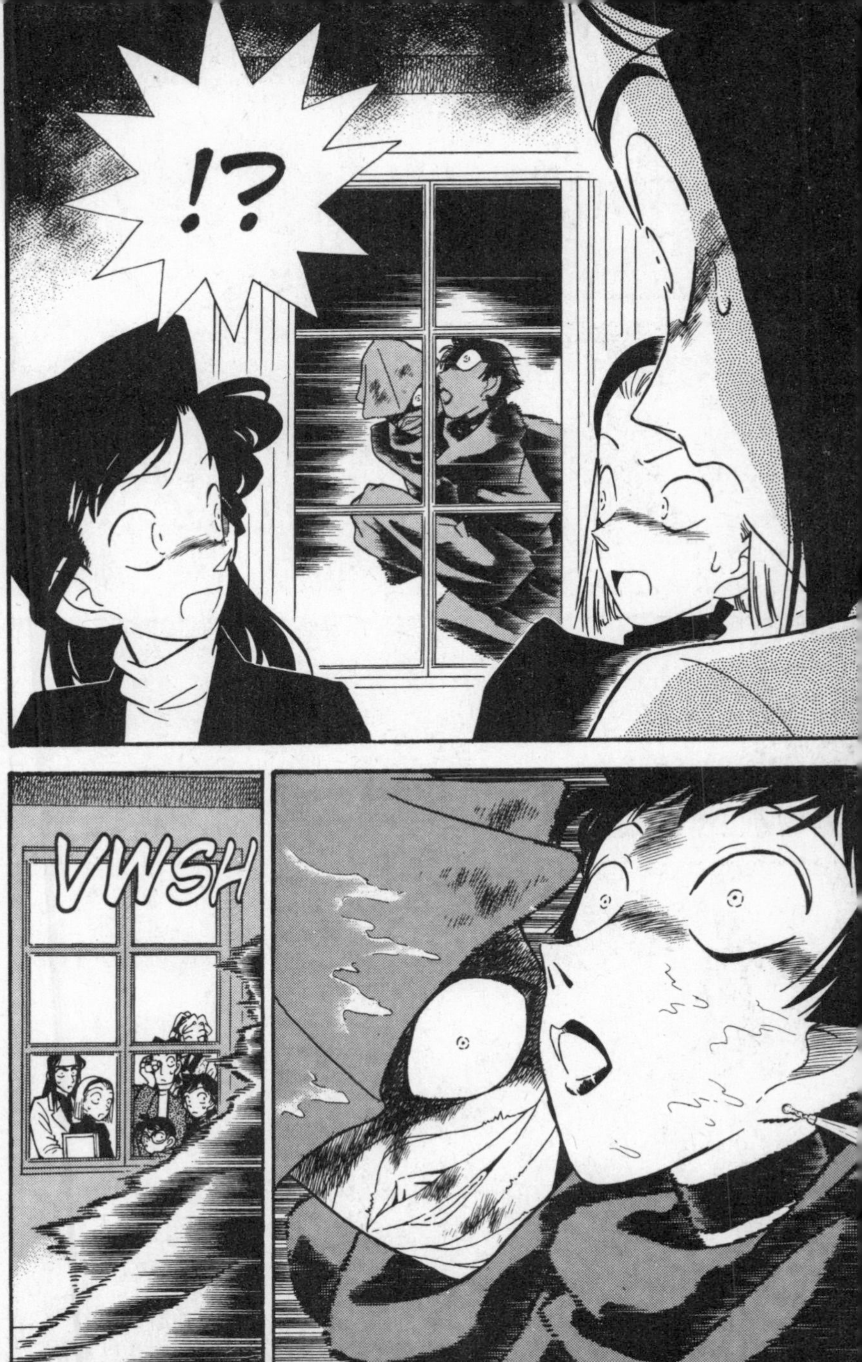
!?
VWSH

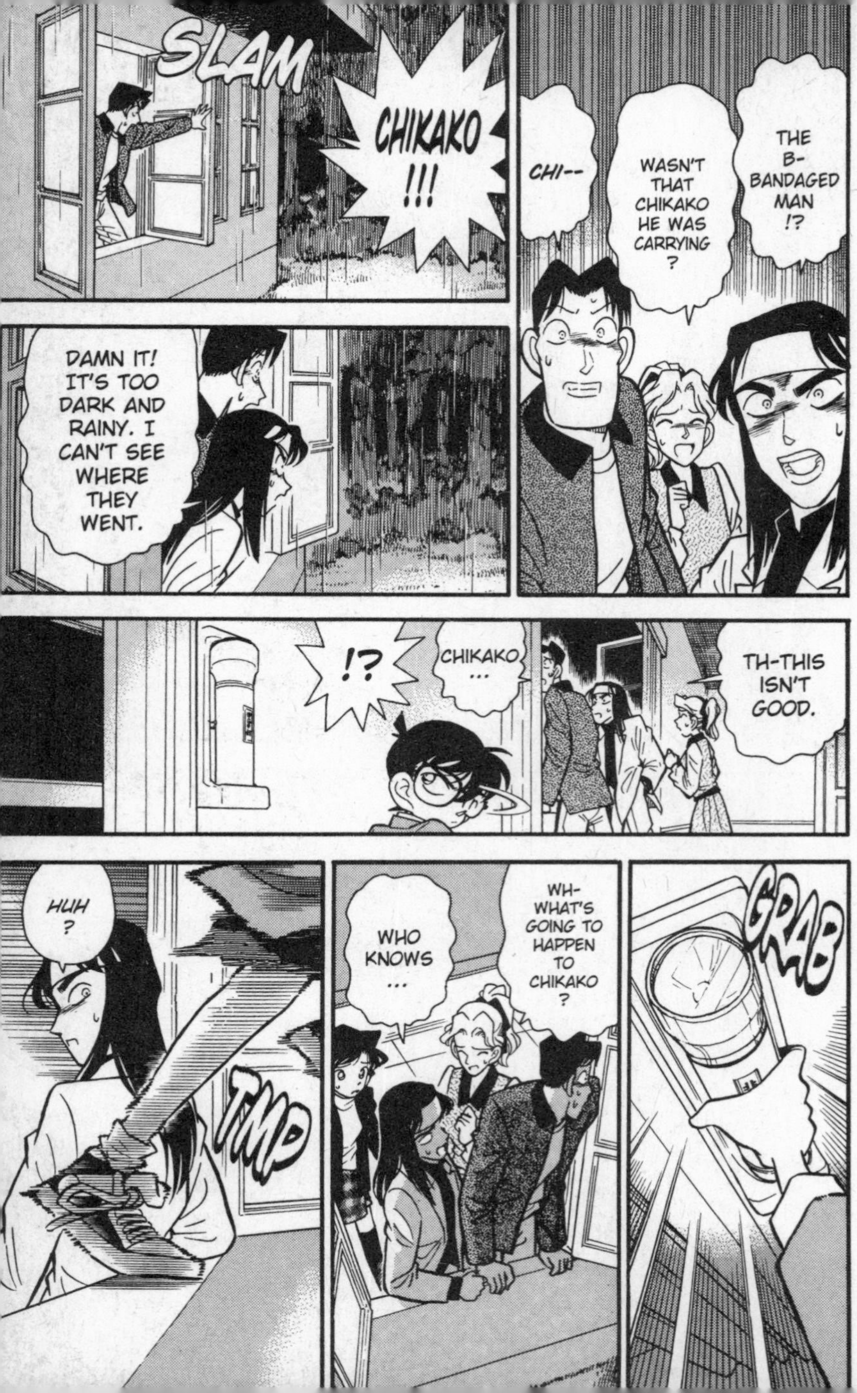
THE B-BANDAGED MAN !?
WASN'T THAT CHIKAKO HE WAS CARRYING ?
CHI--
SLAM
CHIKAKO !!!
DAMN IT! IT'S TOO DARK AND RAINY. I CAN'T SEE WHERE THEY WENT.
TH-THIS ISN'T GOOD.
CHIKAKO ...
!?
GRAB
WH-WHAT'S GOING TO HAPPEN TO CHIKAKO ?
WHO KNOWS ...
HUH ?
TMP

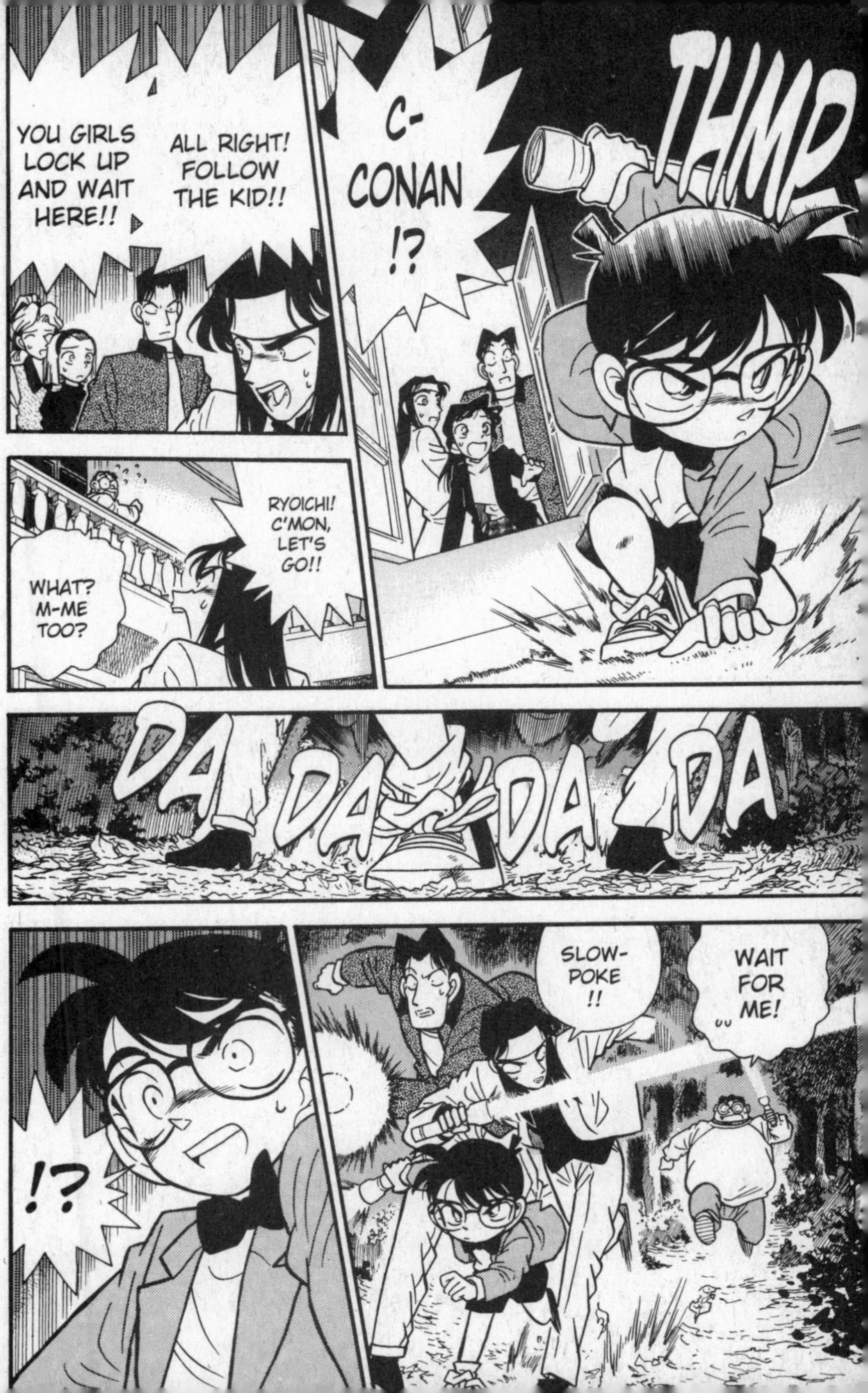
THMP
C-CONAN!?
ALL RIGHT! FOLLOW THE KID!!
YOU GIRLS LOCK UP AND WAIT HERE!!
RYOICHI! C'MON, LET'S GO!!
WHAT? M-ME TOO?
DA DA DA DA
WAIT FOR ME!
SLOW-POKE!!
!?

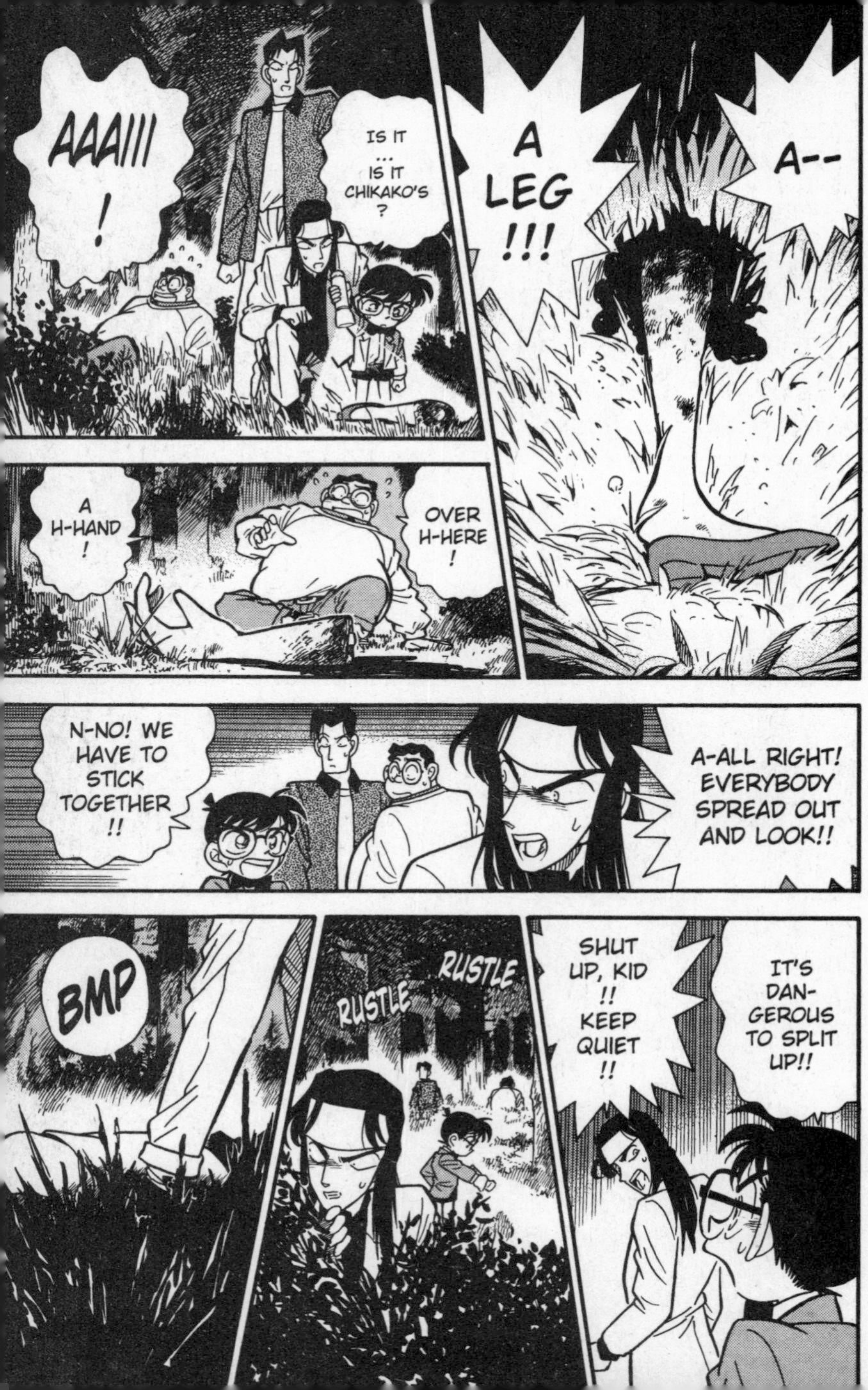

A--
A LEG !!!
IS IT ... IS IT CHIKAKO'S ?
AAAIII !
OVER H-HERE !
A H-HAND !
A-ALL RIGHT! EVERYBODY SPREAD OUT AND LOOK!!
N-NO! WE HAVE TO STICK TOGETHER !!
IT'S DAN-GEROUS TO SPLIT UP!!
SHUT UP, KID !! KEEP QUIET !!
RUSTLE
RUSTLE
BMP

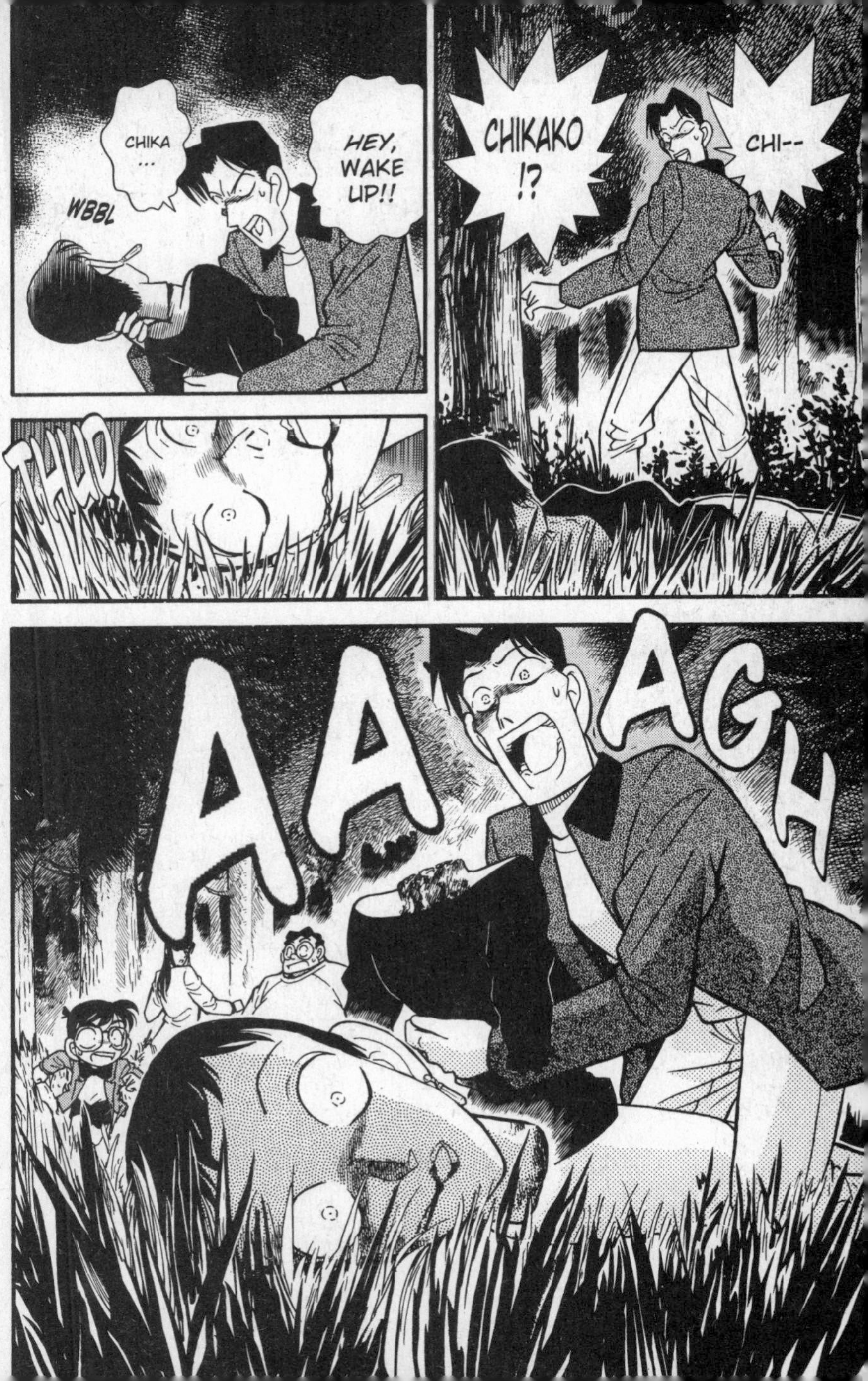

CHIKAKO !?
CHI--
HEY, WAKE UP!!
CHIKA ...
WBBL
THUD
AAAGH

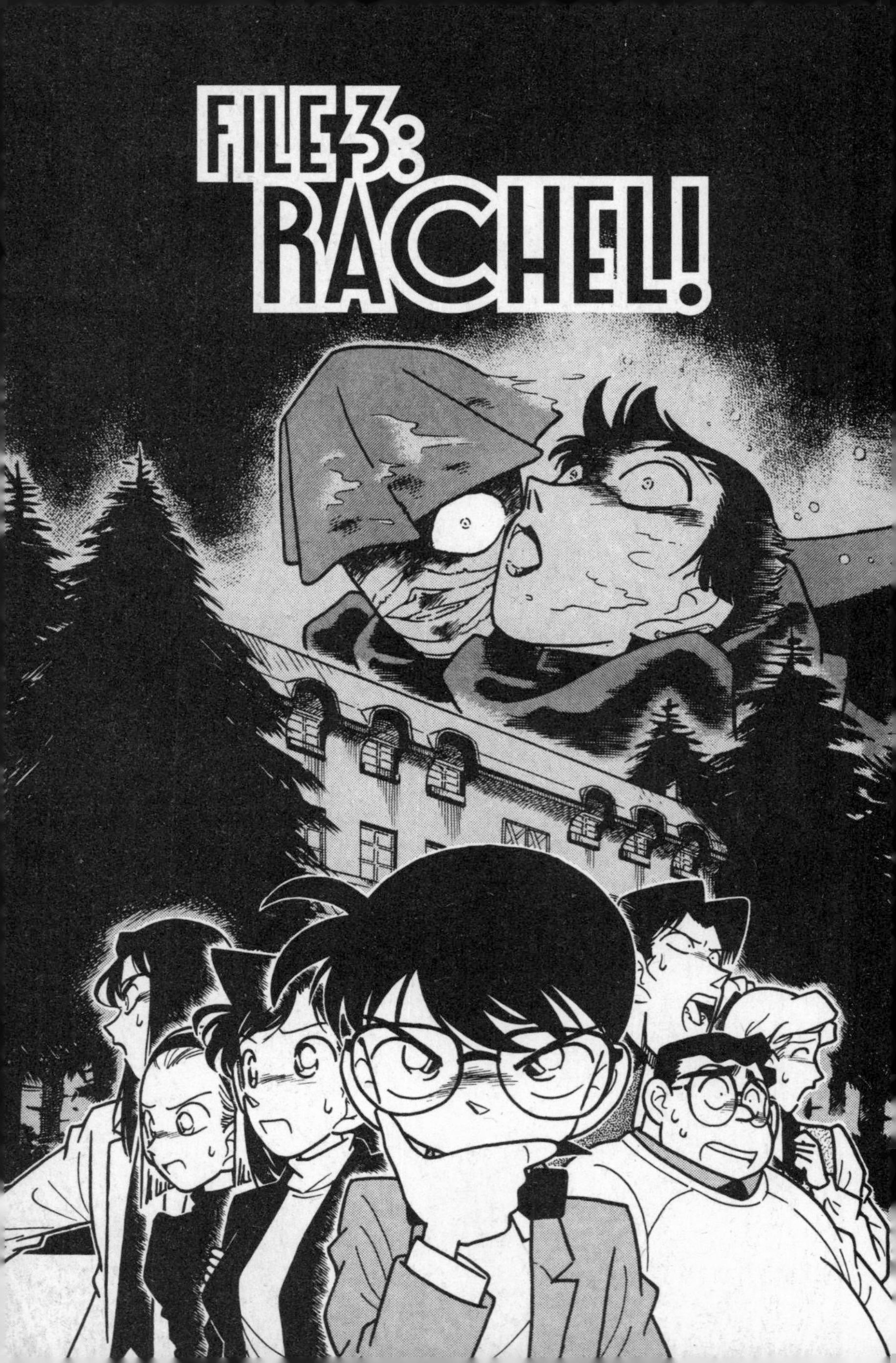
FILE 3:
RACHEL!

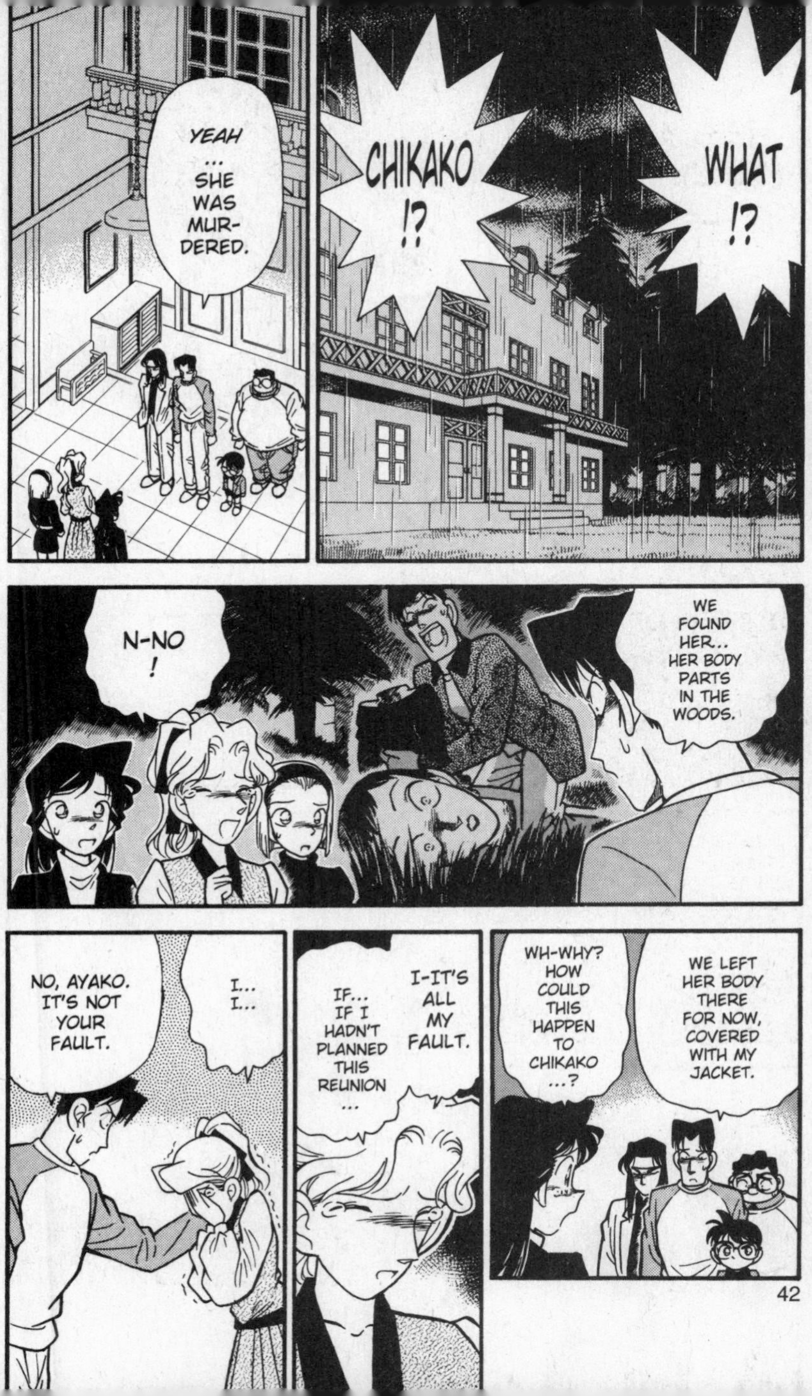

WHAT !?
CHIKAKO !?
YEAH ... SHE WAS MURDERED.
WE FOUND HER.. HER BODY PARTS IN THE WOODS.
N-NO !
WE LEFT HER BODY THERE FOR NOW, COVERED WITH MY JACKET.
WH-WHY? HOW COULD THIS HAPPEN TO CHIKAKO ...?
I-IT'S ALL MY FAULT.
IF... IF I HADN'T PLANNED THIS REUNION ...
I... I...
NO, AYAKO. IT'S NOT YOUR FAULT.

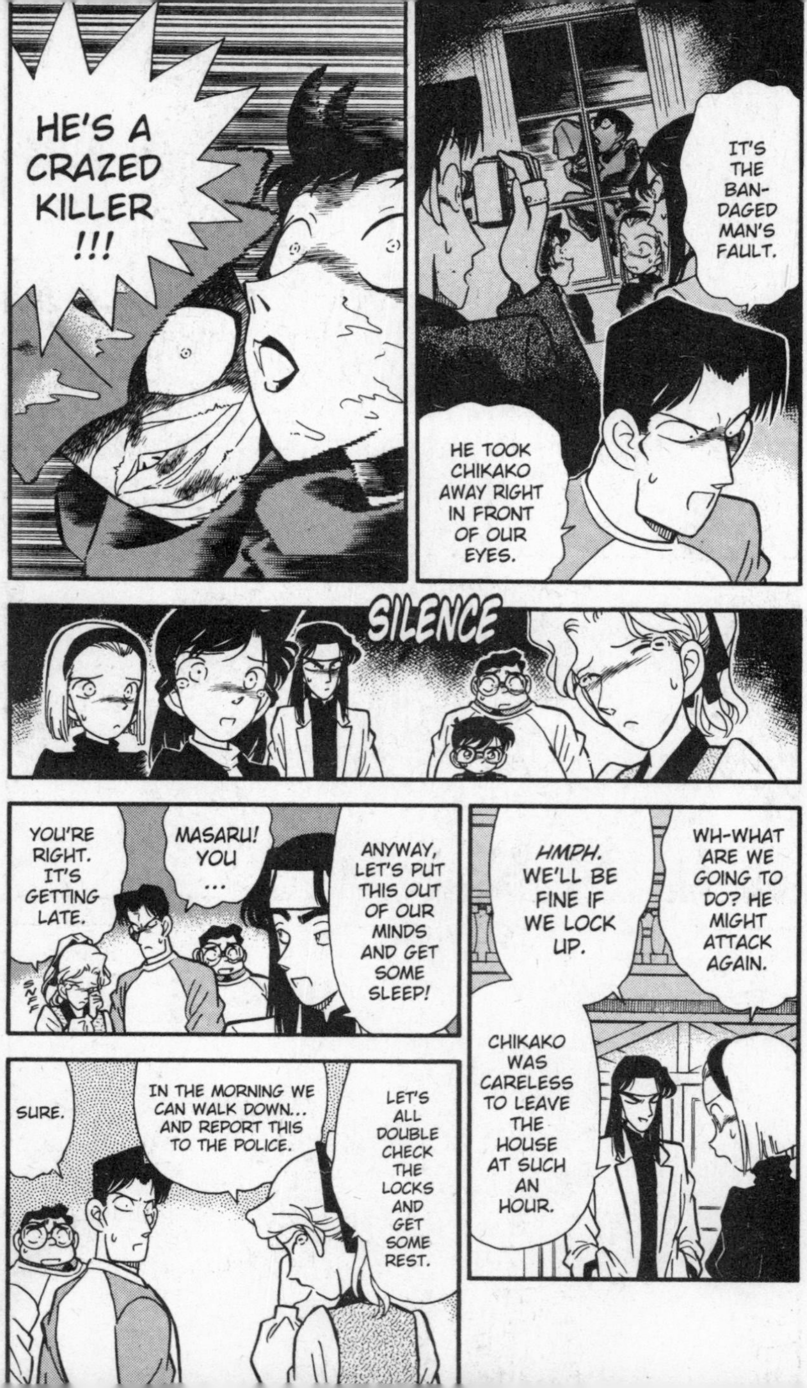
IT'S THE BAN-DAGED MAN'S FAULT.
HE TOOK CHIKAKO AWAY RIGHT IN FRONT OF OUR EYES.
HE'S A CRAZED KILLER !!!
SILENCE
WH-WHAT ARE WE GOING TO DO? HE MIGHT ATTACK AGAIN.
HMPH. WE'LL BE FINE IF WE LOCK UP.
CHIKAKO WAS CARELESS TO LEAVE THE HOUSE AT SUCH AN HOUR.
ANYWAY, LET'S PUT THIS OUT OF OUR MINDS AND GET SOME SLEEP!
MASARU! YOU ...
YOU'RE RIGHT. IT'S GETTING LATE.
SNFF
LET'S ALL DOUBLE CHECK THE LOCKS AND GET SOME REST.
IN THE MORNING WE CAN WALK DOWN... AND REPORT THIS TO THE POLICE.
SURE.

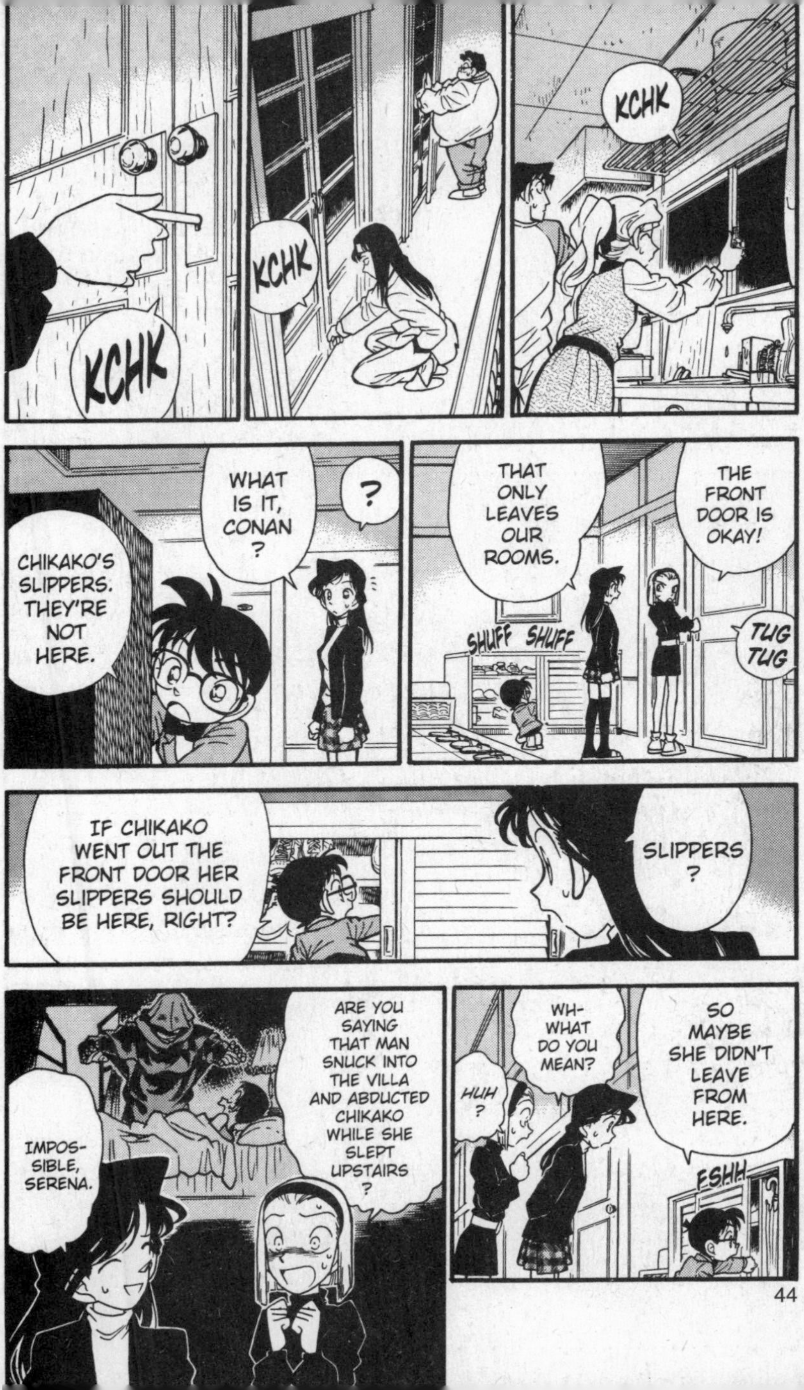
KCHK
KCHK
KCHK
THE FRONT DOOR IS OKAY!
TUG TUG
THAT ONLY LEAVES OUR ROOMS.
SHUFF SHUFF
?
WHAT IS IT, CONAN?
CHIKAKO'S SLIPPERS. THEY'RE NOT HERE.
SLIPPERS?
IF CHIKAKO WENT OUT THE FRONT DOOR HER SLIPPERS SHOULD BE HERE, RIGHT?
SO MAYBE SHE DIDN'T LEAVE FROM HERE.
WH-WHAT DO YOU MEAN?
HUH?
FSHH
ARE YOU SAYING THAT MAN SNUCK INTO THE VILLA AND ABDUCTED CHIKAKO WHILE SHE SLEPT UPSTAIRS?
IMPOSSIBLE, SERENA.

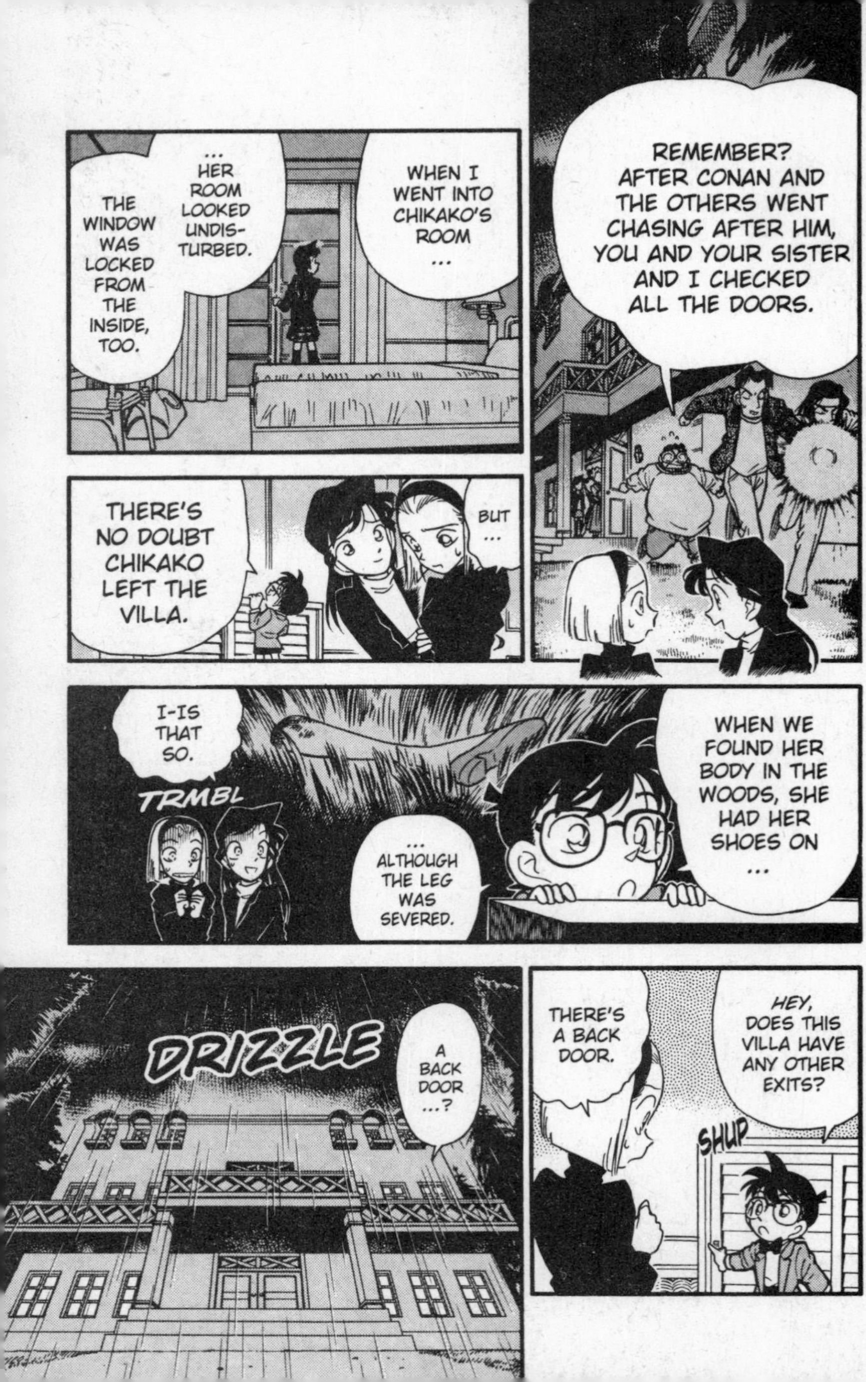
REMEMBER? AFTER CONAN AND THE OTHERS WENT CHASING AFTER HIM, YOU AND YOUR SISTER AND I CHECKED ALL THE DOORS.
WHEN I WENT INTO CHIKAKO'S ROOM ...
... HER ROOM LOOKED UNDIS-TURBED.
THE WINDOW WAS LOCKED FROM THE INSIDE, TOO.
BUT ...
THERE'S NO DOUBT CHIKAKO LEFT THE VILLA.
WHEN WE FOUND HER BODY IN THE WOODS, SHE HAD HER SHOES ON ...
... ALTHOUGH THE LEG WAS SEVERED.
I-IS THAT SO.
TRMBL
HEY, DOES THIS VILLA HAVE ANY OTHER EXITS?
SHUP
THERE'S A BACK DOOR.
DRIZZLE
A BACK DOOR ...?

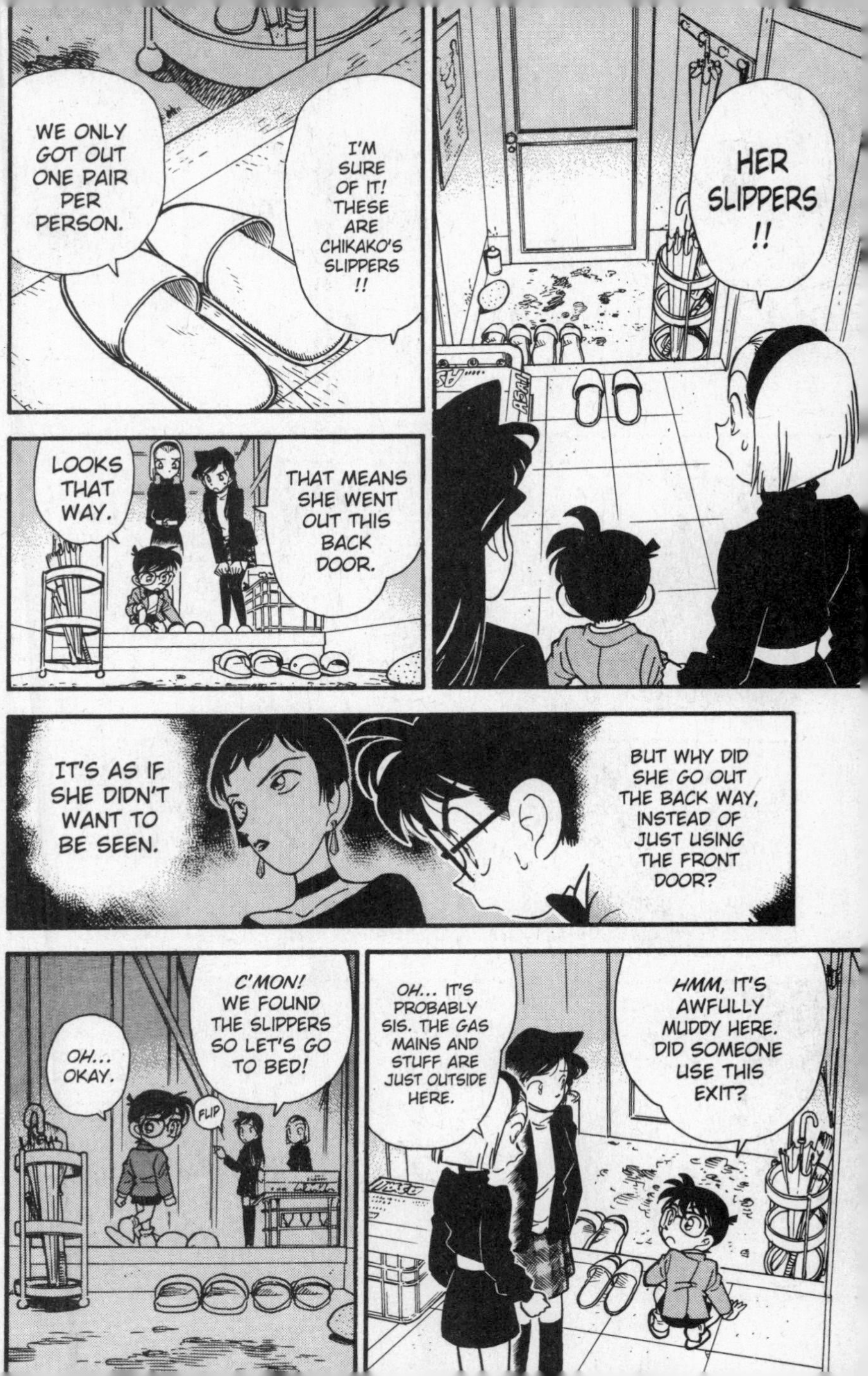
HER SLIPPERS !!
I'M SURE OF IT! THESE ARE CHIKAKO'S SLIPPERS !!
WE ONLY GOT OUT ONE PAIR PER PERSON.
THAT MEANS SHE WENT OUT THIS BACK DOOR.
LOOKS THAT WAY.
BUT WHY DID SHE GO OUT THE BACK WAY, INSTEAD OF JUST USING THE FRONT DOOR?
IT'S AS IF SHE DIDN'T WANT TO BE SEEN.
HMM, IT'S AWFULLY MUDDY HERE. DID SOMEONE USE THIS EXIT?
OH... IT'S PROBABLY SIS. THE GAS MAINS AND STUFF ARE JUST OUTSIDE HERE.
C'MON! WE FOUND THE SLIPPERS SO LET'S GO TO BED!
FLIP
OH... OKAY.

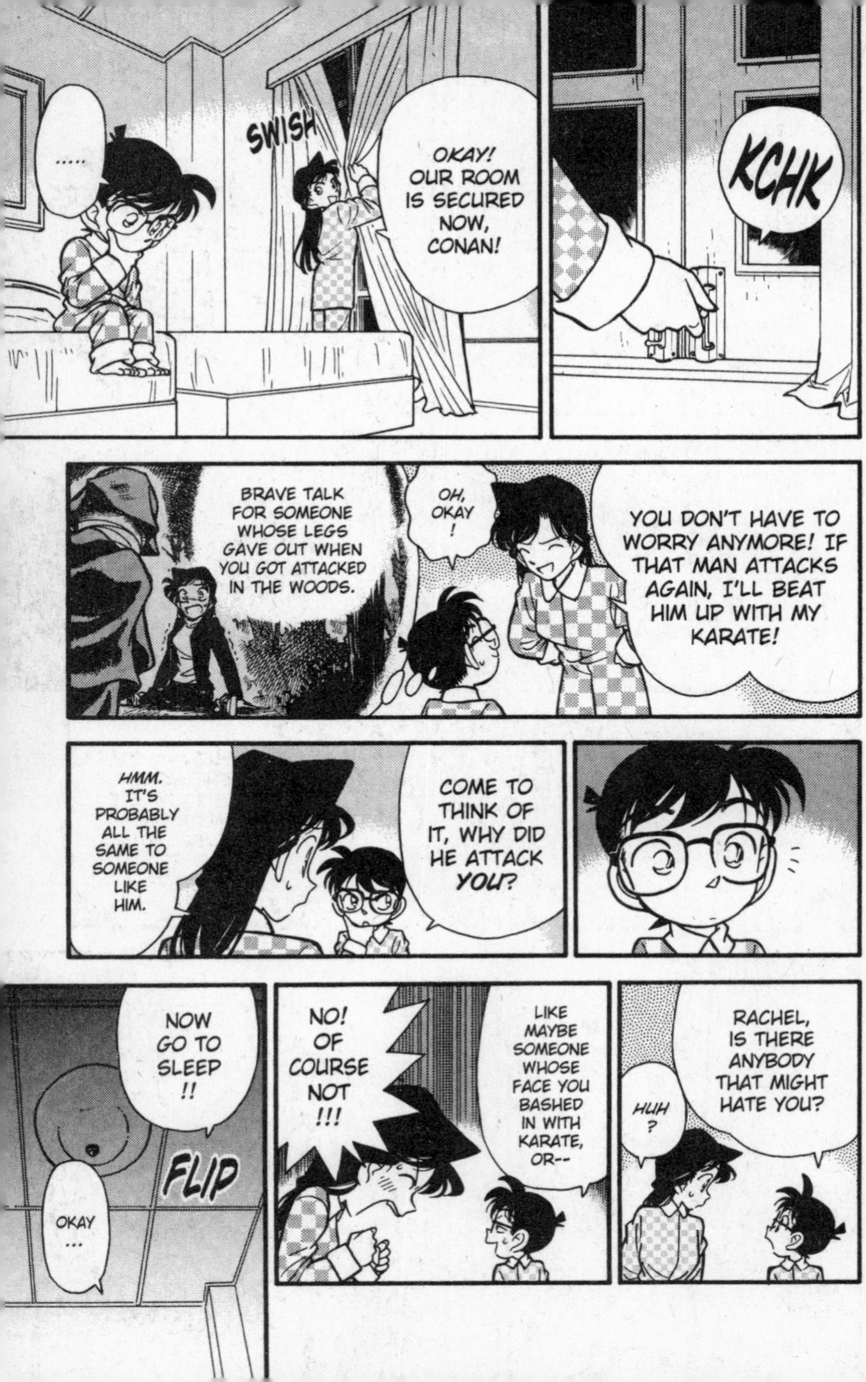
KCHK
OKAY! OUR ROOM IS SECURED NOW, CONAN!
SWISH
.....
YOU DON'T HAVE TO WORRY ANYMORE! IF THAT MAN ATTACKS AGAIN, I'LL BEAT HIM UP WITH MY KARATE!
OH, OKAY!
BRAVE TALK FOR SOMEONE WHOSE LEGS GAVE OUT WHEN YOU GOT ATTACKED IN THE WOODS.
COME TO THINK OF IT, WHY DID HE ATTACK *YOU*?
HMM. IT'S PROBABLY ALL THE SAME TO SOMEONE LIKE HIM.
RACHEL, IS THERE ANYBODY THAT MIGHT HATE YOU?
HUH?
LIKE MAYBE SOMEONE WHOSE FACE YOU BASHED IN WITH KARATE, OR--
NO! OF COURSE NOT!!!
NOW GO TO SLEEP!!
FLIP
OKAY...

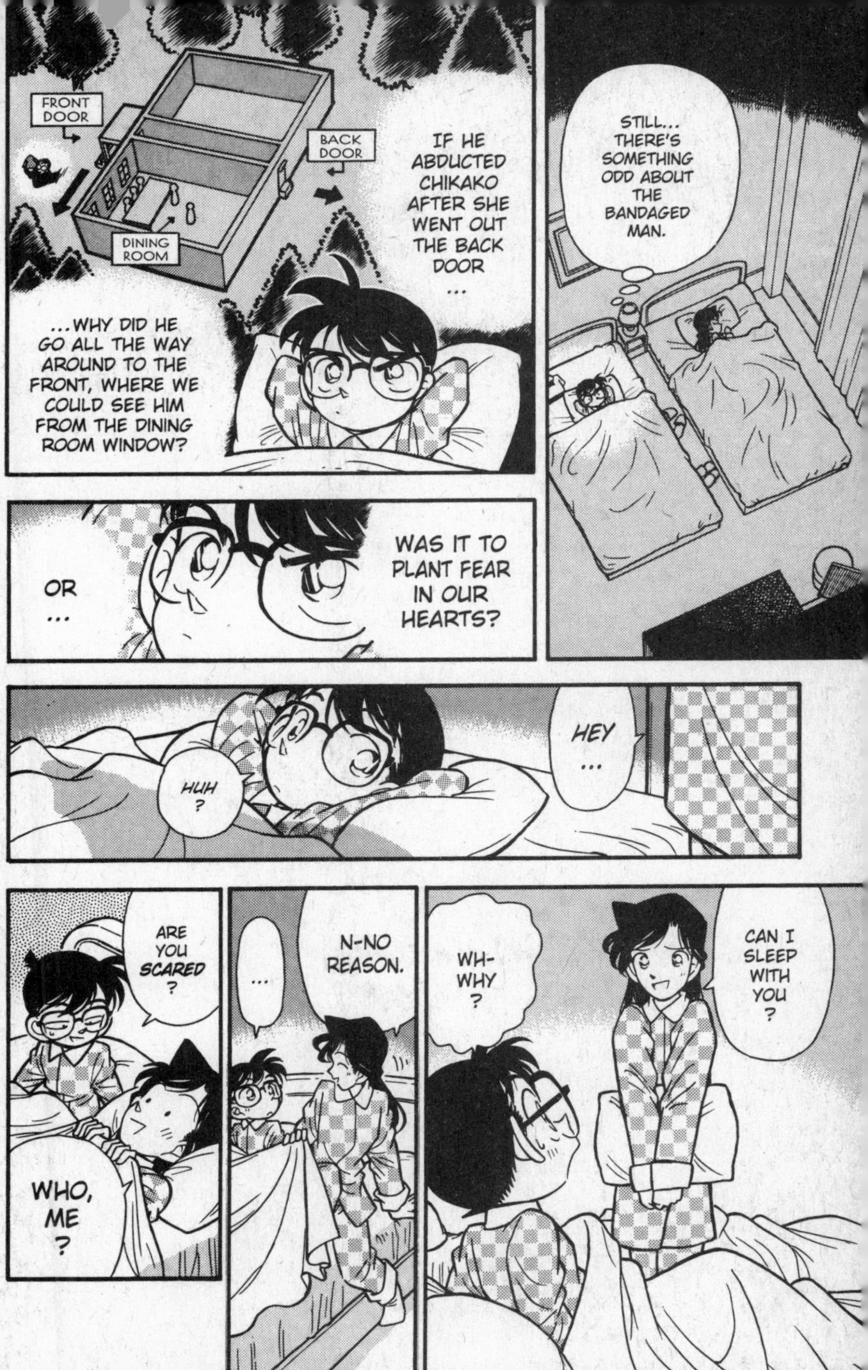
STILL... THERE'S SOMETHING ODD ABOUT THE BANDAGED MAN.
FRONT DOOR
BACK DOOR
DINING ROOM
IF HE ABDUCTED CHIKAKO AFTER SHE WENT OUT THE BACK DOOR ...
...WHY DID HE GO ALL THE WAY AROUND TO THE FRONT, WHERE WE COULD SEE HIM FROM THE DINING ROOM WINDOW?
WAS IT TO PLANT FEAR IN OUR HEARTS?
OR ...
HEY ...
HUH ?
CAN I SLEEP WITH YOU ?
WH- WHY ?
N-NO REASON.
...
ARE YOU SCARED ?
WHO, ME ?

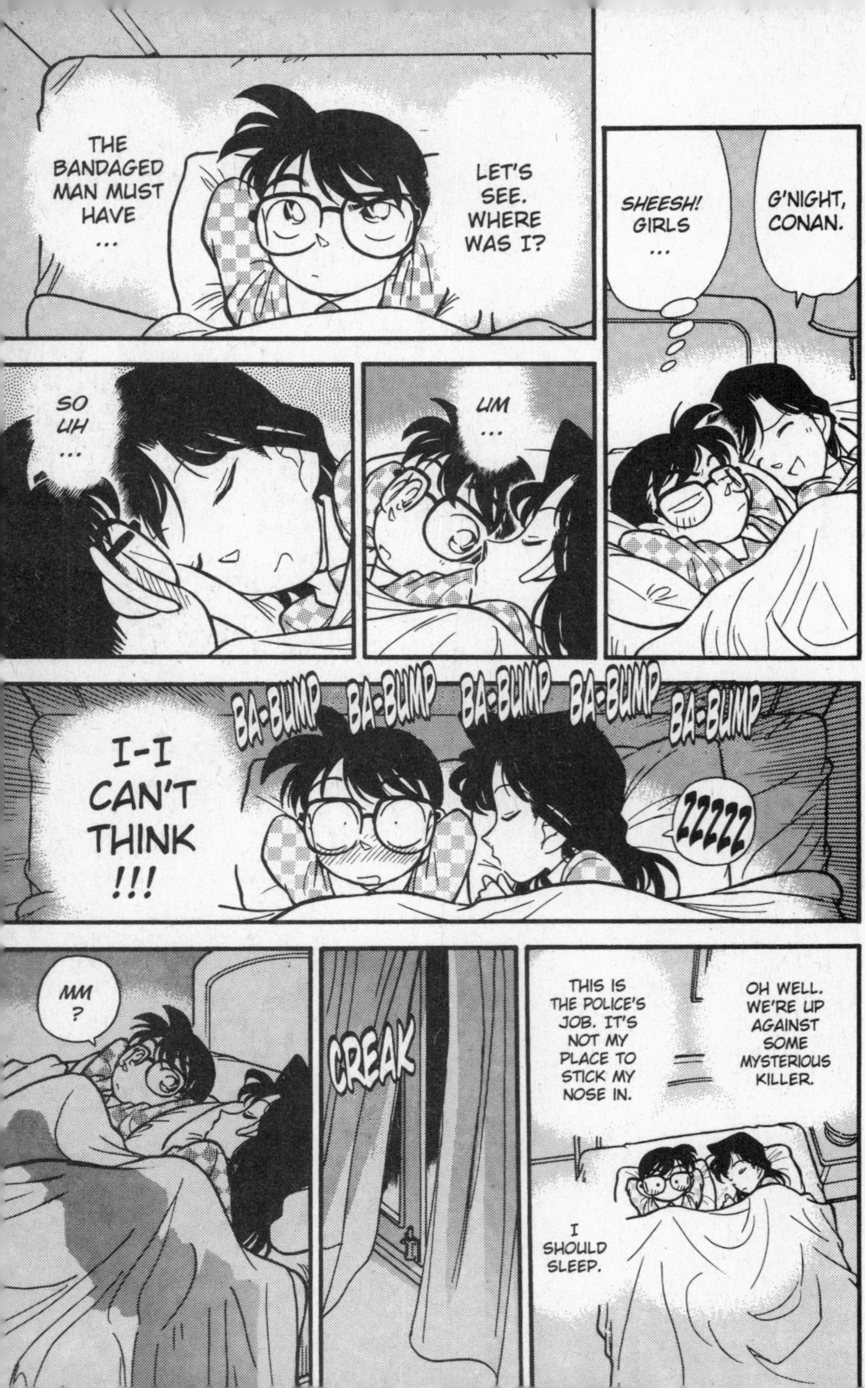
G'NIGHT, CONAN.
SHEESH! GIRLS ...
LET'S SEE. WHERE WAS I?
THE BANDAGED MAN MUST HAVE ...
UM ...
SO UH ...
BA-BUMP
BA-BUMP
BA-BUMP
BA-BUMP
BA-BUMP
ZZZZZ
I-I CAN'T THINK !!!
OH WELL. WE'RE UP AGAINST SOME MYSTERIOUS KILLER.
THIS IS THE POLICE'S JOB. IT'S NOT MY PLACE TO STICK MY NOSE IN.
I SHOULD SLEEP.
CREAK
MM ?

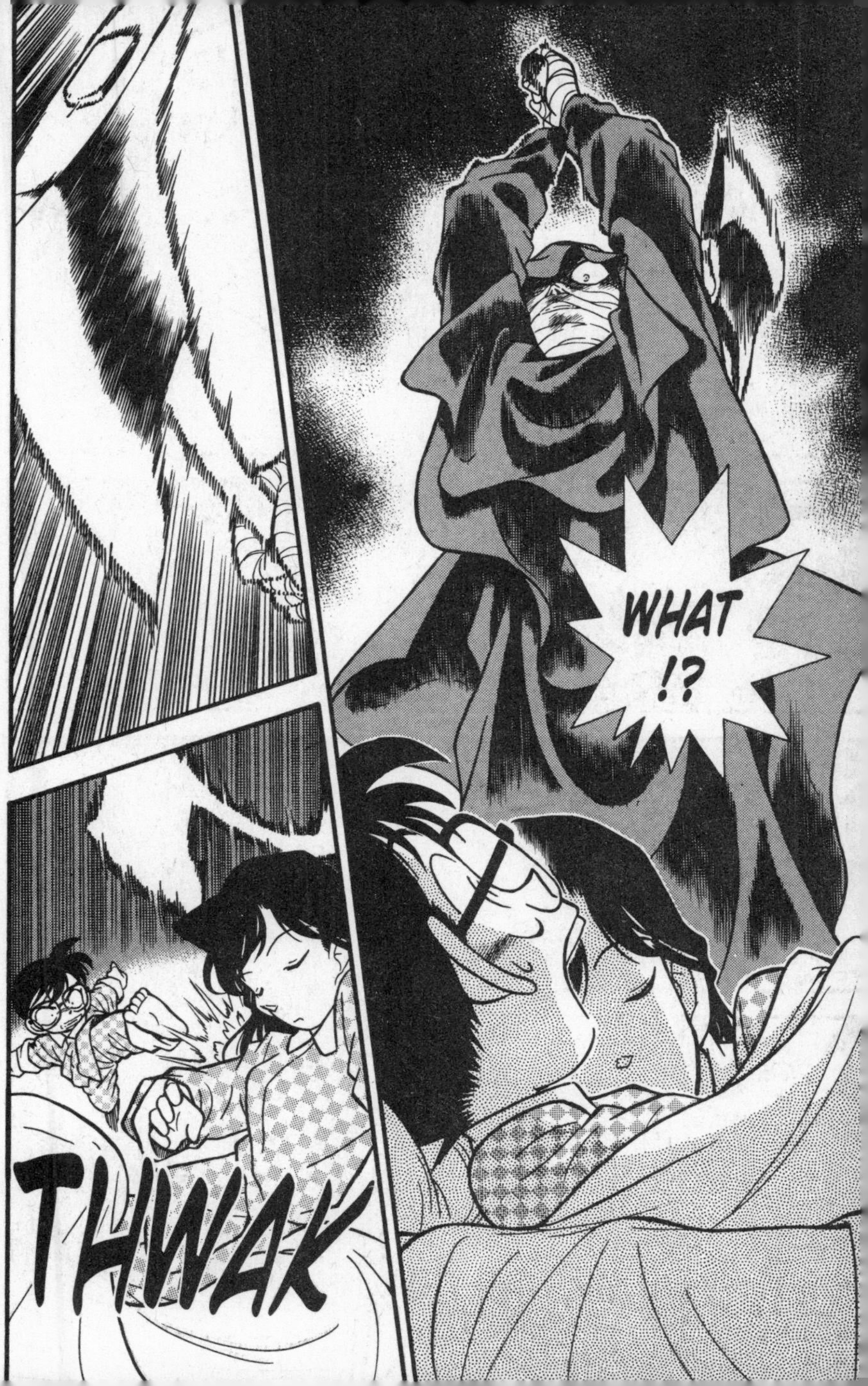
WHAT !?
THWAK

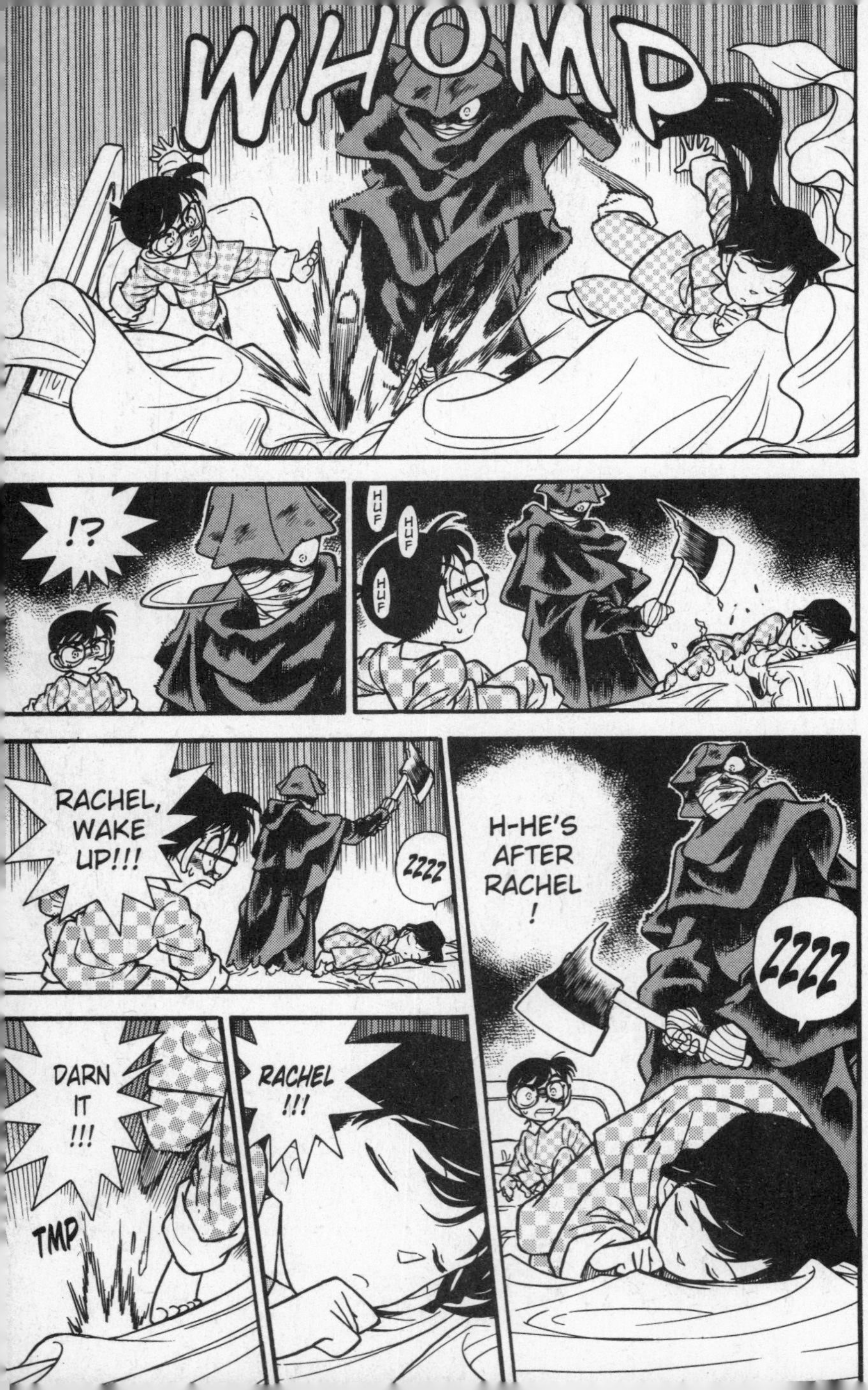
WHOMP
HUF
HUF
HUF
!?
H-HE'S AFTER RACHEL!
ZZZZ
RACHEL, WAKE UP!!!
ZZZZ
RACHEL!!!
DARN IT!!!
TMP

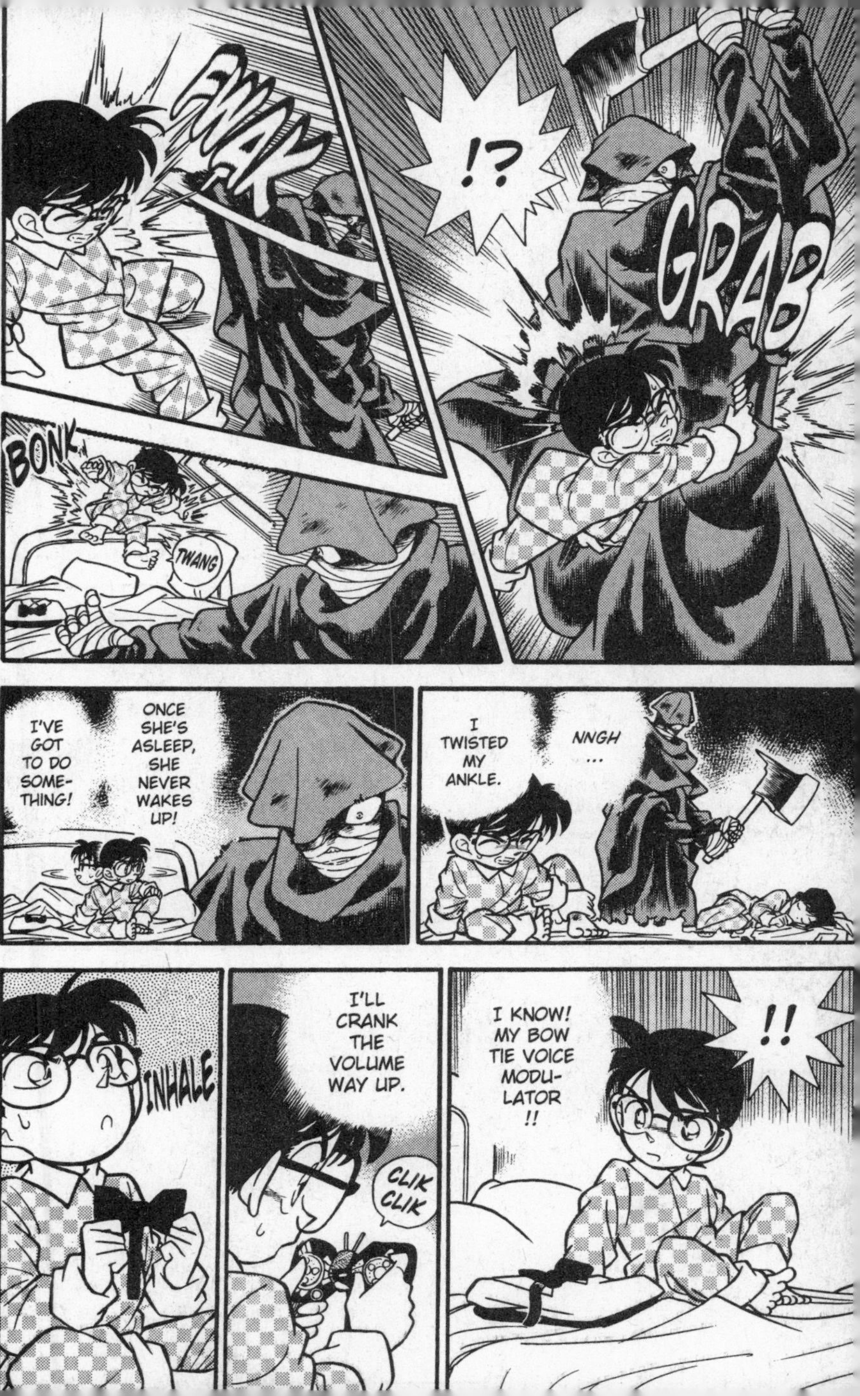
!?
GRAB
SWAK
BONK
TWANG
NNGH ...
I TWISTED MY ANKLE.
ONCE SHE'S ASLEEP, SHE NEVER WAKES UP!
I'VE GOT TO DO SOMETHING!
!!
I KNOW! MY BOW TIE VOICE MODULATOR !!
I'LL CRANK THE VOLUME WAY UP.
CLIK CLIK
INHALE

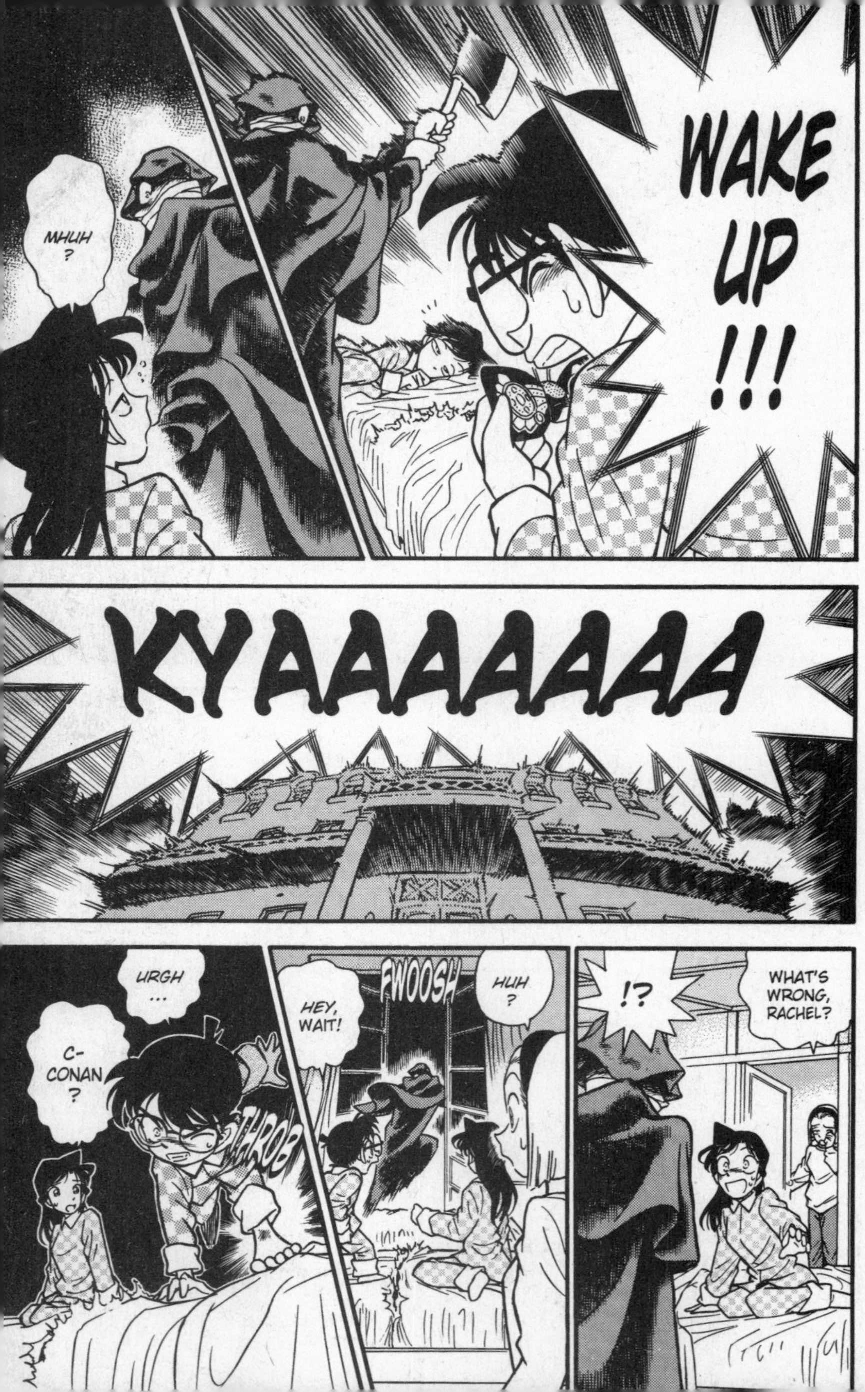
WAKE UP !!!
MHUH ?
KYAAAAAAA
WHAT'S WRONG, RACHEL?
!?
HUH ?
FWOOSH
HEY, WAIT!
URGH ...
C- CONAN ?
THROB

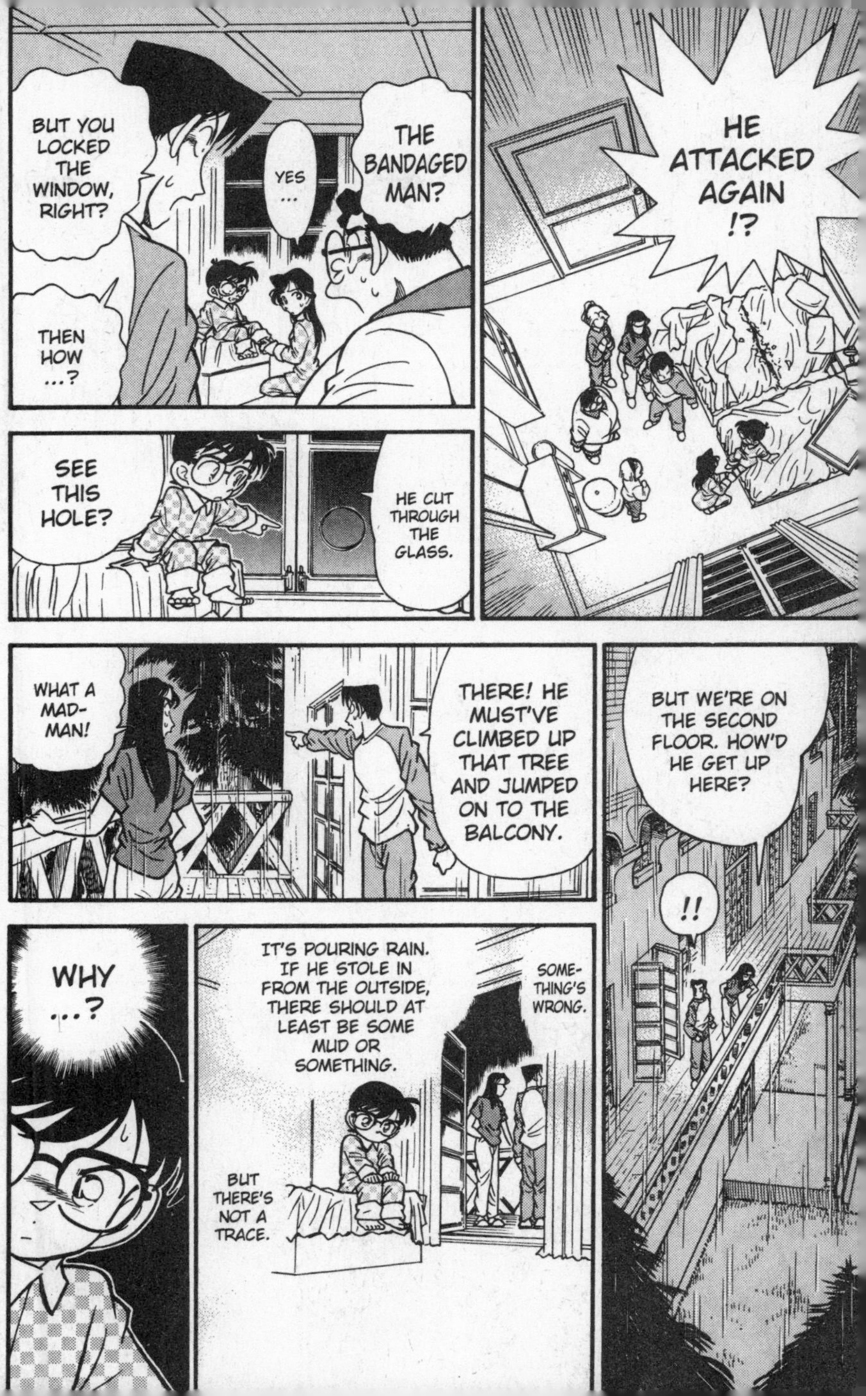
HE ATTACKED AGAIN !?
THE BANDAGED MAN?
YES ...
BUT YOU LOCKED THE WINDOW, RIGHT?
THEN HOW ...?
SEE THIS HOLE?
HE CUT THROUGH THE GLASS.
BUT WE'RE ON THE SECOND FLOOR. HOW'D HE GET UP HERE?
!!
THERE! HE MUST'VE CLIMBED UP THAT TREE AND JUMPED ON TO THE BALCONY.
WHAT A MAD-MAN!
SOME-THING'S WRONG.
IT'S POURING RAIN. IF HE STOLE IN FROM THE OUTSIDE, THERE SHOULD AT LEAST BE SOME MUD OR SOMETHING.
BUT THERE'S NOT A TRACE.
WHY ...?

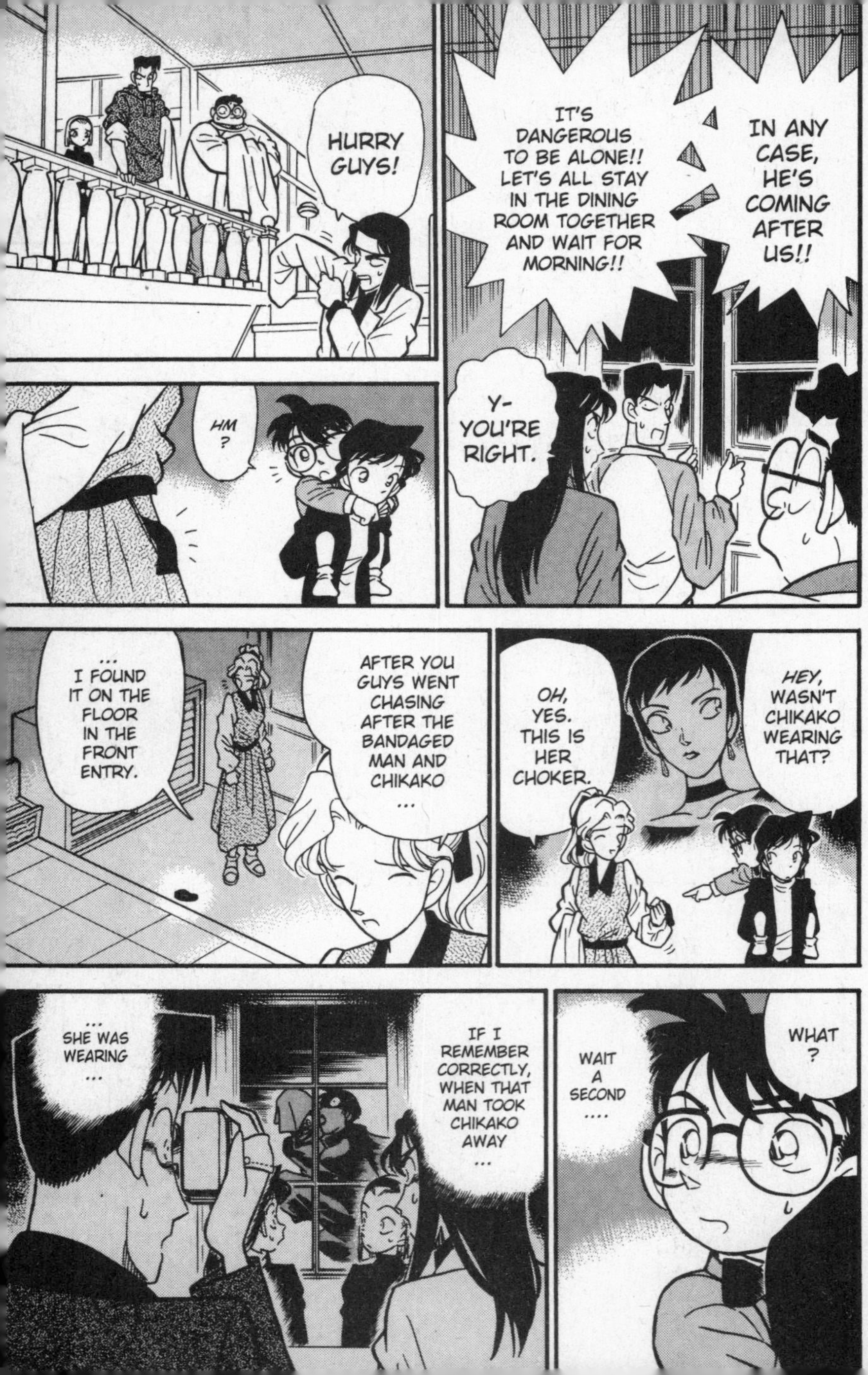
IN ANY CASE, HE'S COMING AFTER US!!
IT'S DANGEROUS TO BE ALONE!! LET'S ALL STAY IN THE DINING ROOM TOGETHER AND WAIT FOR MORNING!!
Y- YOU'RE RIGHT.
HURRY GUYS!
HM ?
HEY, WASN'T CHIKAKO WEARING THAT?
OH, YES. THIS IS HER CHOKER.
AFTER YOU GUYS WENT CHASING AFTER THE BANDAGED MAN AND CHIKAKO ...
... I FOUND IT ON THE FLOOR IN THE FRONT ENTRY.
WHAT ?
WAIT A SECOND ....
IF I REMEMBER CORRECTLY, WHEN THAT MAN TOOK CHIKAKO AWAY ...
... SHE WAS WEARING ...

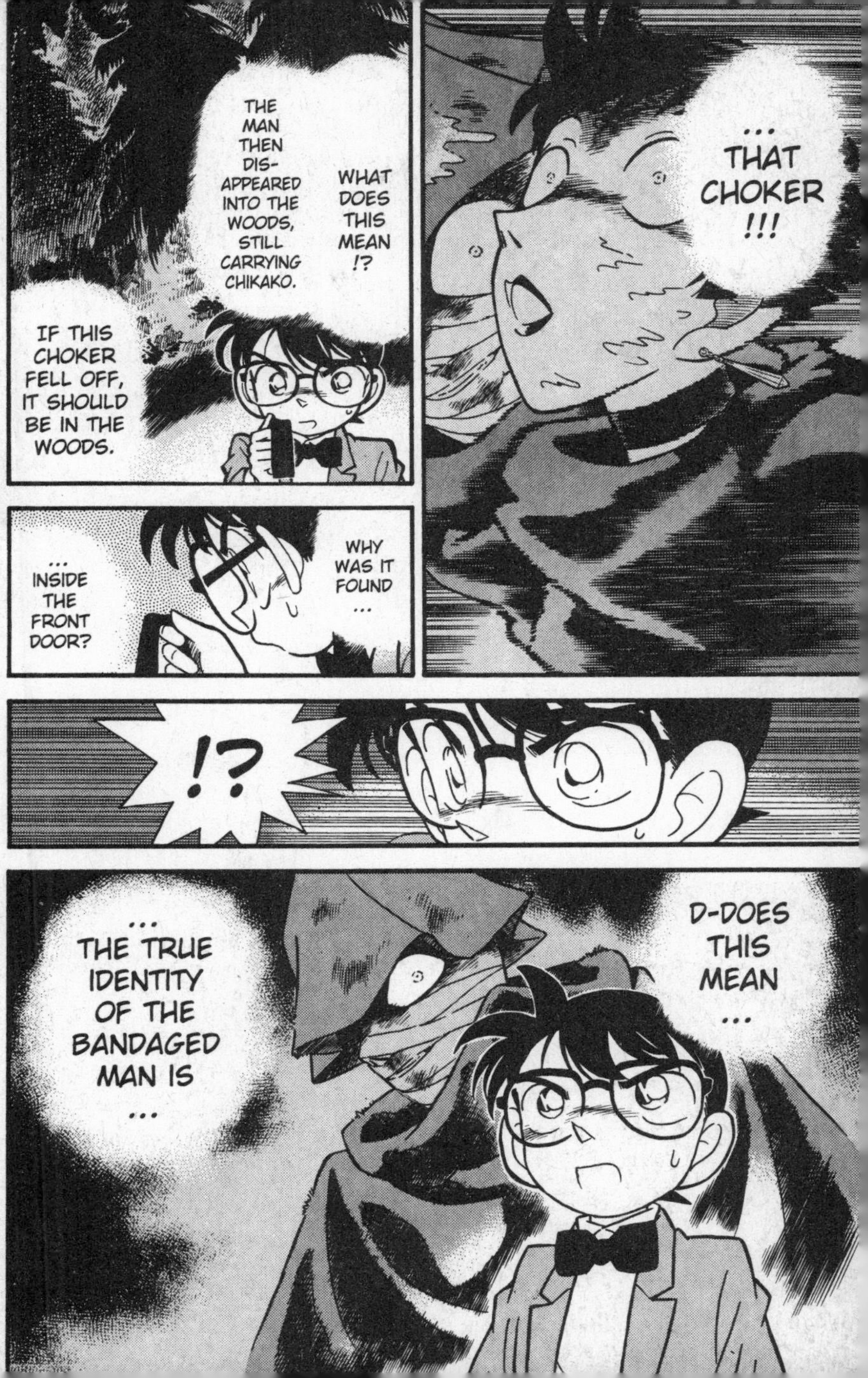
... THAT CHOKER !!!
WHAT DOES THIS MEAN !?
THE MAN THEN DIS- APPEARED INTO THE WOODS, STILL CARRYING CHIKAKO.
IF THIS CHOKER FELL OFF, IT SHOULD BE IN THE WOODS.
WHY WAS IT FOUND ...
... INSIDE THE FRONT DOOR?
!?
D-DOES THIS MEAN ...
... THE TRUE IDENTITY OF THE BANDAGED MAN IS ...

FILE 4:
ASSAULT IN THE DARK!

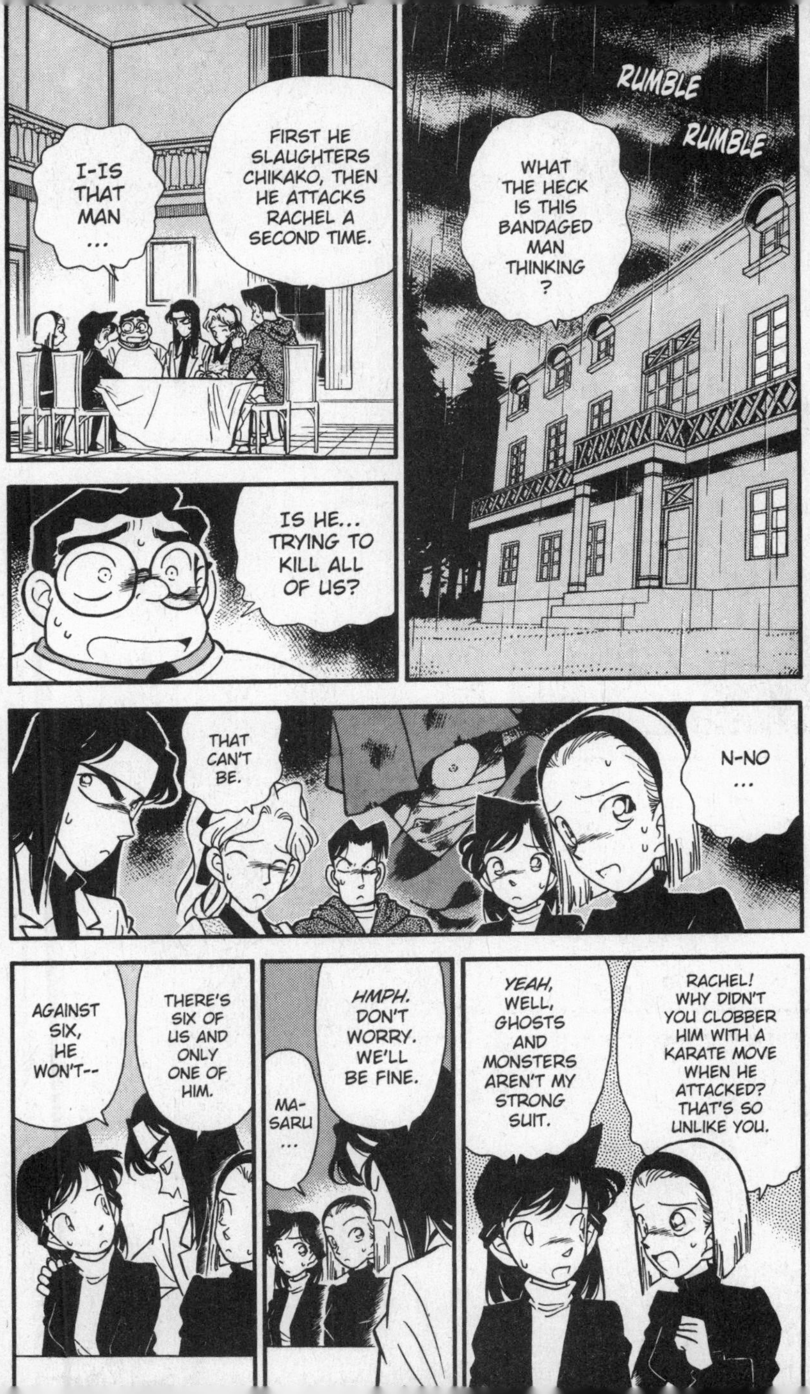
RUMBLE
RUMBLE
WHAT THE HECK IS THIS BANDAGED MAN THINKING?
FIRST HE SLAUGHTERS CHIKAKO, THEN HE ATTACKS RACHEL A SECOND TIME.
I-IS THAT MAN...
IS HE... TRYING TO KILL ALL OF US?
N-NO...
THAT CAN'T BE.
RACHEL! WHY DIDN'T YOU CLOBBER HIM WITH A KARATE MOVE WHEN HE ATTACKED? THAT'S SO UNLIKE YOU.
YEAH, WELL, GHOSTS AND MONSTERS AREN'T MY STRONG SUIT.
HMPH. DON'T WORRY. WE'LL BE FINE.
MA-SARU...
THERE'S SIX OF US AND ONLY ONE OF HIM.
AGAINST SIX, HE WON'T--

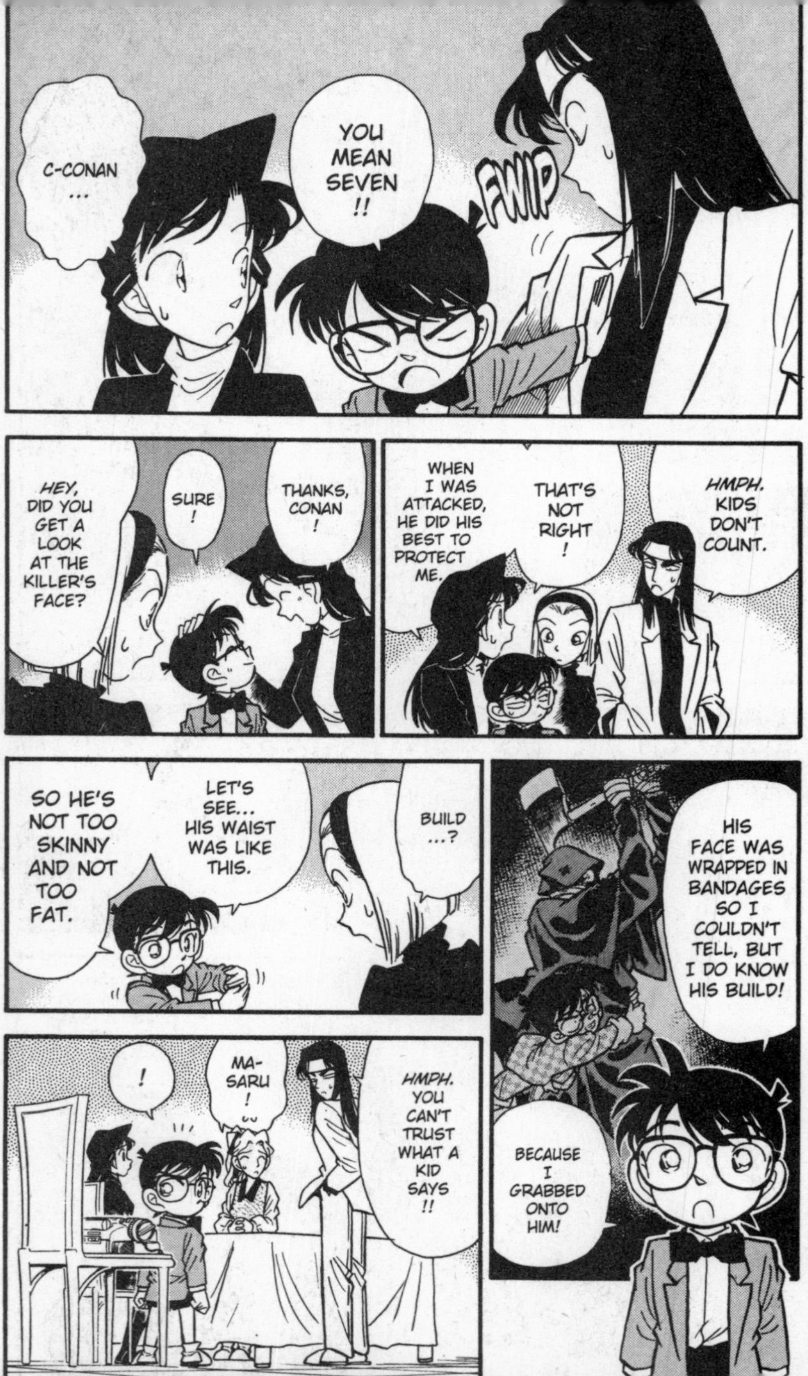
FWIP
YOU MEAN SEVEN !!
C-CONAN ...
HMPH. KIDS DON'T COUNT.
THAT'S NOT RIGHT !
WHEN I WAS ATTACKED, HE DID HIS BEST TO PROTECT ME.
THANKS, CONAN !
SURE !
HEY, DID YOU GET A LOOK AT THE KILLER'S FACE?
HIS FACE WAS WRAPPED IN BANDAGES SO I COULDN'T TELL, BUT I DO KNOW HIS BUILD!
BECAUSE I GRABBED ONTO HIM!
BUILD ...?
LET'S SEE... HIS WAIST WAS LIKE THIS.
SO HE'S NOT TOO SKINNY AND NOT TOO FAT.
HMPH. YOU CAN'T TRUST WHAT A KID SAYS !!
MA-SARU !
!

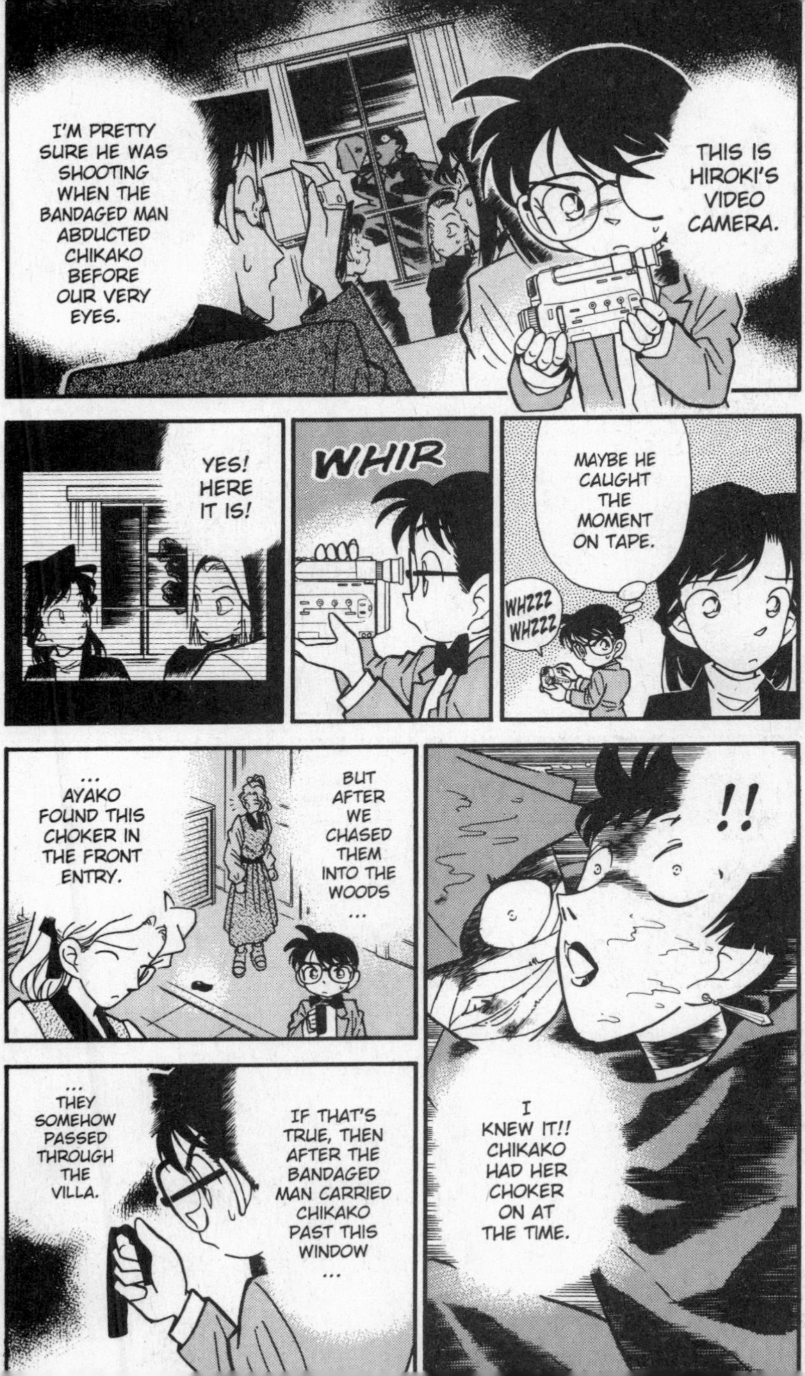
THIS IS HIROKI'S VIDEO CAMERA.
I'M PRETTY SURE HE WAS SHOOTING WHEN THE BANDAGED MAN ABDUCTED CHIKAKO BEFORE OUR VERY EYES.
MAYBE HE CAUGHT THE MOMENT ON TAPE.
WHZZZ WHZZZ
WHIR
YES! HERE IT IS!
!!
I KNEW IT!! CHIKAKO HAD HER CHOKER ON AT THE TIME.
BUT AFTER WE CHASED THEM INTO THE WOODS ...
... AYAKO FOUND THIS CHOKER IN THE FRONT ENTRY.
IF THAT'S TRUE, THEN AFTER THE BANDAGED MAN CARRIED CHIKAKO PAST THIS WINDOW ...
... THEY SOMEHOW PASSED THROUGH THE VILLA.

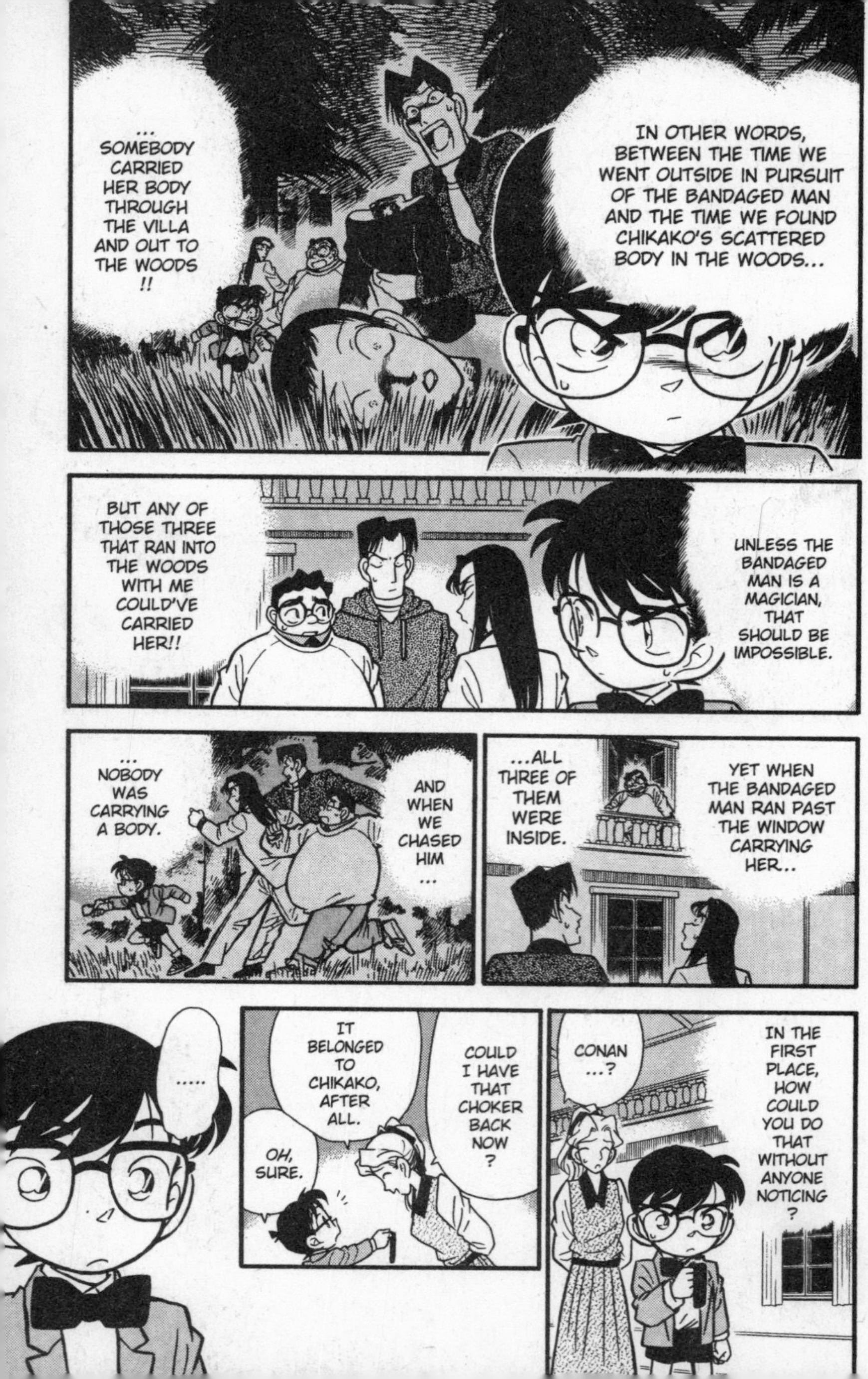
IN OTHER WORDS, BETWEEN THE TIME WE WENT OUTSIDE IN PURSUIT OF THE BANDAGED MAN AND THE TIME WE FOUND CHIKAKO'S SCATTERED BODY IN THE WOODS...
... SOMEBODY CARRIED HER BODY THROUGH THE VILLA AND OUT TO THE WOODS !!
UNLESS THE BANDAGED MAN IS A MAGICIAN, THAT SHOULD BE IMPOSSIBLE.
BUT ANY OF THOSE THREE THAT RAN INTO THE WOODS WITH ME COULD'VE CARRIED HER!!
YET WHEN THE BANDAGED MAN RAN PAST THE WINDOW CARRYING HER..
...ALL THREE OF THEM WERE INSIDE.
AND WHEN WE CHASED HIM ...
... NOBODY WAS CARRYING A BODY.
IN THE FIRST PLACE, HOW COULD YOU DO THAT WITHOUT ANYONE NOTICING ?
CONAN ...?
COULD I HAVE THAT CHOKER BACK NOW ?
IT BELONGED TO CHIKAKO, AFTER ALL.
OH, SURE.
.....

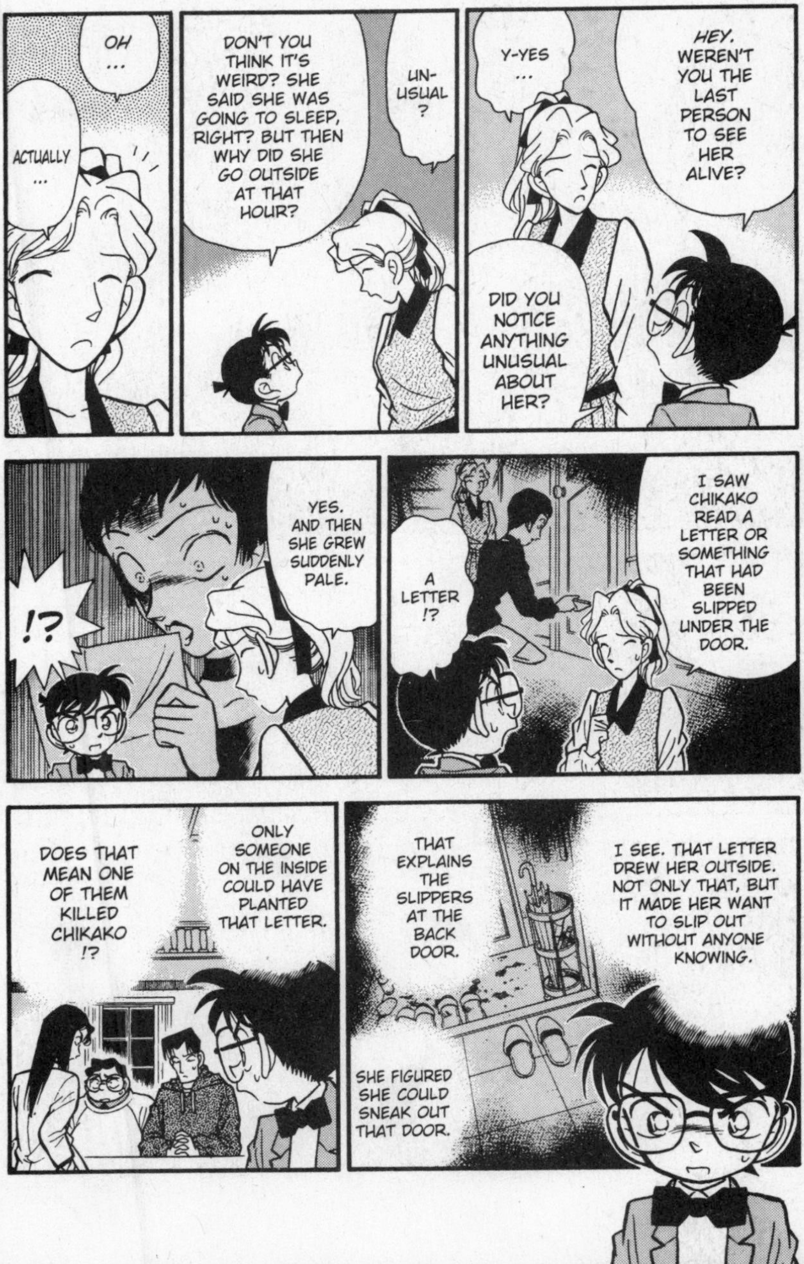

HEY. WEREN'T YOU THE LAST PERSON TO SEE HER ALIVE?
Y-YES ...
DID YOU NOTICE ANYTHING UNUSUAL ABOUT HER?
UN-USUAL ?
DON'T YOU THINK IT'S WEIRD? SHE SAID SHE WAS GOING TO SLEEP, RIGHT? BUT THEN WHY DID SHE GO OUTSIDE AT THAT HOUR?
OH ...
ACTUALLY ...
I SAW CHIKAKO READ A LETTER OR SOMETHING THAT HAD BEEN SLIPPED UNDER THE DOOR.
A LETTER !?
YES. AND THEN SHE GREW SUDDENLY PALE.
!?
I SEE. THAT LETTER DREW HER OUTSIDE. NOT ONLY THAT, BUT IT MADE HER WANT TO SLIP OUT WITHOUT ANYONE KNOWING.
THAT EXPLAINS THE SLIPPERS AT THE BACK DOOR.
SHE FIGURED SHE COULD SNEAK OUT THAT DOOR.
ONLY SOMEONE ON THE INSIDE COULD HAVE PLANTED THAT LETTER.
DOES THAT MEAN ONE OF THEM KILLED CHIKAKO !?

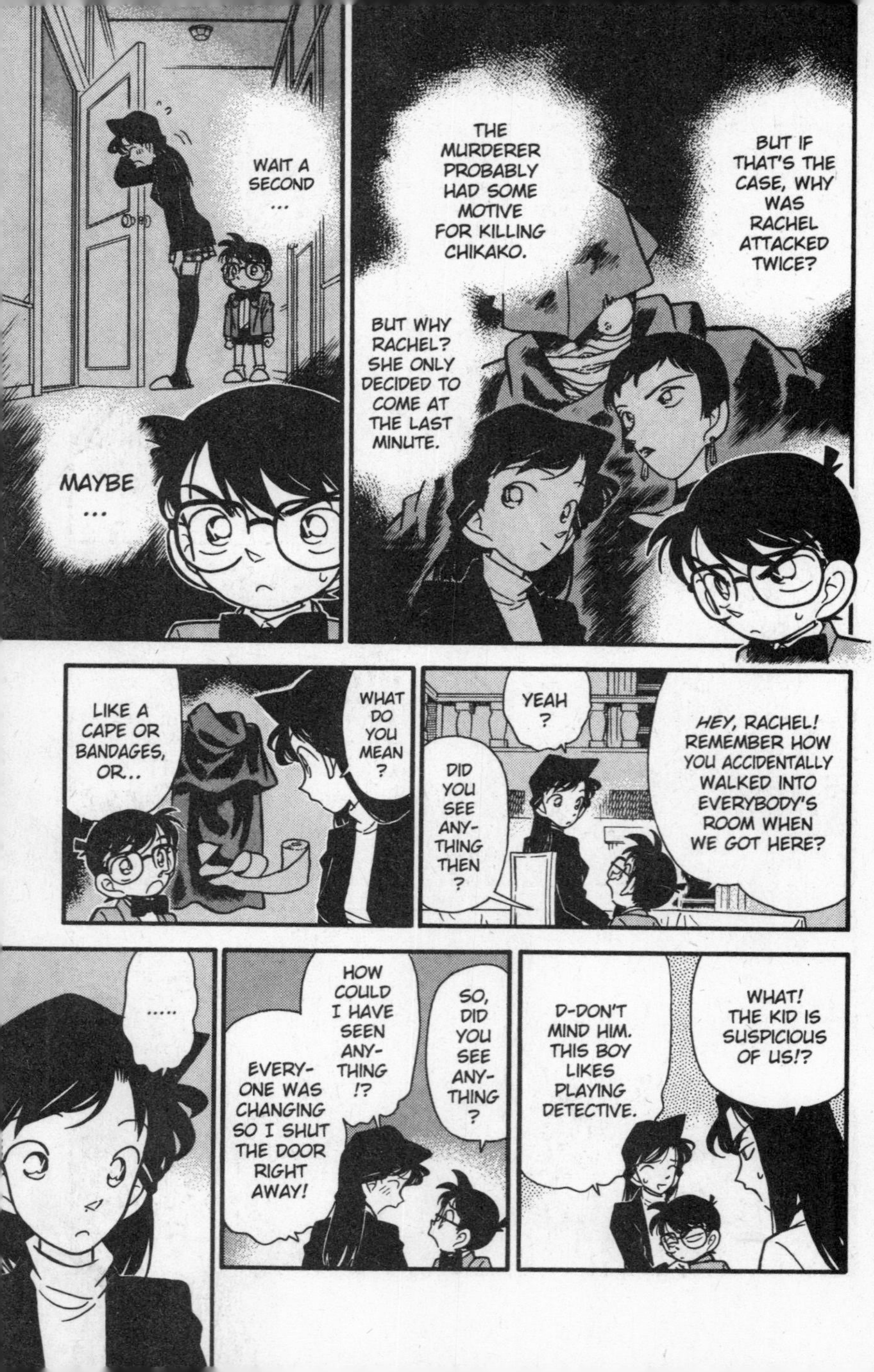
THE MURDERER PROBABLY HAD SOME MOTIVE FOR KILLING CHIKAKO.
BUT IF THAT'S THE CASE, WHY WAS RACHEL ATTACKED TWICE?
BUT WHY RACHEL? SHE ONLY DECIDED TO COME AT THE LAST MINUTE.
WAIT A SECOND ...
MAYBE ...
HEY, RACHEL! REMEMBER HOW YOU ACCIDENTALLY WALKED INTO EVERYBODY'S ROOM WHEN WE GOT HERE?
YEAH ?
DID YOU SEE ANYTHING THEN ?
WHAT DO YOU MEAN ?
LIKE A CAPE OR BANDAGES, OR...
WHAT! THE KID IS SUSPICIOUS OF US!?
D-DON'T MIND HIM. THIS BOY LIKES PLAYING DETECTIVE.
SO, DID YOU SEE ANYTHING ?
HOW COULD I HAVE SEEN ANYTHING !?
EVERYONE WAS CHANGING SO I SHUT THE DOOR RIGHT AWAY!
.....

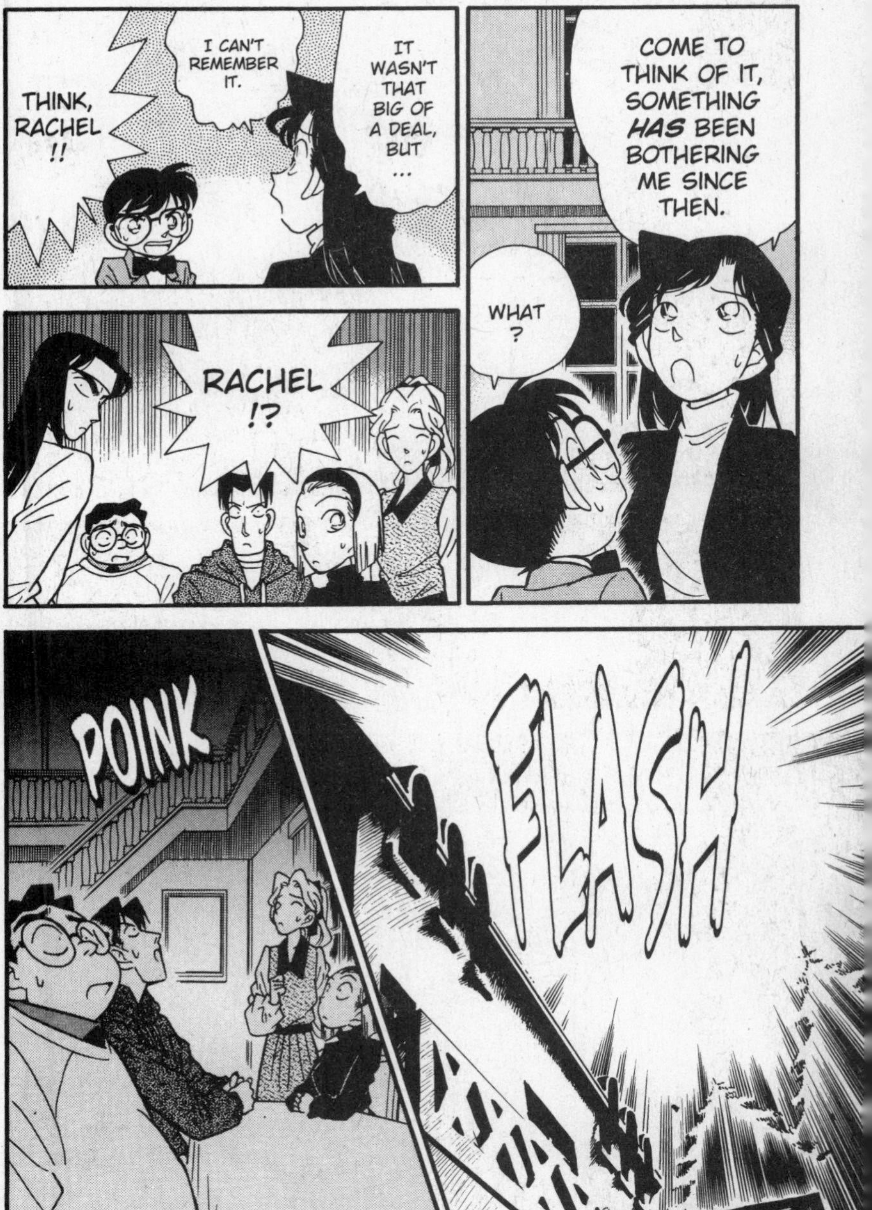
COME TO THINK OF IT, SOMETHING **HAS** BEEN BOTHERING ME SINCE THEN.
WHAT?
IT WASN'T THAT BIG OF A DEAL, BUT ...
I CAN'T REMEMBER IT.
THINK, RACHEL!!
RACHEL!?
FLASH
POINK

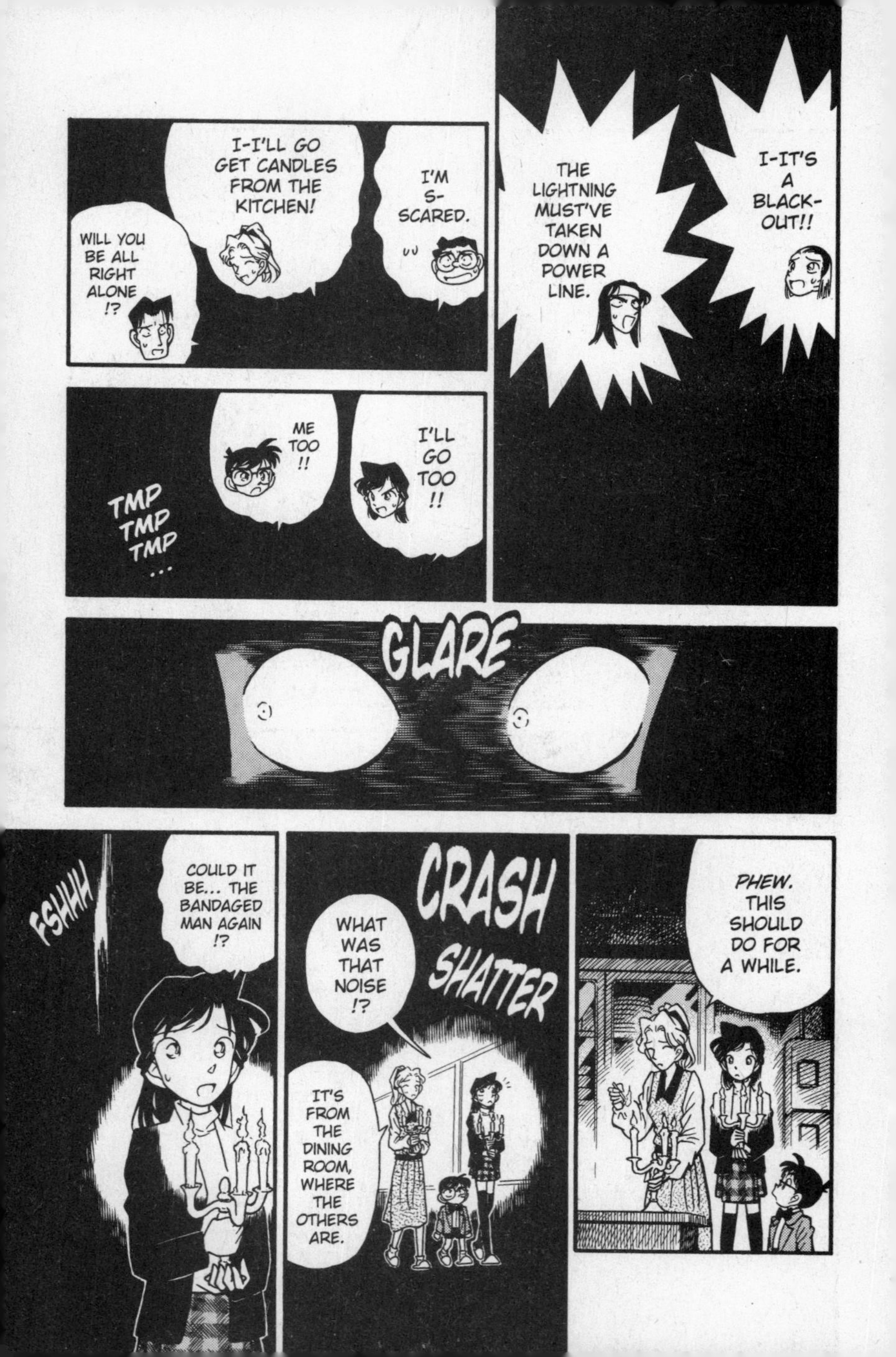
I-IT'S A BLACK-OUT!!
THE LIGHTNING MUST'VE TAKEN DOWN A POWER LINE.
I'M S-SCARED.
I-I'LL GO GET CANDLES FROM THE KITCHEN!
WILL YOU BE ALL RIGHT ALONE!?
I'LL GO TOO!!
ME TOO!!
TMP TMP TMP...
GLARE
PHEW. THIS SHOULD DO FOR A WHILE.
CRASH
SHATTER
WHAT WAS THAT NOISE!?
IT'S FROM THE DINING ROOM, WHERE THE OTHERS ARE.
FSHHH
COULD IT BE... THE BANDAGED MAN AGAIN!?

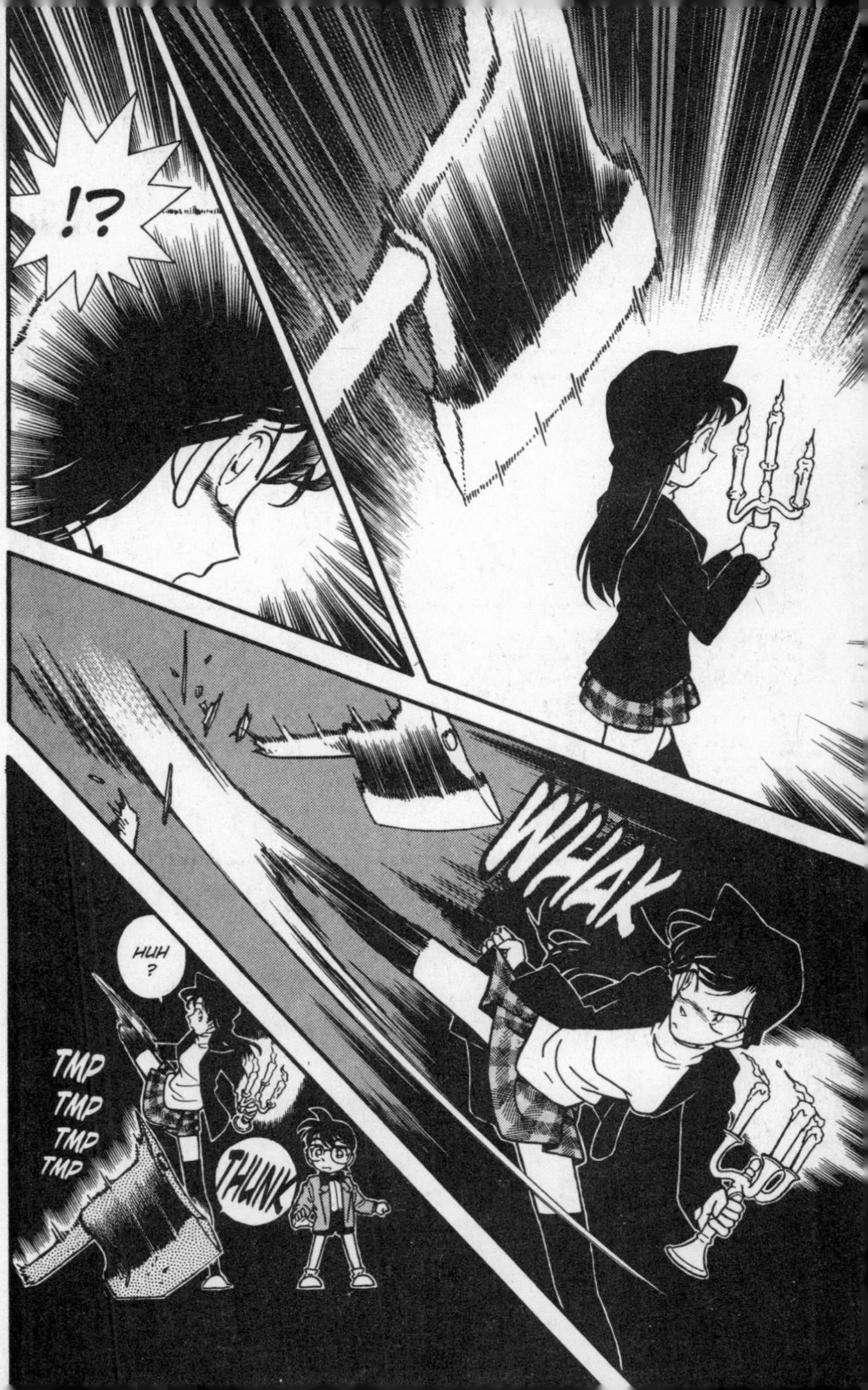
!?
WHAK
HUH ?
TMP TMP TMP TMP
THUNK

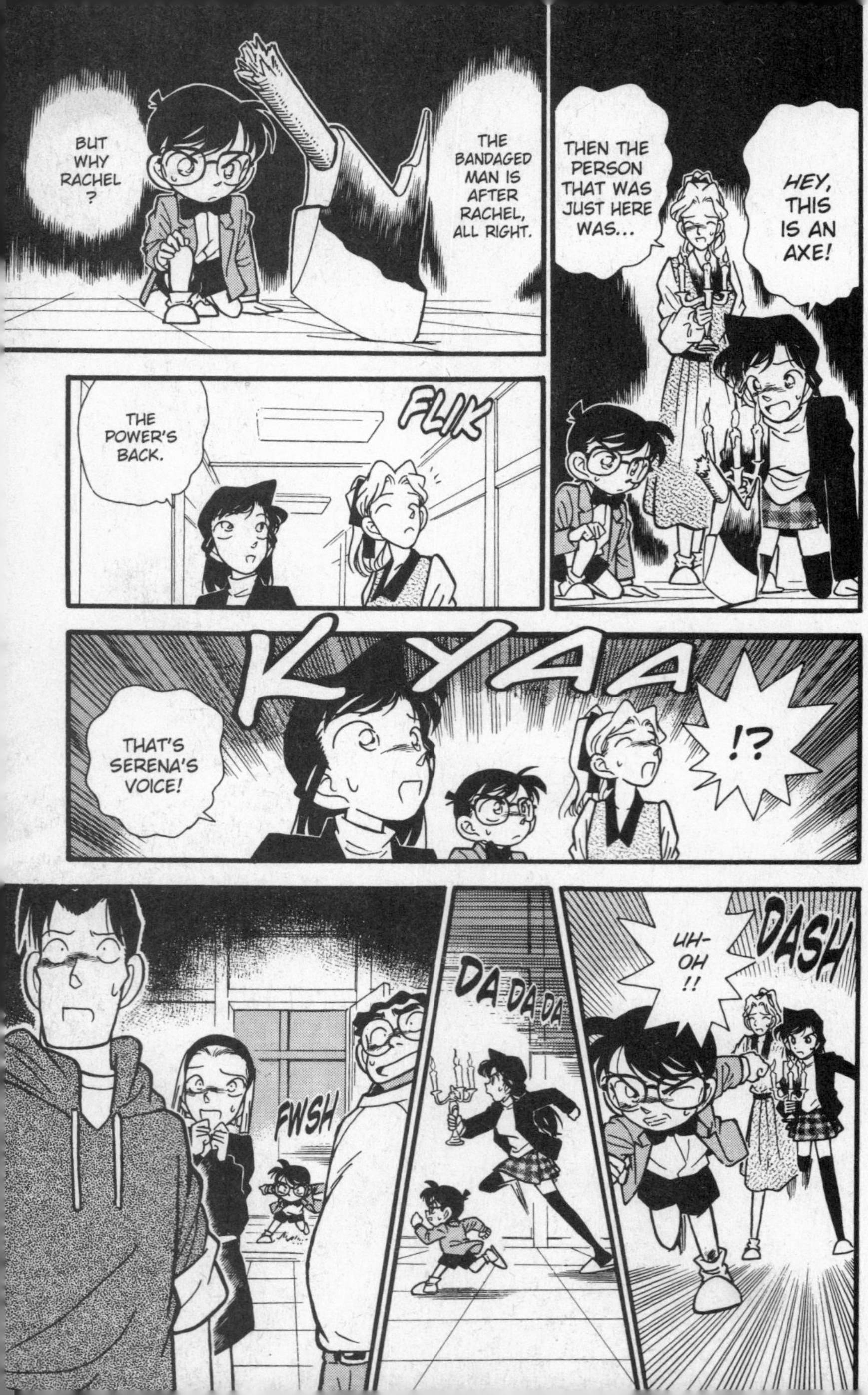
HEY, THIS IS AN AXE!
THEN THE PERSON THAT WAS JUST HERE WAS...
THE BANDAGED MAN IS AFTER RACHEL, ALL RIGHT.
BUT WHY RACHEL ?
FLIK
THE POWER'S BACK.
KYAA
!?
THAT'S SERENA'S VOICE!
DASH
UH-OH !!
DA DA DA
FWSH

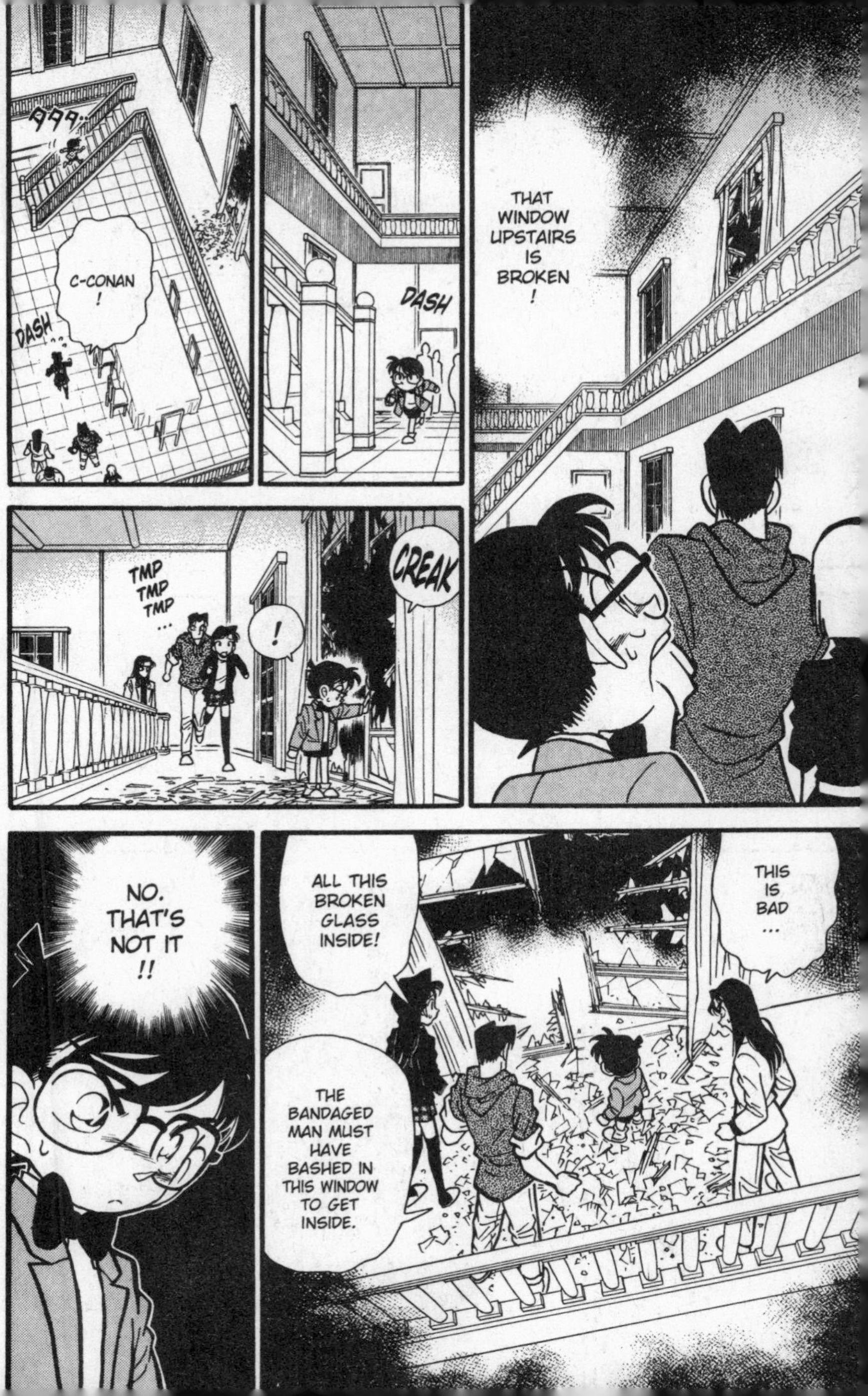
THAT WINDOW UPSTAIRS IS BROKEN!
DASH
C-CONAN!
DASH
CREAK
!
TMP TMP TMP...
THIS IS BAD...
ALL THIS BROKEN GLASS INSIDE!
THE BANDAGED MAN MUST HAVE BASHED IN THIS WINDOW TO GET INSIDE.
NO. THAT'S NOT IT!!

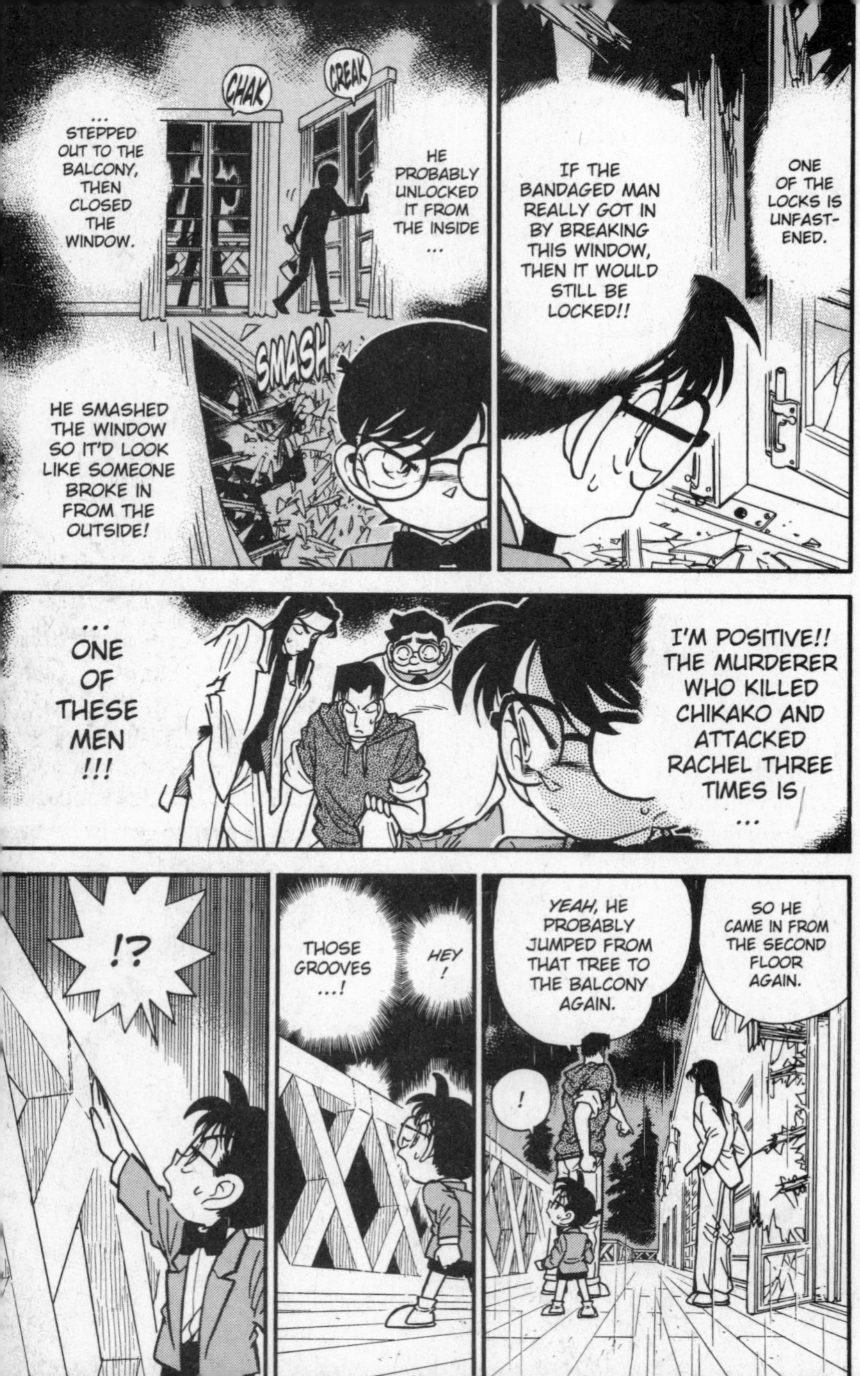
ONE OF THE LOCKS IS UNFASTENED.
IF THE BANDAGED MAN REALLY GOT IN BY BREAKING THIS WINDOW, THEN IT WOULD STILL BE LOCKED!!
HE PROBABLY UNLOCKED IT FROM THE INSIDE ...
CREAK
CHAK
... STEPPED OUT TO THE BALCONY, THEN CLOSED THE WINDOW.
SMASH
HE SMASHED THE WINDOW SO IT'D LOOK LIKE SOMEONE BROKE IN FROM THE OUTSIDE!
I'M POSITIVE!! THE MURDERER WHO KILLED CHIKAKO AND ATTACKED RACHEL THREE TIMES IS ...
... ONE OF THESE MEN !!!
SO HE CAME IN FROM THE SECOND FLOOR AGAIN.
YEAH, HE PROBABLY JUMPED FROM THAT TREE TO THE BALCONY AGAIN.
!
HEY !
THOSE GROOVES ...!
!?

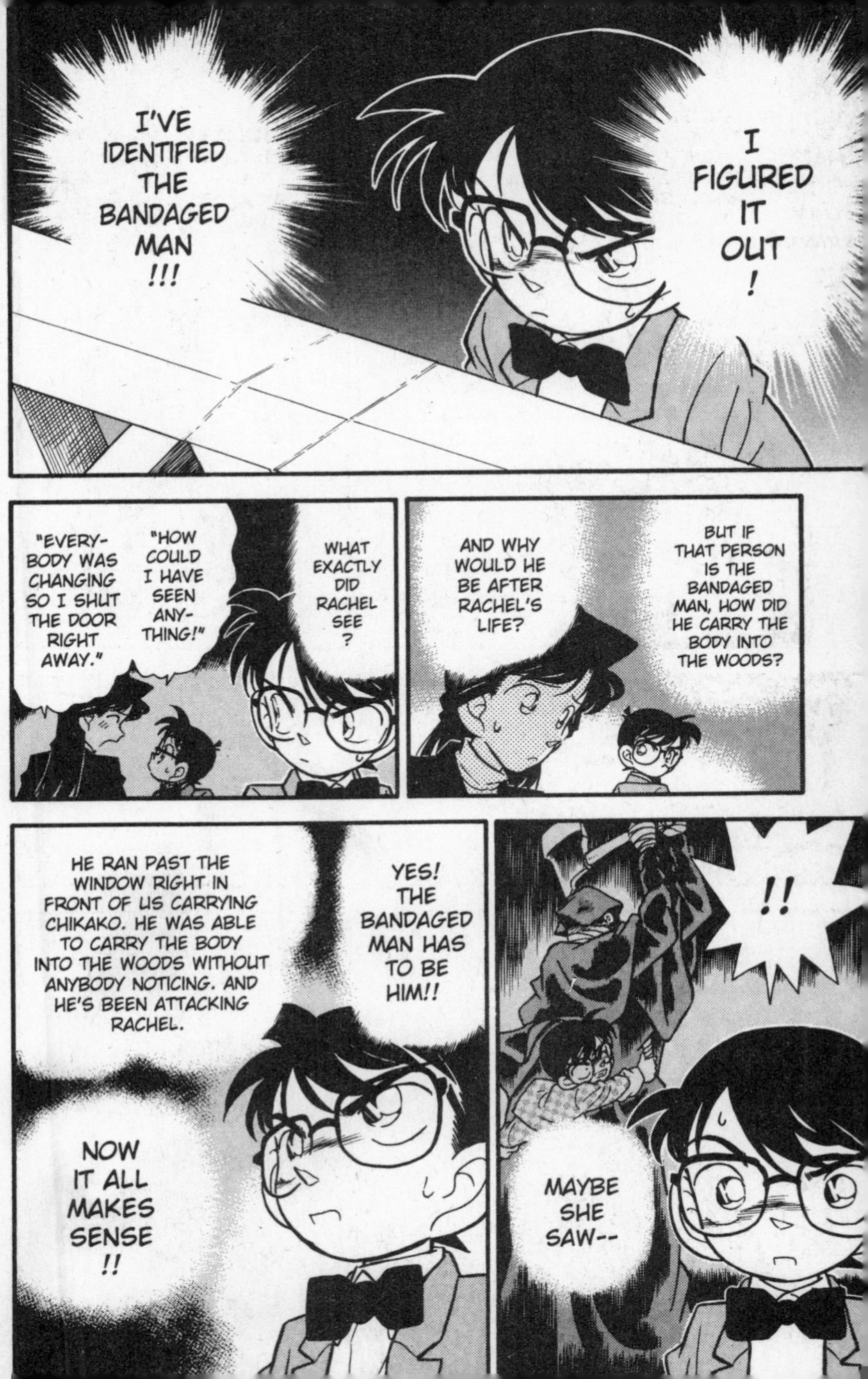
I FIGURED IT OUT !
I'VE IDENTIFIED THE BANDAGED MAN !!!
BUT IF THAT PERSON IS THE BANDAGED MAN, HOW DID HE CARRY THE BODY INTO THE WOODS?
AND WHY WOULD HE BE AFTER RACHEL'S LIFE?
WHAT EXACTLY DID RACHEL SEE ?
"HOW COULD I HAVE SEEN ANY-THING!"
"EVERY-BODY WAS CHANGING SO I SHUT THE DOOR RIGHT AWAY."
!!
MAYBE SHE SAW--
YES! THE BANDAGED MAN HAS TO BE HIM!!
HE RAN PAST THE WINDOW RIGHT IN FRONT OF US CARRYING CHIKAKO. HE WAS ABLE TO CARRY THE BODY INTO THE WOODS WITHOUT ANYBODY NOTICING. AND HE'S BEEN ATTACKING RACHEL.
NOW IT ALL MAKES SENSE !!

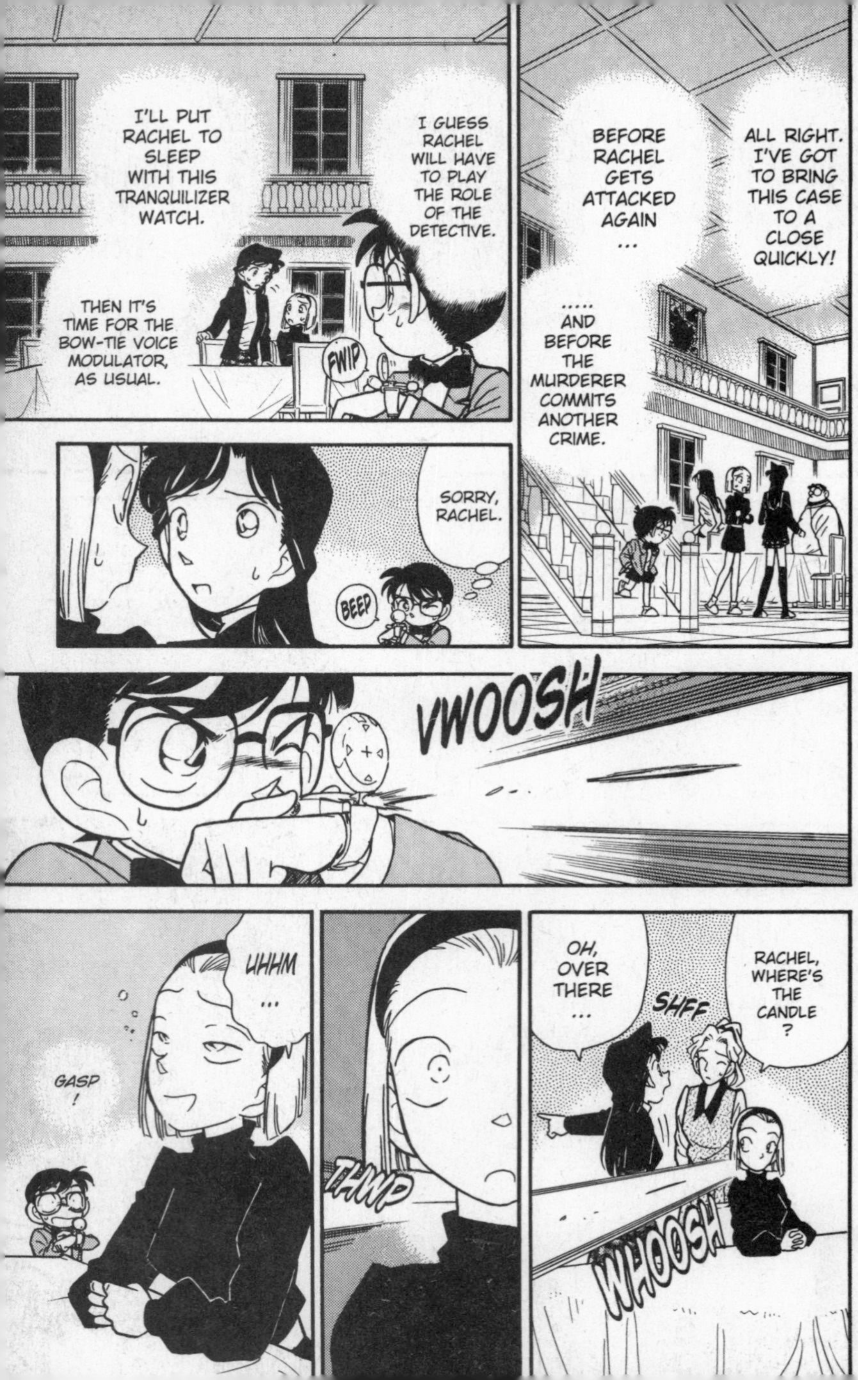

ALL RIGHT. I'VE GOT TO BRING THIS CASE TO A CLOSE QUICKLY!
BEFORE RACHEL GETS ATTACKED AGAIN ...
..... AND BEFORE THE MURDERER COMMITS ANOTHER CRIME.
I GUESS RACHEL WILL HAVE TO PLAY THE ROLE OF THE DETECTIVE.
I'LL PUT RACHEL TO SLEEP WITH THIS TRANQUILIZER WATCH.
FWIP
THEN IT'S TIME FOR THE BOW-TIE VOICE MODULATOR, AS USUAL.
SORRY, RACHEL.
BEEP
VWOOSH
RACHEL, WHERE'S THE CANDLE ?
SHFF
OH, OVER THERE ...
WHOOSH
THMP
UHHM ...
GASP !

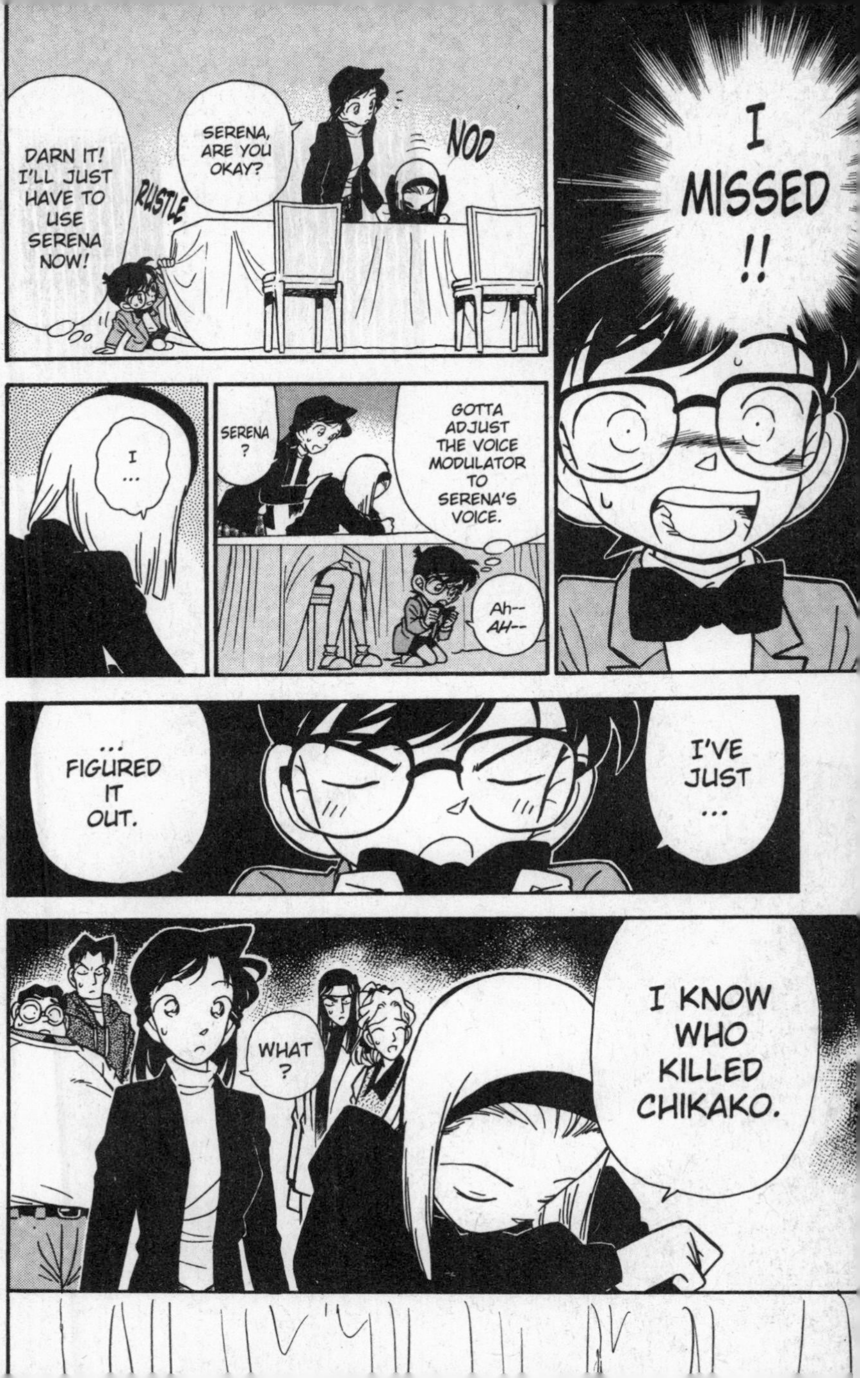
I MISSED!!
NOD
SERENA, ARE YOU OKAY?
RUSTLE
DARN IT! I'LL JUST HAVE TO USE SERENA NOW!
GOTTA ADJUST THE VOICE MODULATOR TO SERENA'S VOICE.
SERENA?
Ah-- AH--
I ...
I'VE JUST ...
... FIGURED IT OUT.
I KNOW WHO KILLED CHIKAKO.
WHAT?

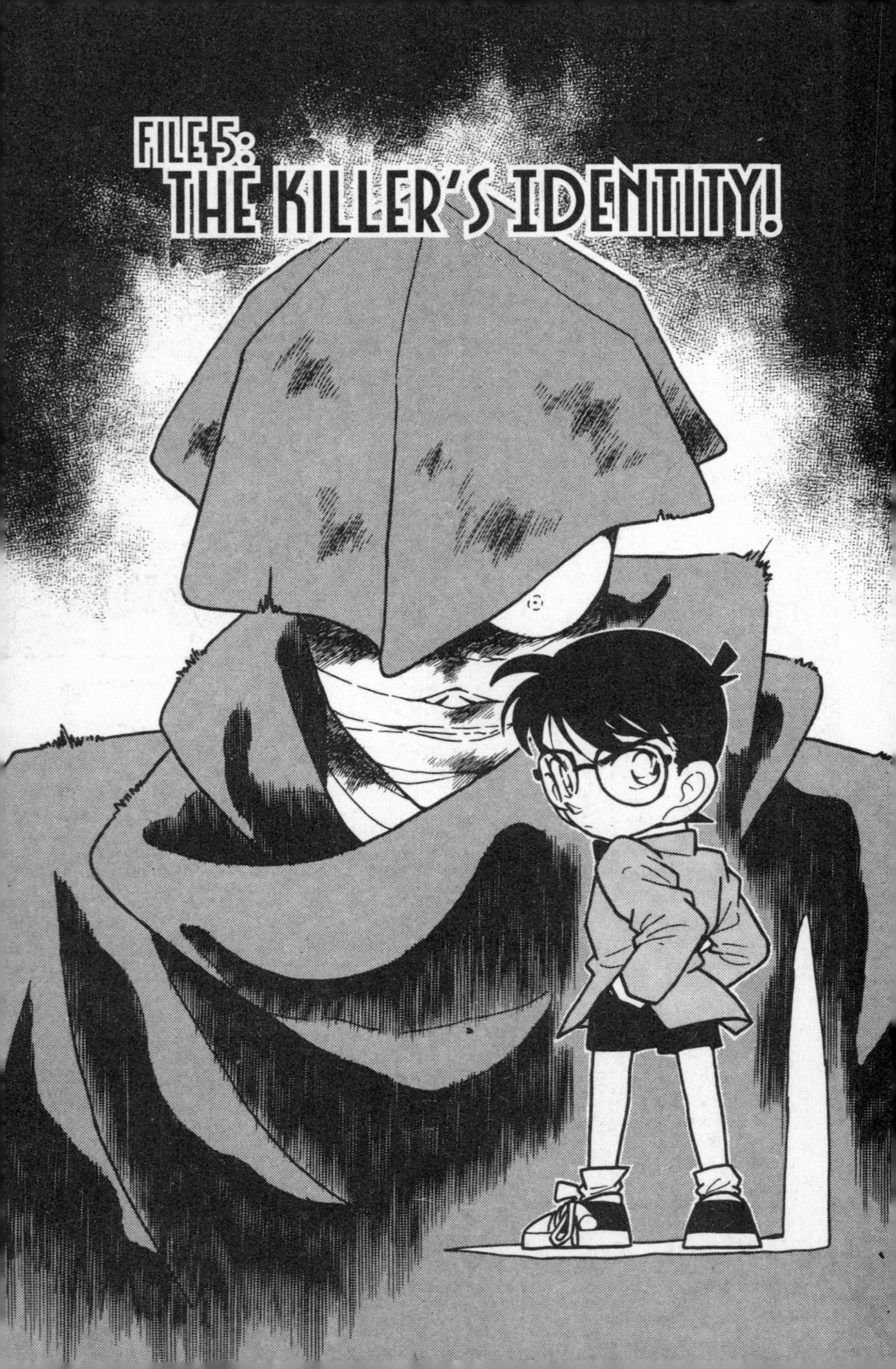
FILE 5:
THE KILLER'S IDENTITY!

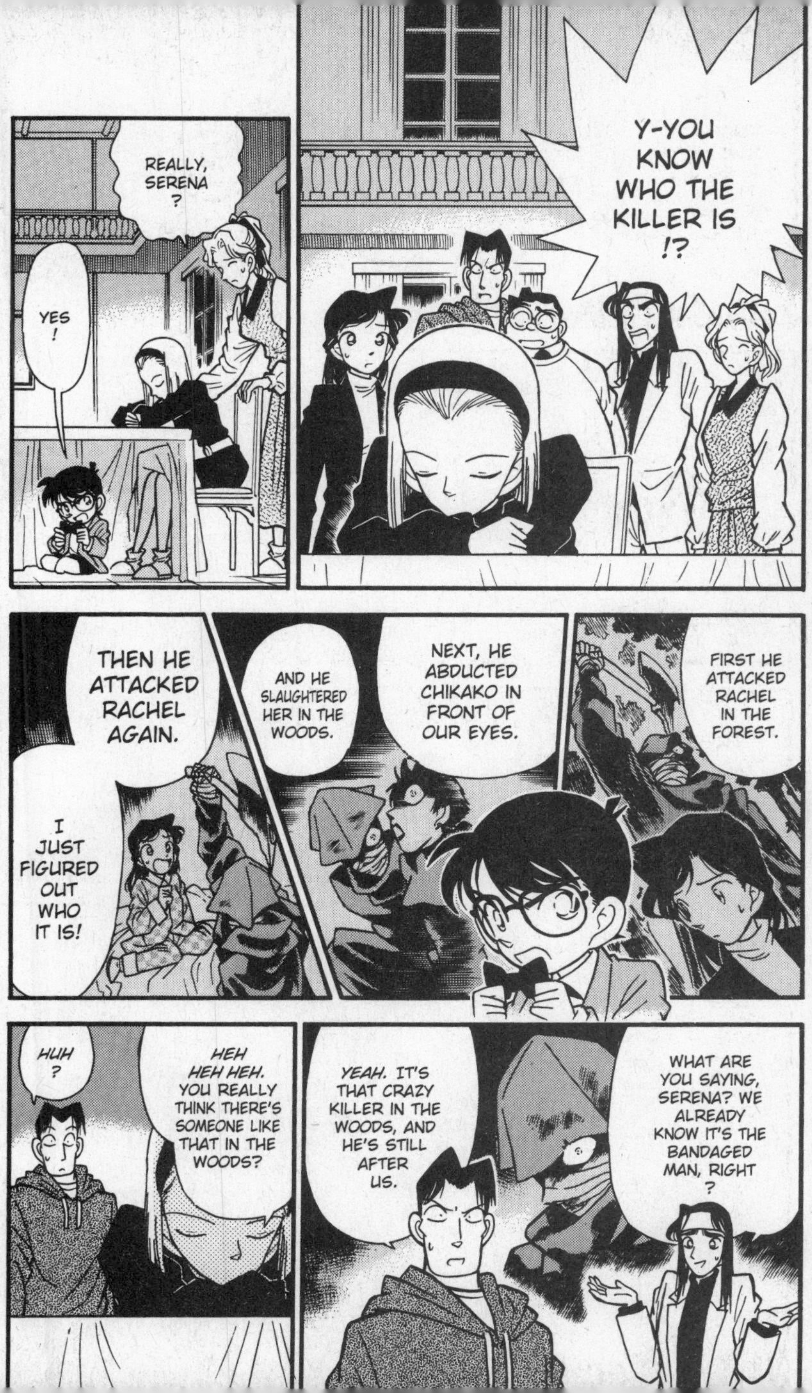
Y-YOU KNOW WHO THE KILLER IS !?
REALLY, SERENA ?
YES !
FIRST HE ATTACKED RACHEL IN THE FOREST.
NEXT, HE ABDUCTED CHIKAKO IN FRONT OF OUR EYES.
AND HE SLAUGHTERED HER IN THE WOODS.
THEN HE ATTACKED RACHEL AGAIN.
I JUST FIGURED OUT WHO IT IS!
WHAT ARE YOU SAYING, SERENA? WE ALREADY KNOW IT'S THE BANDAGED MAN, RIGHT ?
YEAH. IT'S THAT CRAZY KILLER IN THE WOODS, AND HE'S STILL AFTER US.
HEH HEH HEH. YOU REALLY THINK THERE'S SOMEONE LIKE THAT IN THE WOODS?
HUH ?

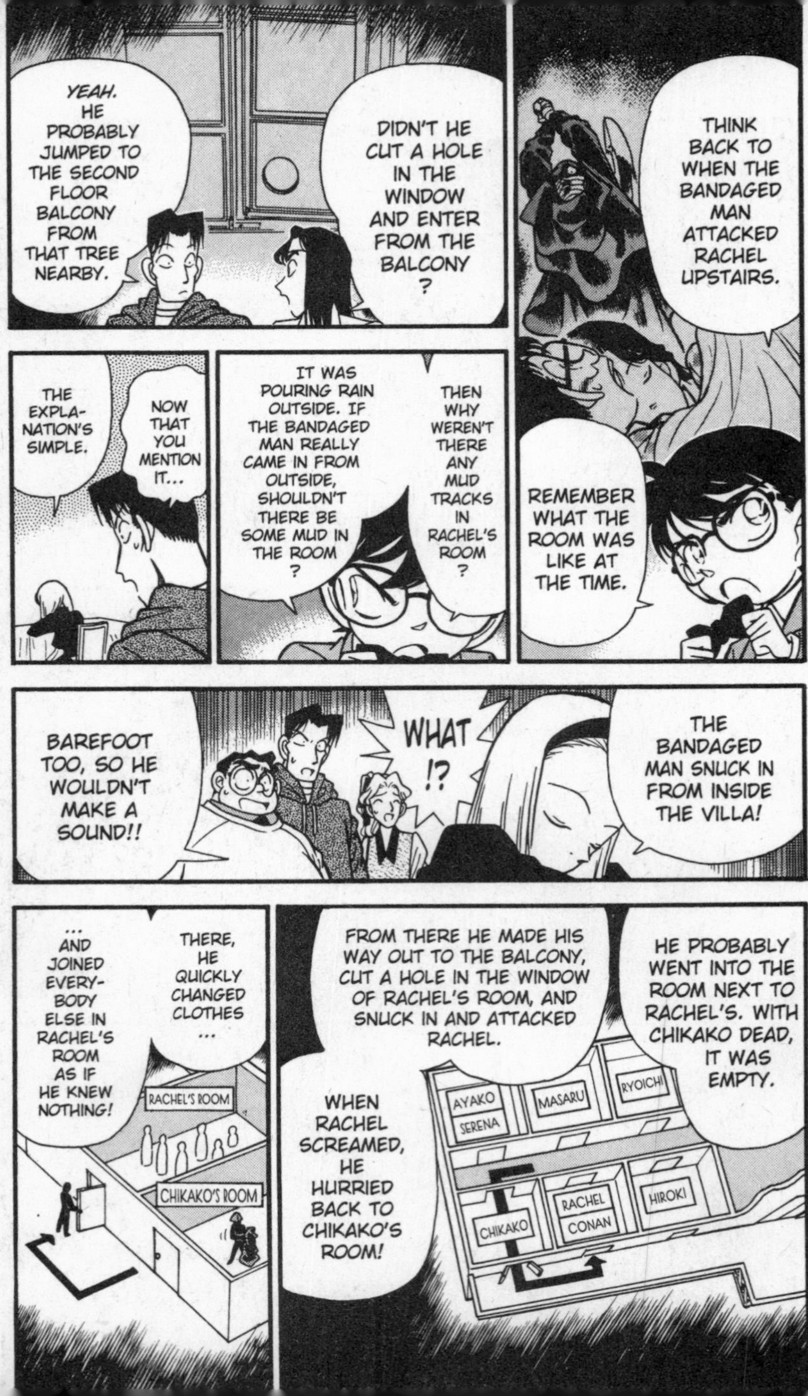
THINK BACK TO WHEN THE BANDAGED MAN ATTACKED RACHEL UPSTAIRS.
DIDN'T HE CUT A HOLE IN THE WINDOW AND ENTER FROM THE BALCONY ?
YEAH. HE PROBABLY JUMPED TO THE SECOND FLOOR BALCONY FROM THAT TREE NEARBY.
REMEMBER WHAT THE ROOM WAS LIKE AT THE TIME.
THEN WHY WEREN'T THERE ANY MUD TRACKS IN RACHEL'S ROOM ?
IT WAS POURING RAIN OUTSIDE. IF THE BANDAGED MAN REALLY CAME IN FROM OUTSIDE, SHOULDN'T THERE BE SOME MUD IN THE ROOM ?
NOW THAT YOU MENTION IT...
THE EXPLA-NATION'S SIMPLE.
THE BANDAGED MAN SNUCK IN FROM INSIDE THE VILLA!
WHAT !?
BAREFOOT TOO, SO HE WOULDN'T MAKE A SOUND!!
HE PROBABLY WENT INTO THE ROOM NEXT TO RACHEL'S. WITH CHIKAKO DEAD, IT WAS EMPTY.
FROM THERE HE MADE HIS WAY OUT TO THE BALCONY, CUT A HOLE IN THE WINDOW OF RACHEL'S ROOM, AND SNUCK IN AND ATTACKED RACHEL.
RYOICHI
MASARU
AYAKO
SERENA
HIROKI
RACHEL
CONAN
CHIKAKO
WHEN RACHEL SCREAMED, HE HURRIED BACK TO CHIKAKO'S ROOM!
THERE, HE QUICKLY CHANGED CLOTHES ...
... AND JOINED EVERY-BODY ELSE IN RACHEL'S ROOM AS IF HE KNEW NOTHING!
RACHEL'S ROOM
CHIKAKO'S ROOM

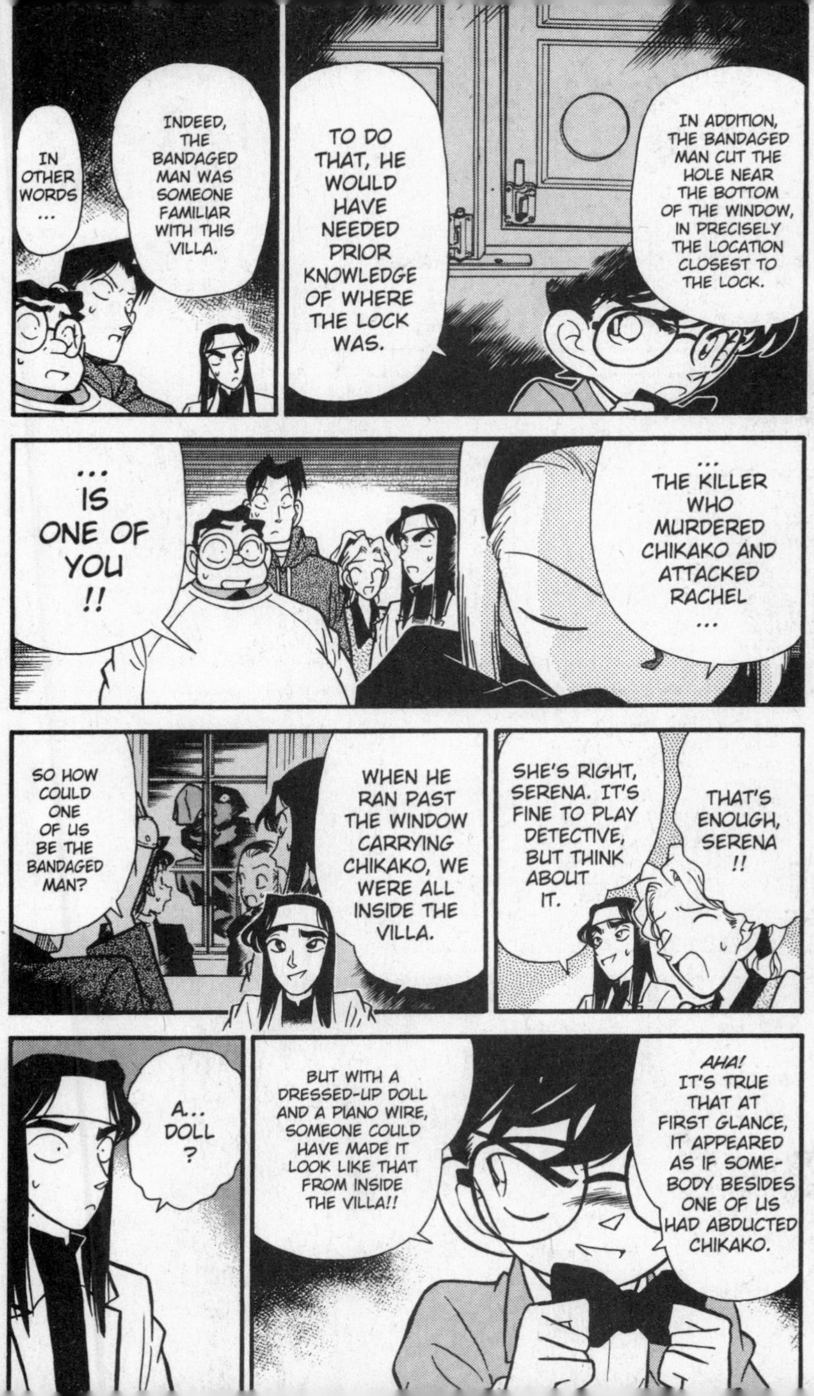
IN ADDITION, THE BANDAGED MAN CUT THE HOLE NEAR THE BOTTOM OF THE WINDOW, IN PRECISELY THE LOCATION CLOSEST TO THE LOCK.
TO DO THAT, HE WOULD HAVE NEEDED PRIOR KNOWLEDGE OF WHERE THE LOCK WAS.
INDEED, THE BANDAGED MAN WAS SOMEONE FAMILIAR WITH THIS VILLA.
IN OTHER WORDS ...
... THE KILLER WHO MURDERED CHIKAKO AND ATTACKED RACHEL ...
... IS ONE OF YOU !!
THAT'S ENOUGH, SERENA !!
SHE'S RIGHT, SERENA. IT'S FINE TO PLAY DETECTIVE, BUT THINK ABOUT IT.
WHEN HE RAN PAST THE WINDOW CARRYING CHIKAKO, WE WERE ALL INSIDE THE VILLA.
SO HOW COULD ONE OF US BE THE BANDAGED MAN?
AHA! IT'S TRUE THAT AT FIRST GLANCE, IT APPEARED AS IF SOMEBODY BESIDES ONE OF US HAD ABDUCTED CHIKAKO.
BUT WITH A DRESSED-UP DOLL AND A PIANO WIRE, SOMEONE COULD HAVE MADE IT LOOK LIKE THAT FROM INSIDE THE VILLA!!
A... DOLL ?

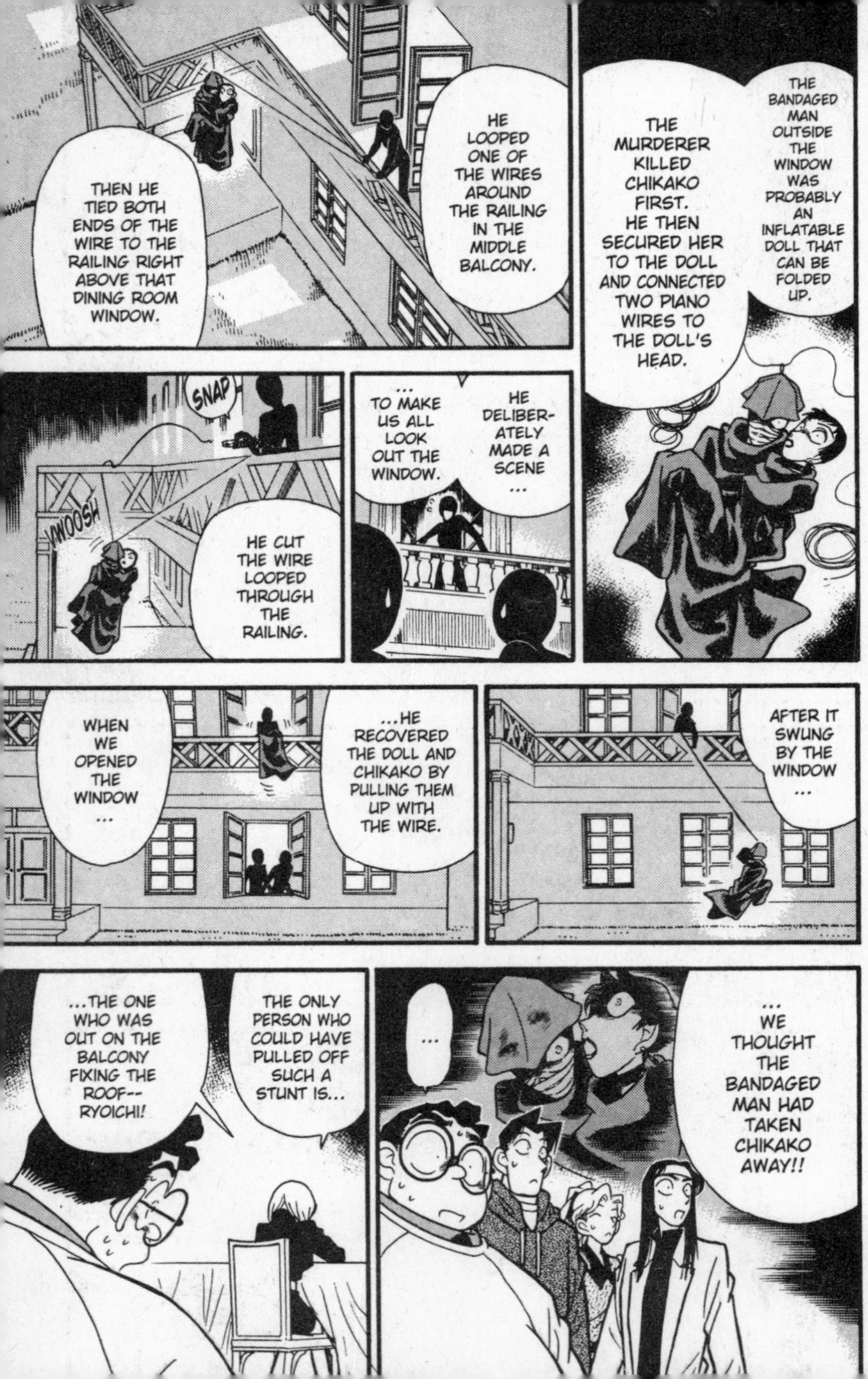
THE BANDAGED MAN OUTSIDE THE WINDOW WAS PROBABLY AN INFLATABLE DOLL THAT CAN BE FOLDED UP.
THE MURDERER KILLED CHIKAKO FIRST. HE THEN SECURED HER TO THE DOLL AND CONNECTED TWO PIANO WIRES TO THE DOLL'S HEAD.
HE LOOPED ONE OF THE WIRES AROUND THE RAILING IN THE MIDDLE BALCONY.
THEN HE TIED BOTH ENDS OF THE WIRE TO THE RAILING RIGHT ABOVE THAT DINING ROOM WINDOW.
HE DELIBER-ATELY MADE A SCENE ...
... TO MAKE US ALL LOOK OUT THE WINDOW.
SNAP
VWOOSH
HE CUT THE WIRE LOOPED THROUGH THE RAILING.
AFTER IT SWUNG BY THE WINDOW ...
...HE RECOVERED THE DOLL AND CHIKAKO BY PULLING THEM UP WITH THE WIRE.
WHEN WE OPENED THE WINDOW ...
... WE THOUGHT THE BANDAGED MAN HAD TAKEN CHIKAKO AWAY!!
...
THE ONLY PERSON WHO COULD HAVE PULLED OFF SUCH A STUNT IS...
...THE ONE WHO WAS OUT ON THE BALCONY FIXING THE ROOF-- RYOICHI!

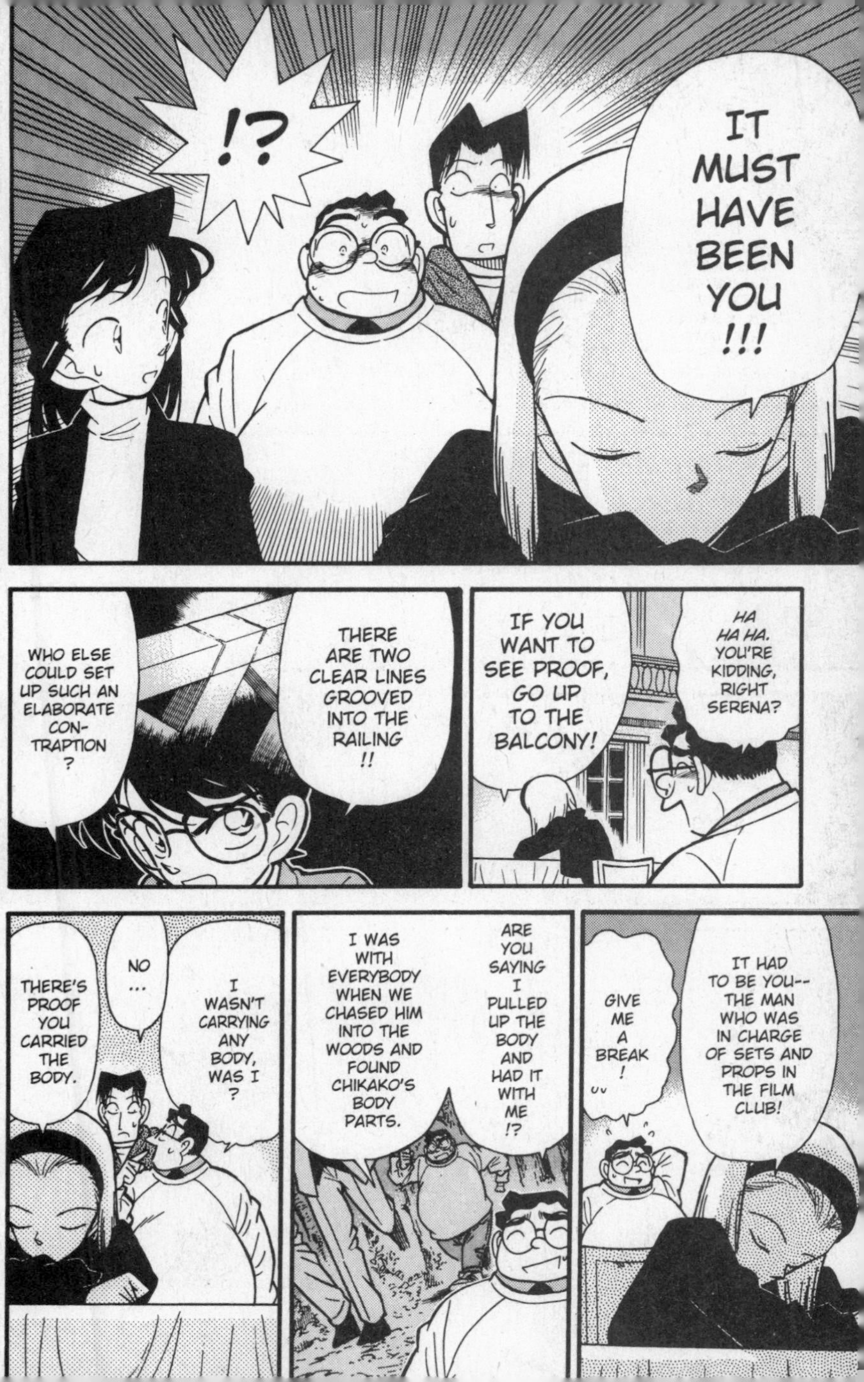
IT MUST HAVE BEEN YOU!!!
!?
HA HA HA. YOU'RE KIDDING, RIGHT SERENA?
IF YOU WANT TO SEE PROOF, GO UP TO THE BALCONY!
THERE ARE TWO CLEAR LINES GROOVED INTO THE RAILING!!
WHO ELSE COULD SET UP SUCH AN ELABORATE CON-TRAPTION?
IT HAD TO BE YOU--THE MAN WHO WAS IN CHARGE OF SETS AND PROPS IN THE FILM CLUB!
GIVE ME A BREAK!
ARE YOU SAYING I PULLED UP THE BODY AND HAD IT WITH ME!?
I WAS WITH EVERYBODY WHEN WE CHASED HIM INTO THE WOODS AND FOUND CHIKAKO'S BODY PARTS.
I WASN'T CARRYING ANY BODY, WAS I?
NO...
THERE'S PROOF YOU CARRIED THE BODY.

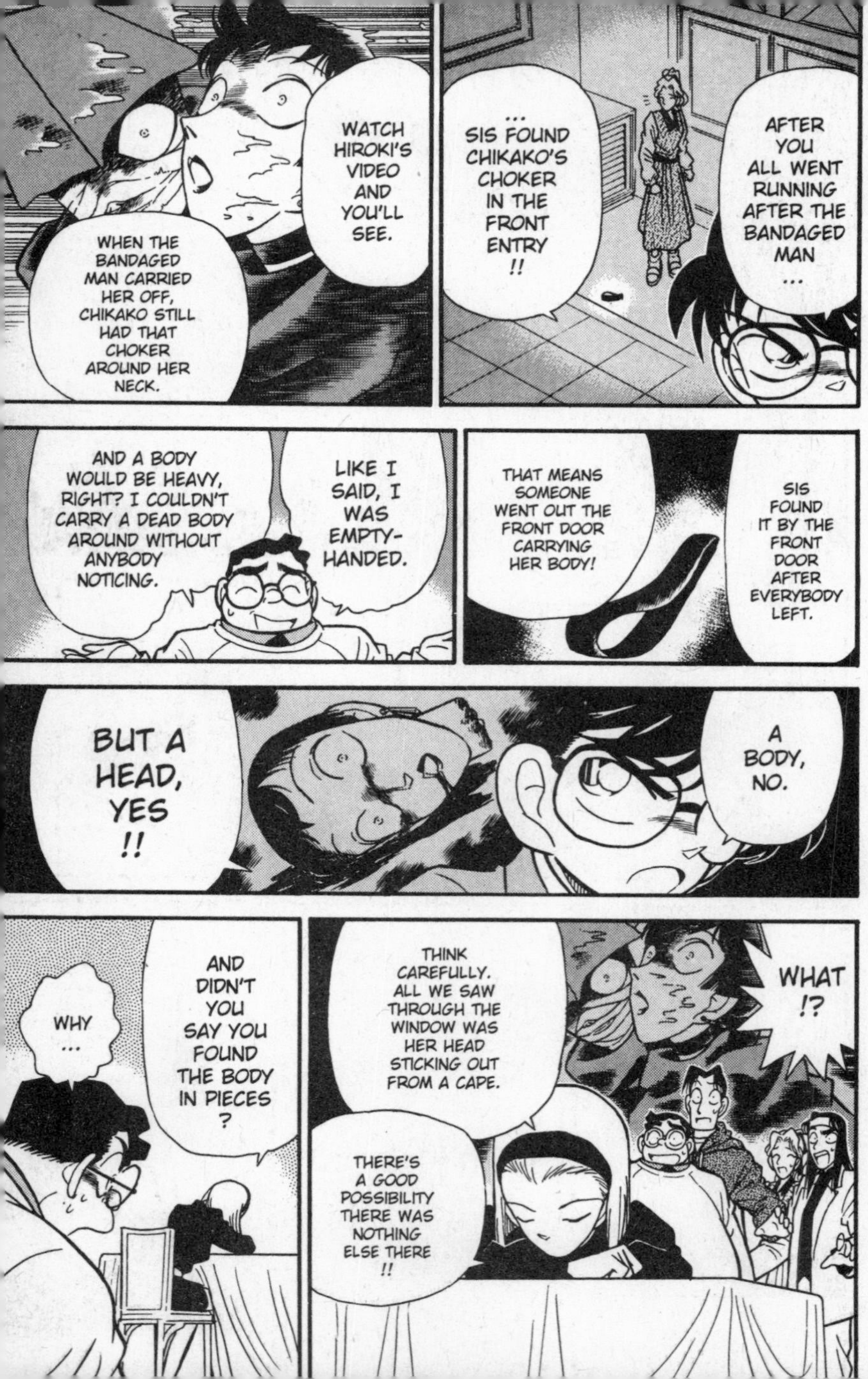
AFTER YOU ALL WENT RUNNING AFTER THE BANDAGED MAN ...
... SIS FOUND CHIKAKO'S CHOKER IN THE FRONT ENTRY !!
WATCH HIROKI'S VIDEO AND YOU'LL SEE.
WHEN THE BANDAGED MAN CARRIED HER OFF, CHIKAKO STILL HAD THAT CHOKER AROUND HER NECK.
SIS FOUND IT BY THE FRONT DOOR AFTER EVERYBODY LEFT.
THAT MEANS SOMEONE WENT OUT THE FRONT DOOR CARRYING HER BODY!
LIKE I SAID, I WAS EMPTY-HANDED.
AND A BODY WOULD BE HEAVY, RIGHT? I COULDN'T CARRY A DEAD BODY AROUND WITHOUT ANYBODY NOTICING.
A BODY, NO.
BUT A HEAD, YES !!
WHAT !?
THINK CAREFULLY. ALL WE SAW THROUGH THE WINDOW WAS HER HEAD STICKING OUT FROM A CAPE.
THERE'S A GOOD POSSIBILITY THERE WAS NOTHING ELSE THERE !!
AND DIDN'T YOU SAY YOU FOUND THE BODY IN PIECES ?
WHY ...

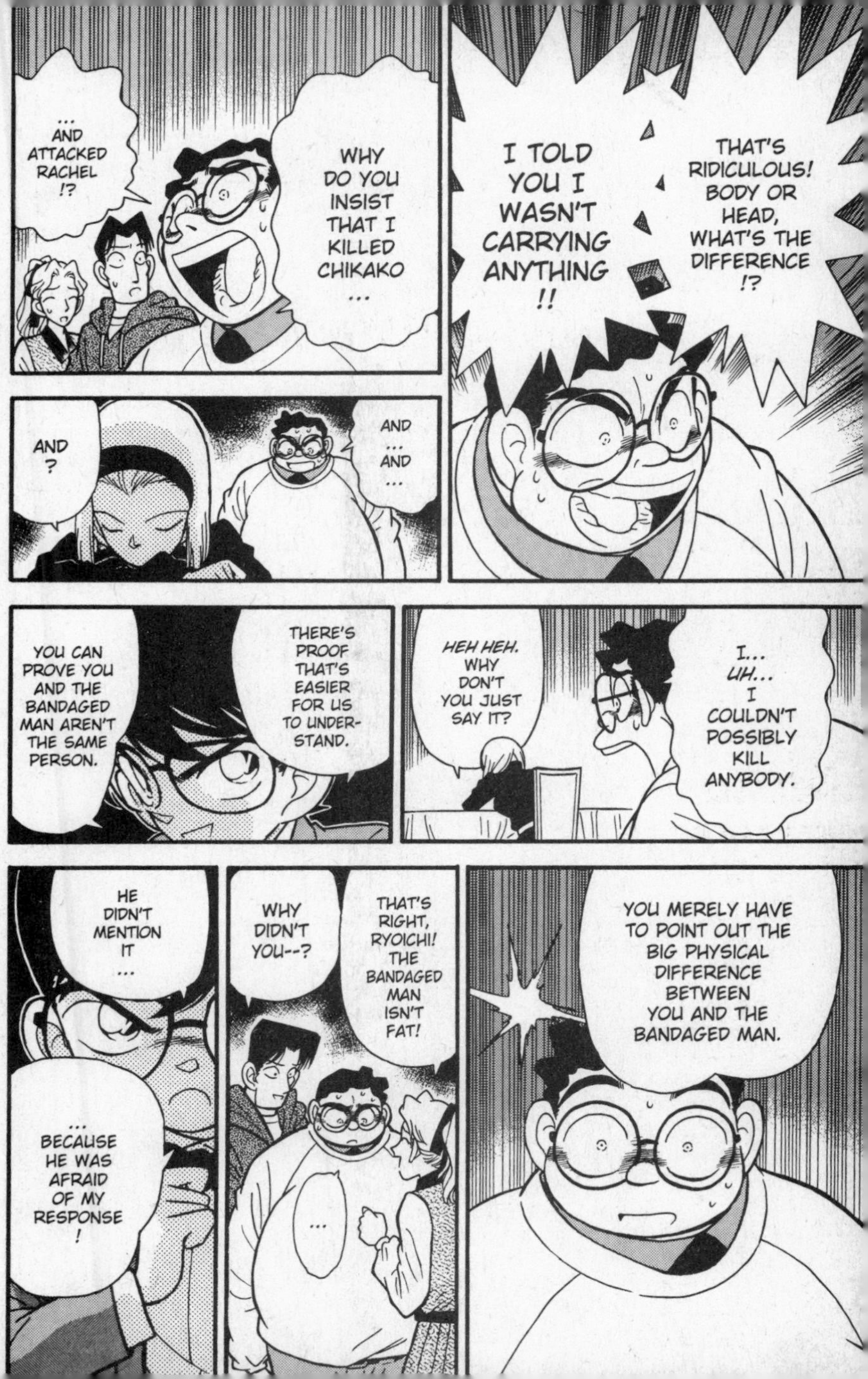
THAT'S RIDICULOUS! BODY OR HEAD, WHAT'S THE DIFFERENCE!?
I TOLD YOU I WASN'T CARRYING ANYTHING!!
WHY DO YOU INSIST THAT I KILLED CHIKAKO...
...AND ATTACKED RACHEL!?
AND... AND...
AND?
I... UH... I COULDN'T POSSIBLY KILL ANYBODY.
HEH HEH. WHY DON'T YOU JUST SAY IT?
THERE'S PROOF THAT'S EASIER FOR US TO UNDERSTAND.
YOU CAN PROVE YOU AND THE BANDAGED MAN AREN'T THE SAME PERSON.
YOU MERELY HAVE TO POINT OUT THE BIG PHYSICAL DIFFERENCE BETWEEN YOU AND THE BANDAGED MAN.
THAT'S RIGHT, RYOICHI! THE BANDAGED MAN ISN'T FAT!
WHY DIDN'T YOU--?
...
HE DIDN'T MENTION IT...
...BECAUSE HE WAS AFRAID OF MY RESPONSE!

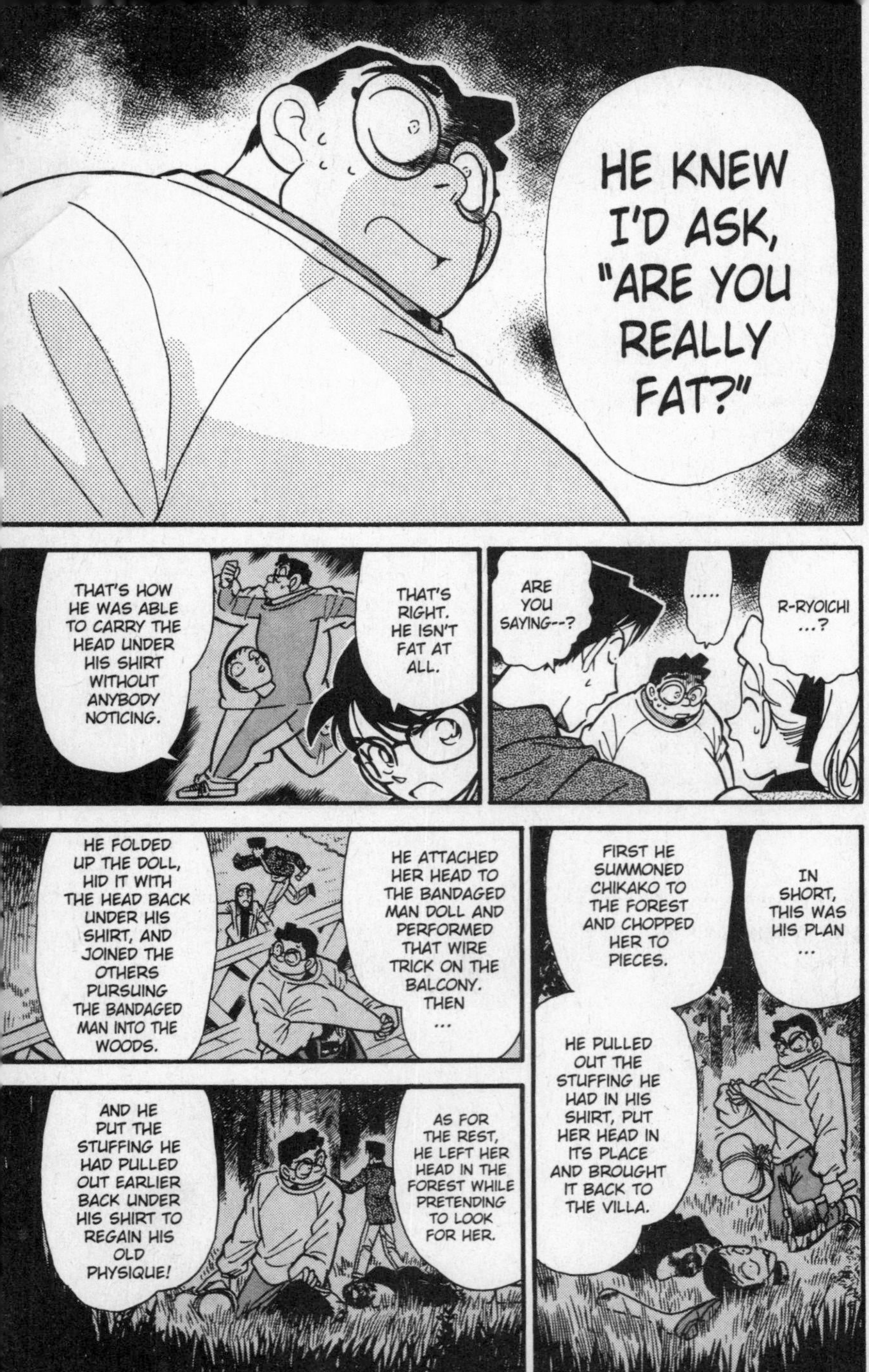
HE KNEW I'D ASK, "ARE YOU REALLY FAT?"
R-RYOICHI ...?
.....
ARE YOU SAYING--?
THAT'S RIGHT. HE ISN'T FAT AT ALL.
THAT'S HOW HE WAS ABLE TO CARRY THE HEAD UNDER HIS SHIRT WITHOUT ANYBODY NOTICING.
IN SHORT, THIS WAS HIS PLAN ...
FIRST HE SUMMONED CHIKAKO TO THE FOREST AND CHOPPED HER TO PIECES.
HE PULLED OUT THE STUFFING HE HAD IN HIS SHIRT, PUT HER HEAD IN ITS PLACE AND BROUGHT IT BACK TO THE VILLA.
HE ATTACHED HER HEAD TO THE BANDAGED MAN DOLL AND PERFORMED THAT WIRE TRICK ON THE BALCONY. THEN ...
HE FOLDED UP THE DOLL, HID IT WITH THE HEAD BACK UNDER HIS SHIRT, AND JOINED THE OTHERS PURSUING THE BANDAGED MAN INTO THE WOODS.
AS FOR THE REST, HE LEFT HER HEAD IN THE FOREST WHILE PRETENDING TO LOOK FOR HER.
AND HE PUT THE STUFFING HE HAD PULLED OUT EARLIER BACK UNDER HIS SHIRT TO REGAIN HIS OLD PHYSIQUE!

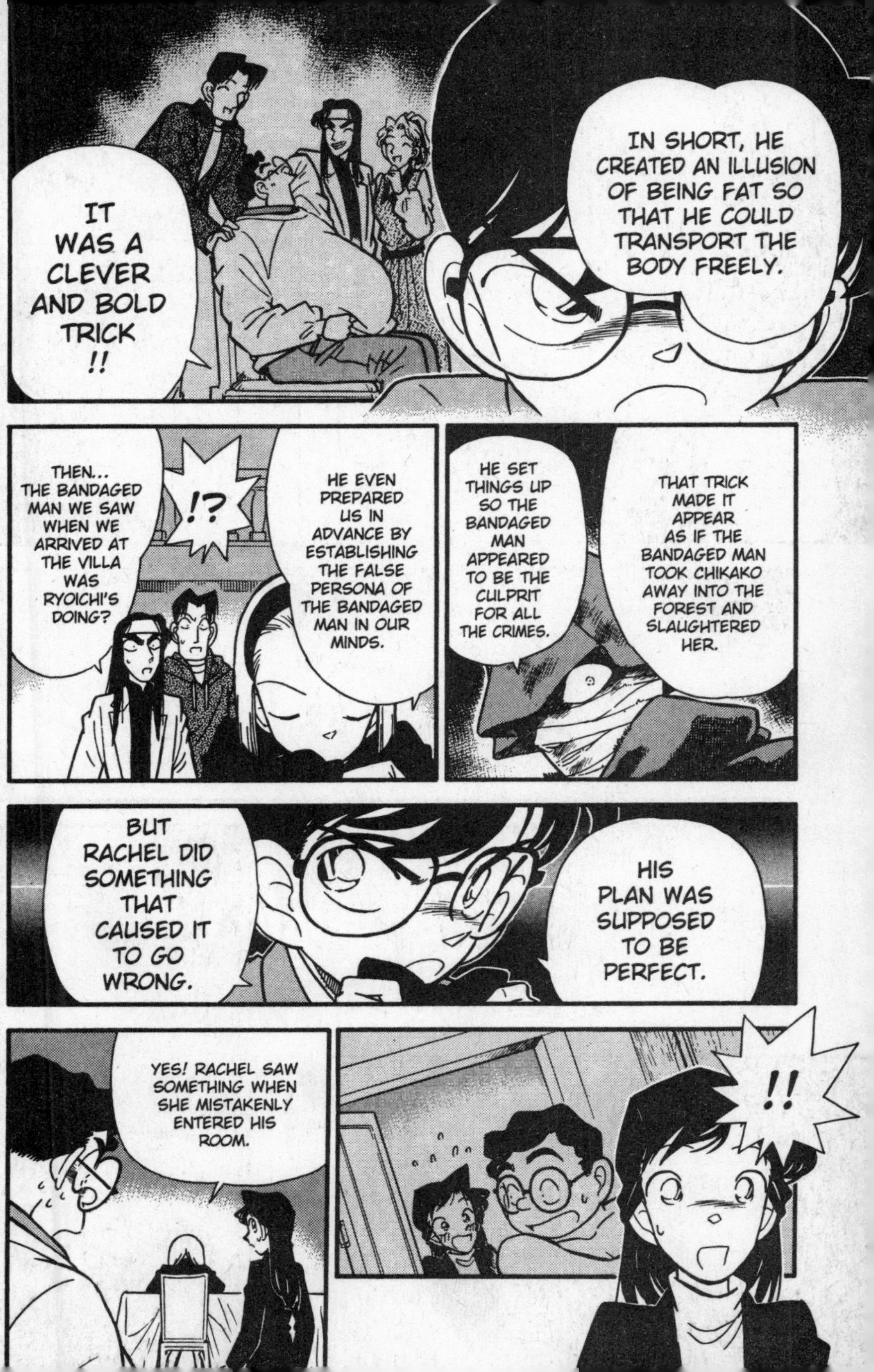
IN SHORT, HE CREATED AN ILLUSION OF BEING FAT SO THAT HE COULD TRANSPORT THE BODY FREELY.
IT WAS A CLEVER AND BOLD TRICK !!
THAT TRICK MADE IT APPEAR AS IF THE BANDAGED MAN TOOK CHIKAKO AWAY INTO THE FOREST AND SLAUGHTERED HER.
HE SET THINGS UP SO THE BANDAGED MAN APPEARED TO BE THE CULPRIT FOR ALL THE CRIMES.
HE EVEN PREPARED US IN ADVANCE BY ESTABLISHING THE FALSE PERSONA OF THE BANDAGED MAN IN OUR MINDS.
!?
THEN... THE BANDAGED MAN WE SAW WHEN WE ARRIVED AT THE VILLA WAS RYOICHI'S DOING?
HIS PLAN WAS SUPPOSED TO BE PERFECT.
BUT RACHEL DID SOMETHING THAT CAUSED IT TO GO WRONG.
!!
YES! RACHEL SAW SOMETHING WHEN SHE MISTAKENLY ENTERED HIS ROOM.

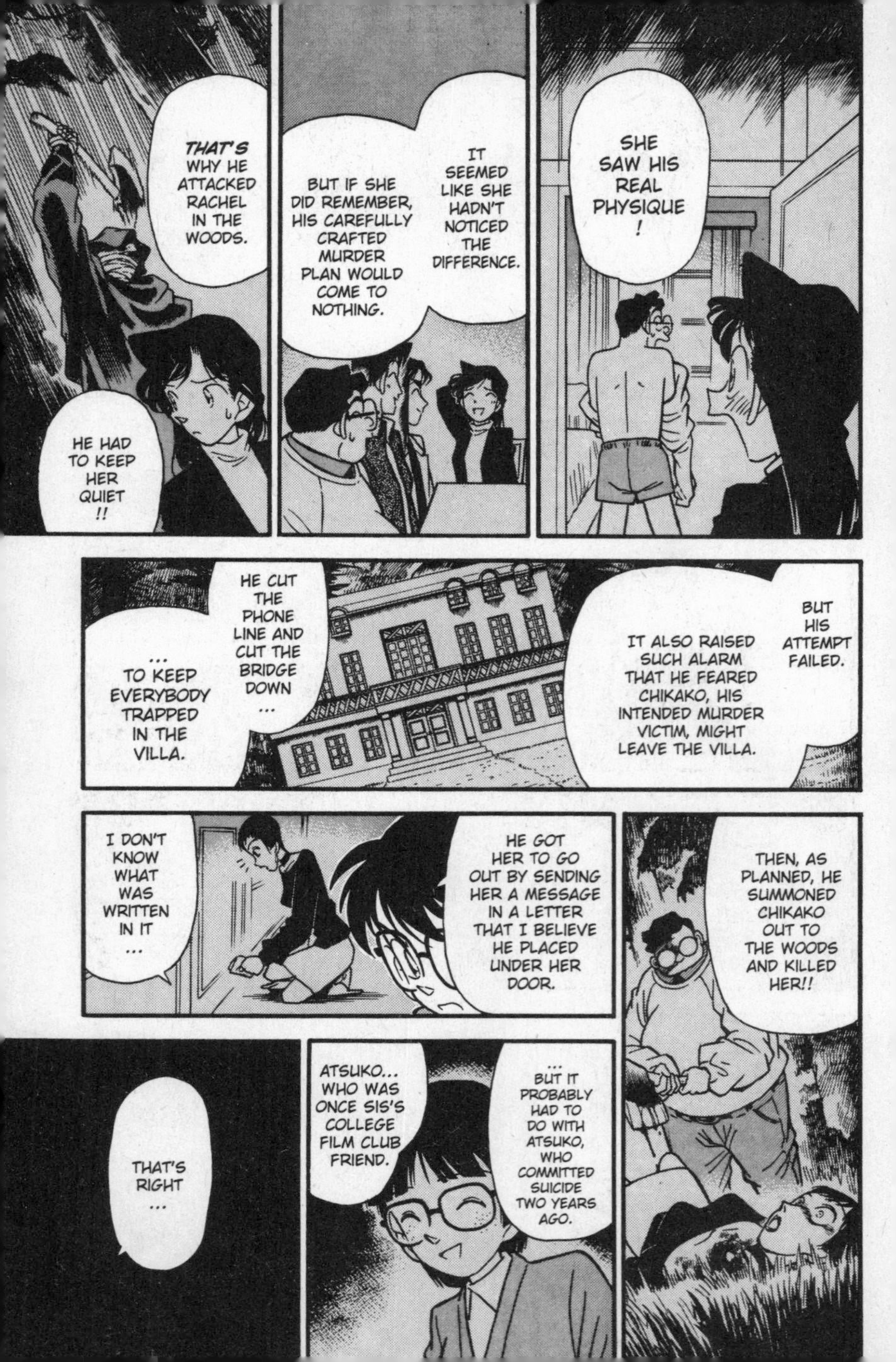
SHE SAW HIS REAL PHYSIQUE !
IT SEEMED LIKE SHE HADN'T NOTICED THE DIFFERENCE.
BUT IF SHE DID REMEMBER, HIS CAREFULLY CRAFTED MURDER PLAN WOULD COME TO NOTHING.
THAT'S WHY HE ATTACKED RACHEL IN THE WOODS.
HE HAD TO KEEP HER QUIET !!
BUT HIS ATTEMPT FAILED.
IT ALSO RAISED SUCH ALARM THAT HE FEARED CHIKAKO, HIS INTENDED MURDER VICTIM, MIGHT LEAVE THE VILLA.
HE CUT THE PHONE LINE AND CUT THE BRIDGE DOWN ...
... TO KEEP EVERYBODY TRAPPED IN THE VILLA.
THEN, AS PLANNED, HE SUMMONED CHIKAKO OUT TO THE WOODS AND KILLED HER!!
HE GOT HER TO GO OUT BY SENDING HER A MESSAGE IN A LETTER THAT I BELIEVE HE PLACED UNDER HER DOOR.
I DON'T KNOW WHAT WAS WRITTEN IN IT ...
... BUT IT PROBABLY HAD TO DO WITH ATSUKO, WHO COMMITTED SUICIDE TWO YEARS AGO.
ATSUKO... WHO WAS ONCE SIS'S COLLEGE FILM CLUB FRIEND.
THAT'S RIGHT ...

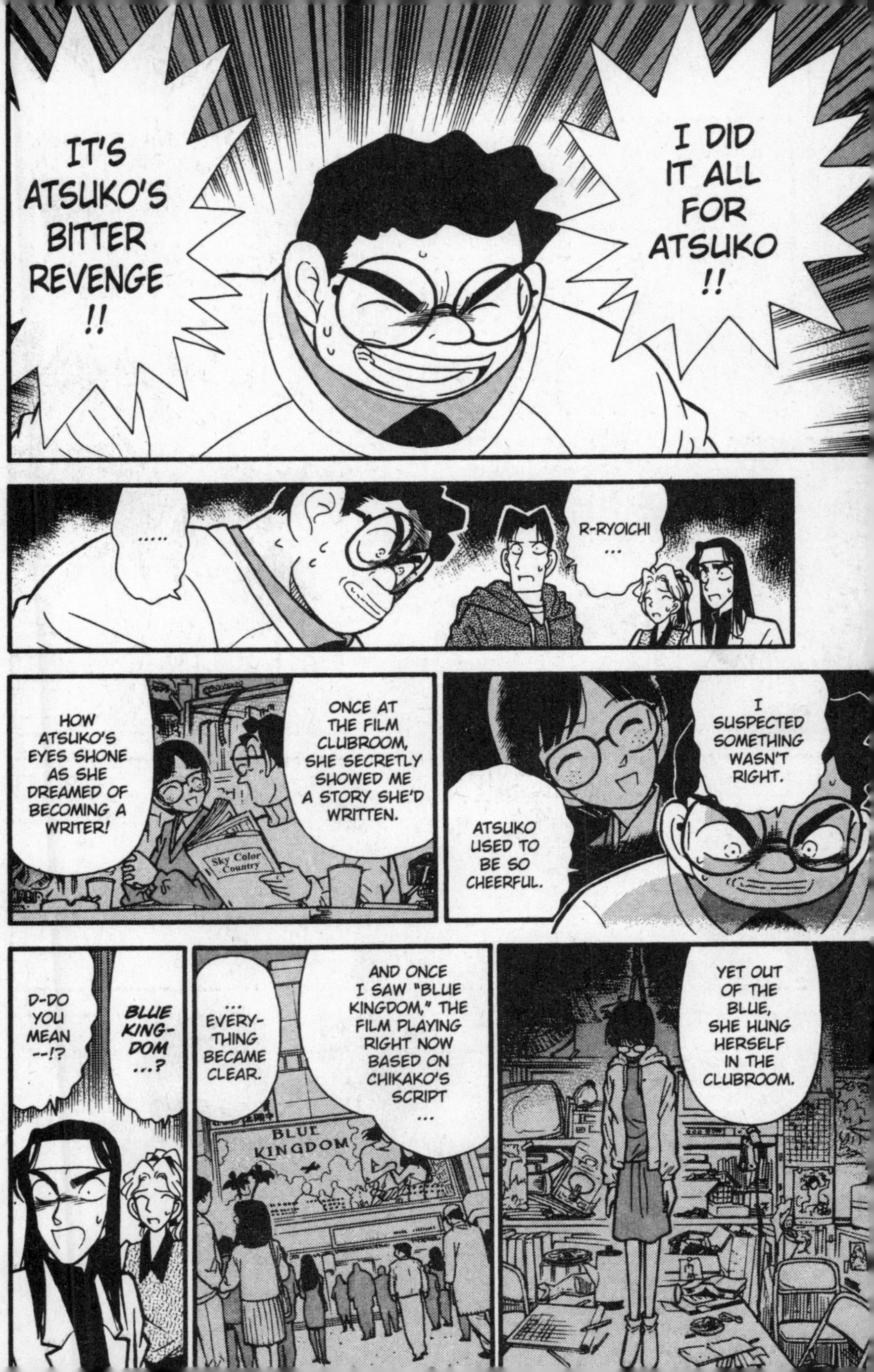
I DID IT ALL FOR ATSUKO!!
IT'S ATSUKO'S BITTER REVENGE!!
R-RYOICHI...
.....
I SUSPECTED SOMETHING WASN'T RIGHT.
ATSUKO USED TO BE SO CHEERFUL.
ONCE AT THE FILM CLUBROOM, SHE SECRETLY SHOWED ME A STORY SHE'D WRITTEN.
HOW ATSUKO'S EYES SHONE AS SHE DREAMED OF BECOMING A WRITER!
Sky Color Country
YET OUT OF THE BLUE, SHE HUNG HERSELF IN THE CLUBROOM.
AND ONCE I SAW "BLUE KINGDOM," THE FILM PLAYING RIGHT NOW BASED ON CHIKAKO'S SCRIPT...
...EVERYTHING BECAME CLEAR.
BLUE KINGDOM
BLUE KINGDOM...?
D-DO YOU MEAN--!?

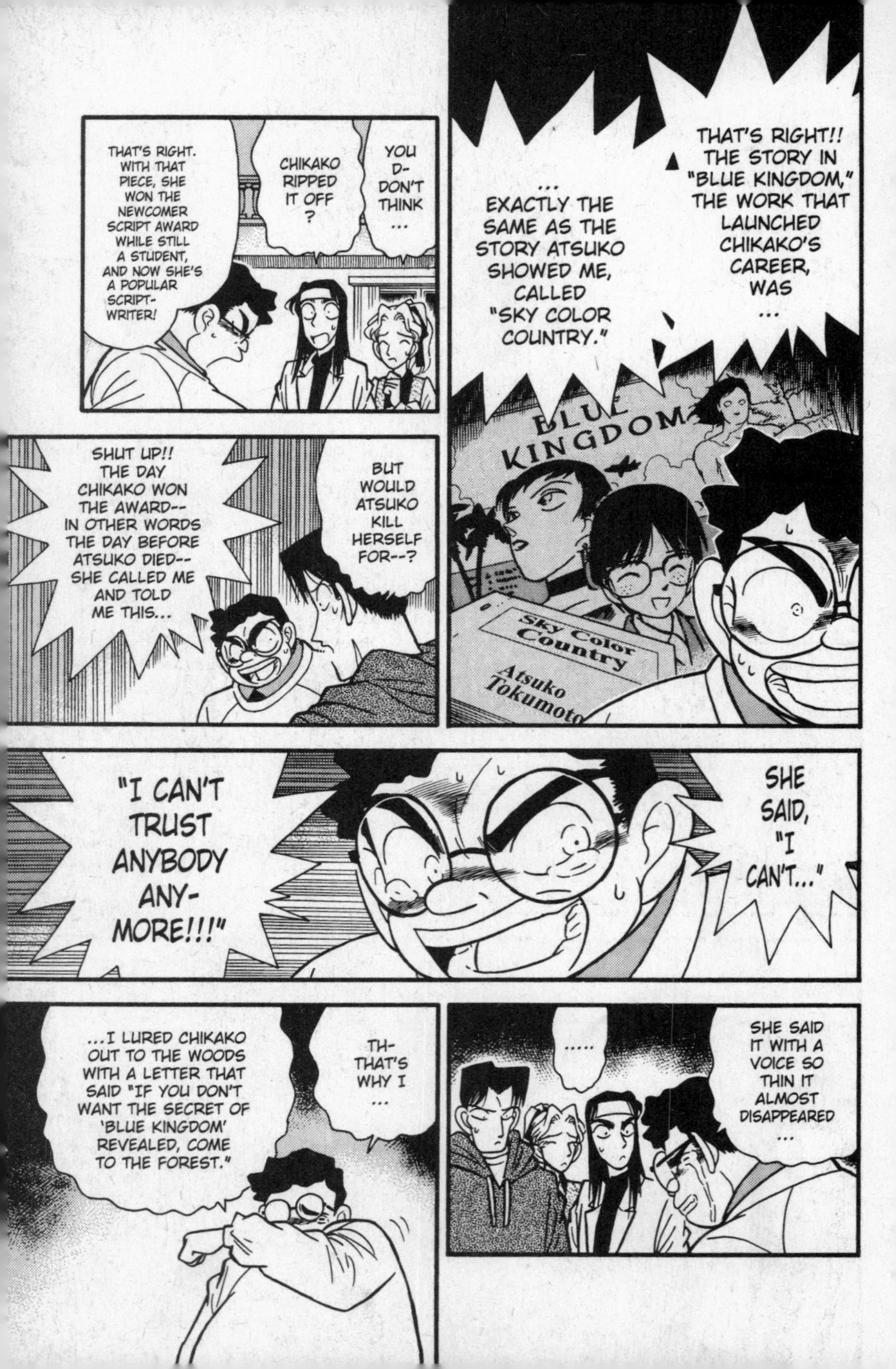
THAT'S RIGHT!! THE STORY IN "BLUE KINGDOM," THE WORK THAT LAUNCHED CHIKAKO'S CAREER, WAS ...
... EXACTLY THE SAME AS THE STORY ATSUKO SHOWED ME, CALLED "SKY COLOR COUNTRY."
BLUE KINGDOM
Sky Color Country
Atsuko Tokumoto
YOU D-DON'T THINK ...
CHIKAKO RIPPED IT OFF ?
THAT'S RIGHT. WITH THAT PIECE, SHE WON THE NEWCOMER SCRIPT AWARD WHILE STILL A STUDENT, AND NOW SHE'S A POPULAR SCRIPT-WRITER!
BUT WOULD ATSUKO KILL HERSELF FOR--?
SHUT UP!! THE DAY CHIKAKO WON THE AWARD-- IN OTHER WORDS THE DAY BEFORE ATSUKO DIED-- SHE CALLED ME AND TOLD ME THIS...
SHE SAID, "I CAN'T..."
"I CAN'T TRUST ANYBODY ANY-MORE!!!"
SHE SAID IT WITH A VOICE SO THIN IT ALMOST DISAPPEARED ...
.....
TH-THAT'S WHY I ...
...I LURED CHIKAKO OUT TO THE WOODS WITH A LETTER THAT SAID "IF YOU DON'T WANT THE SECRET OF 'BLUE KINGDOM' REVEALED, COME TO THE FOREST."

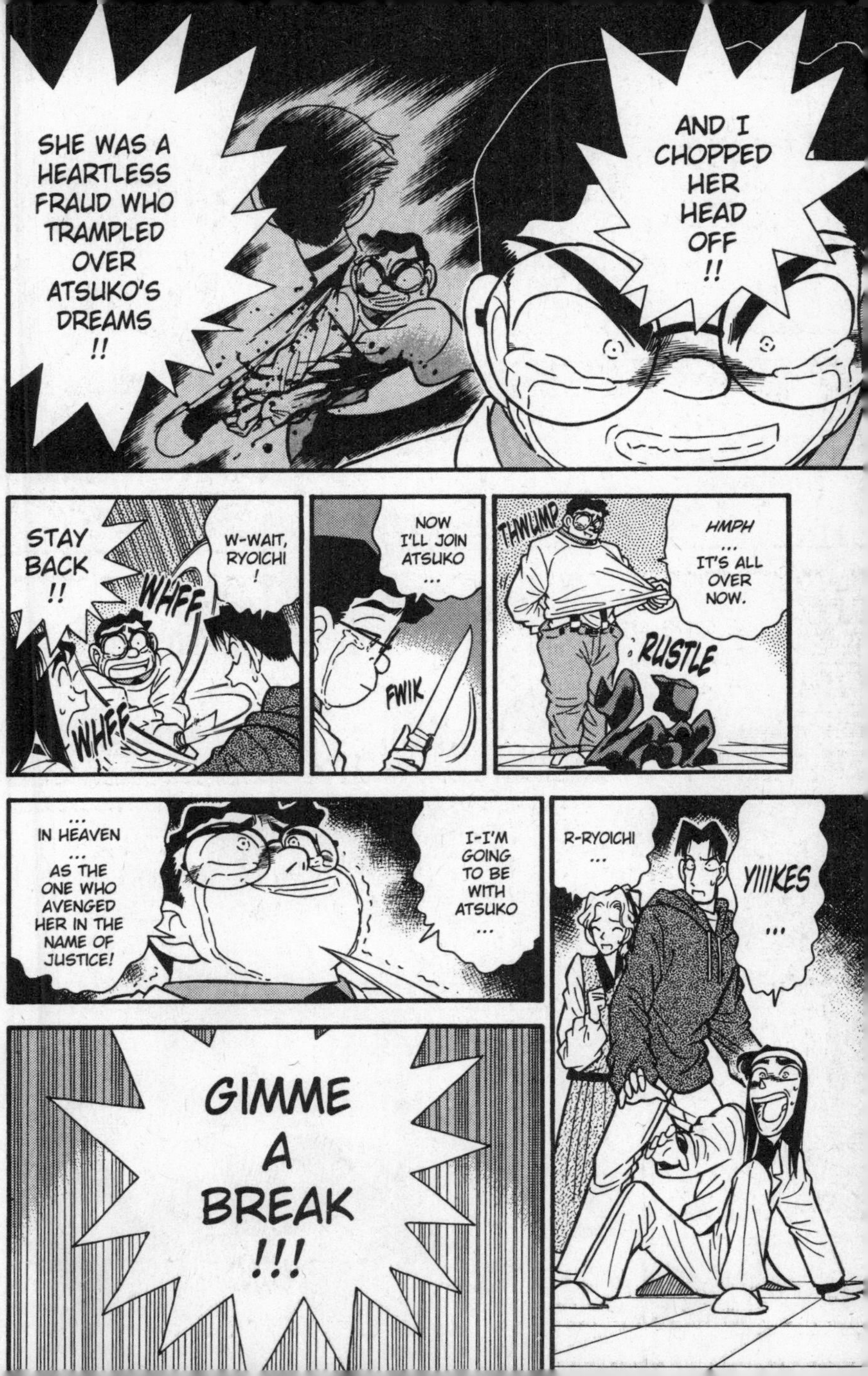
AND I CHOPPED HER HEAD OFF !!
SHE WAS A HEARTLESS FRAUD WHO TRAMPLED OVER ATSUKO'S DREAMS !!
HMPH ... IT'S ALL OVER NOW.
THWUMP
RUSTLE
NOW I'LL JOIN ATSUKO ...
FWIK
W-WAIT, RYOICHI !
STAY BACK !!
WHFF
WHFF
YIIIKES ...
R-RYOICHI ...
I-I'M GOING TO BE WITH ATSUKO ...
... IN HEAVEN ... AS THE ONE WHO AVENGED HER IN THE NAME OF JUSTICE!
GIMME A BREAK !!!

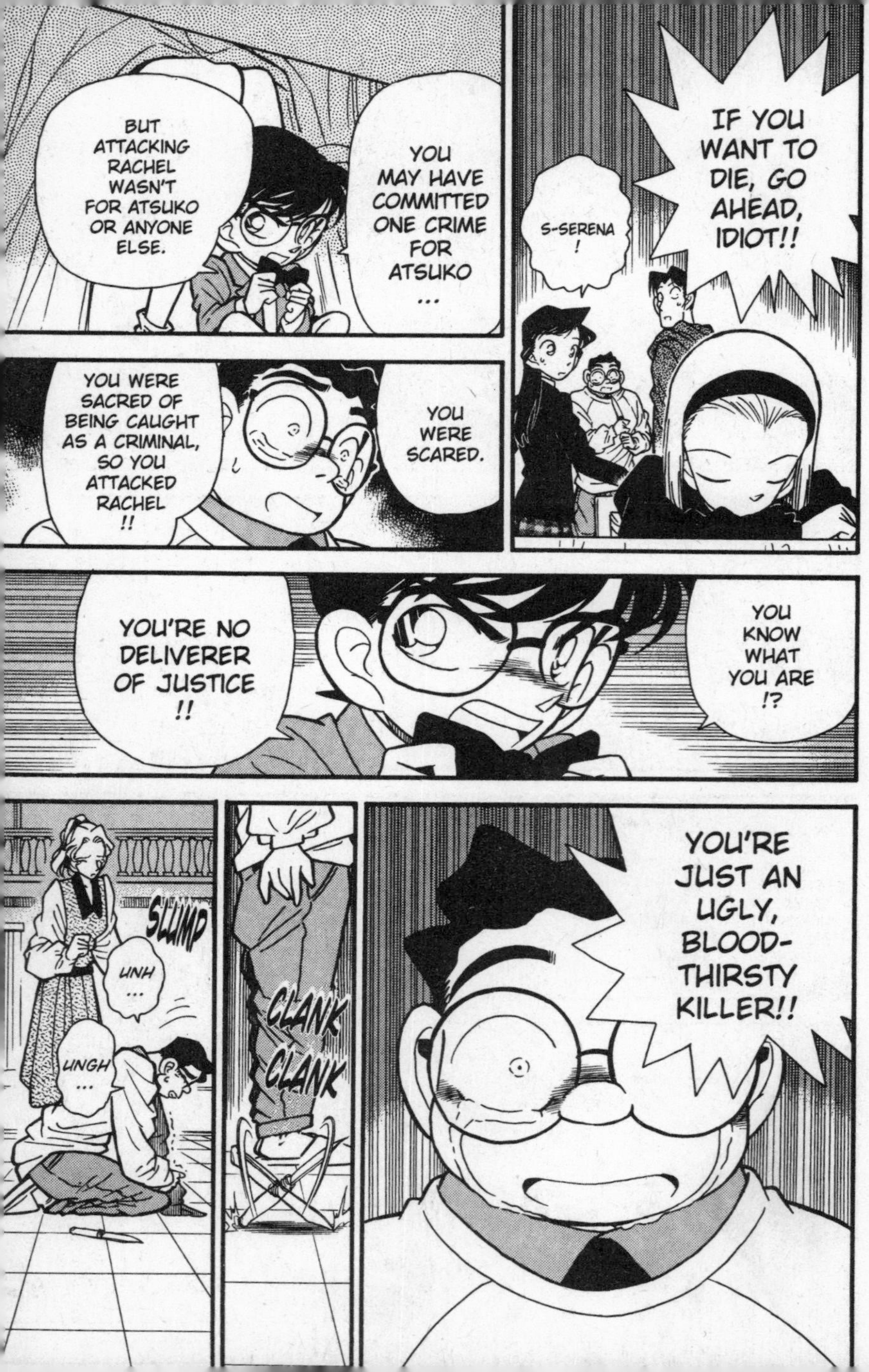
IF YOU WANT TO DIE, GO AHEAD, IDIOT!!
S-SERENA!
YOU MAY HAVE COMMITTED ONE CRIME FOR ATSUKO...
BUT ATTACKING RACHEL WASN'T FOR ATSUKO OR ANYONE ELSE.
YOU WERE SCARED.
YOU WERE SACRED OF BEING CAUGHT AS A CRIMINAL, SO YOU ATTACKED RACHEL!!
YOU KNOW WHAT YOU ARE!?
YOU'RE NO DELIVERER OF JUSTICE!!
YOU'RE JUST AN UGLY, BLOOD-THIRSTY KILLER!!
CLANK
CLANK
SLUMP
UNH...
UNGH...

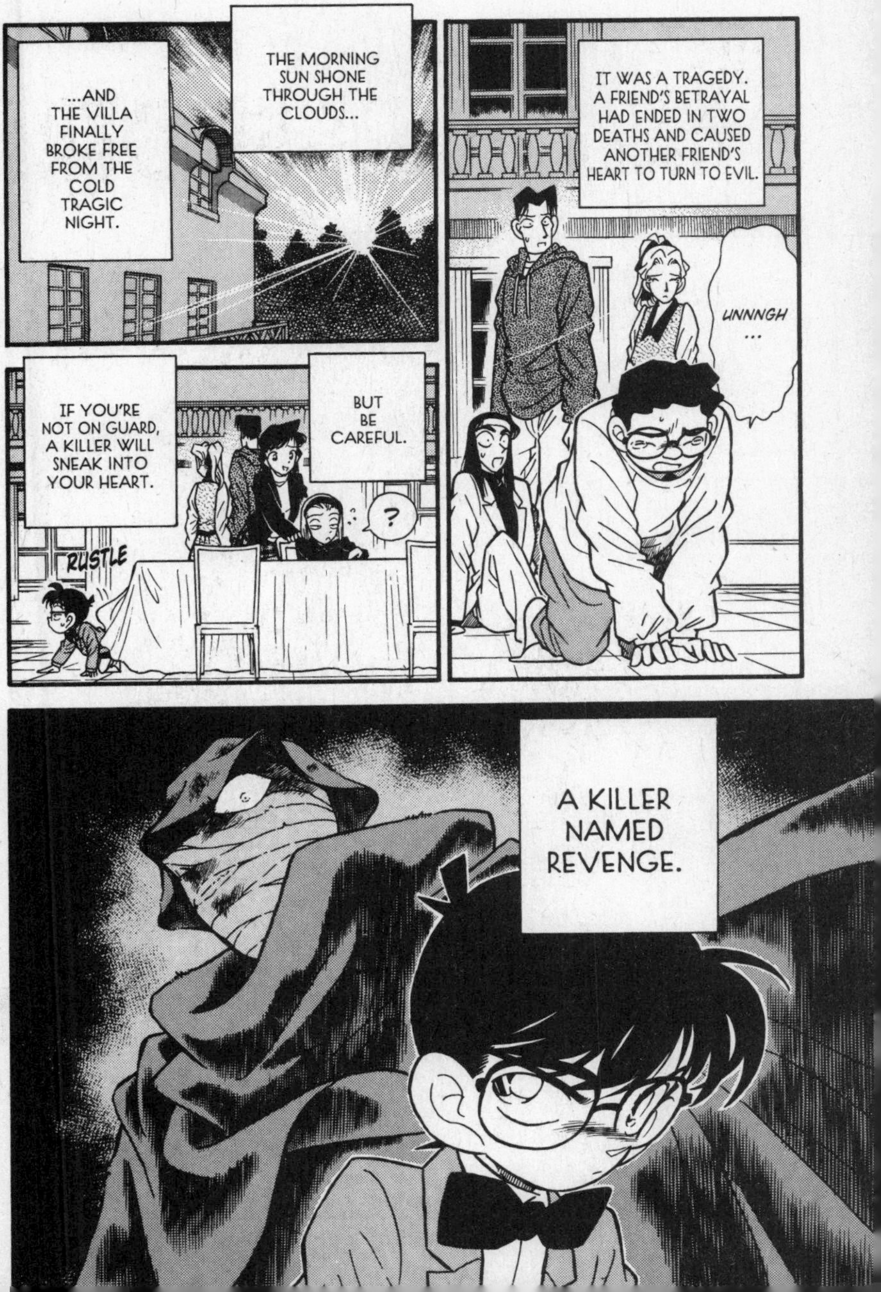
IT WAS A TRAGEDY. A FRIEND'S BETRAYAL HAD ENDED IN TWO DEATHS AND CAUSED ANOTHER FRIEND'S HEART TO TURN TO EVIL.
UNNNGH ...
THE MORNING SUN SHONE THROUGH THE CLOUDS...
...AND THE VILLA FINALLY BROKE FREE FROM THE COLD TRAGIC NIGHT.
BUT BE CAREFUL.
IF YOU'RE NOT ON GUARD, A KILLER WILL SNEAK INTO YOUR HEART.
?
RUSTLE
A KILLER NAMED REVENGE.

FILE 6: KARAOKE MURDER!

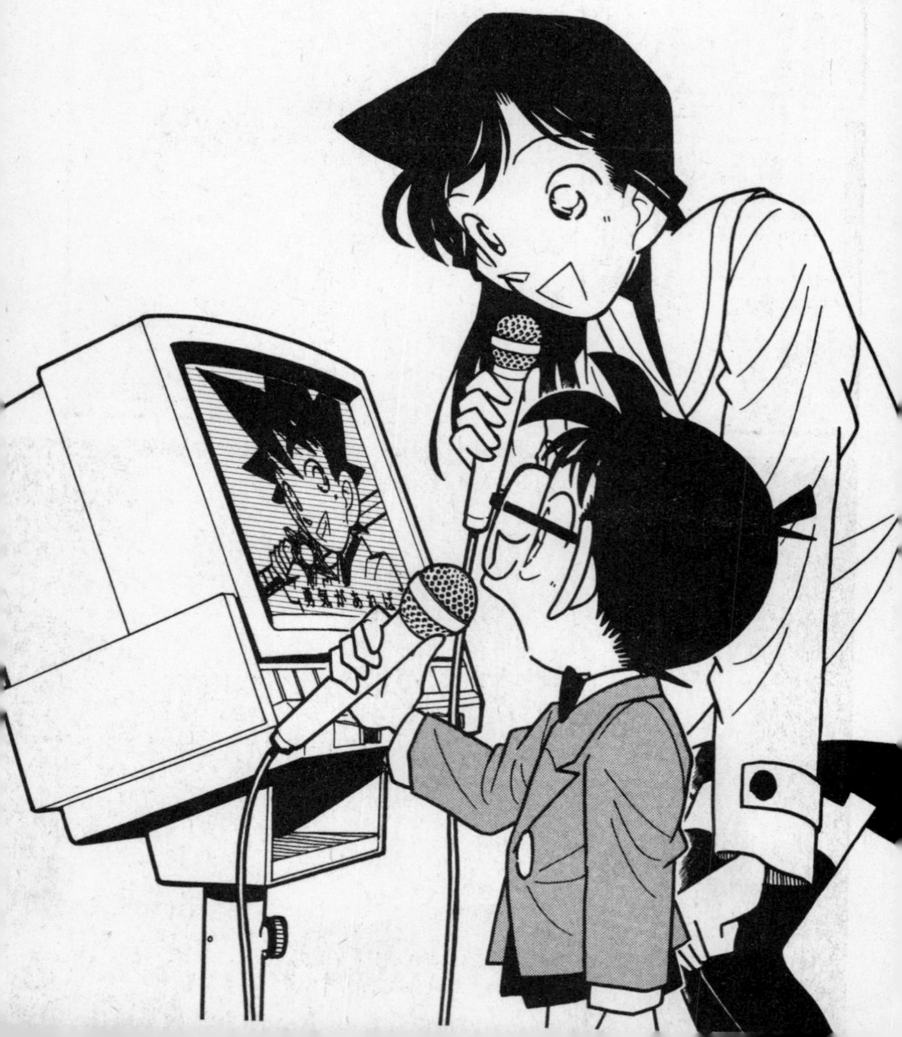
勇気があれば

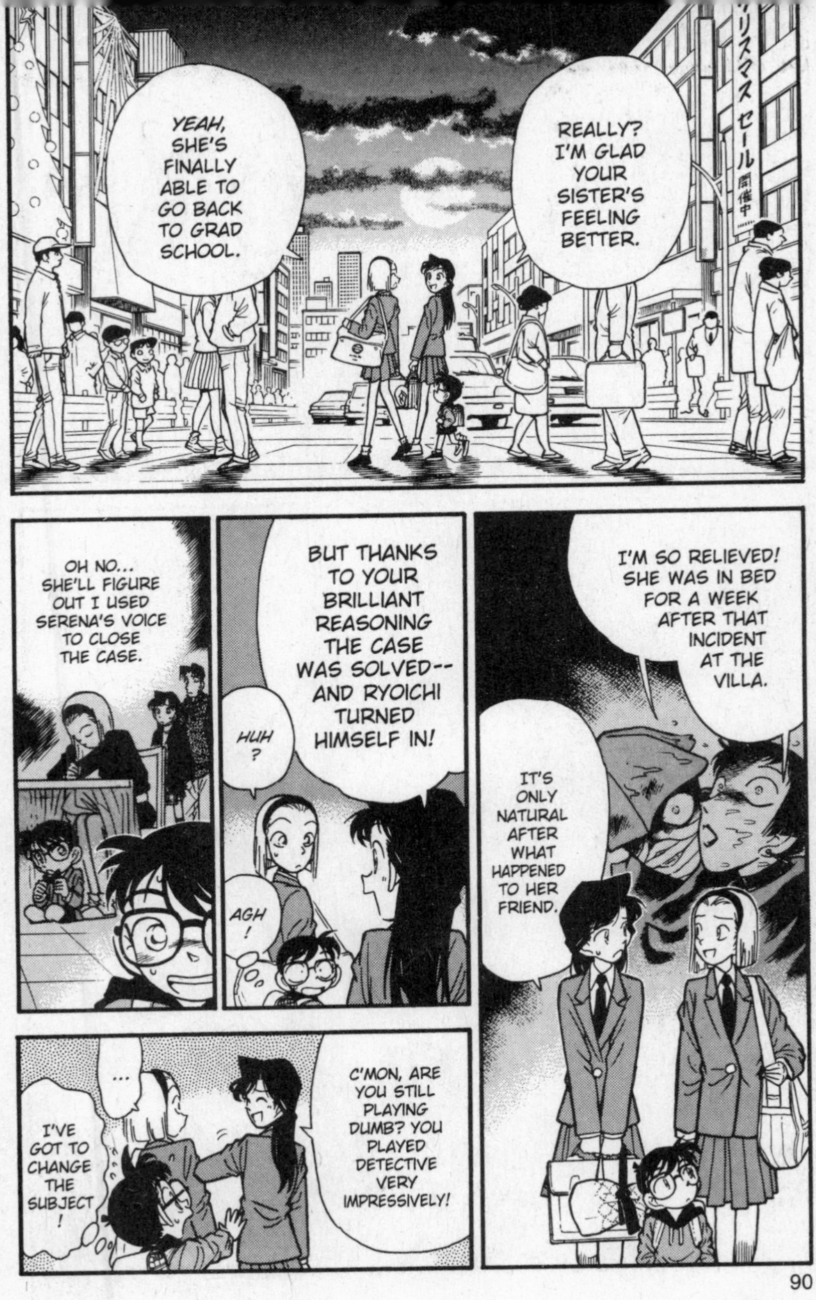
リスマス セール 開催中
REALLY? I'M GLAD YOUR SISTER'S FEELING BETTER.
YEAH, SHE'S FINALLY ABLE TO GO BACK TO GRAD SCHOOL.
I'M SO RELIEVED! SHE WAS IN BED FOR A WEEK AFTER THAT INCIDENT AT THE VILLA.
IT'S ONLY NATURAL AFTER WHAT HAPPENED TO HER FRIEND.
BUT THANKS TO YOUR BRILLIANT REASONING THE CASE WAS SOLVED-- AND RYOICHI TURNED HIMSELF IN!
HUH ?
AGH !
OH NO... SHE'LL FIGURE OUT I USED SERENA'S VOICE TO CLOSE THE CASE.
C'MON, ARE YOU STILL PLAYING DUMB? YOU PLAYED DETECTIVE VERY IMPRESSIVELY!
...
I'VE GOT TO CHANGE THE SUBJECT !

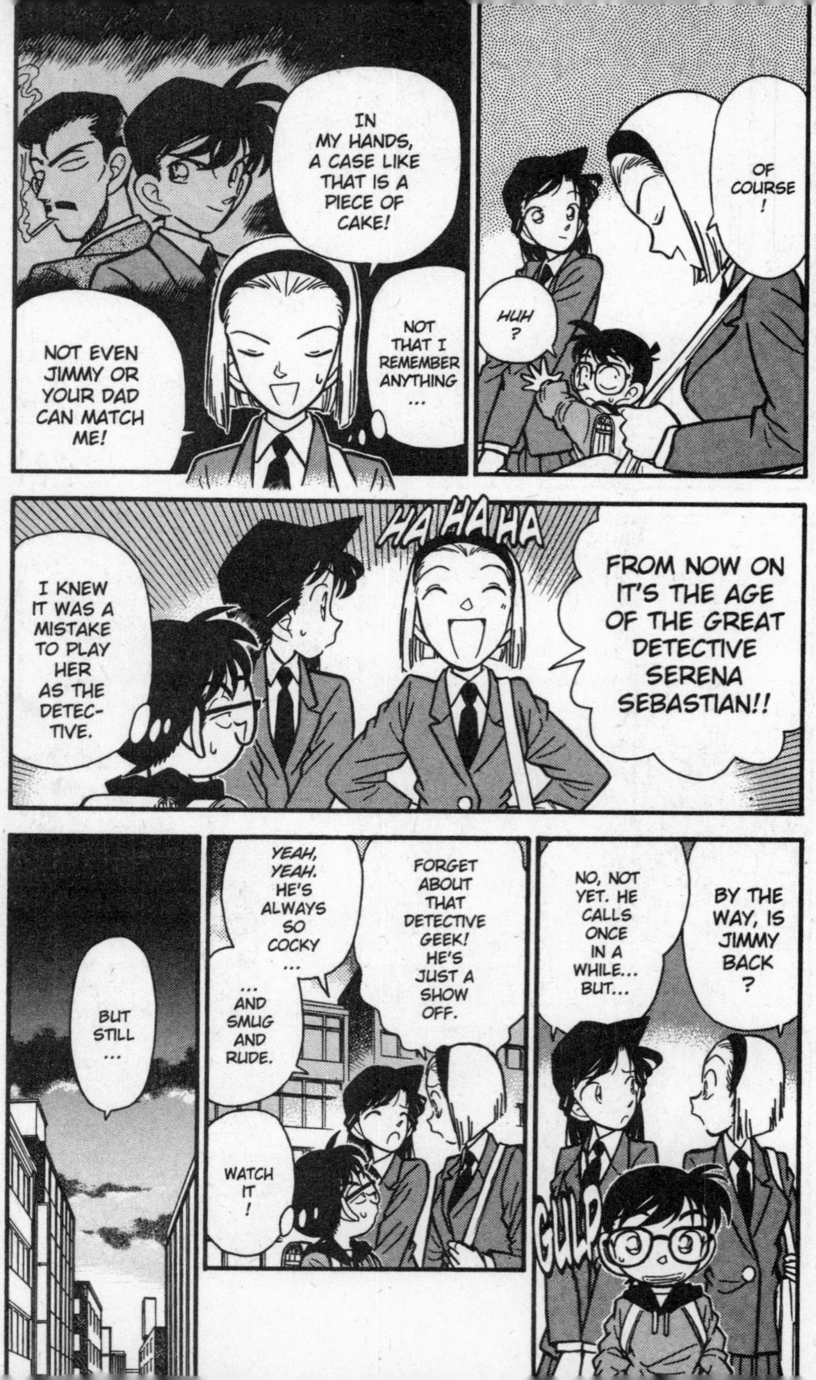
OF COURSE!
HUH?
IN MY HANDS, A CASE LIKE THAT IS A PIECE OF CAKE!
NOT THAT I REMEMBER ANYTHING...
NOT EVEN JIMMY OR YOUR DAD CAN MATCH ME!
FROM NOW ON IT'S THE AGE OF THE GREAT DETECTIVE SERENA SEBASTIAN!!
HA HA HA
I KNEW IT WAS A MISTAKE TO PLAY HER AS THE DETEC-TIVE.
BY THE WAY, IS JIMMY BACK?
NO, NOT YET. HE CALLS ONCE IN A WHILE... BUT...
GULP
FORGET ABOUT THAT DETECTIVE GEEK! HE'S JUST A SHOW OFF.
YEAH, YEAH. HE'S ALWAYS SO COCKY...
...AND SMUG AND RUDE.
WATCH IT!
BUT STILL...

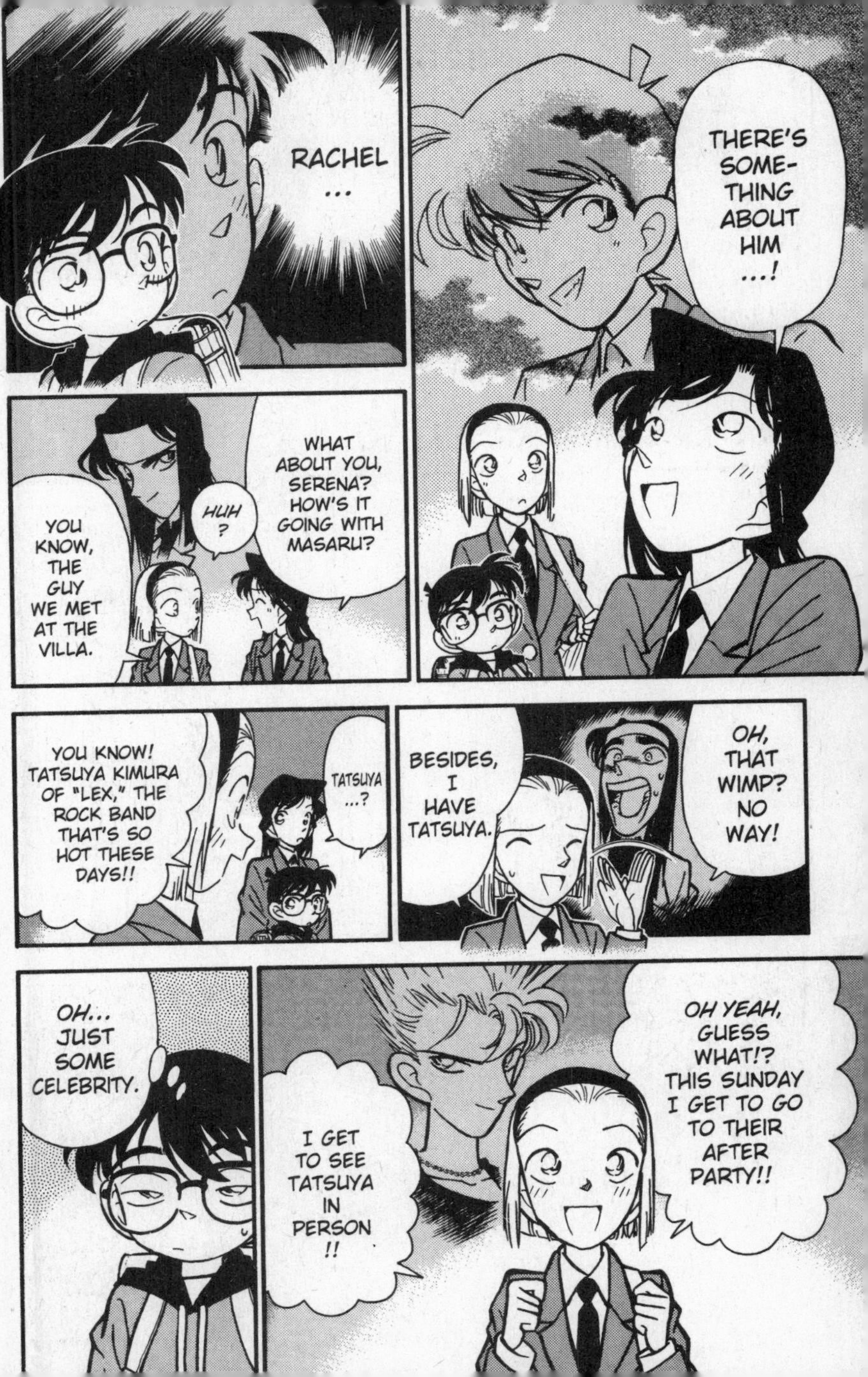
THERE'S SOME-THING ABOUT HIM ...!
RACHEL ...
WHAT ABOUT YOU, SERENA? HOW'S IT GOING WITH MASARU?
HUH?
YOU KNOW, THE GUY WE MET AT THE VILLA.
OH, THAT WIMP? NO WAY!
BESIDES, I HAVE TATSUYA.
TATSUYA ...?
YOU KNOW! TATSUYA KIMURA OF "LEX," THE ROCK BAND THAT'S SO HOT THESE DAYS!!
OH YEAH, GUESS WHAT!? THIS SUNDAY I GET TO GO TO THEIR AFTER PARTY!!
I GET TO SEE TATSUYA IN PERSON !!
OH... JUST SOME CELEBRITY.

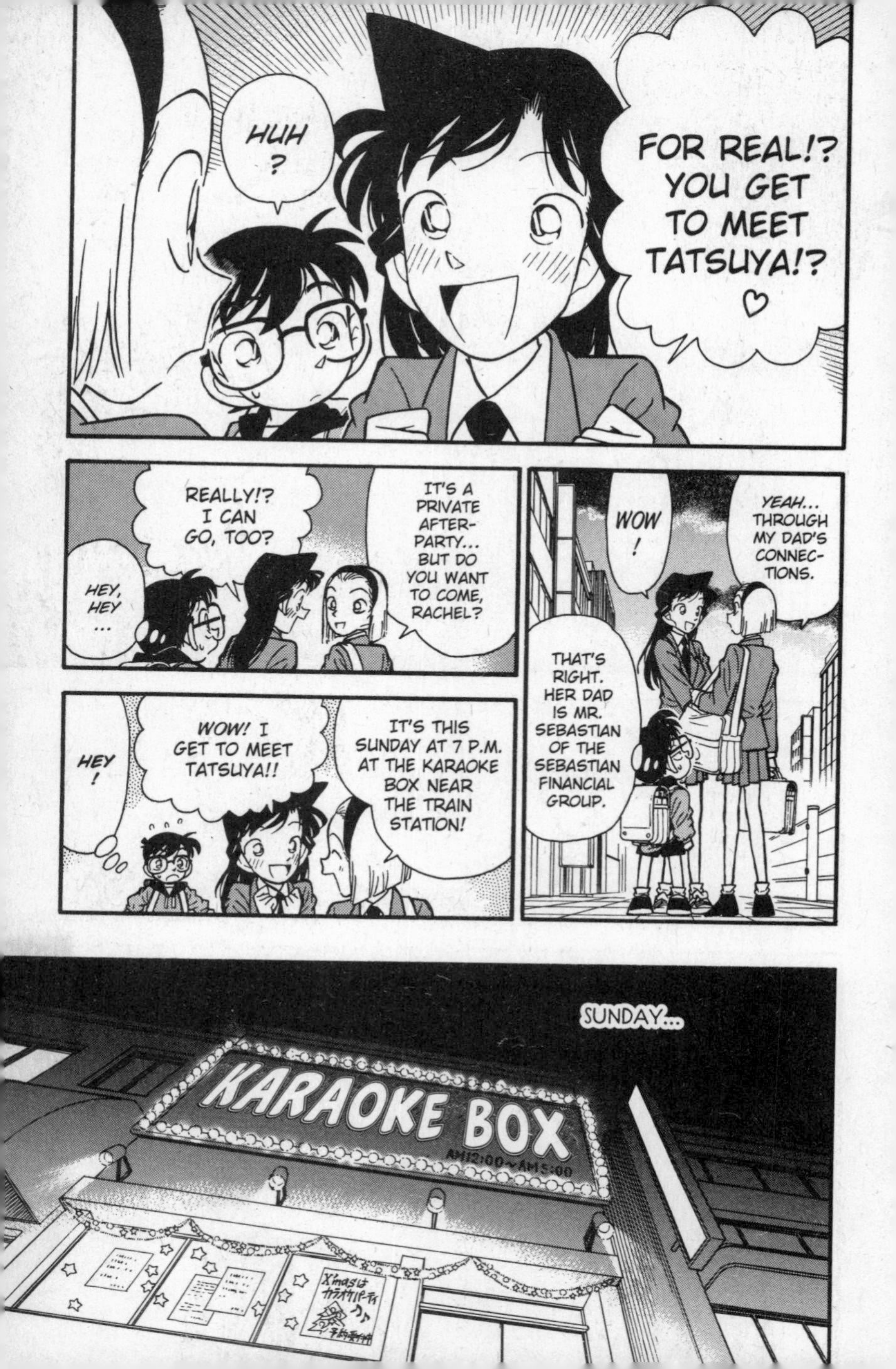
FOR REAL!? YOU GET TO MEET TATSUYA!? ♡
HUH ?
YEAH... THROUGH MY DAD'S CONNEC- TIONS.
WOW !
THAT'S RIGHT. HER DAD IS MR. SEBASTIAN OF THE SEBASTIAN FINANCIAL GROUP.
IT'S A PRIVATE AFTER- PARTY... BUT DO YOU WANT TO COME, RACHEL?
REALLY!? I CAN GO, TOO?
HEY, HEY ...
IT'S THIS SUNDAY AT 7 P.M. AT THE KARAOKE BOX NEAR THE TRAIN STATION!
WOW! I GET TO MEET TATSUYA!!
HEY !
SUNDAY...
KARAOKE BOX
AM12:00~AM5:00
X'masは
カラオケパーティ

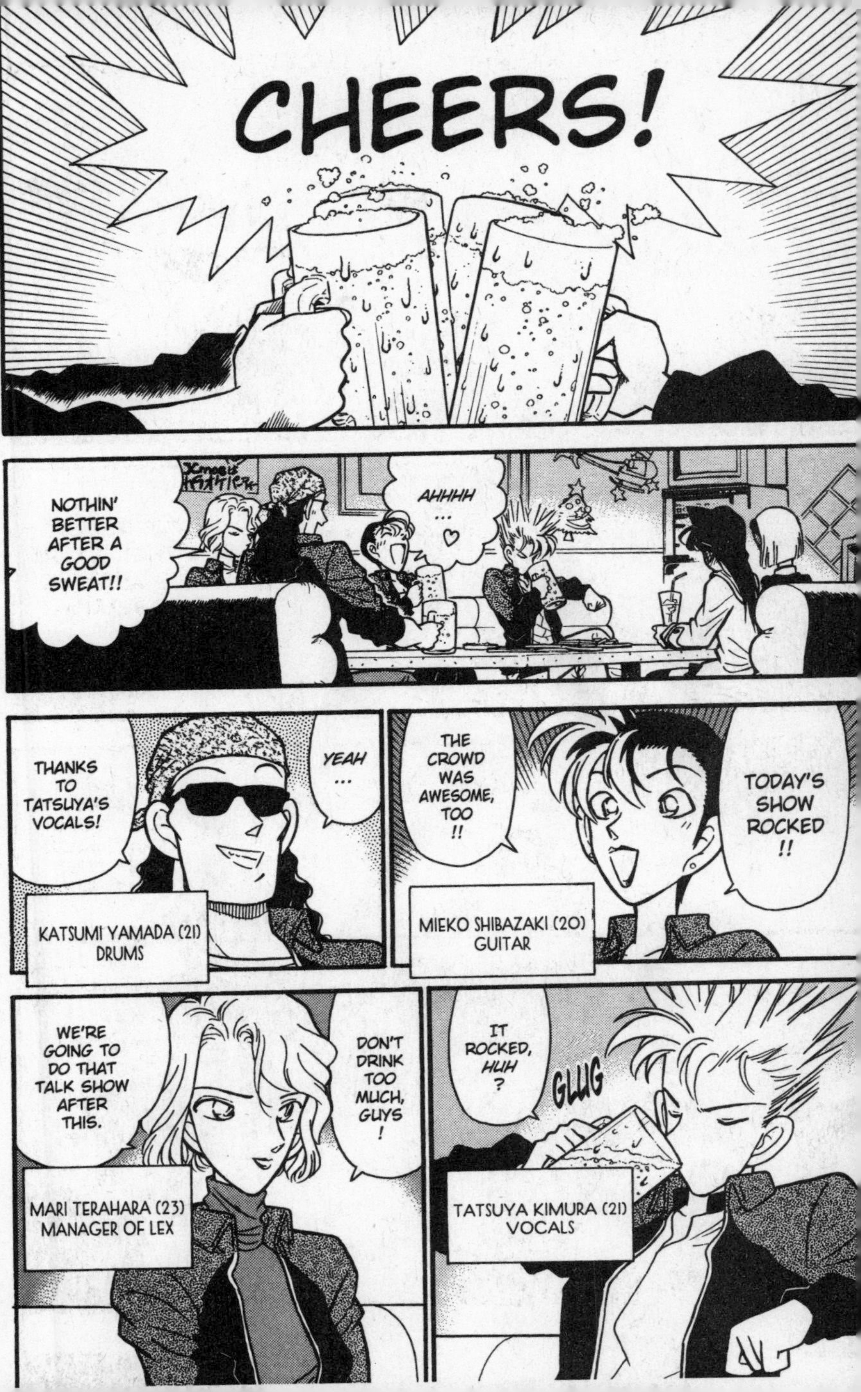
CHEERS!
AHHHH ... ♥
NOTHIN' BETTER AFTER A GOOD SWEAT!!
TODAY'S SHOW ROCKED!!
THE CROWD WAS AWESOME, TOO!!
MIEKO SHIBAZAKI (20) GUITAR
YEAH ...
THANKS TO TATSUYA'S VOCALS!
KATSUMI YAMADA (21) DRUMS
IT ROCKED, HUH?
GLUG
TATSUYA KIMURA (21) VOCALS
DON'T DRINK TOO MUCH, GUYS!
WE'RE GOING TO DO THAT TALK SHOW AFTER THIS.
MARI TERAHARA (23) MANAGER OF LEX

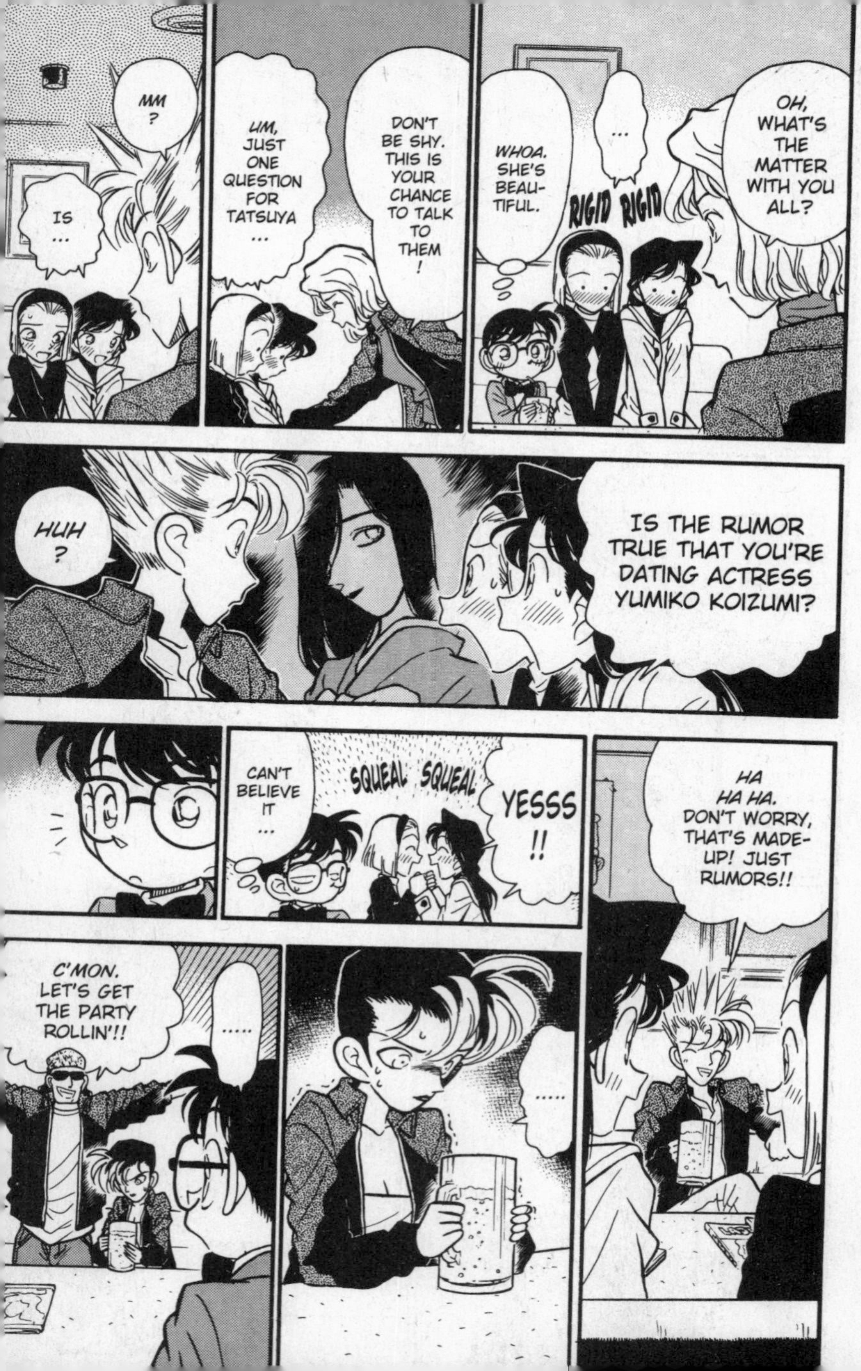
OH, WHAT'S THE MATTER WITH YOU ALL?
...
RIGID RIGID
WHOA. SHE'S BEAU-TIFUL.
DON'T BE SHY. THIS IS YOUR CHANCE TO TALK TO THEM!
UM, JUST ONE QUESTION FOR TATSUYA ...
MM ?
IS ...
IS THE RUMOR TRUE THAT YOU'RE DATING ACTRESS YUMIKO KOIZUMI?
HUH ?
HA HA HA. DON'T WORRY, THAT'S MADE-UP! JUST RUMORS!!
YESSS !!
SQUEAL SQUEAL
CAN'T BELIEVE IT ...
.....
C'MON. LET'S GET THE PARTY ROLLIN'!!
.....

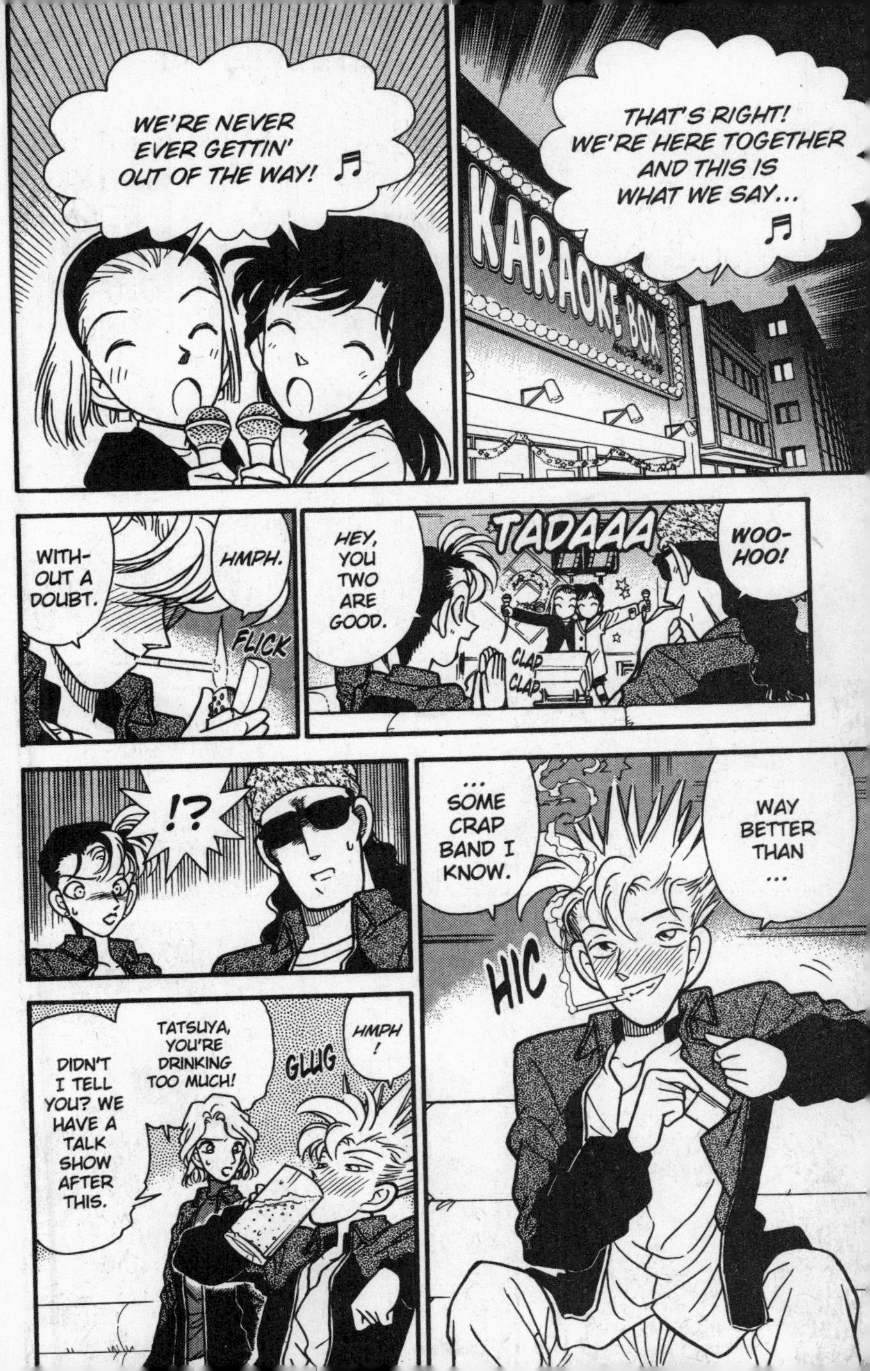
THAT'S RIGHT! WE'RE HERE TOGETHER AND THIS IS WHAT WE SAY... ♪
KARAOKE BOX
WE'RE NEVER EVER GETTIN' OUT OF THE WAY! ♫
TADAAA
WOO-HOO!
HEY, YOU TWO ARE GOOD.
CLAP CLAP
HMPH.
WITH-OUT A DOUBT.
FLICK
WAY BETTER THAN ...
... SOME CRAP BAND I KNOW.
HIC
!?
HMPH!
GLUG
TATSUYA, YOU'RE DRINKING TOO MUCH!
DIDN'T I TELL YOU? WE HAVE A TALK SHOW AFTER THIS.

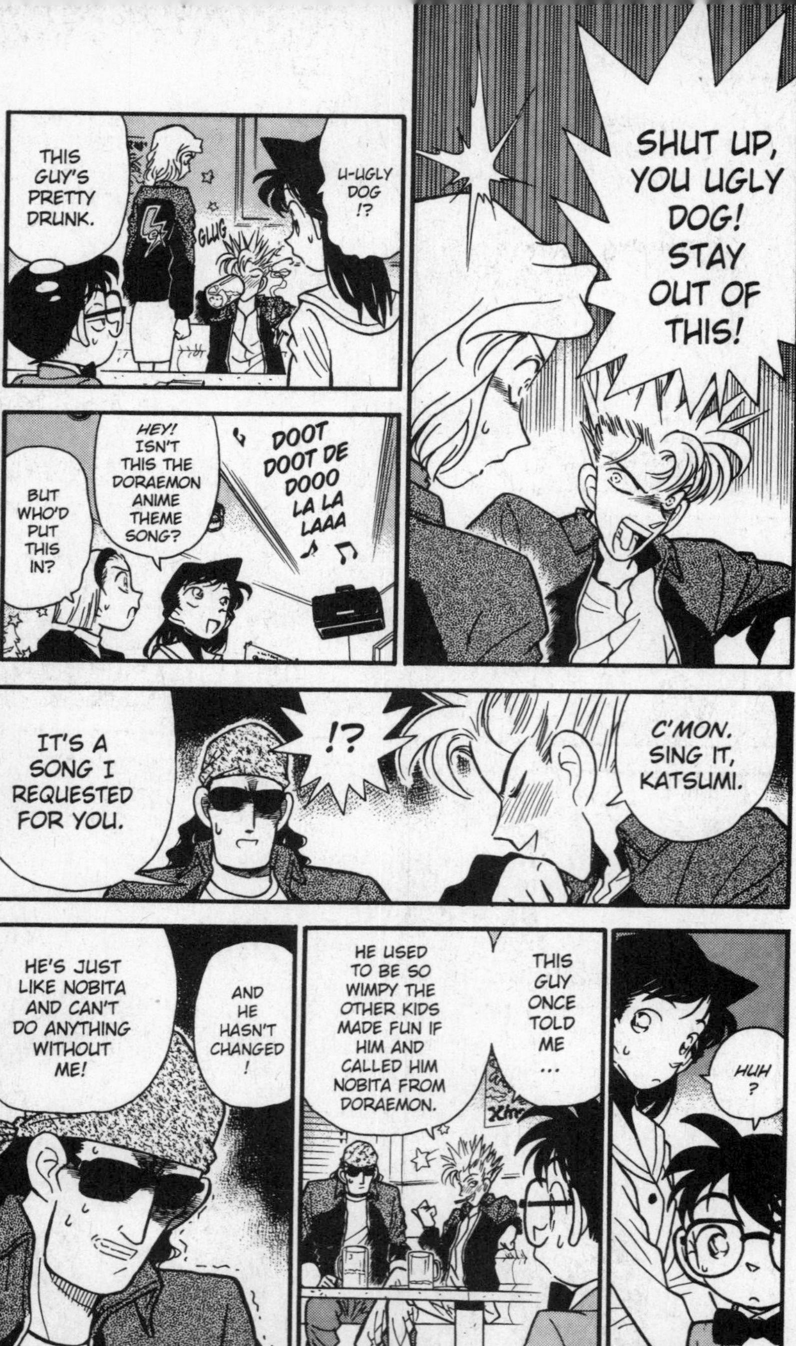
SHUT UP, YOU UGLY DOG! STAY OUT OF THIS!
U-UGLY DOG !?
GLUG
THIS GUY'S PRETTY DRUNK.
DOOT DOOT DE DOOO LA LA LAAA
HEY! ISN'T THIS THE DORAEMON ANIME THEME SONG?
BUT WHO'D PUT THIS IN?
C'MON. SING IT, KATSUMI.
!?
IT'S A SONG I REQUESTED FOR YOU.
HUH ?
THIS GUY ONCE TOLD ME ...
HE USED TO BE SO WIMPY THE OTHER KIDS MADE FUN IF HIM AND CALLED HIM NOBITA FROM DORAEMON.
AND HE HASN'T CHANGED !
HE'S JUST LIKE NOBITA AND CAN'T DO ANYTHING WITHOUT ME!

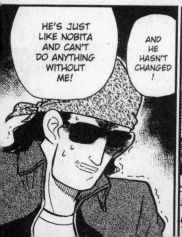

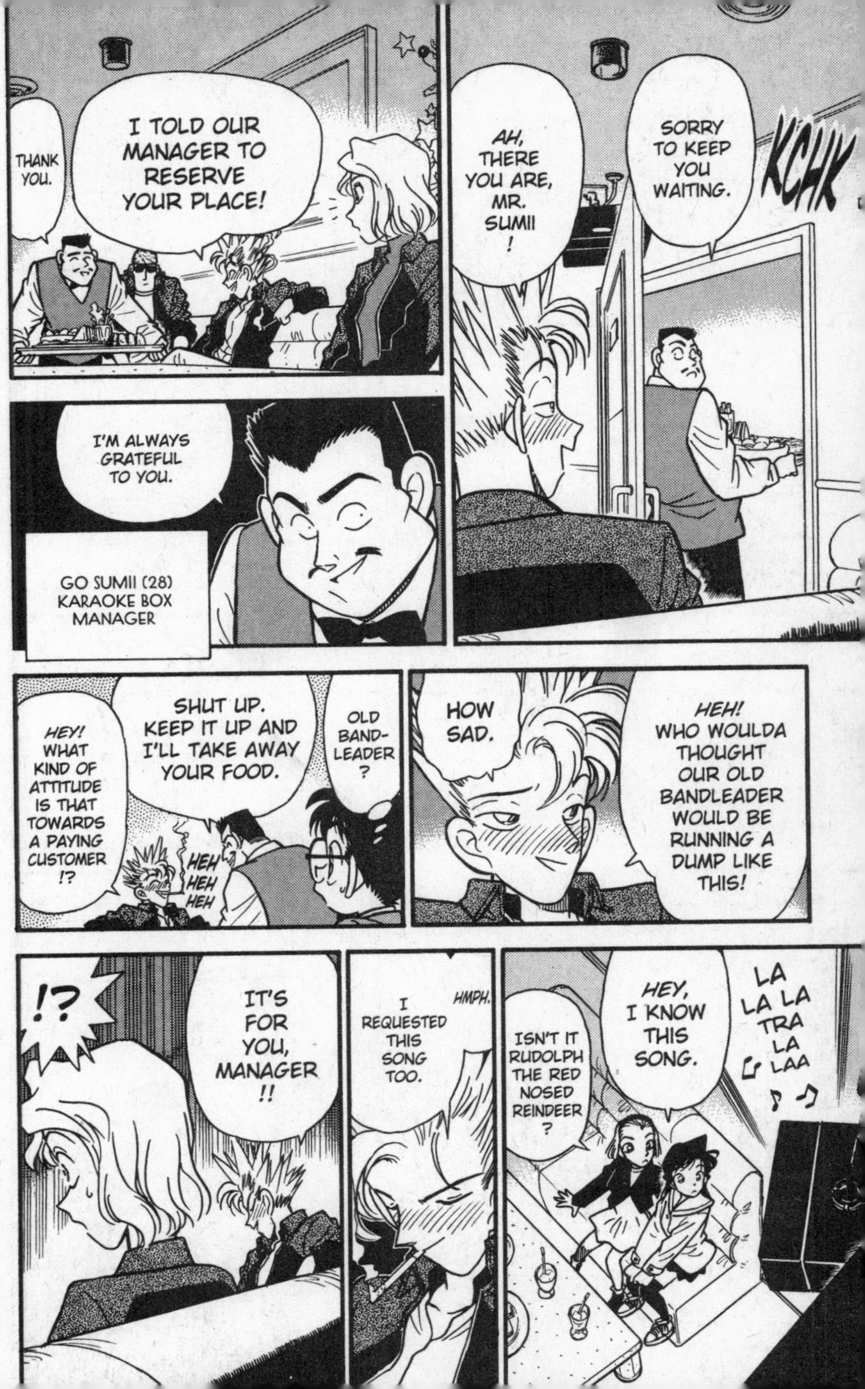
KCHK
SORRY TO KEEP YOU WAITING.
AH, THERE YOU ARE, MR. SUMII!
I TOLD OUR MANAGER TO RESERVE YOUR PLACE!
THANK YOU.
I'M ALWAYS GRATEFUL TO YOU.
GO SUMII (28) KARAOKE BOX MANAGER
HEH! WHO WOULDA THOUGHT OUR OLD BANDLEADER WOULD BE RUNNING A DUMP LIKE THIS!
HOW SAD.
OLD BAND-LEADER?
SHUT UP. KEEP IT UP AND I'LL TAKE AWAY YOUR FOOD.
HEH HEH HEH
HEY! WHAT KIND OF ATTITUDE IS THAT TOWARDS A PAYING CUSTOMER!?
LA LA LA TRA LA LAA
HEY, I KNOW THIS SONG.
ISN'T IT RUDOLPH THE RED NOSED REINDEER?
HMPH.
I REQUESTED THIS SONG TOO.
IT'S FOR YOU, MANAGER!!
!?

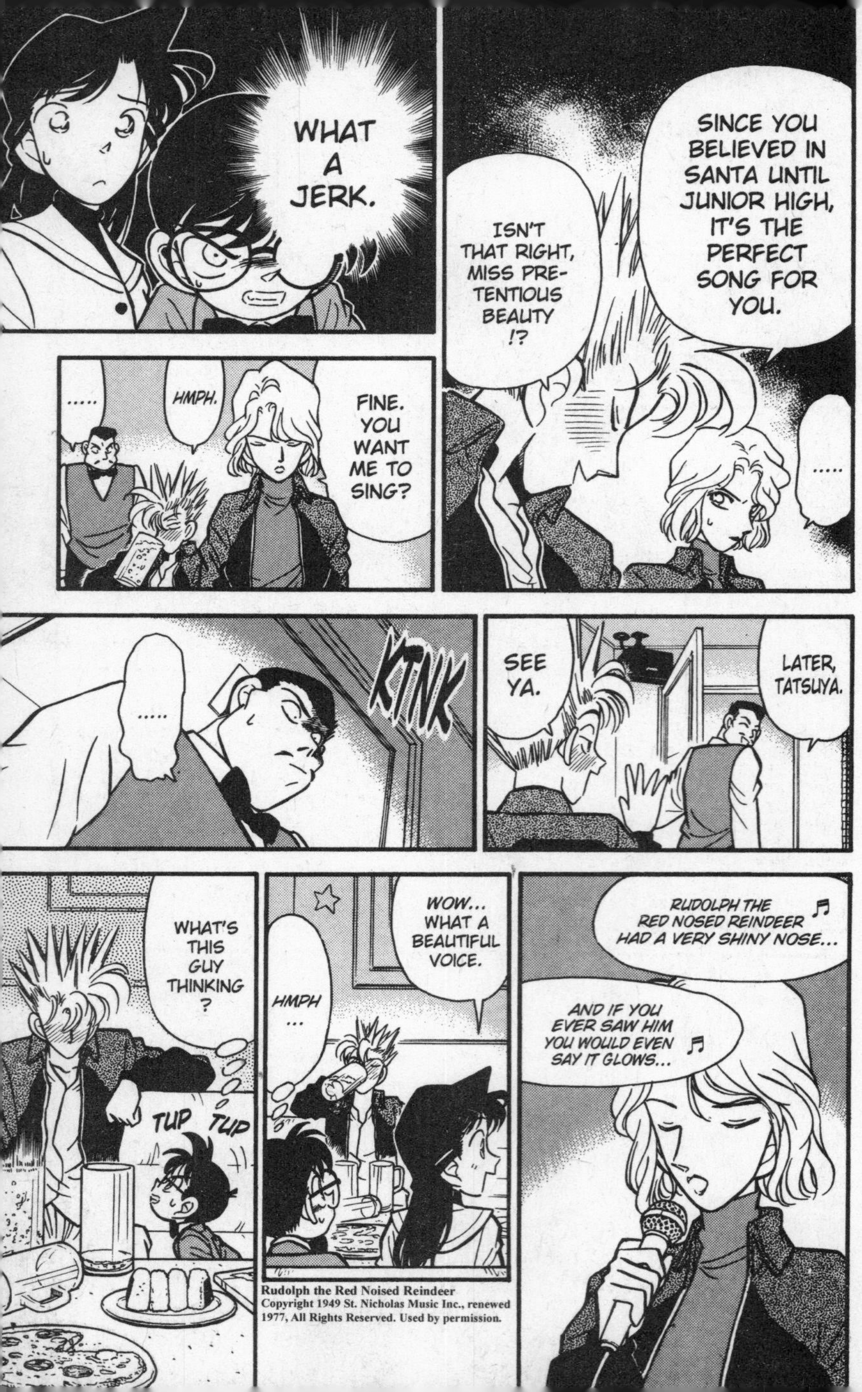
SINCE YOU BELIEVED IN SANTA UNTIL JUNIOR HIGH, IT'S THE PERFECT SONG FOR YOU.
ISN'T THAT RIGHT, MISS PRE-TENTIOUS BEAUTY !?
.....
WHAT A JERK.
FINE. YOU WANT ME TO SING?
HMPH.
.....
LATER, TATSUYA.
SEE YA.
KTNK
.....
RUDOLPH THE RED NOSED REINDEER HAD A VERY SHINY NOSE...
AND IF YOU EVER SAW HIM YOU WOULD EVEN SAY IT GLOWS...
WOW... WHAT A BEAUTIFUL VOICE.
HMPH ...
WHAT'S THIS GUY THINKING ?
TUP TUP

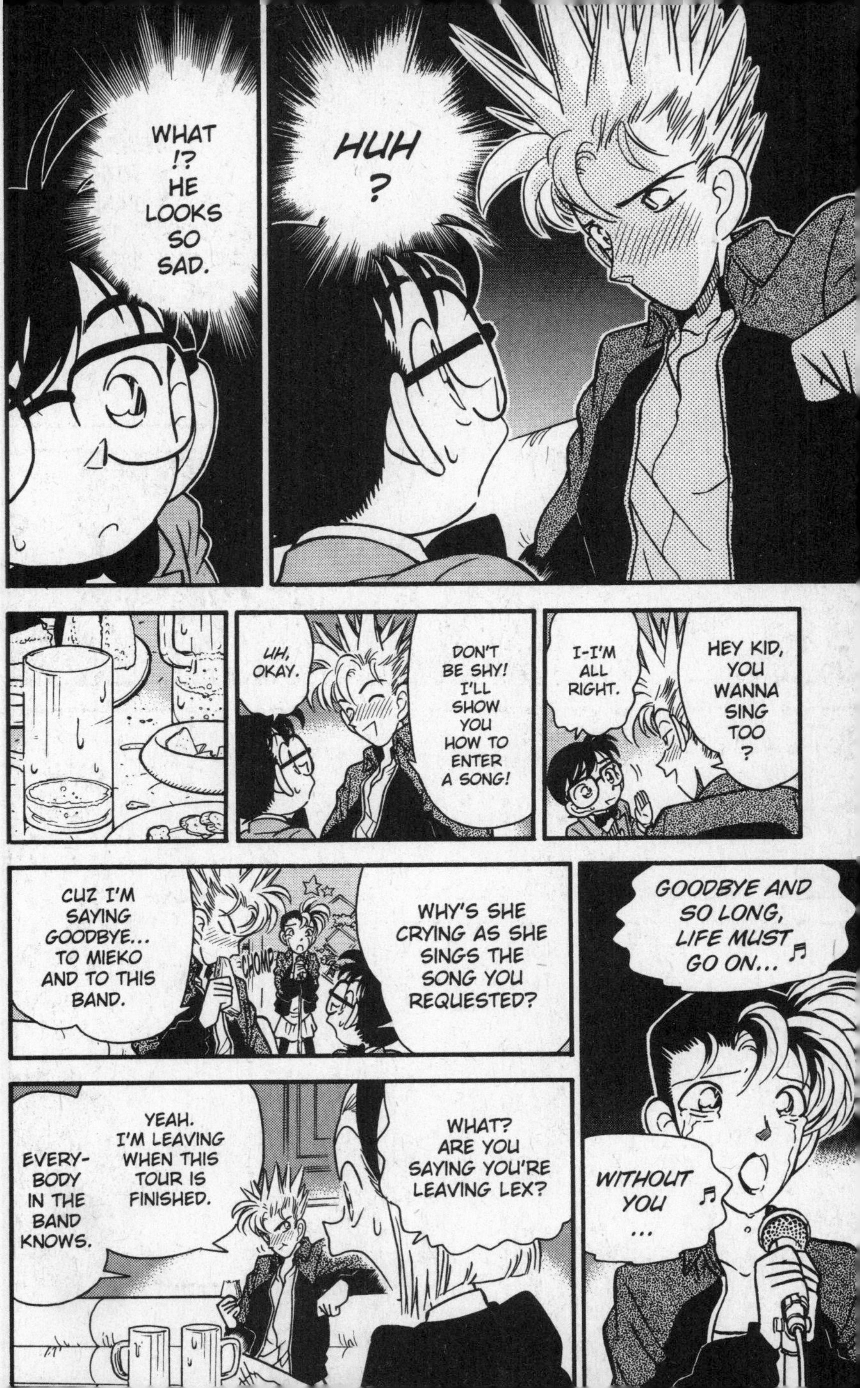
HUH ?
WHAT !? HE LOOKS SO SAD.
HEY KID, YOU WANNA SING TOO ?
I-I'M ALL RIGHT.
DON'T BE SHY! I'LL SHOW YOU HOW TO ENTER A SONG!
UH, OKAY.
GOODBYE AND SO LONG, LIFE MUST GO ON... ♪
WITHOUT YOU ♪ ...
WHY'S SHE CRYING AS SHE SINGS THE SONG YOU REQUESTED?
CHOMP
CUZ I'M SAYING GOODBYE... TO MIEKO AND TO THIS BAND.
WHAT? ARE YOU SAYING YOU'RE LEAVING LEX?
YEAH. I'M LEAVING WHEN THIS TOUR IS FINISHED.
EVERY-BODY IN THE BAND KNOWS.

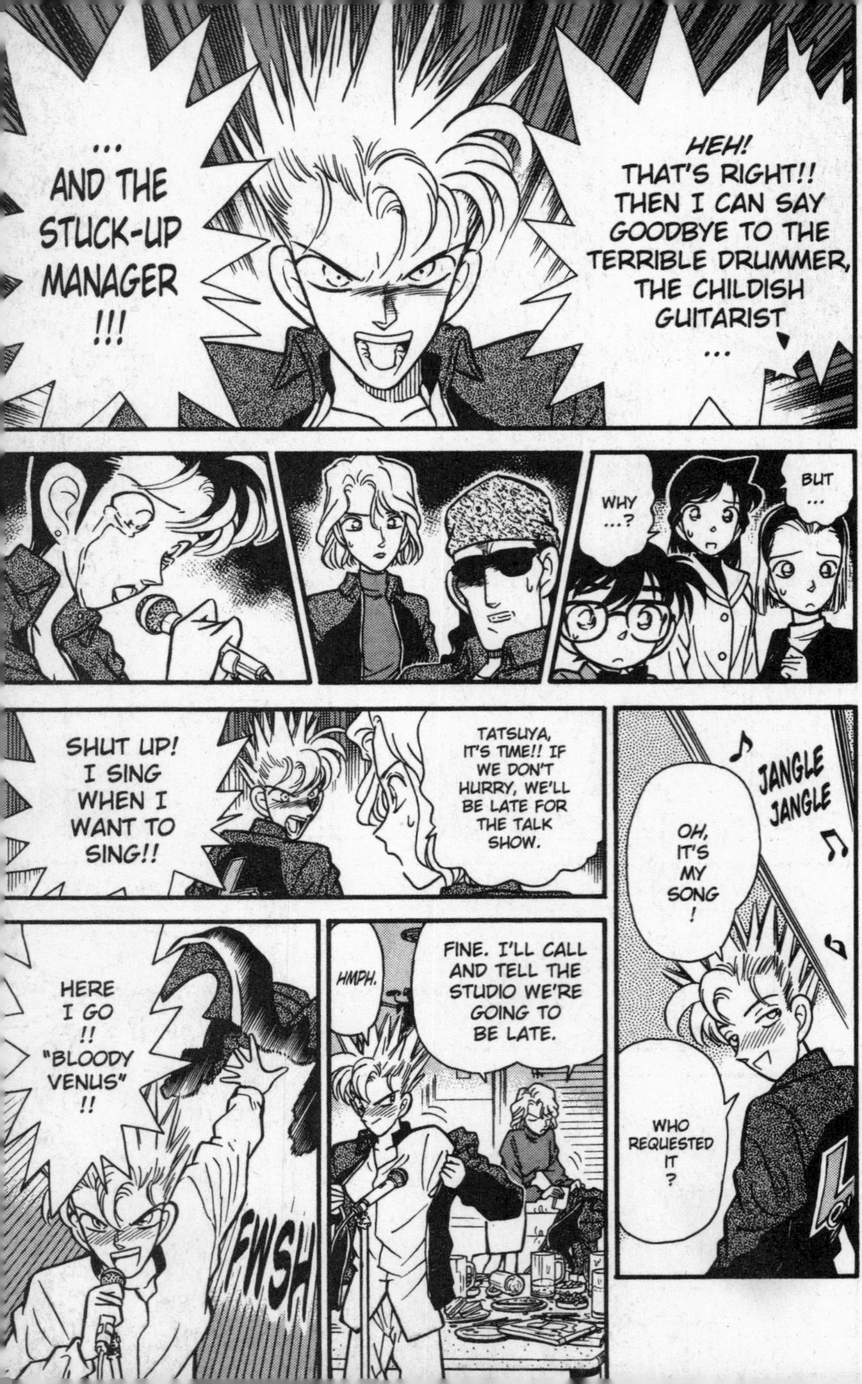
HEH! THAT'S RIGHT!! THEN I CAN SAY GOODBYE TO THE TERRIBLE DRUMMER, THE CHILDISH GUITARIST ...
... AND THE STUCK-UP MANAGER !!!
BUT ...
WHY ...?
JANGLE JANGLE
OH, IT'S MY SONG !
WHO REQUESTED IT ?
TATSUYA, IT'S TIME!! IF WE DON'T HURRY, WE'LL BE LATE FOR THE TALK SHOW.
SHUT UP! I SING WHEN I WANT TO SING!!
FINE. I'LL CALL AND TELL THE STUDIO WE'RE GOING TO BE LATE.
HMPH.
HERE I GO !! "BLOODY VENUS" !!
FWSH

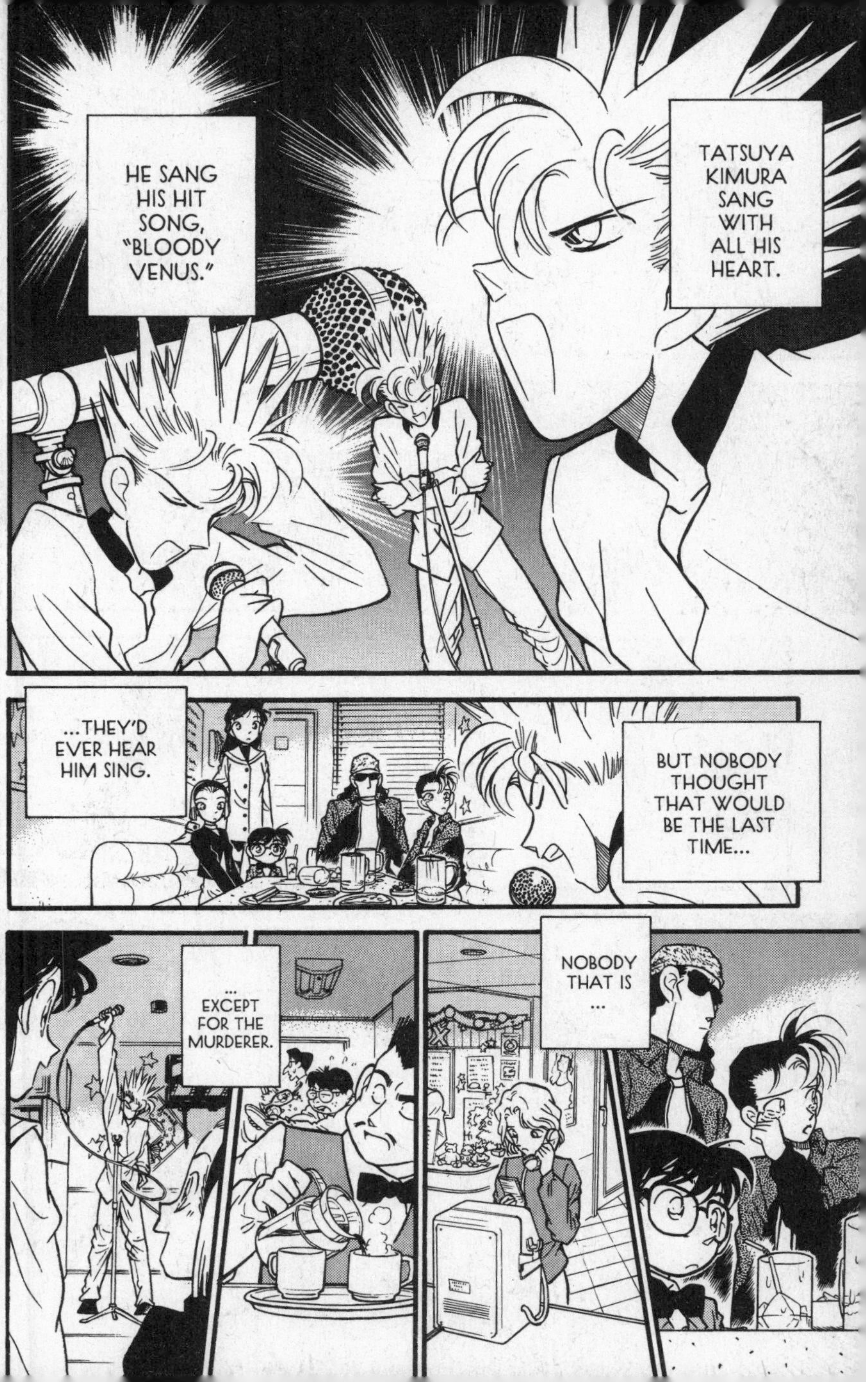
TATSUYA KIMURA SANG WITH ALL HIS HEART.
HE SANG HIS HIT SONG, "BLOODY VENUS."
BUT NOBODY THOUGHT THAT WOULD BE THE LAST TIME...
...THEY'D EVER HEAR HIM SING.
NOBODY THAT IS ...
... EXCEPT FOR THE MURDERER.

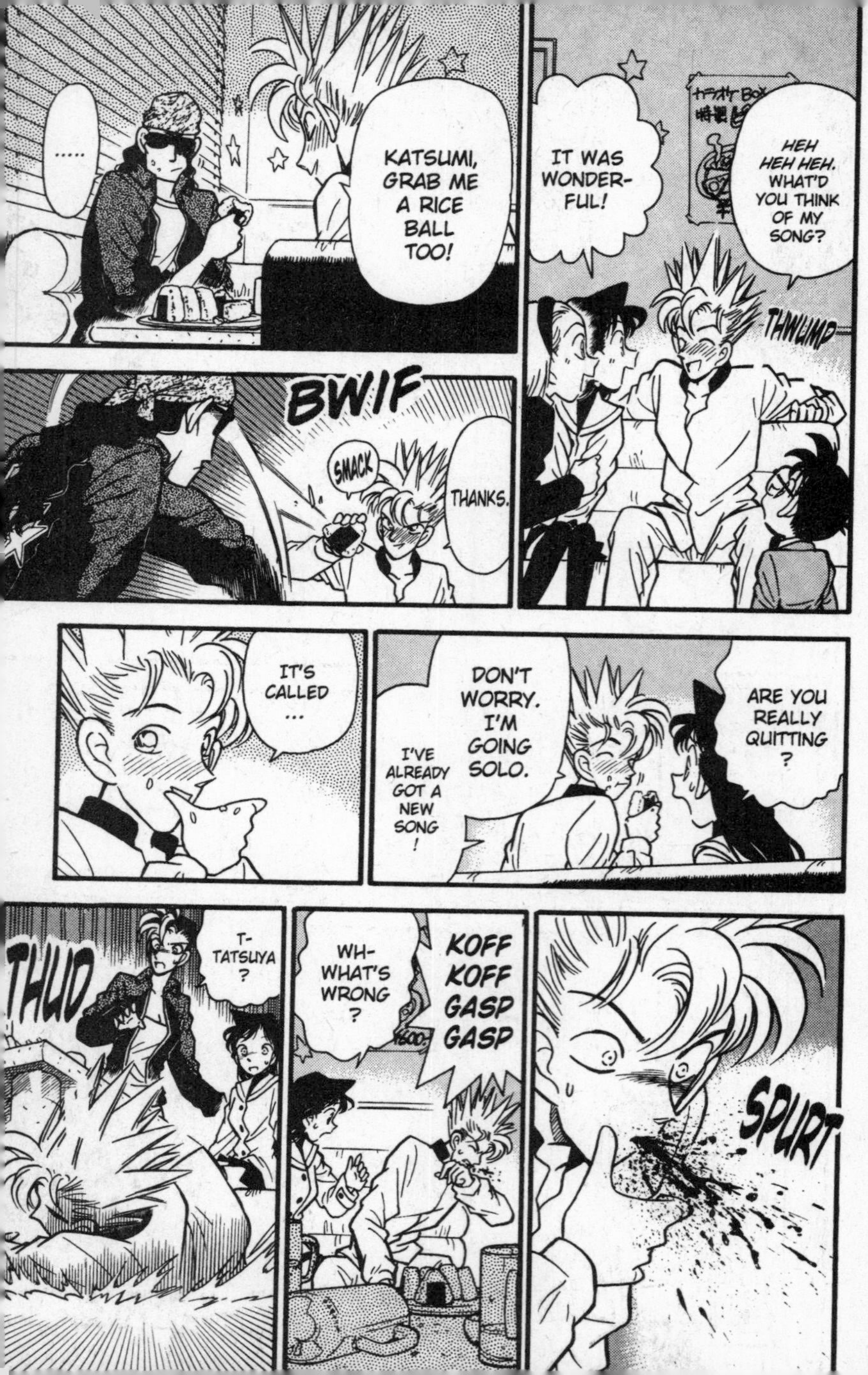
HEH HEH HEH. WHAT'D YOU THINK OF MY SONG?
IT WAS WONDERFUL!
THWUMP
KATSUMI, GRAB ME A RICE BALL TOO!
......
BWIF
THANKS.
SMACK
ARE YOU REALLY QUITTING?
DON'T WORRY. I'M GOING SOLO.
I'VE ALREADY GOT A NEW SONG!
IT'S CALLED ...
SPURT
KOFF KOFF GASP GASP
WH- WHAT'S WRONG?
T- TATSUYA?
THUD

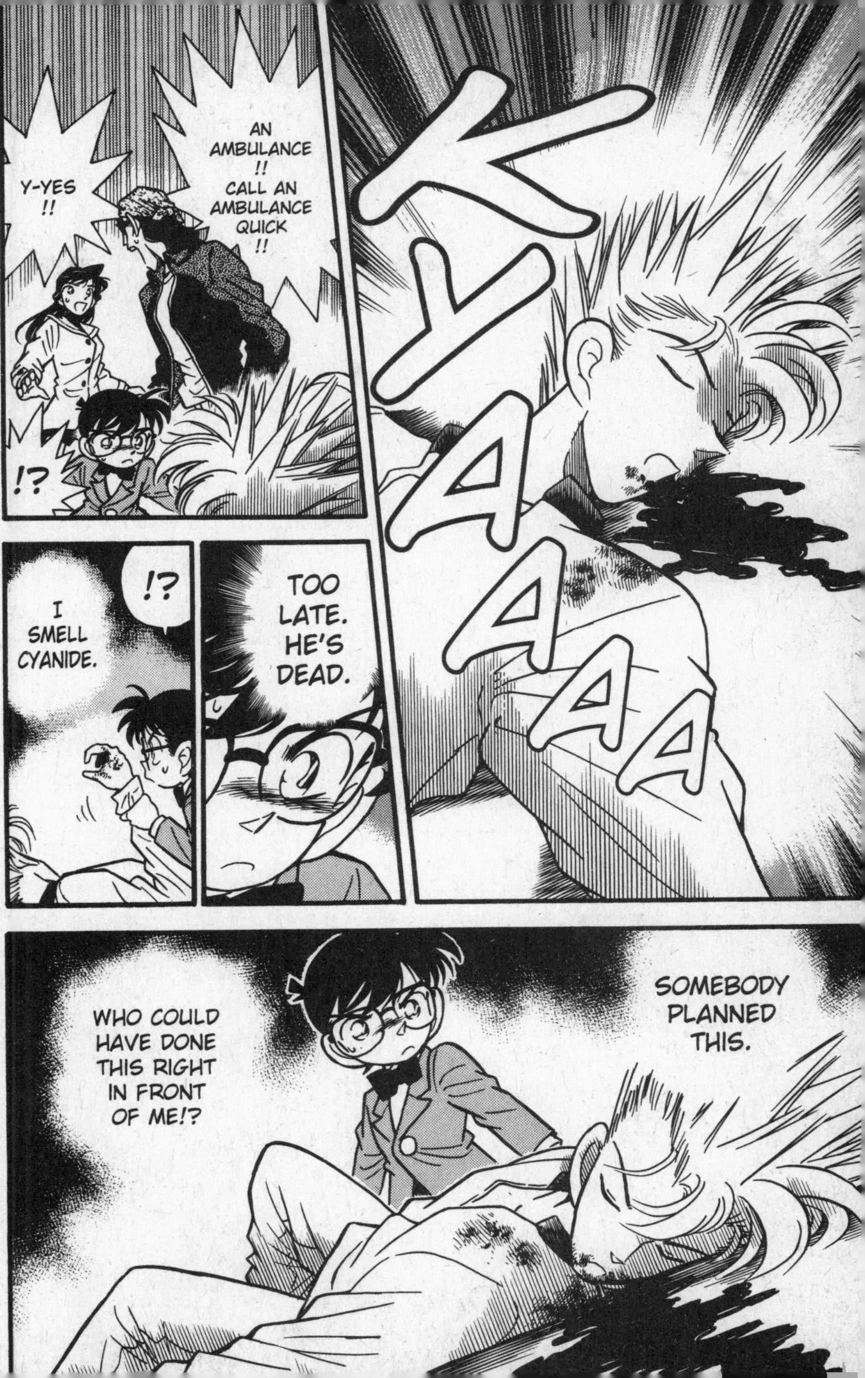

YAAAAAA
AN AMBULANCE!! CALL AN AMBULANCE QUICK!!
Y-YES!!
!?
TOO LATE. HE'S DEAD.
!?
I SMELL CYANIDE.
SOMEBODY PLANNED THIS.
WHO COULD HAVE DONE THIS RIGHT IN FRONT OF ME!?

FILE 7:
MURDER OR SUICIDE?

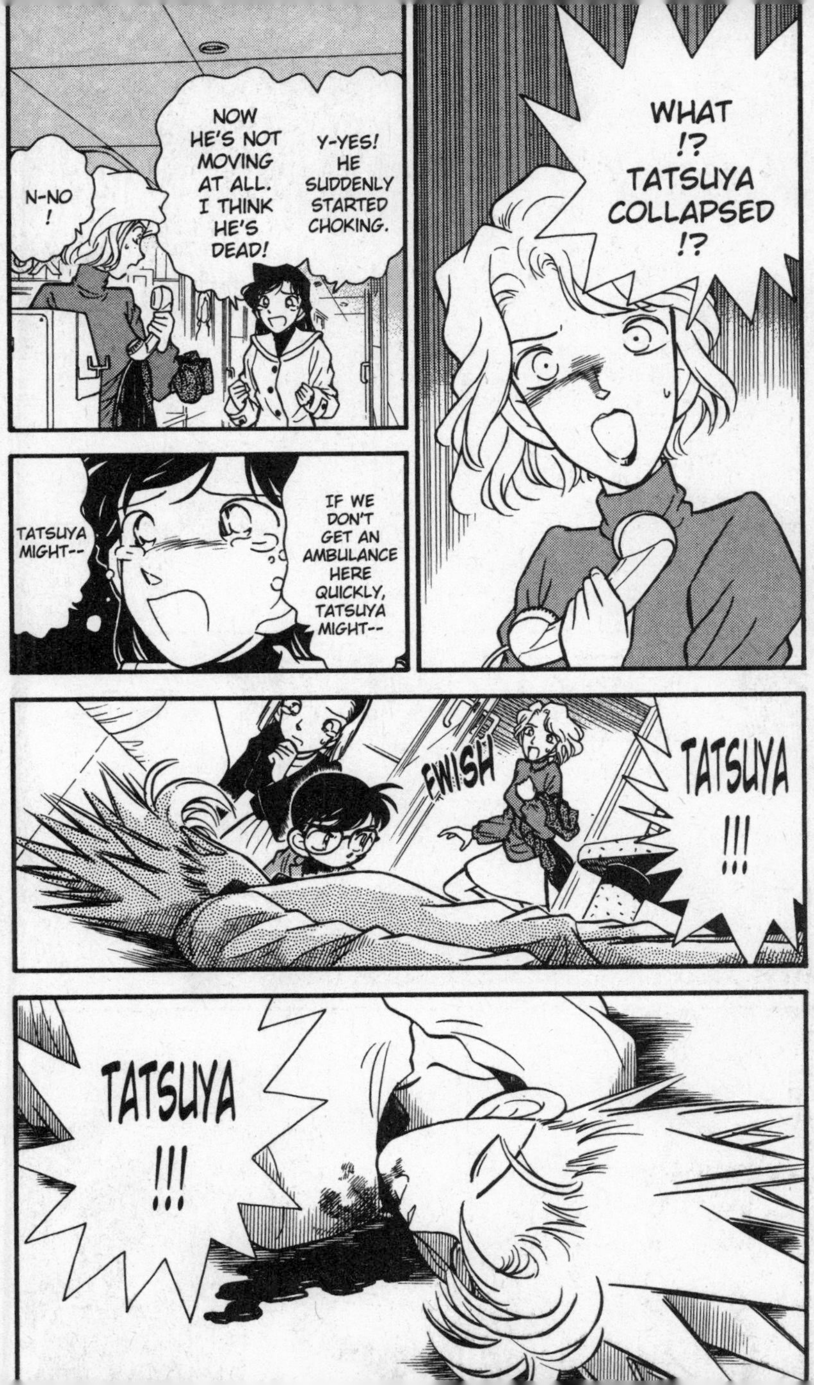
WHAT!? TATSUYA COLLAPSED!?
Y-YES! HE SUDDENLY STARTED CHOKING.
NOW HE'S NOT MOVING AT ALL. I THINK HE'S DEAD!
N-NO!
IF WE DON'T GET AN AMBULANCE HERE QUICKLY, TATSUYA MIGHT--
TATSUYA MIGHT--
TATSUYA!!!
FWISH
TATSUYA!!!

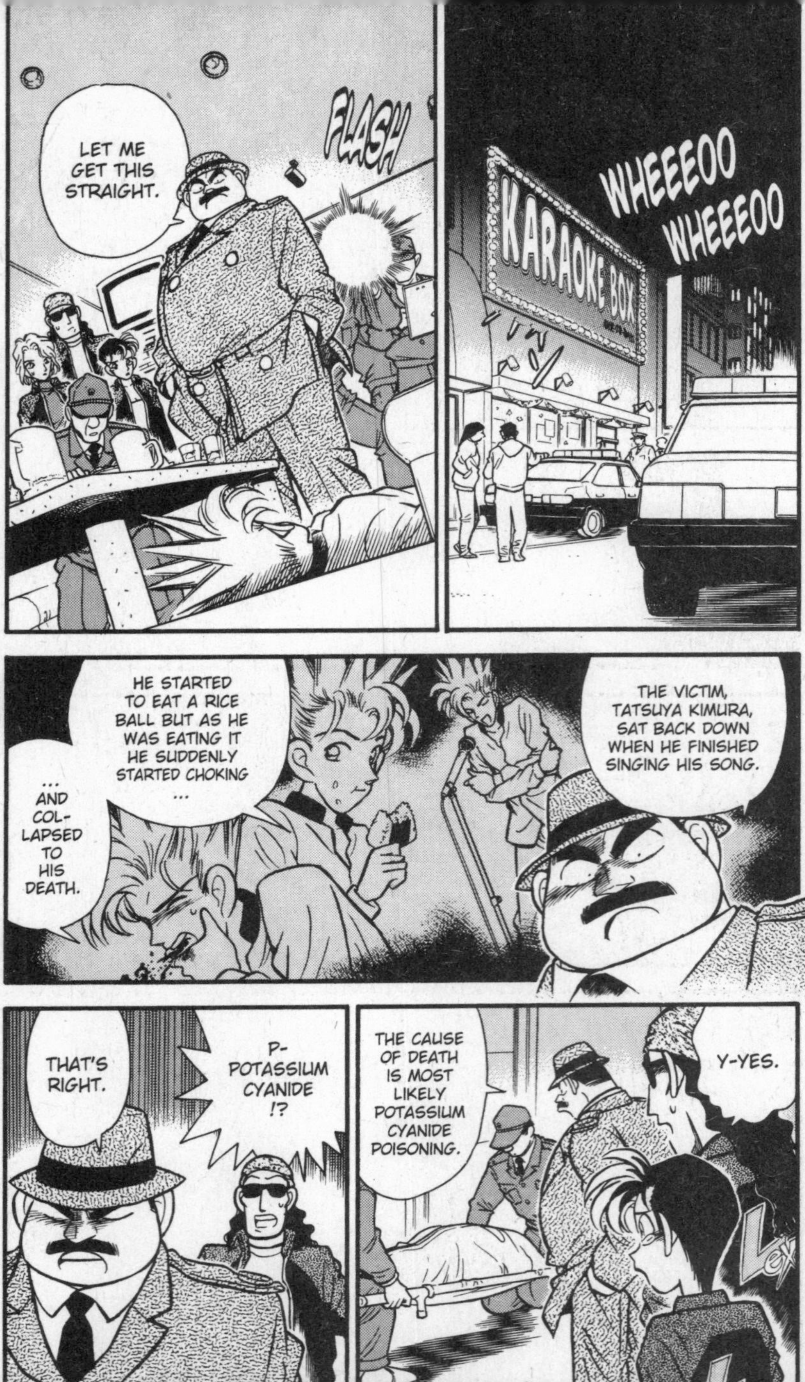
WHEEEOO
WHEEEOO
KARAOKE BOX
FLASH
LET ME GET THIS STRAIGHT.
THE VICTIM, TATSUYA KIMURA, SAT BACK DOWN WHEN HE FINISHED SINGING HIS SONG.
HE STARTED TO EAT A RICE BALL BUT AS HE WAS EATING IT HE SUDDENLY STARTED CHOKING ...
... AND COL-LAPSED TO HIS DEATH.
Y-YES.
THE CAUSE OF DEATH IS MOST LIKELY POTASSIUM CYANIDE POISONING.
P-POTASSIUM CYANIDE !?
THAT'S RIGHT.

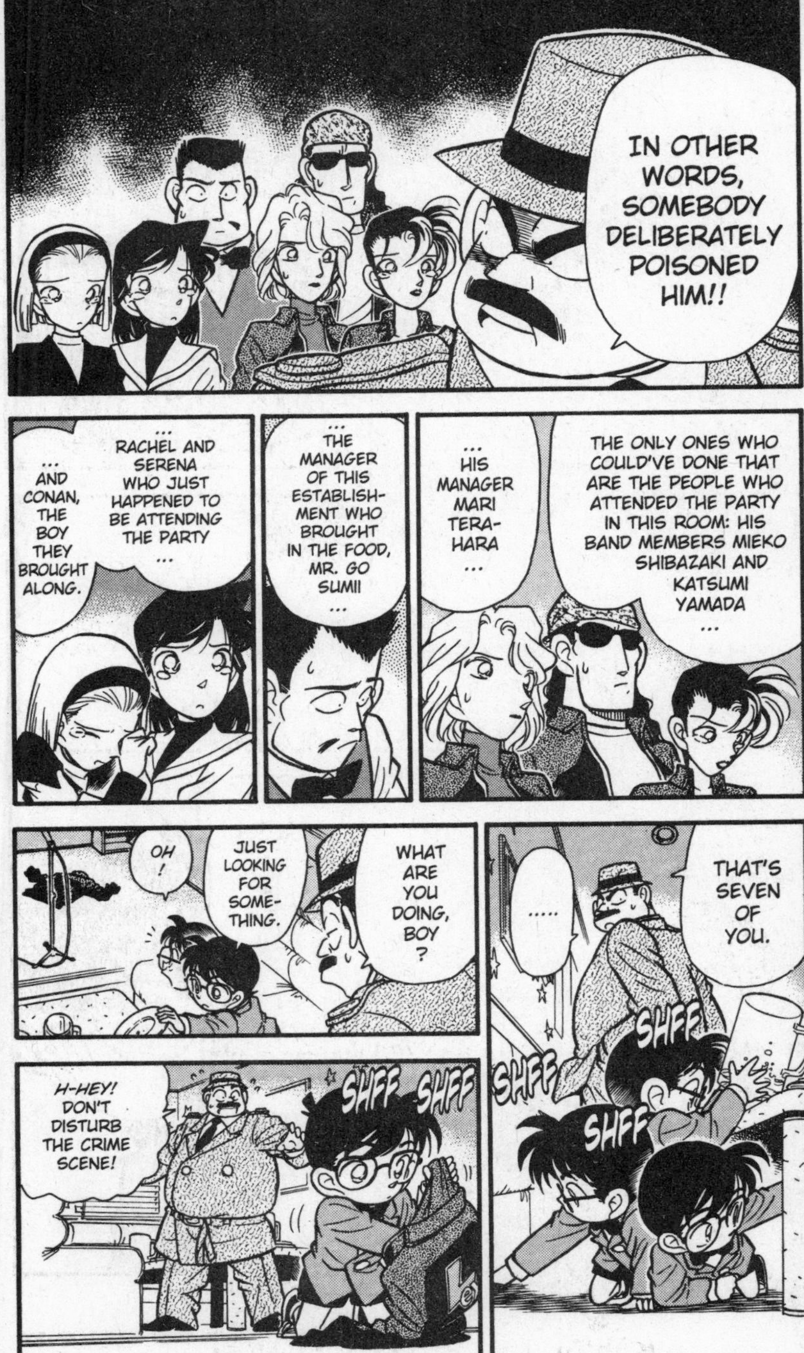
IN OTHER WORDS, SOMEBODY DELIBERATELY POISONED HIM!!
THE ONLY ONES WHO COULD'VE DONE THAT ARE THE PEOPLE WHO ATTENDED THE PARTY IN THIS ROOM: HIS BAND MEMBERS MIEKO SHIBAZAKI AND KATSUMI YAMADA ...
... HIS MANAGER MARI TERA-HARA ...
... THE MANAGER OF THIS ESTABLISH-MENT WHO BROUGHT IN THE FOOD, MR. GO SUMII ...
... RACHEL AND SERENA WHO JUST HAPPENED TO BE ATTENDING THE PARTY ...
... AND CONAN, THE BOY THEY BROUGHT ALONG.
THAT'S SEVEN OF YOU.
.....
SHFF
SHFF
SHFF
WHAT ARE YOU DOING, BOY?
JUST LOOKING FOR SOMETHING.
OH!
H-HEY! DON'T DISTURB THE CRIME SCENE!
SHFF
SHFF

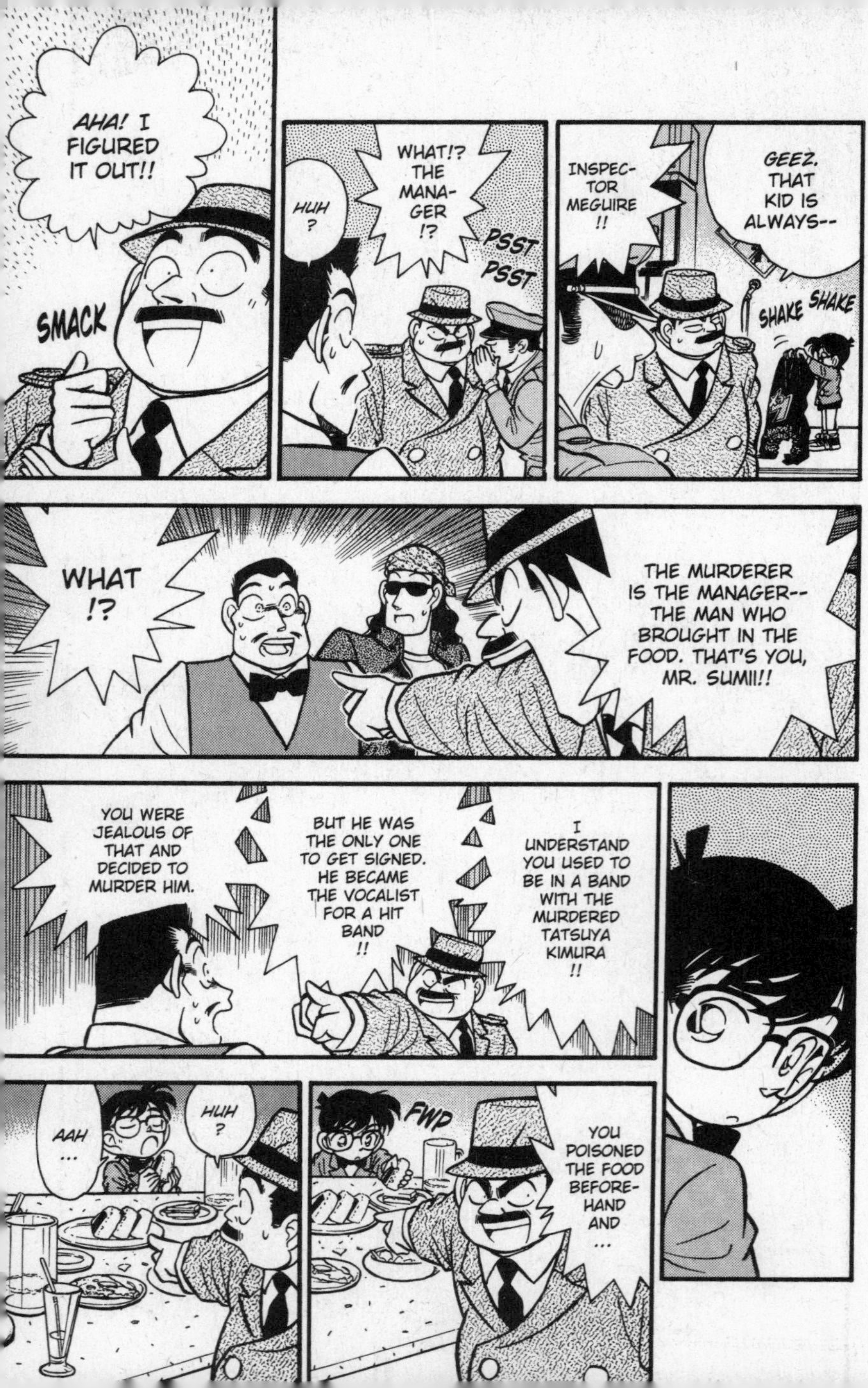
GEEZ. THAT KID IS ALWAYS--
INSPECTOR MEGUIRE!!
SHAKE SHAKE
WHAT!? THE MANAGER!?
HUH?
PSST PSST
AHA! I FIGURED IT OUT!!
SMACK
THE MURDERER IS THE MANAGER-- THE MAN WHO BROUGHT IN THE FOOD. THAT'S YOU, MR. SUMII!!
WHAT!?
I UNDERSTAND YOU USED TO BE IN A BAND WITH THE MURDERED TATSUYA KIMURA!!
BUT HE WAS THE ONLY ONE TO GET SIGNED. HE BECAME THE VOCALIST FOR A HIT BAND!!
YOU WERE JEALOUS OF THAT AND DECIDED TO MURDER HIM.
FWP
YOU POISONED THE FOOD BEFOREHAND AND...
HUH?
AAH...

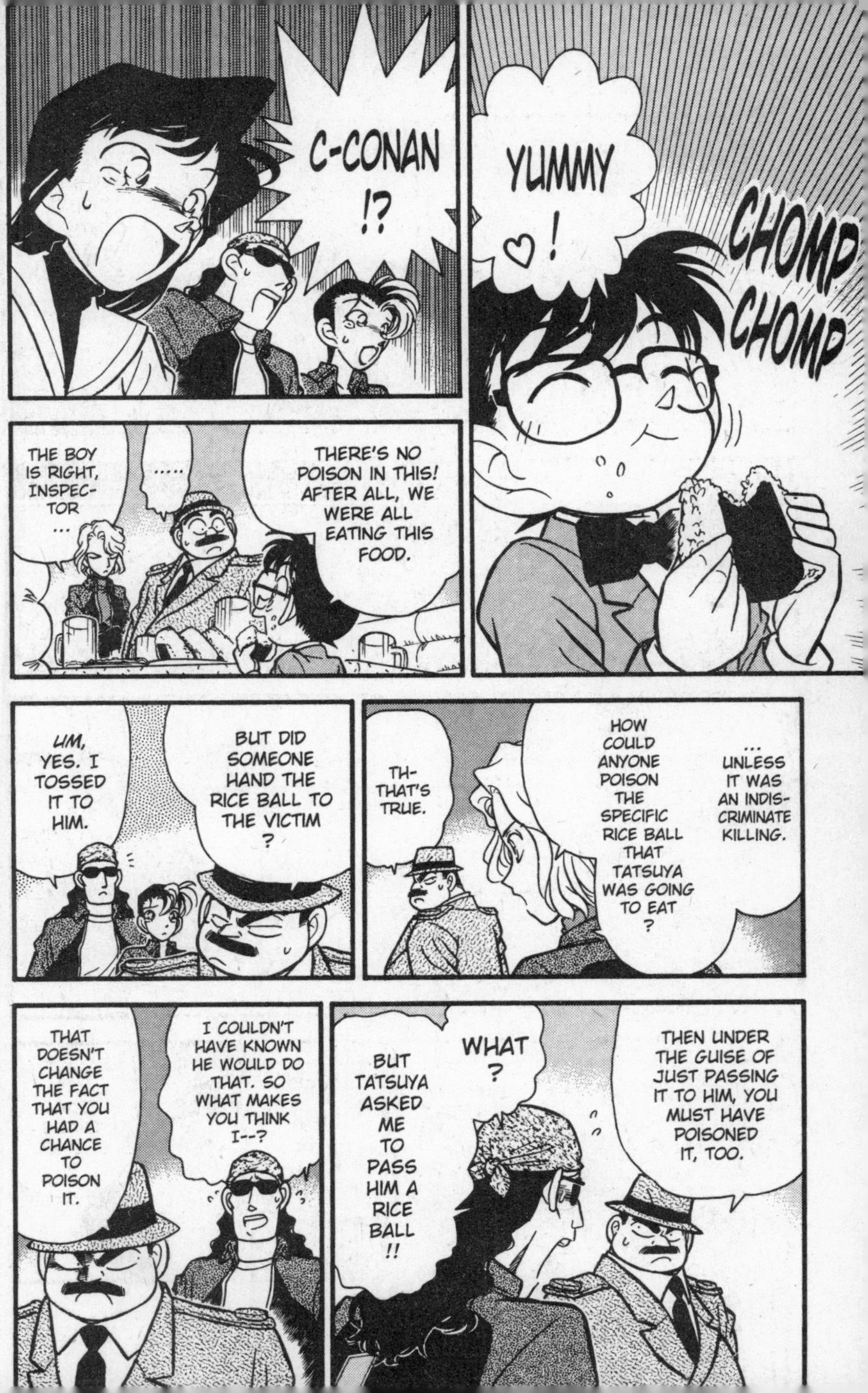
YUMMY ♡!
CHOMP CHOMP
C-CONAN !?
THERE'S NO POISON IN THIS! AFTER ALL, WE WERE ALL EATING THIS FOOD.
......
THE BOY IS RIGHT, INSPECTOR ...
HOW COULD ANYONE POISON THE SPECIFIC RICE BALL THAT TATSUYA WAS GOING TO EAT ?
... UNLESS IT WAS AN INDIS-CRIMINATE KILLING.
TH-THAT'S TRUE.
BUT DID SOMEONE HAND THE RICE BALL TO THE VICTIM ?
UM, YES. I TOSSED IT TO HIM.
THEN UNDER THE GUISE OF JUST PASSING IT TO HIM, YOU MUST HAVE POISONED IT, TOO.
WHAT ?
BUT TATSUYA ASKED ME TO PASS HIM A RICE BALL !!
I COULDN'T HAVE KNOWN HE WOULD DO THAT. SO WHAT MAKES YOU THINK I--?
THAT DOESN'T CHANGE THE FACT THAT YOU HAD A CHANCE TO POISON IT.

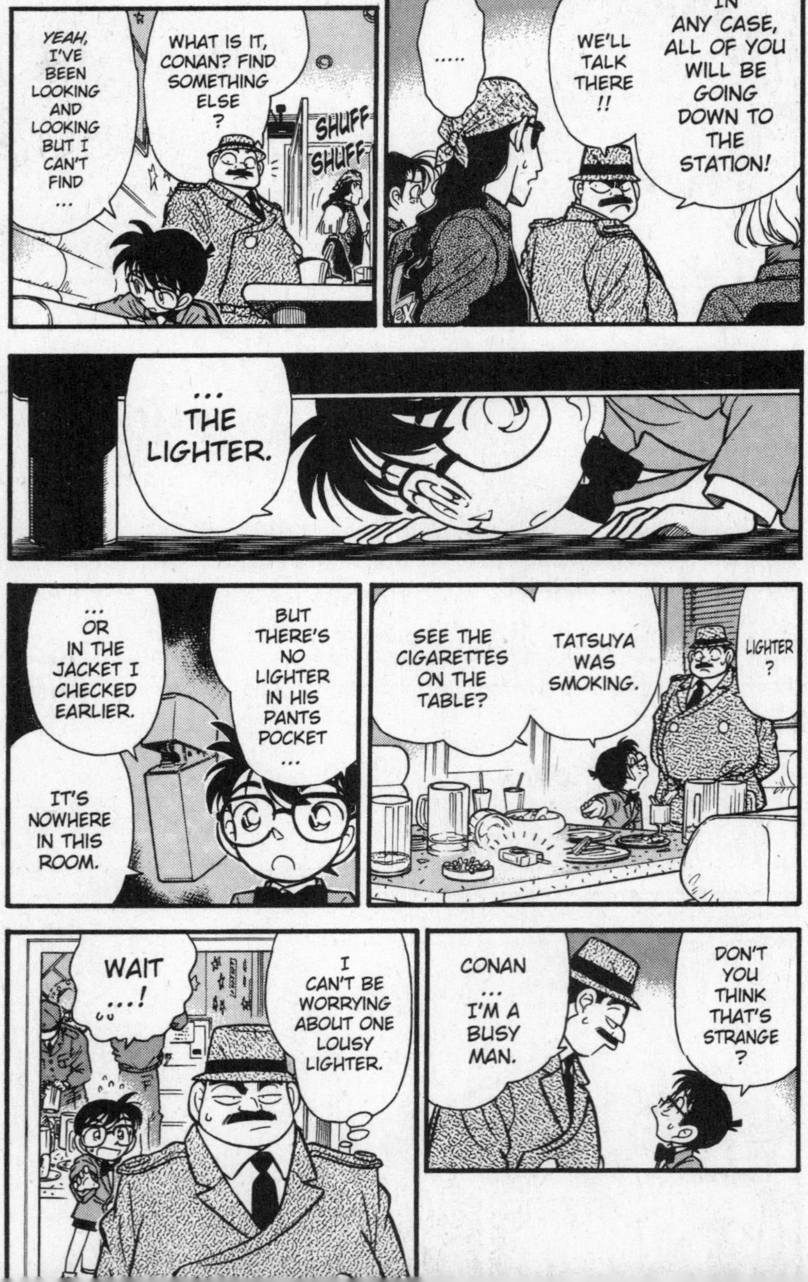
IN ANY CASE, ALL OF YOU WILL BE GOING DOWN TO THE STATION!
WE'LL TALK THERE !!
.....
WHAT IS IT, CONAN? FIND SOMETHING ELSE ?
SHUFF SHUFF
YEAH, I'VE BEEN LOOKING AND LOOKING BUT I CAN'T FIND ...
... THE LIGHTER.
LIGHTER ?
TATSUYA WAS SMOKING.
SEE THE CIGARETTES ON THE TABLE?
BUT THERE'S NO LIGHTER IN HIS PANTS POCKET ...
... OR IN THE JACKET I CHECKED EARLIER.
IT'S NOWHERE IN THIS ROOM.
DON'T YOU THINK THAT'S STRANGE ?
CONAN ... I'M A BUSY MAN.
I CAN'T BE WORRYING ABOUT ONE LOUSY LIGHTER.
WAIT ...!

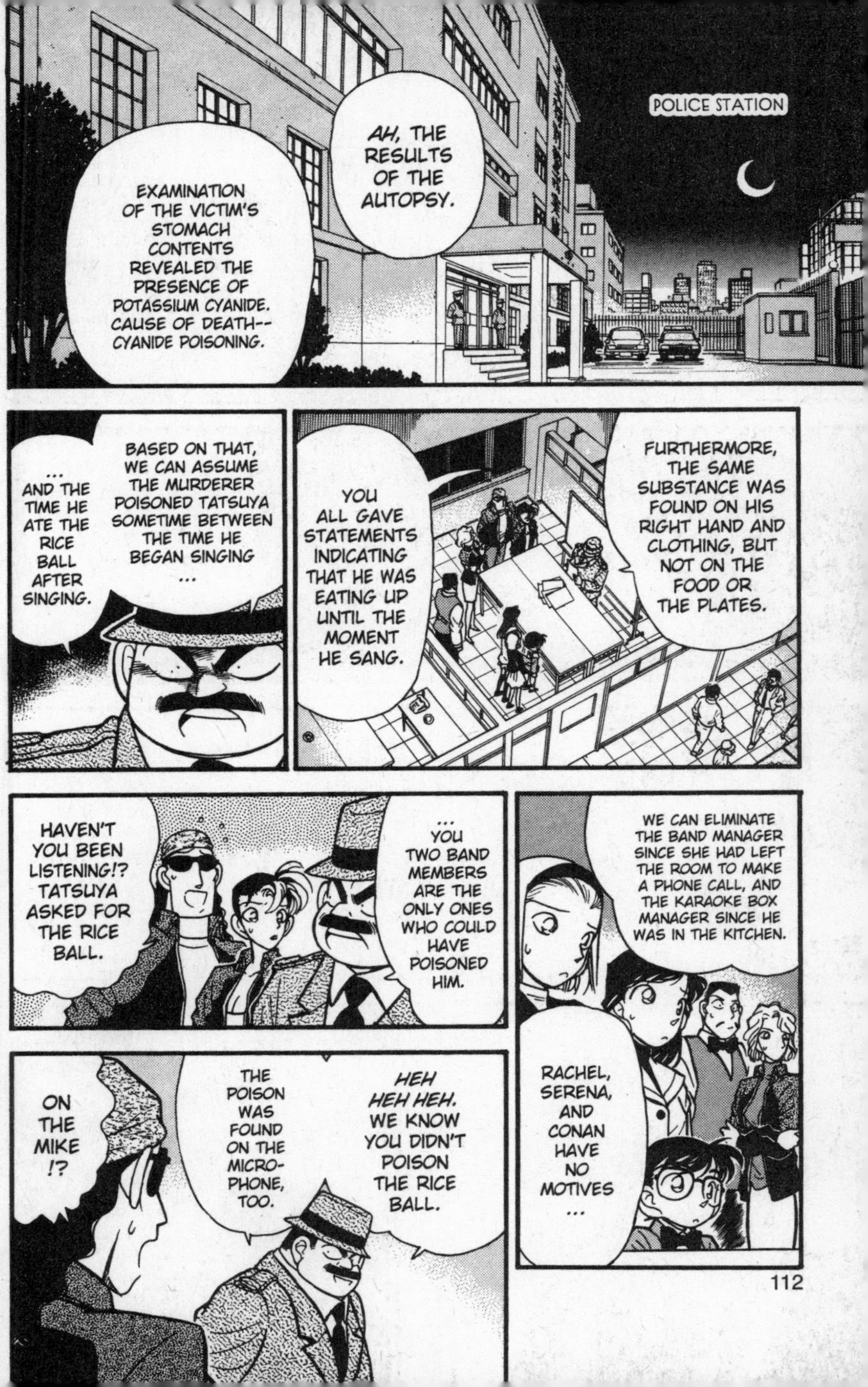
POLICE STATION
AH, THE RESULTS OF THE AUTOPSY.
EXAMINATION OF THE VICTIM'S STOMACH CONTENTS REVEALED THE PRESENCE OF POTASSIUM CYANIDE. CAUSE OF DEATH--CYANIDE POISONING.
FURTHERMORE, THE SAME SUBSTANCE WAS FOUND ON HIS RIGHT HAND AND CLOTHING, BUT NOT ON THE FOOD OR THE PLATES.
YOU ALL GAVE STATEMENTS INDICATING THAT HE WAS EATING UP UNTIL THE MOMENT HE SANG.
BASED ON THAT, WE CAN ASSUME THE MURDERER POISONED TATSUYA SOMETIME BETWEEN THE TIME HE BEGAN SINGING ...
... AND THE TIME HE ATE THE RICE BALL AFTER SINGING.
WE CAN ELIMINATE THE BAND MANAGER SINCE SHE HAD LEFT THE ROOM TO MAKE A PHONE CALL, AND THE KARAOKE BOX MANAGER SINCE HE WAS IN THE KITCHEN.
RACHEL, SERENA, AND CONAN HAVE NO MOTIVES ...
... YOU TWO BAND MEMBERS ARE THE ONLY ONES WHO COULD HAVE POISONED HIM.
HAVEN'T YOU BEEN LISTENING!? TATSUYA ASKED FOR THE RICE BALL.
HEH HEH HEH. WE KNOW YOU DIDN'T POISON THE RICE BALL.
THE POISON WAS FOUND ON THE MICRO-PHONE, TOO.
ON THE MIKE !?

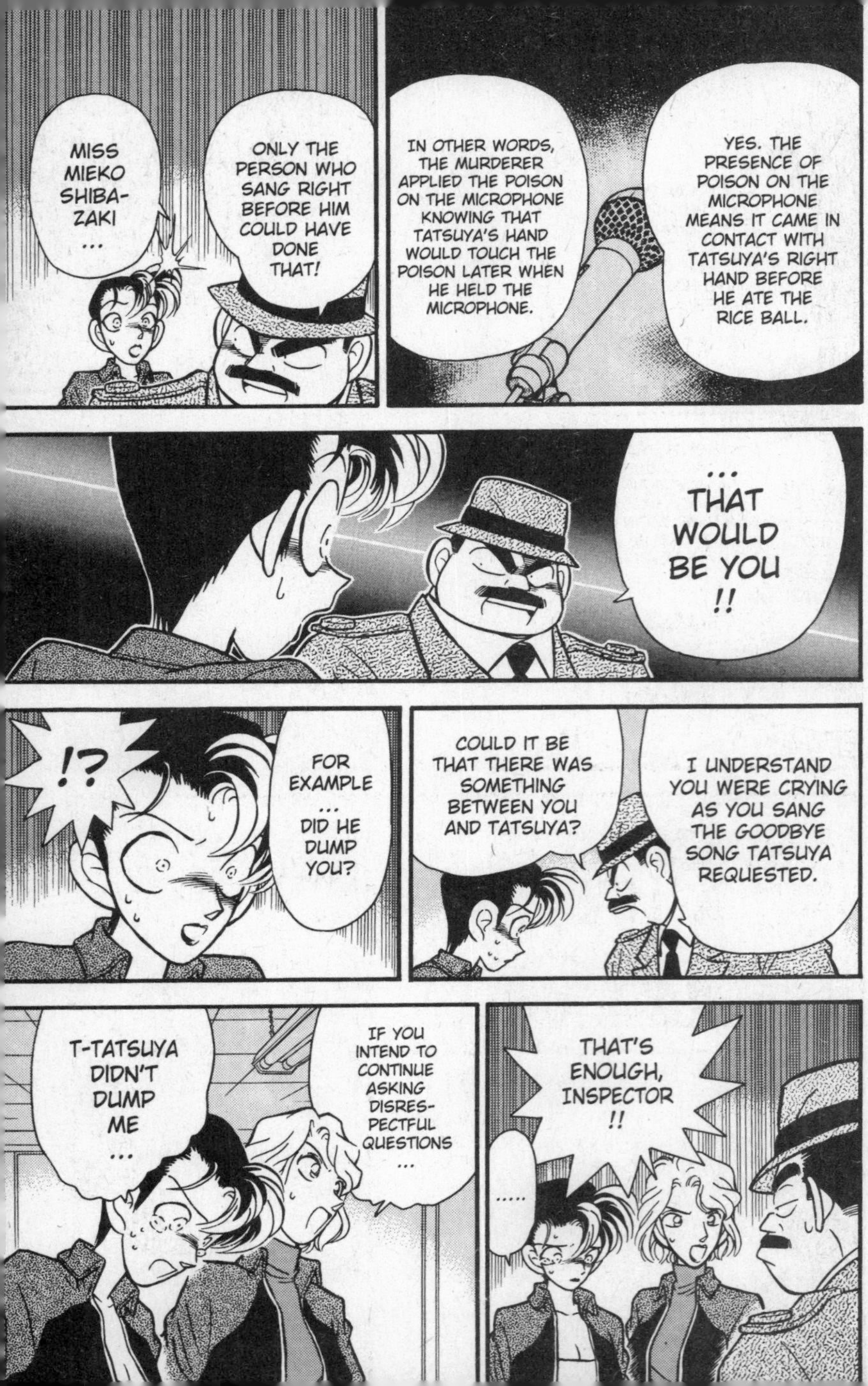
YES. THE PRESENCE OF POISON ON THE MICROPHONE MEANS IT CAME IN CONTACT WITH TATSUYA'S RIGHT HAND BEFORE HE ATE THE RICE BALL.
IN OTHER WORDS, THE MURDERER APPLIED THE POISON ON THE MICROPHONE KNOWING THAT TATSUYA'S HAND WOULD TOUCH THE POISON LATER WHEN HE HELD THE MICROPHONE.
ONLY THE PERSON WHO SANG RIGHT BEFORE HIM COULD HAVE DONE THAT!
MISS MIEKO SHIBAZAKI ...
... THAT WOULD BE YOU !!
I UNDERSTAND YOU WERE CRYING AS YOU SANG THE GOODBYE SONG TATSUYA REQUESTED.
COULD IT BE THAT THERE WAS SOMETHING BETWEEN YOU AND TATSUYA?
FOR EXAMPLE ... DID HE DUMP YOU?
!?
THAT'S ENOUGH, INSPECTOR !!
.....
IF YOU INTEND TO CONTINUE ASKING DISRESPECTFUL QUESTIONS ...
T-TATSUYA DIDN'T DUMP ME ...

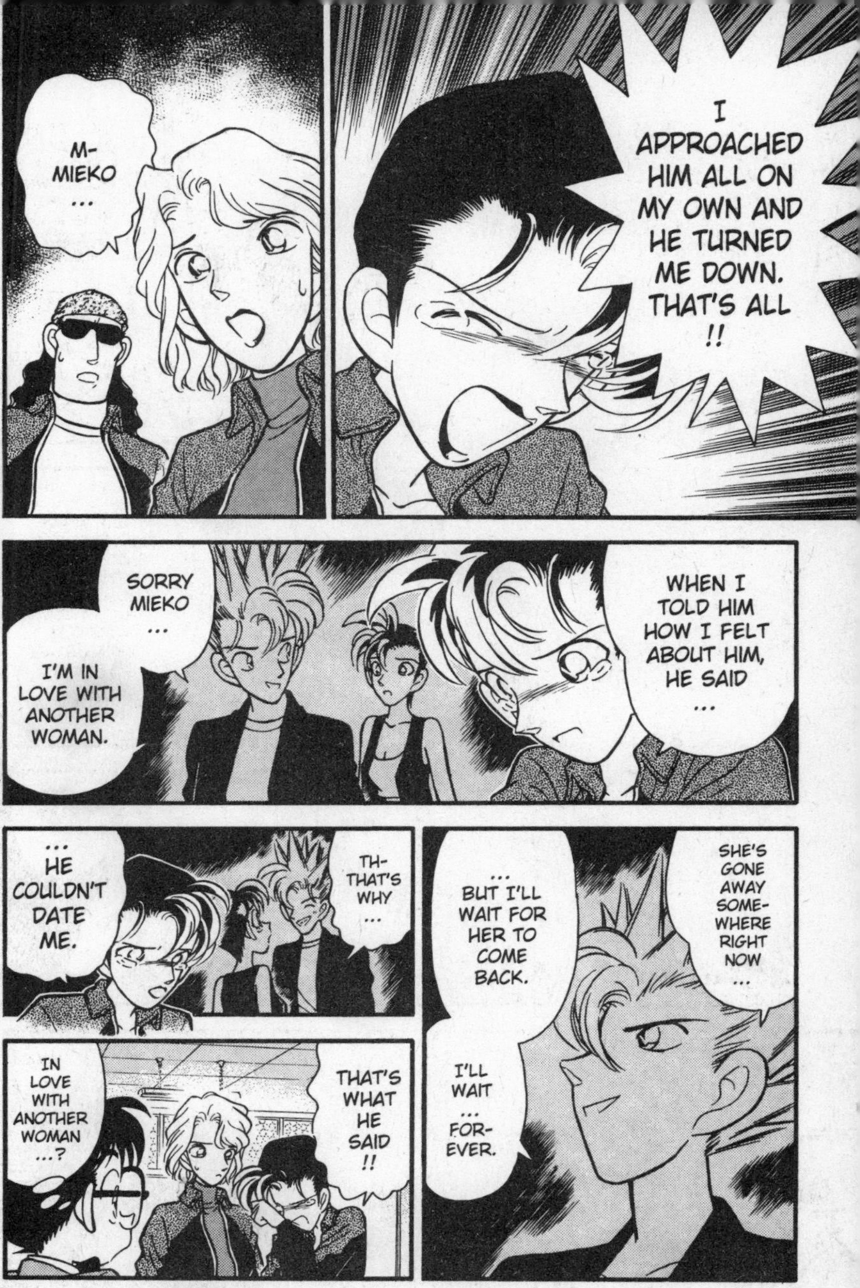
I APPROACHED HIM ALL ON MY OWN AND HE TURNED ME DOWN. THAT'S ALL !!
M-MIEKO ...
WHEN I TOLD HIM HOW I FELT ABOUT HIM, HE SAID ...
SORRY MIEKO ...
I'M IN LOVE WITH ANOTHER WOMAN.
SHE'S GONE AWAY SOMEWHERE RIGHT NOW ...
... BUT I'LL WAIT FOR HER TO COME BACK.
I'LL WAIT ... FOREVER.
TH-THAT'S WHY ...
... HE COULDN'T DATE ME.
THAT'S WHAT HE SAID !!
IN LOVE WITH ANOTHER WOMAN ...?

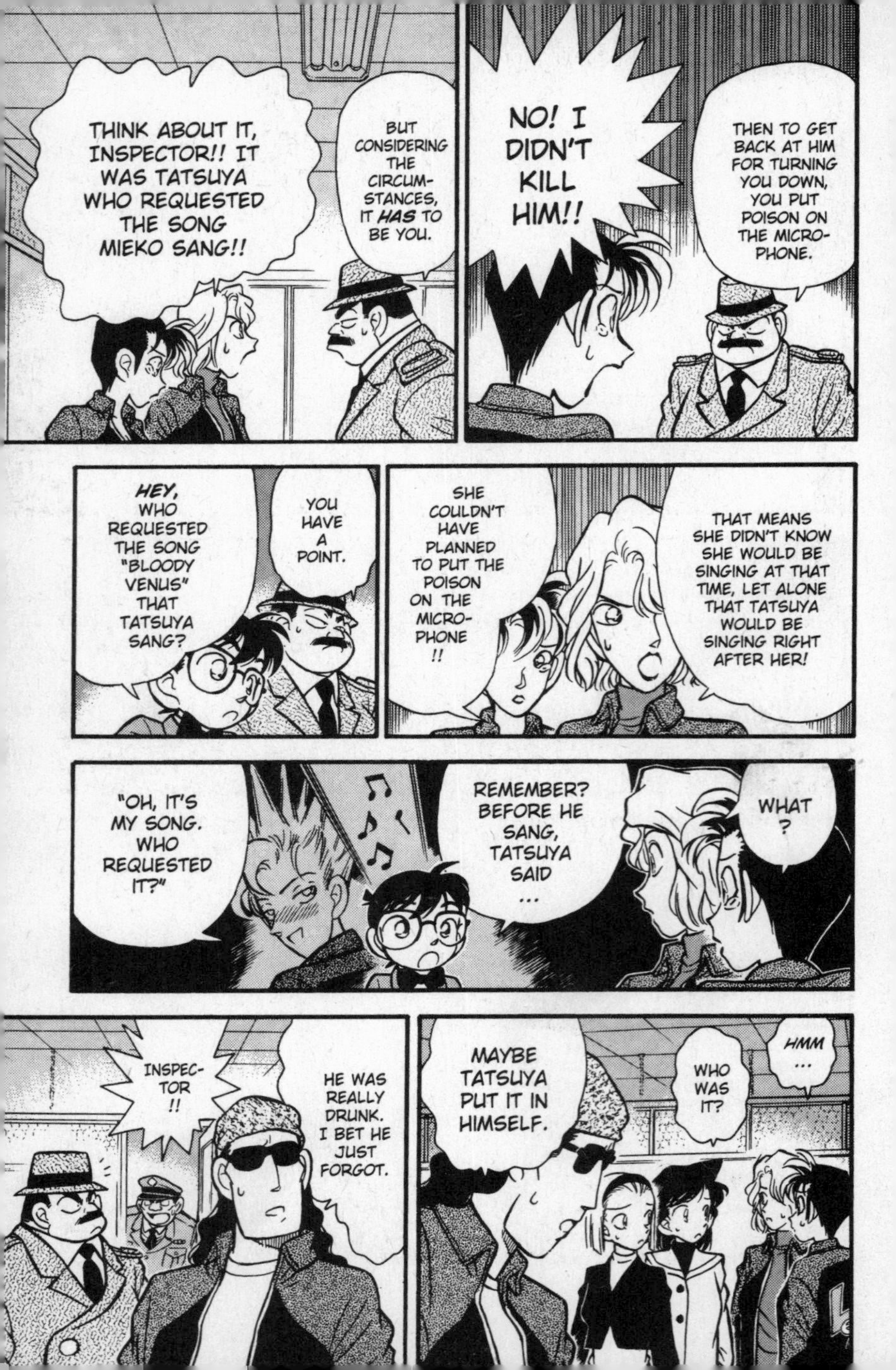
THEN TO GET BACK AT HIM FOR TURNING YOU DOWN, YOU PUT POISON ON THE MICROPHONE.
NO! I DIDN'T KILL HIM!!
BUT CONSIDERING THE CIRCUMSTANCES, IT *HAS* TO BE YOU.
THINK ABOUT IT, INSPECTOR!! IT WAS TATSUYA WHO REQUESTED THE SONG MIEKO SANG!!
THAT MEANS SHE DIDN'T KNOW SHE WOULD BE SINGING AT THAT TIME, LET ALONE THAT TATSUYA WOULD BE SINGING RIGHT AFTER HER!
SHE COULDN'T HAVE PLANNED TO PUT THE POISON ON THE MICROPHONE !!
YOU HAVE A POINT.
HEY, WHO REQUESTED THE SONG "BLOODY VENUS" THAT TATSUYA SANG?
WHAT ?
REMEMBER? BEFORE HE SANG, TATSUYA SAID ...
"OH, IT'S MY SONG. WHO REQUESTED IT?"
HMM ...
WHO WAS IT?
MAYBE TATSUYA PUT IT IN HIMSELF.
HE WAS REALLY DRUNK. I BET HE JUST FORGOT.
INSPECTOR !!

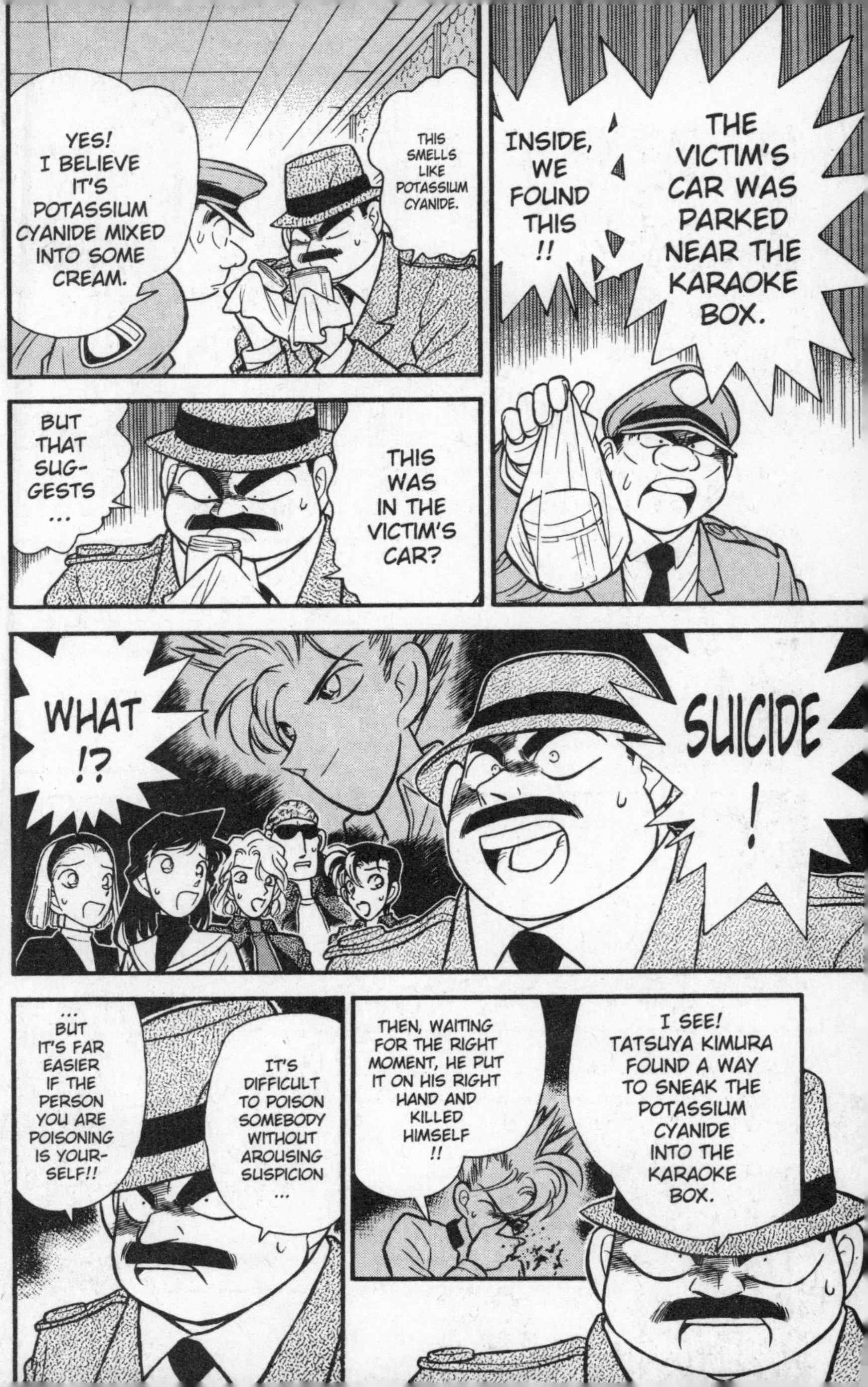
THE VICTIM'S CAR WAS PARKED NEAR THE KARAOKE BOX.
INSIDE, WE FOUND THIS!!
THIS SMELLS LIKE POTASSIUM CYANIDE.
YES! I BELIEVE IT'S POTASSIUM CYANIDE MIXED INTO SOME CREAM.
THIS WAS IN THE VICTIM'S CAR?
BUT THAT SUG-GESTS...
SUICIDE!
WHAT!?
I SEE! TATSUYA KIMURA FOUND A WAY TO SNEAK THE POTASSIUM CYANIDE INTO THE KARAOKE BOX.
THEN, WAITING FOR THE RIGHT MOMENT, HE PUT IT ON HIS RIGHT HAND AND KILLED HIMSELF!!
IT'S DIFFICULT TO POISON SOMEBODY WITHOUT AROUSING SUSPICION...
...BUT IT'S FAR EASIER IF THE PERSON YOU ARE POISONING IS YOUR-SELF!!

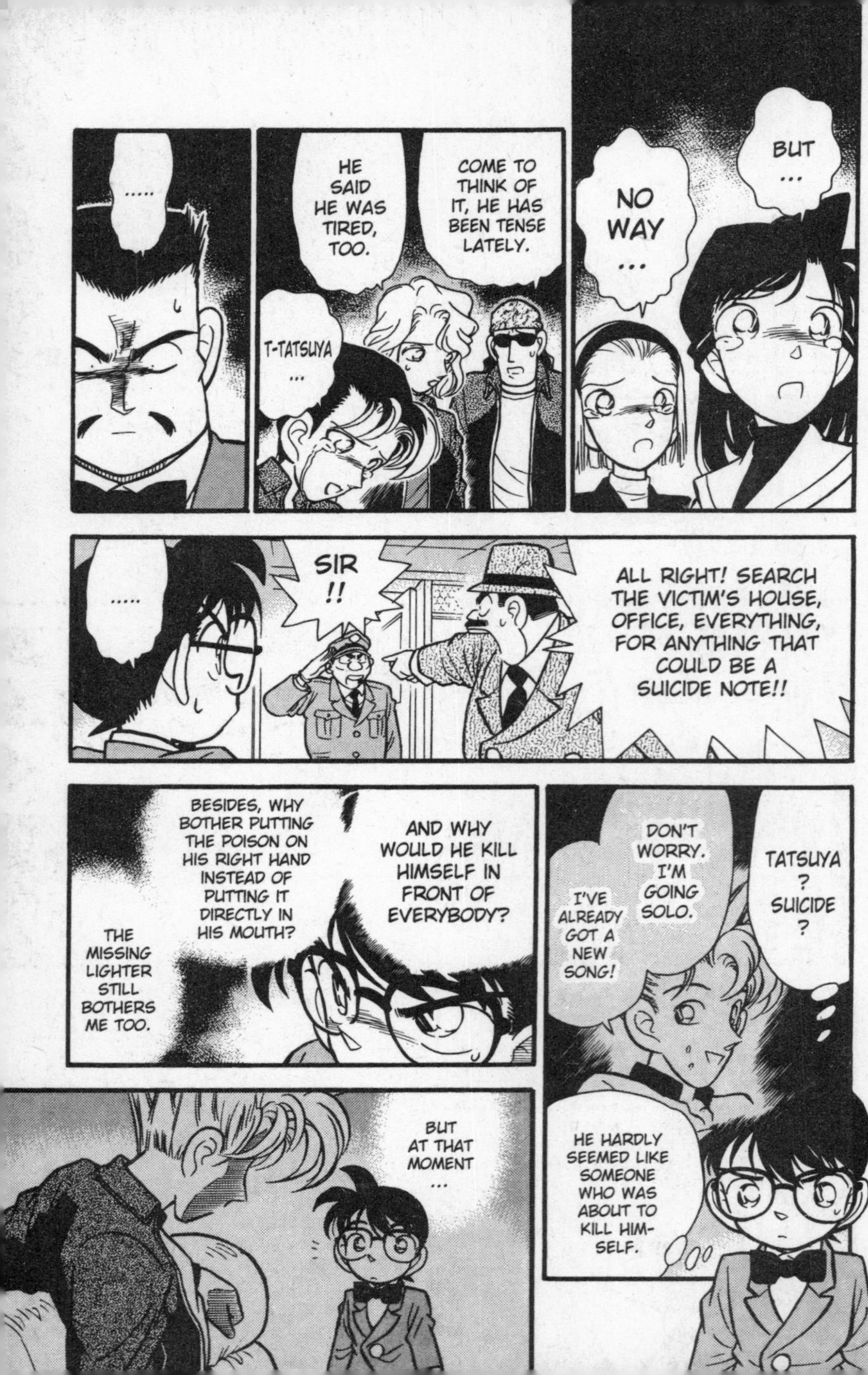
BUT ...
NO WAY ...
COME TO THINK OF IT, HE HAS BEEN TENSE LATELY.
HE SAID HE WAS TIRED, TOO.
T-TATSUYA ...
.....
ALL RIGHT! SEARCH THE VICTIM'S HOUSE, OFFICE, EVERYTHING, FOR ANYTHING THAT COULD BE A SUICIDE NOTE!!
SIR !!
.....
TATSUYA ? SUICIDE ?
DON'T WORRY. I'M GOING SOLO.
I'VE ALREADY GOT A NEW SONG!
AND WHY WOULD HE KILL HIMSELF IN FRONT OF EVERYBODY?
BESIDES, WHY BOTHER PUTTING THE POISON ON HIS RIGHT HAND INSTEAD OF PUTTING IT DIRECTLY IN HIS MOUTH?
THE MISSING LIGHTER STILL BOTHERS ME TOO.
HE HARDLY SEEMED LIKE SOMEONE WHO WAS ABOUT TO KILL HIM-SELF.
BUT AT THAT MOMENT ...

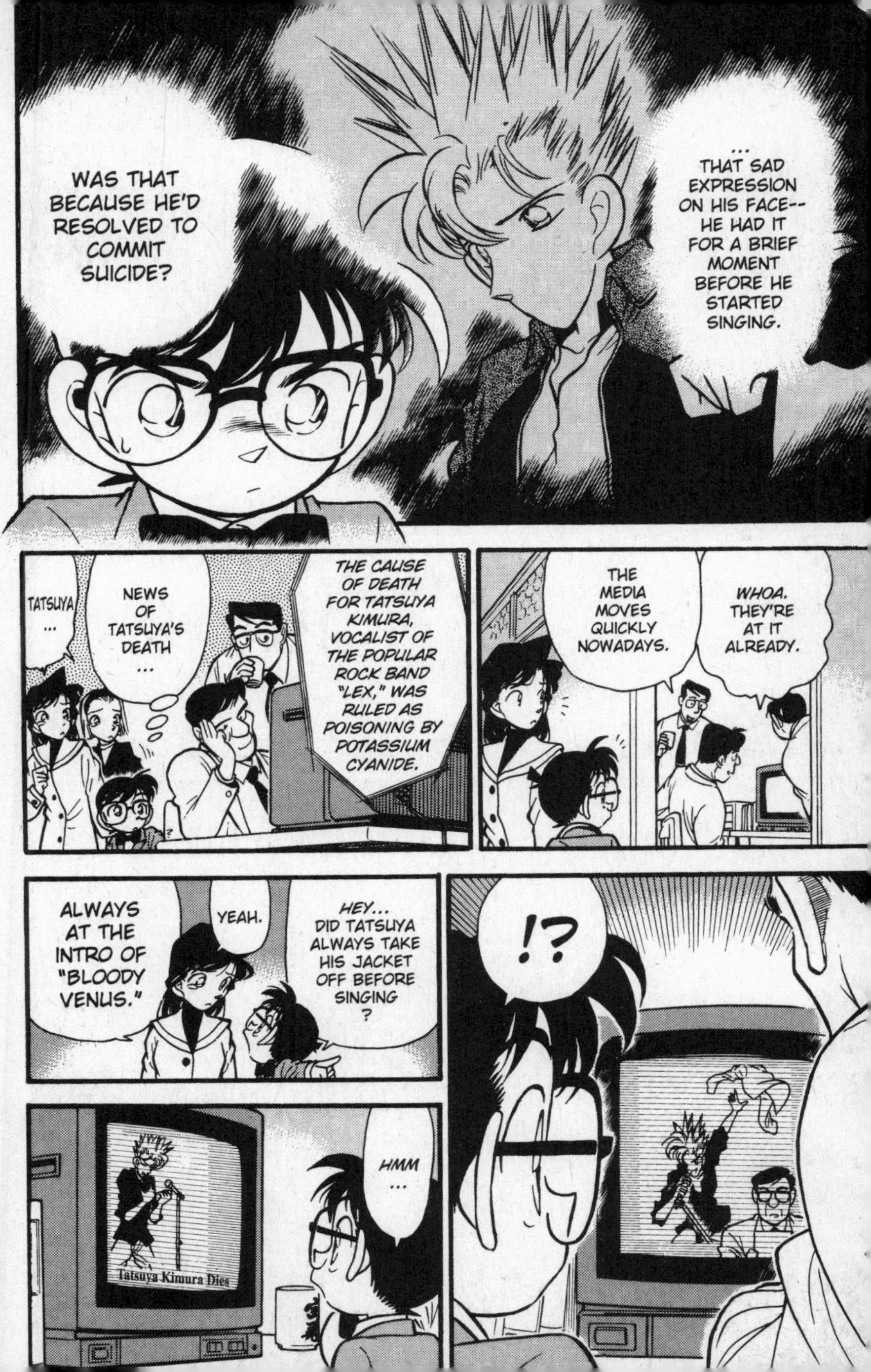
... THAT SAD EXPRESSION ON HIS FACE-- HE HAD IT FOR A BRIEF MOMENT BEFORE HE STARTED SINGING.
WAS THAT BECAUSE HE'D RESOLVED TO COMMIT SUICIDE?
WHOA. THEY'RE AT IT ALREADY.
THE MEDIA MOVES QUICKLY NOWADAYS.
THE CAUSE OF DEATH FOR TATSUYA KIMURA, VOCALIST OF THE POPULAR ROCK BAND "LEX," WAS RULED AS POISONING BY POTASSIUM CYANIDE.
NEWS OF TATSUYA'S DEATH ...
TATSUYA ...
!?
HEY... DID TATSUYA ALWAYS TAKE HIS JACKET OFF BEFORE SINGING ?
YEAH.
ALWAYS AT THE INTRO OF "BLOODY VENUS."
HMM ...
Tatsuya Kimura Dies

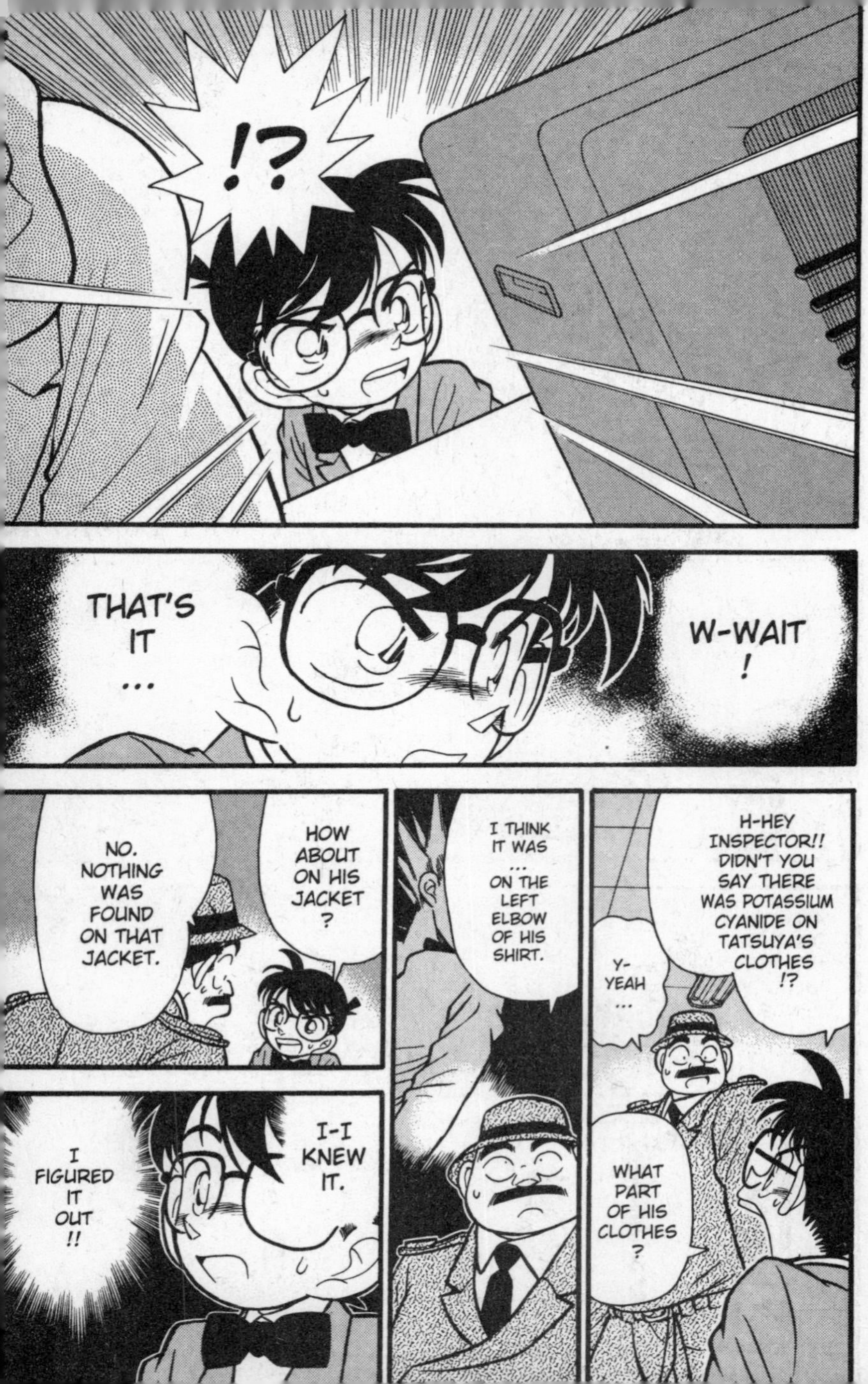

!?
W-WAIT !
THAT'S IT ...
H-HEY INSPECTOR!! DIDN'T YOU SAY THERE WAS POTASSIUM CYANIDE ON TATSUYA'S CLOTHES !?
Y-YEAH ...
WHAT PART OF HIS CLOTHES ?
I THINK IT WAS ... ON THE LEFT ELBOW OF HIS SHIRT.
HOW ABOUT ON HIS JACKET ?
NO. NOTHING WAS FOUND ON THAT JACKET.
I-I KNEW IT.
I FIGURED IT OUT !!

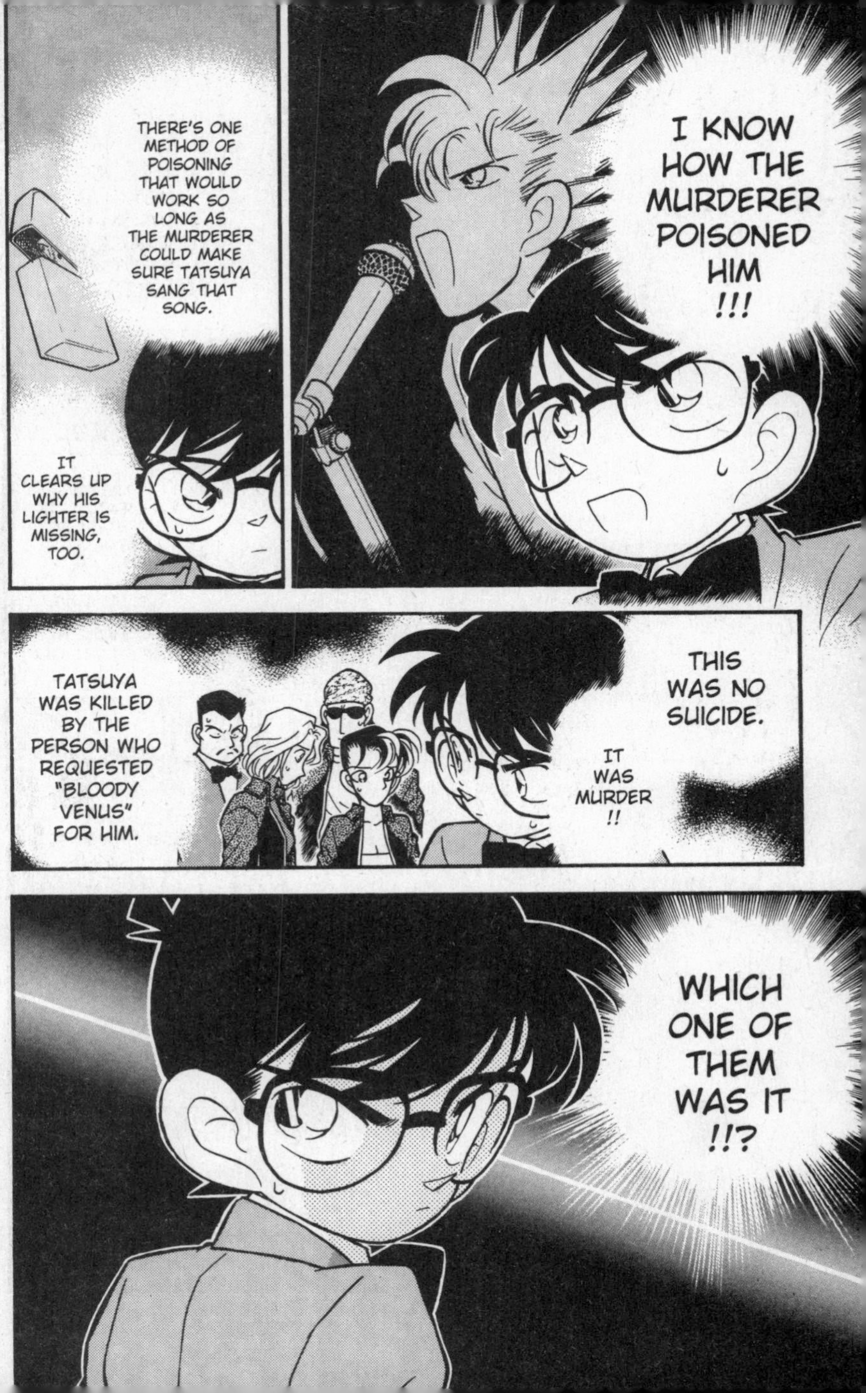
I KNOW HOW THE MURDERER POISONED HIM !!!
THERE'S ONE METHOD OF POISONING THAT WOULD WORK SO LONG AS THE MURDERER COULD MAKE SURE TATSUYA SANG THAT SONG.
IT CLEARS UP WHY HIS LIGHTER IS MISSING, TOO.
THIS WAS NO SUICIDE.
IT WAS MURDER !!
TATSUYA WAS KILLED BY THE PERSON WHO REQUESTED "BLOODY VENUS" FOR HIM.
WHICH ONE OF THEM WAS IT !!?

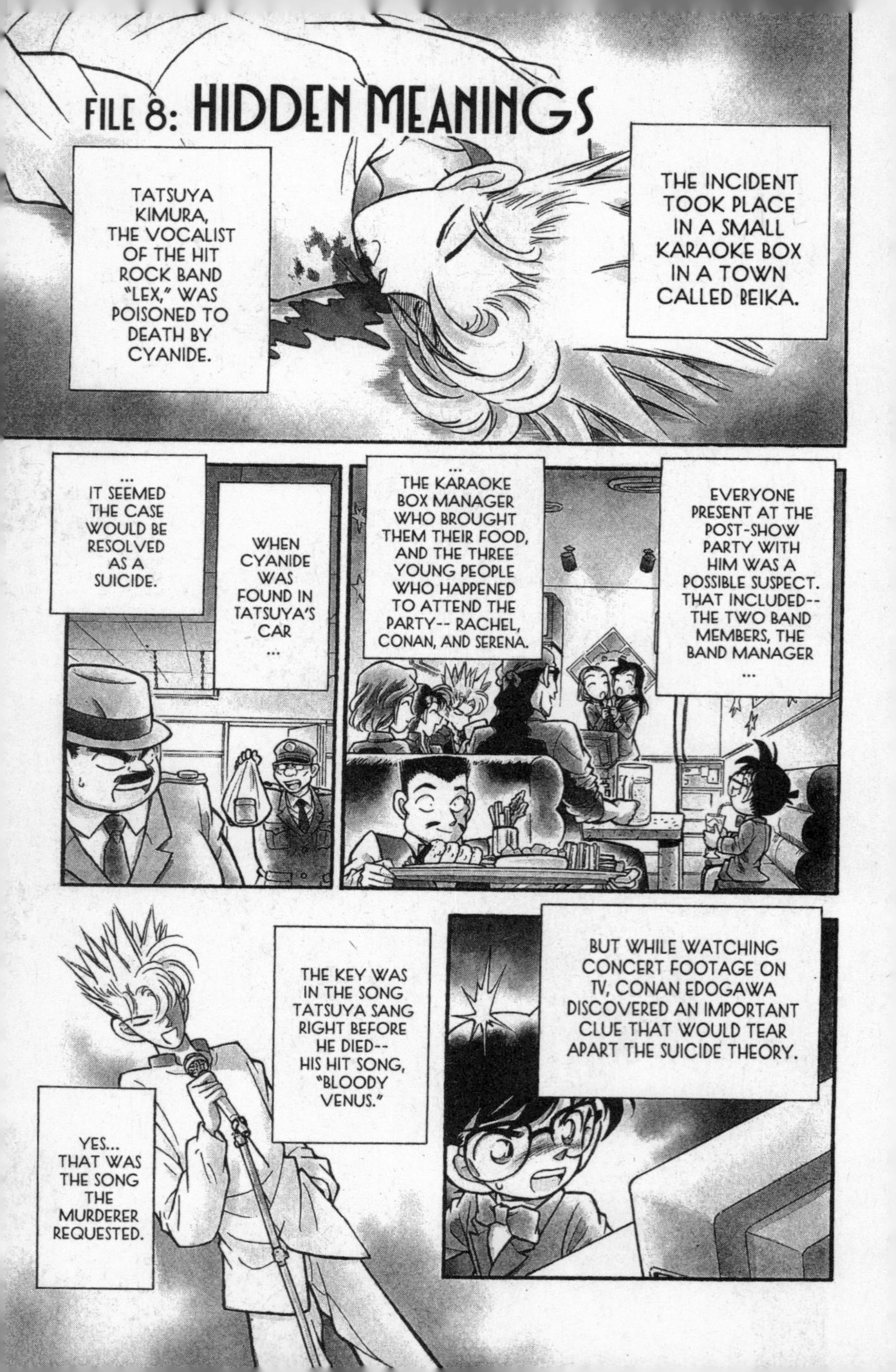
FILE 8: HIDDEN MEANINGS
THE INCIDENT TOOK PLACE IN A SMALL KARAOKE BOX IN A TOWN CALLED BEIKA.
TATSUYA KIMURA, THE VOCALIST OF THE HIT ROCK BAND "LEX," WAS POISONED TO DEATH BY CYANIDE.
EVERYONE PRESENT AT THE POST-SHOW PARTY WITH HIM WAS A POSSIBLE SUSPECT. THAT INCLUDED-- THE TWO BAND MEMBERS, THE BAND MANAGER ...
... THE KARAOKE BOX MANAGER WHO BROUGHT THEM THEIR FOOD, AND THE THREE YOUNG PEOPLE WHO HAPPENED TO ATTEND THE PARTY-- RACHEL, CONAN, AND SERENA.
WHEN CYANIDE WAS FOUND IN TATSUYA'S CAR ...
... IT SEEMED THE CASE WOULD BE RESOLVED AS A SUICIDE.
BUT WHILE WATCHING CONCERT FOOTAGE ON TV, CONAN EDOGAWA DISCOVERED AN IMPORTANT CLUE THAT WOULD TEAR APART THE SUICIDE THEORY.
THE KEY WAS IN THE SONG TATSUYA SANG RIGHT BEFORE HE DIED-- HIS HIT SONG, "BLOODY VENUS."
YES... THAT WAS THE SONG THE MURDERER REQUESTED.

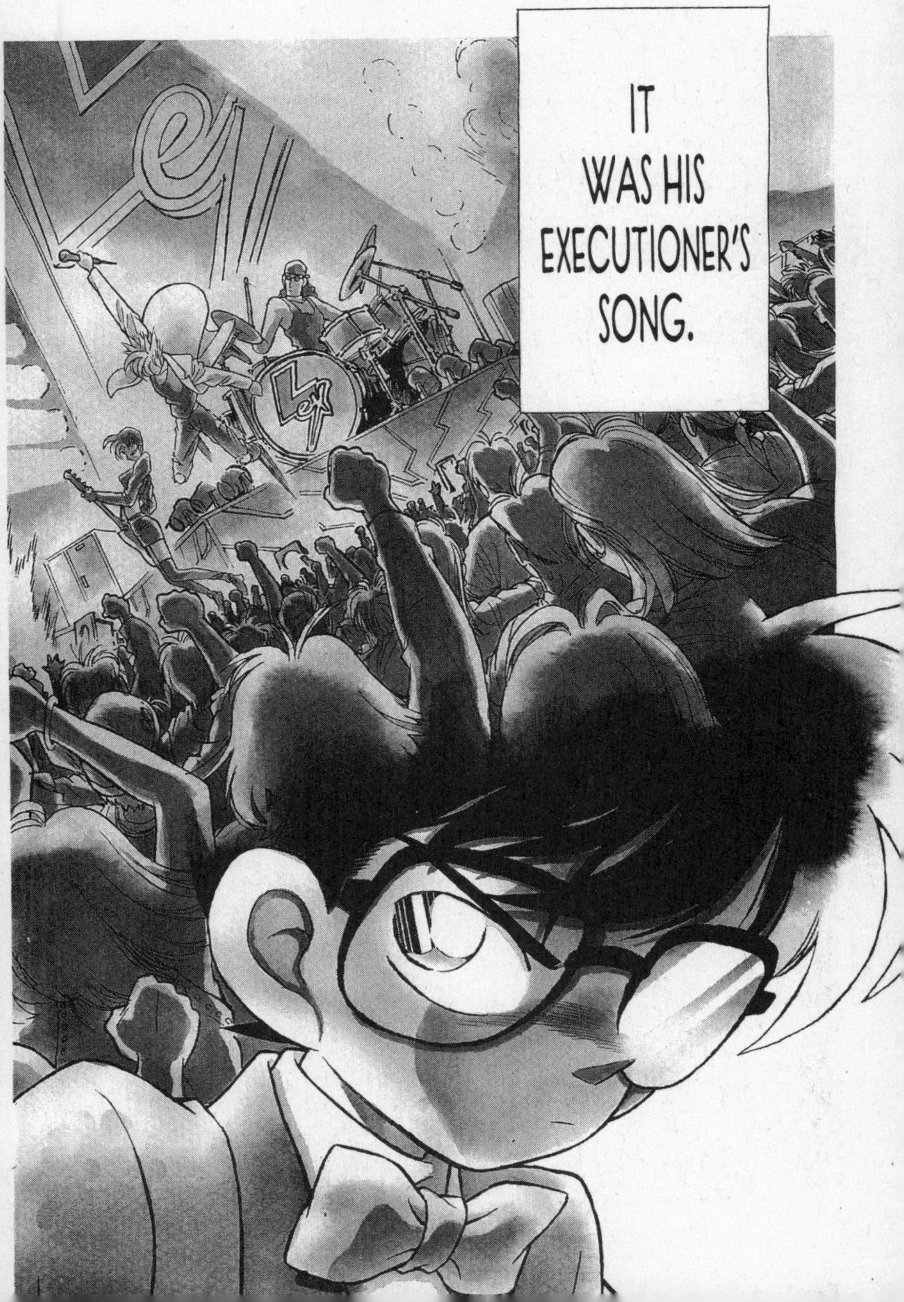
IT WAS HIS EXECUTIONER'S SONG.

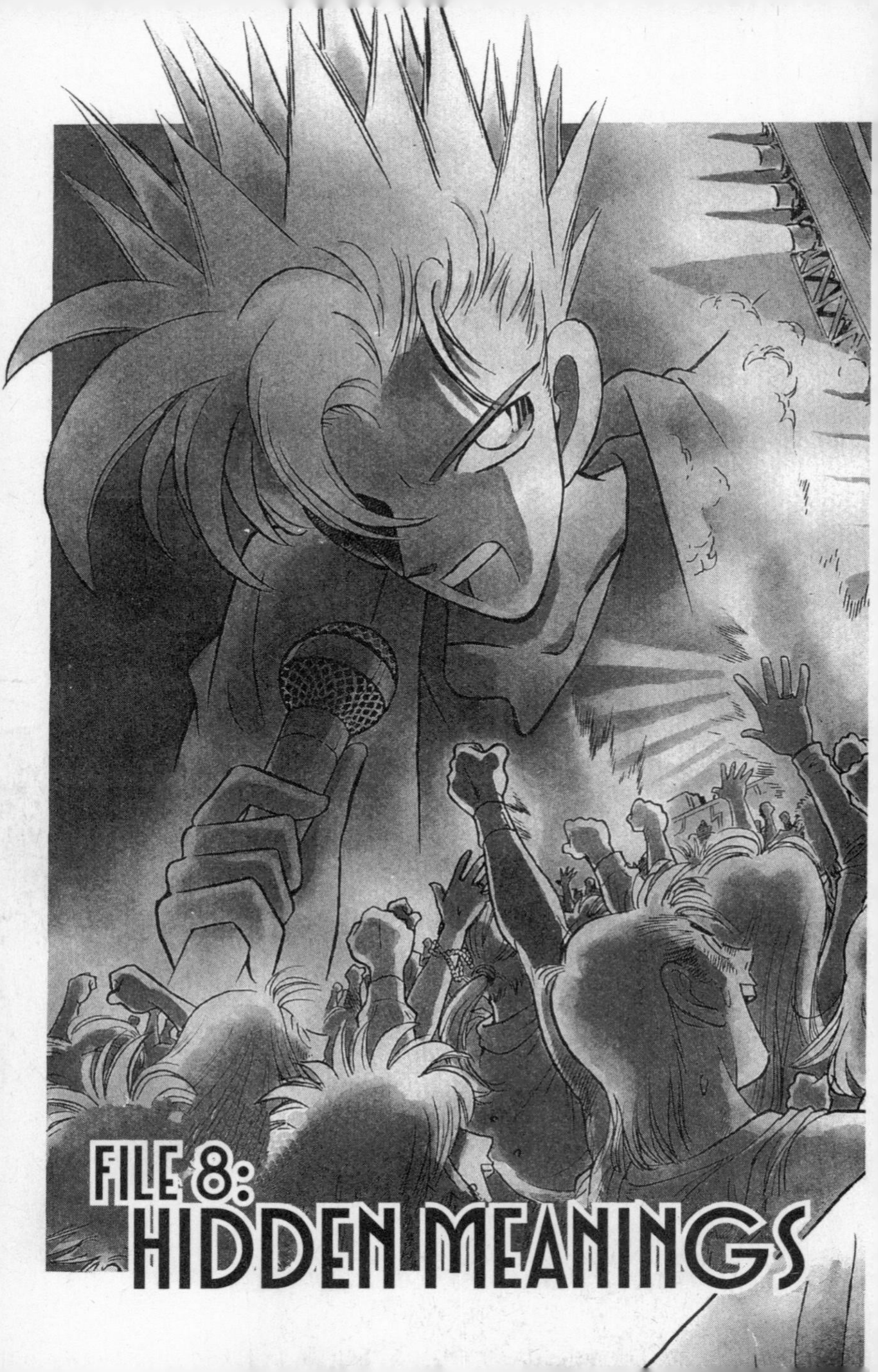
FILE 8:
HIDDEN MEANINGS

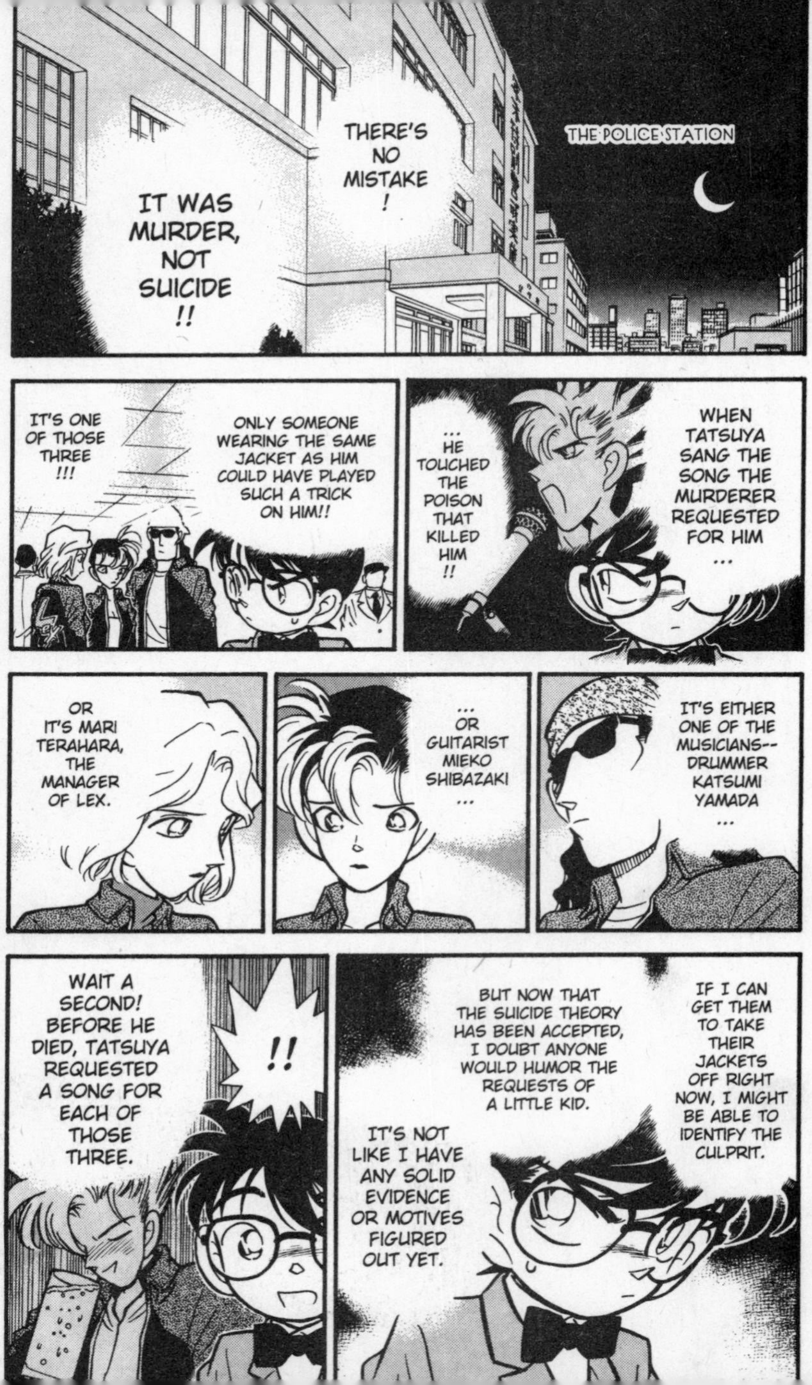
THE POLICE STATION
THERE'S NO MISTAKE !
IT WAS MURDER, NOT SUICIDE !!
WHEN TATSUYA SANG THE SONG THE MURDERER REQUESTED FOR HIM ...
... HE TOUCHED THE POISON THAT KILLED HIM !!
ONLY SOMEONE WEARING THE SAME JACKET AS HIM COULD HAVE PLAYED SUCH A TRICK ON HIM!!
IT'S ONE OF THOSE THREE !!!
IT'S EITHER ONE OF THE MUSICIANS-- DRUMMER KATSUMI YAMADA ...
... OR GUITARIST MIEKO SHIBAZAKI ...
OR IT'S MARI TERAHARA, THE MANAGER OF LEX.
IF I CAN GET THEM TO TAKE THEIR JACKETS OFF RIGHT NOW, I MIGHT BE ABLE TO IDENTIFY THE CULPRIT.
BUT NOW THAT THE SUICIDE THEORY HAS BEEN ACCEPTED, I DOUBT ANYONE WOULD HUMOR THE REQUESTS OF A LITTLE KID.
IT'S NOT LIKE I HAVE ANY SOLID EVIDENCE OR MOTIVES FIGURED OUT YET.
!!
WAIT A SECOND! BEFORE HE DIED, TATSUYA REQUESTED A SONG FOR EACH OF THOSE THREE.

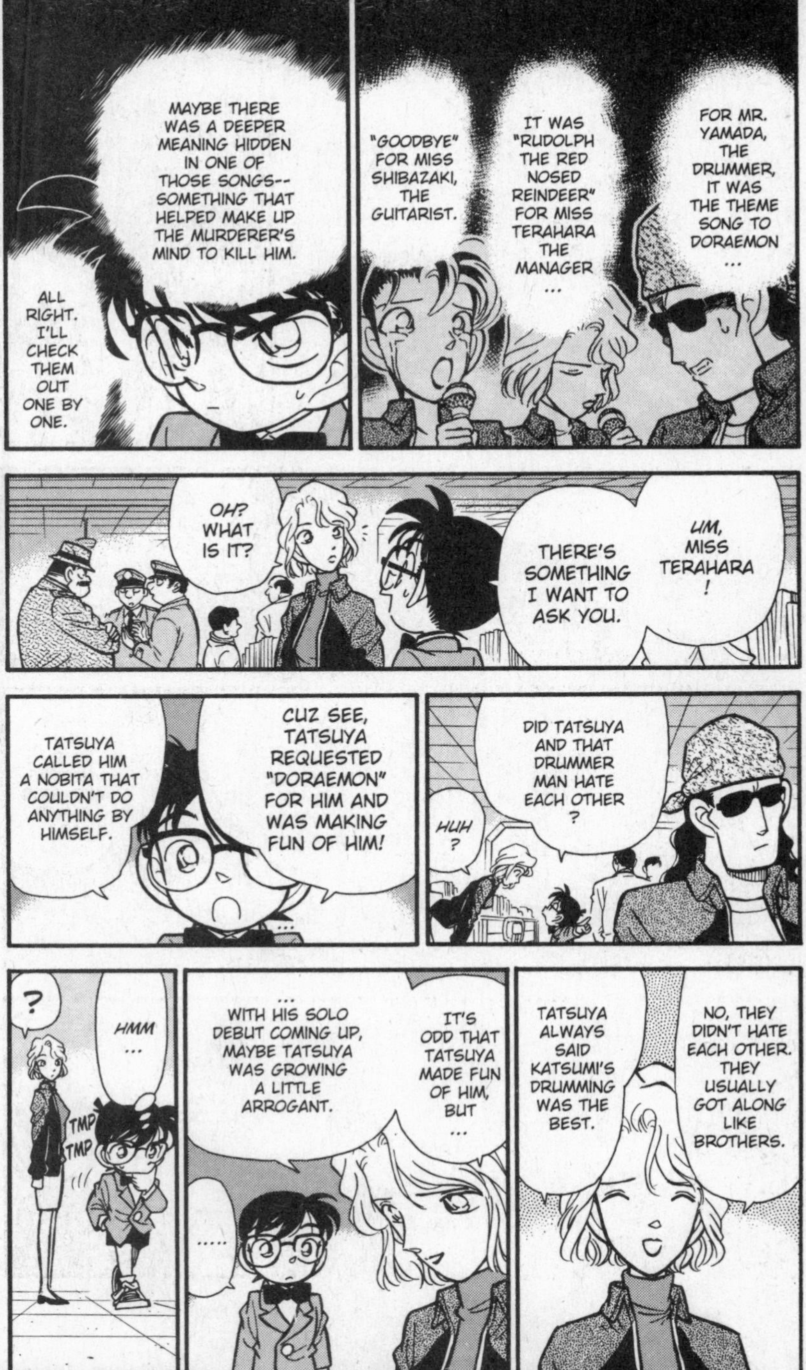
FOR MR. YAMADA, THE DRUMMER, IT WAS THE THEME SONG TO DORAEMON ...
IT WAS "RUDOLPH THE RED NOSED REINDEER" FOR MISS TERAHARA THE MANAGER ...
"GOODBYE" FOR MISS SHIBAZAKI, THE GUITARIST.
MAYBE THERE WAS A DEEPER MEANING HIDDEN IN ONE OF THOSE SONGS-- SOMETHING THAT HELPED MAKE UP THE MURDERER'S MIND TO KILL HIM.
ALL RIGHT. I'LL CHECK THEM OUT ONE BY ONE.
UM, MISS TERAHARA!
THERE'S SOMETHING I WANT TO ASK YOU.
OH? WHAT IS IT?
DID TATSUYA AND THAT DRUMMER MAN HATE EACH OTHER?
HUH?
CUZ SEE, TATSUYA REQUESTED "DORAEMON" FOR HIM AND WAS MAKING FUN OF HIM!
TATSUYA CALLED HIM A NOBITA THAT COULDN'T DO ANYTHING BY HIMSELF.
...
NO, THEY DIDN'T HATE EACH OTHER. THEY USUALLY GOT ALONG LIKE BROTHERS.
TATSUYA ALWAYS SAID KATSUMI'S DRUMMING WAS THE BEST.
IT'S ODD THAT TATSUYA MADE FUN OF HIM, BUT ...
... WITH HIS SOLO DEBUT COMING UP, MAYBE TATSUYA WAS GROWING A LITTLE ARROGANT.
.....
HMM ...
?
TMP TMP

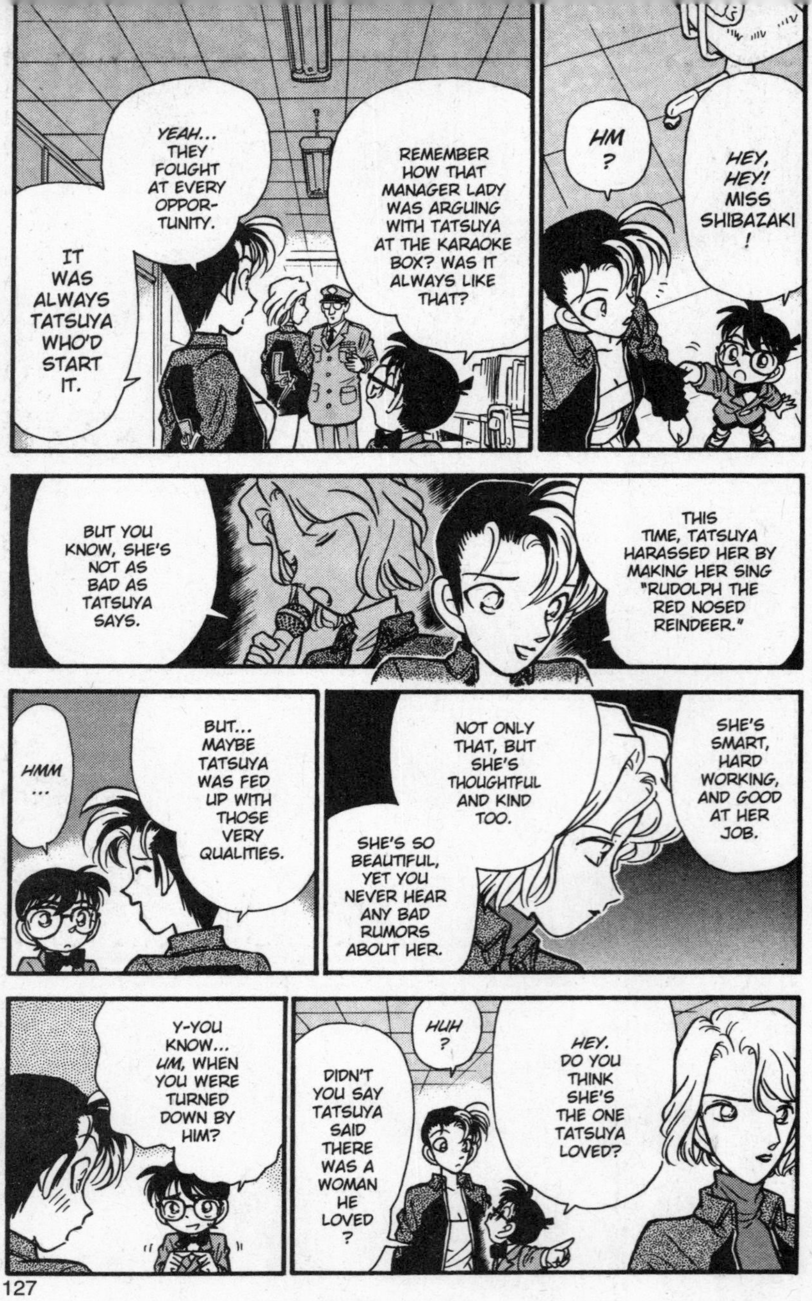
HEY, HEY! MISS SHIBAZAKI!
HM?
REMEMBER HOW THAT MANAGER LADY WAS ARGUING WITH TATSUYA AT THE KARAOKE BOX? WAS IT ALWAYS LIKE THAT?
YEAH... THEY FOUGHT AT EVERY OPPOR-TUNITY.
IT WAS ALWAYS TATSUYA WHO'D START IT.
THIS TIME, TATSUYA HARASSED HER BY MAKING HER SING "RUDOLPH THE RED NOSED REINDEER."
BUT YOU KNOW, SHE'S NOT AS BAD AS TATSUYA SAYS.
SHE'S SMART, HARD WORKING, AND GOOD AT HER JOB.
NOT ONLY THAT, BUT SHE'S THOUGHTFUL AND KIND TOO.
SHE'S SO BEAUTIFUL, YET YOU NEVER HEAR ANY BAD RUMORS ABOUT HER.
BUT... MAYBE TATSUYA WAS FED UP WITH THOSE VERY QUALITIES.
HMM...
HEY. DO YOU THINK SHE'S THE ONE TATSUYA LOVED?
HUH?
DIDN'T YOU SAY TATSUYA SAID THERE WAS A WOMAN HE LOVED?
Y-YOU KNOW... UM, WHEN YOU WERE TURNED DOWN BY HIM?

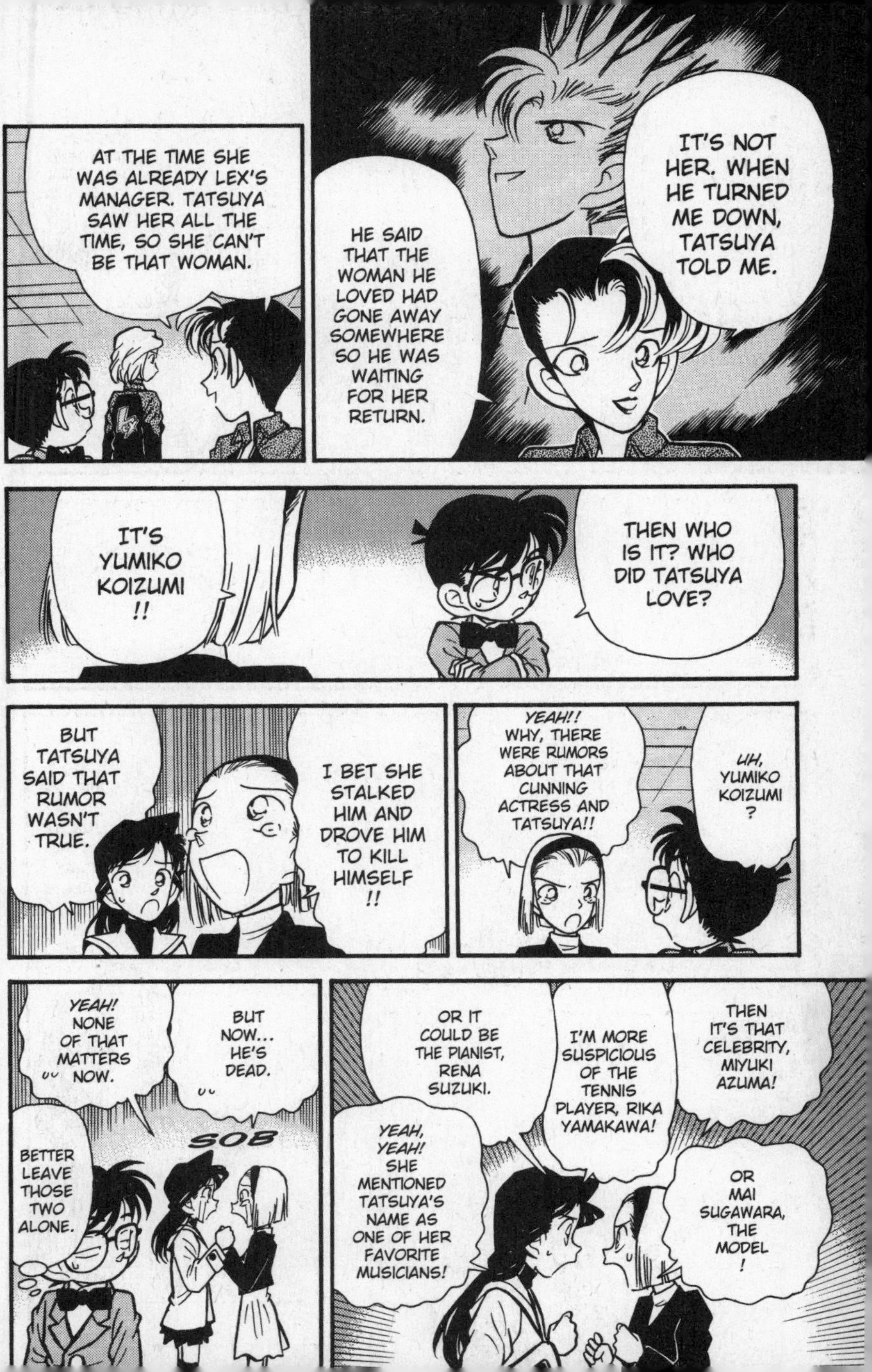
IT'S NOT HER. WHEN HE TURNED ME DOWN, TATSUYA TOLD ME.
HE SAID THAT THE WOMAN HE LOVED HAD GONE AWAY SOMEWHERE SO HE WAS WAITING FOR HER RETURN.
AT THE TIME SHE WAS ALREADY LEX'S MANAGER. TATSUYA SAW HER ALL THE TIME, SO SHE CAN'T BE THAT WOMAN.
THEN WHO IS IT? WHO DID TATSUYA LOVE?
IT'S YUMIKO KOIZUMI !!
UH, YUMIKO KOIZUMI ?
YEAH!! WHY, THERE WERE RUMORS ABOUT THAT CUNNING ACTRESS AND TATSUYA!!
I BET SHE STALKED HIM AND DROVE HIM TO KILL HIMSELF !!
BUT TATSUYA SAID THAT RUMOR WASN'T TRUE.
THEN IT'S THAT CELEBRITY, MIYUKI AZUMA!
I'M MORE SUSPICIOUS OF THE TENNIS PLAYER, RIKA YAMAKAWA!
OR IT COULD BE THE PIANIST, RENA SUZUKI.
OR MAI SUGAWARA, THE MODEL !
YEAH, YEAH! SHE MENTIONED TATSUYA'S NAME AS ONE OF HER FAVORITE MUSICIANS!
BUT NOW... HE'S DEAD.
YEAH! NONE OF THAT MATTERS NOW.
SOB
BETTER LEAVE THOSE TWO ALONE.

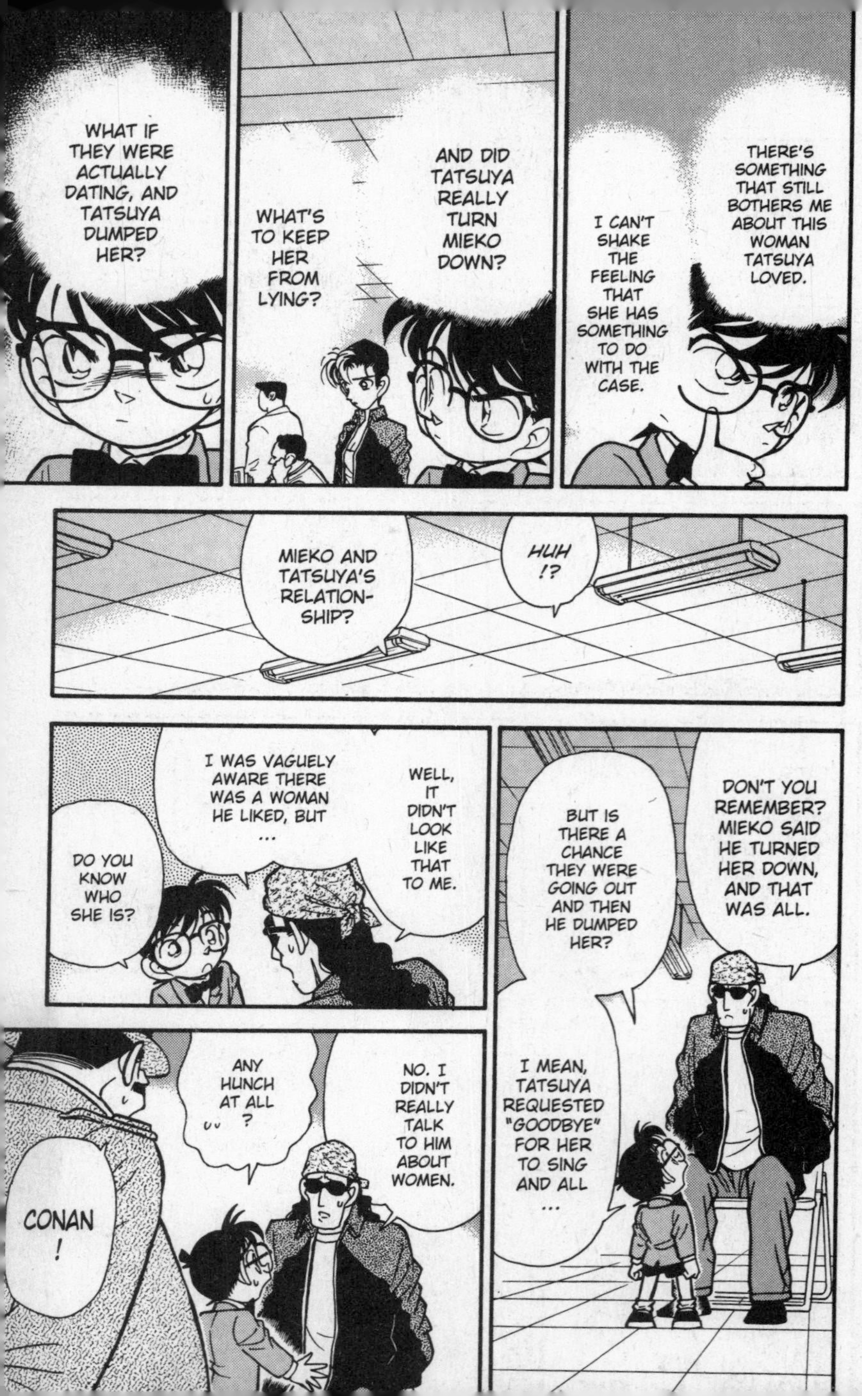
THERE'S SOMETHING THAT STILL BOTHERS ME ABOUT THIS WOMAN TATSUYA LOVED.
I CAN'T SHAKE THE FEELING THAT SHE HAS SOMETHING TO DO WITH THE CASE.
AND DID TATSUYA REALLY TURN MIEKO DOWN?
WHAT'S TO KEEP HER FROM LYING?
WHAT IF THEY WERE ACTUALLY DATING, AND TATSUYA DUMPED HER?
HUH!?
MIEKO AND TATSUYA'S RELATIONSHIP?
DON'T YOU REMEMBER? MIEKO SAID HE TURNED HER DOWN, AND THAT WAS ALL.
BUT IS THERE A CHANCE THEY WERE GOING OUT AND THEN HE DUMPED HER?
I MEAN, TATSUYA REQUESTED "GOODBYE" FOR HER TO SING AND ALL ...
WELL, IT DIDN'T LOOK LIKE THAT TO ME.
I WAS VAGUELY AWARE THERE WAS A WOMAN HE LIKED, BUT ...
DO YOU KNOW WHO SHE IS?
NO. I DIDN'T REALLY TALK TO HIM ABOUT WOMEN.
ANY HUNCH AT ALL ?
CONAN!

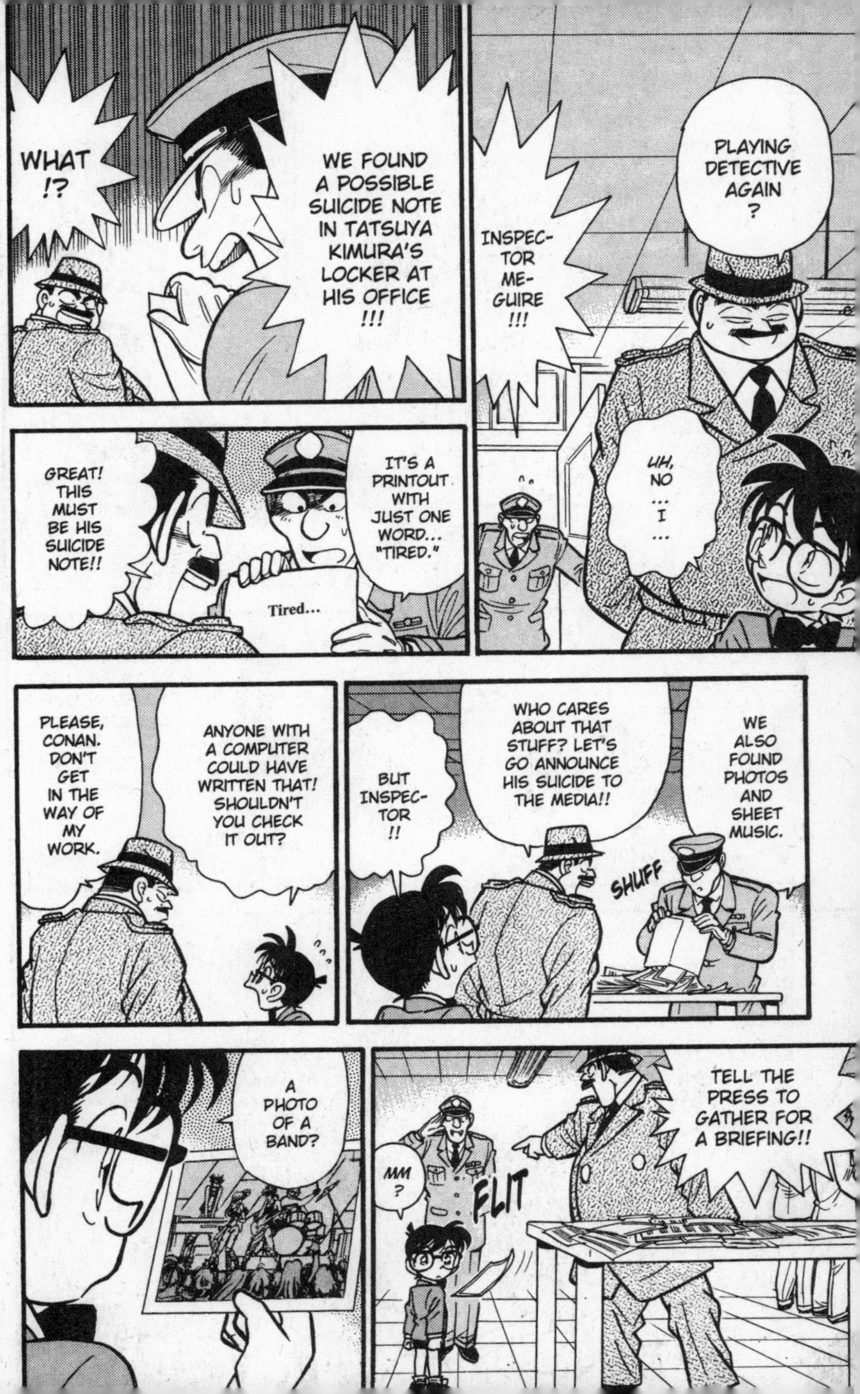
PLAYING DETECTIVE AGAIN ?
UH, NO ... I ...
INSPECTOR MEGUIRE !!!
WE FOUND A POSSIBLE SUICIDE NOTE IN TATSUYA KIMURA'S LOCKER AT HIS OFFICE !!!
WHAT !?
IT'S A PRINTOUT WITH JUST ONE WORD... "TIRED."
Tired...
GREAT! THIS MUST BE HIS SUICIDE NOTE!!
WE ALSO FOUND PHOTOS AND SHEET MUSIC.
SHUFF
WHO CARES ABOUT THAT STUFF? LET'S GO ANNOUNCE HIS SUICIDE TO THE MEDIA!!
BUT INSPECTOR !!
ANYONE WITH A COMPUTER COULD HAVE WRITTEN THAT! SHOULDN'T YOU CHECK IT OUT?
PLEASE, CONAN. DON'T GET IN THE WAY OF MY WORK.
TELL THE PRESS TO GATHER FOR A BRIEFING!!
MM ?
FLIT
A PHOTO OF A BAND?

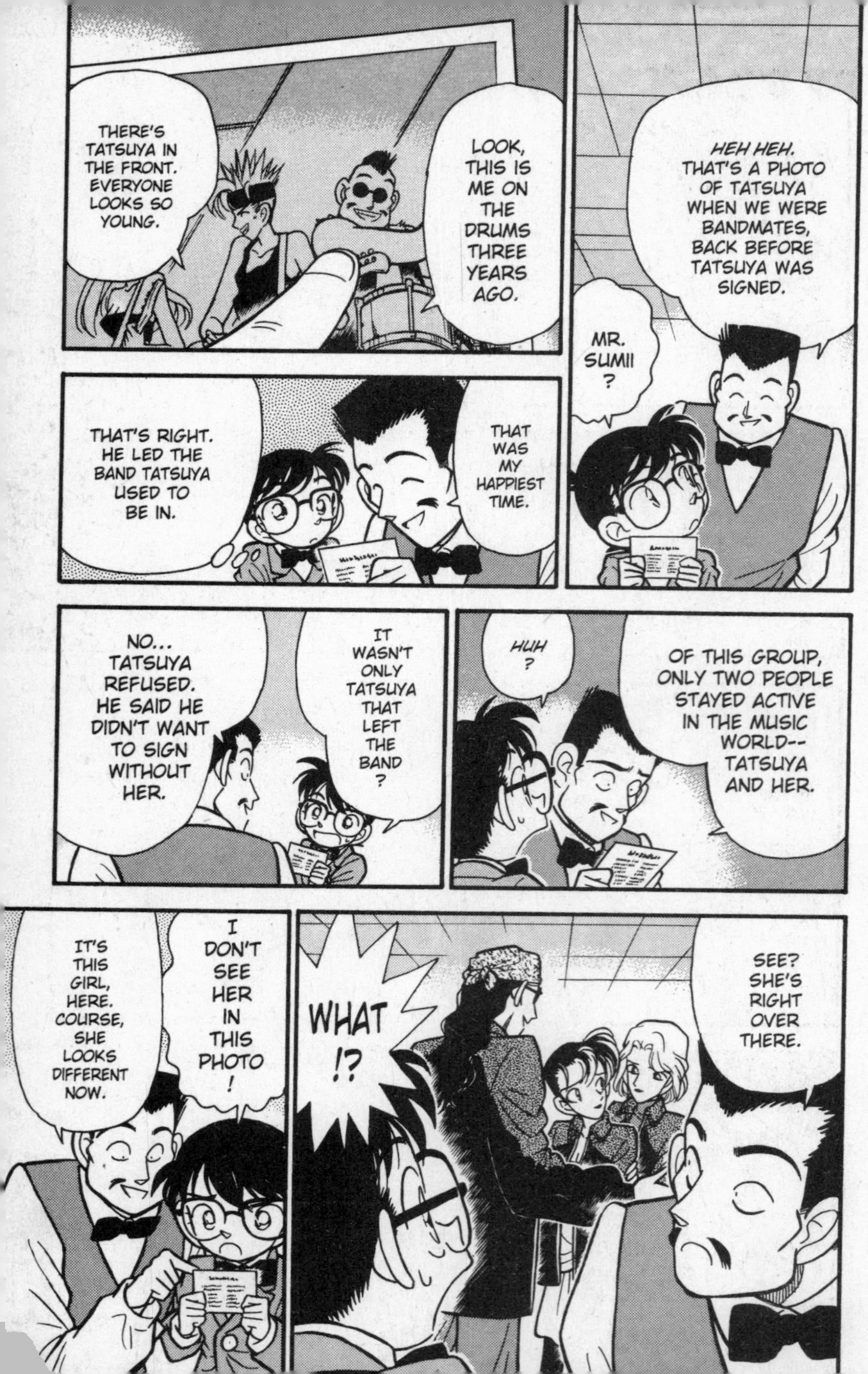
HEH HEH. THAT'S A PHOTO OF TATSUYA WHEN WE WERE BANDMATES, BACK BEFORE TATSUYA WAS SIGNED.
MR. SUMII?
LOOK, THIS IS ME ON THE DRUMS THREE YEARS AGO.
THERE'S TATSUYA IN THE FRONT. EVERYONE LOOKS SO YOUNG.
THAT WAS MY HAPPIEST TIME.
THAT'S RIGHT. HE LED THE BAND TATSUYA USED TO BE IN.
OF THIS GROUP, ONLY TWO PEOPLE STAYED ACTIVE IN THE MUSIC WORLD-- TATSUYA AND HER.
HUH?
IT WASN'T ONLY TATSUYA THAT LEFT THE BAND?
NO... TATSUYA REFUSED. HE SAID HE DIDN'T WANT TO SIGN WITHOUT HER.
SEE? SHE'S RIGHT OVER THERE.
WHAT!?
I DON'T SEE HER IN THIS PHOTO!
IT'S THIS GIRL, HERE. COURSE, SHE LOOKS DIFFERENT NOW.

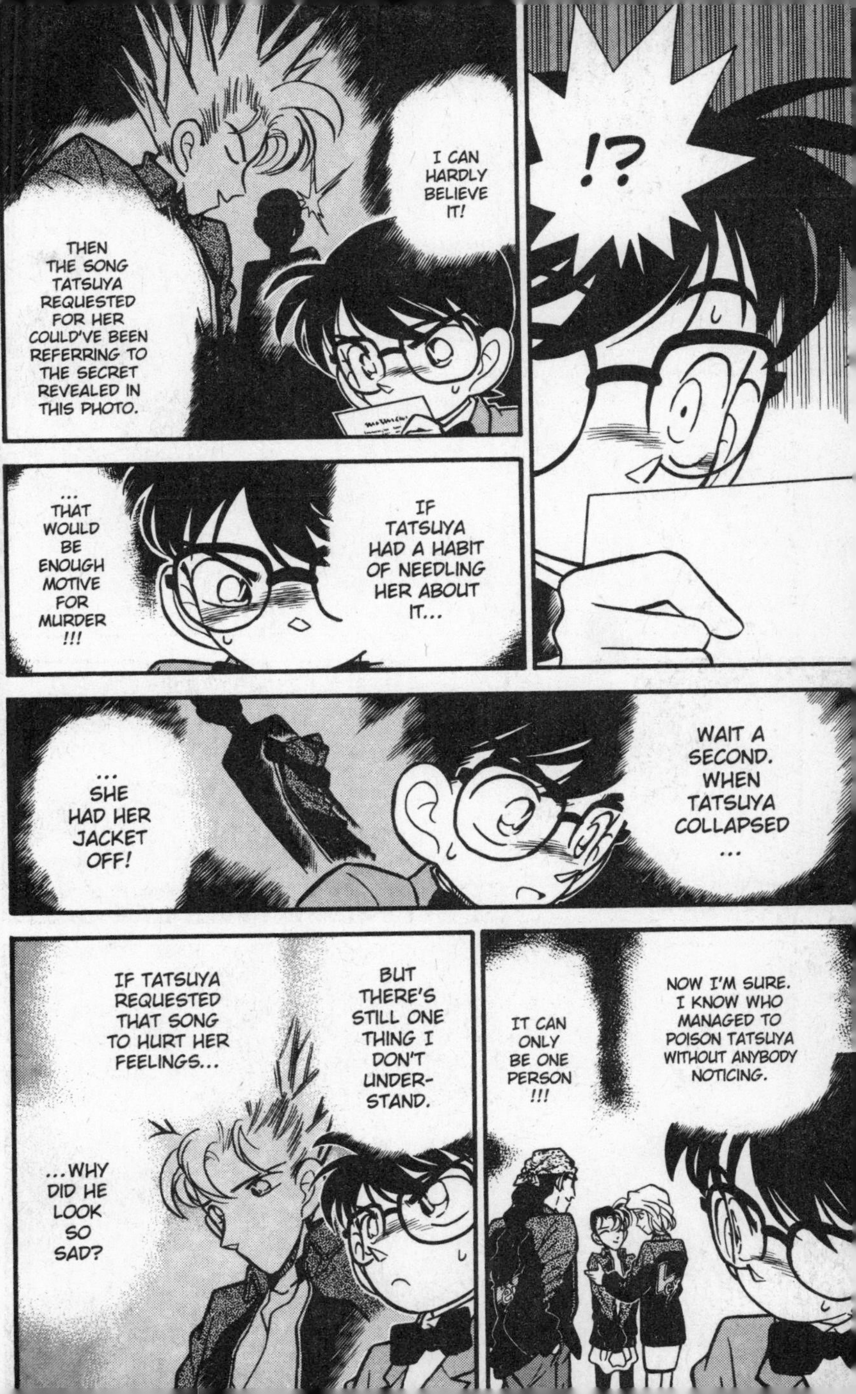
!?
I CAN HARDLY BELIEVE IT!
THEN THE SONG TATSUYA REQUESTED FOR HER COULD'VE BEEN REFERRING TO THE SECRET REVEALED IN THIS PHOTO.
IF TATSUYA HAD A HABIT OF NEEDLING HER ABOUT IT...
...THAT WOULD BE ENOUGH MOTIVE FOR MURDER!!!
WAIT A SECOND. WHEN TATSUYA COLLAPSED...
...SHE HAD HER JACKET OFF!
NOW I'M SURE. I KNOW WHO MANAGED TO POISON TATSUYA WITHOUT ANYBODY NOTICING.
IT CAN ONLY BE ONE PERSON!!!
BUT THERE'S STILL ONE THING I DON'T UNDER-STAND.
IF TATSUYA REQUESTED THAT SONG TO HURT HER FEELINGS...
...WHY DID HE LOOK SO SAD?

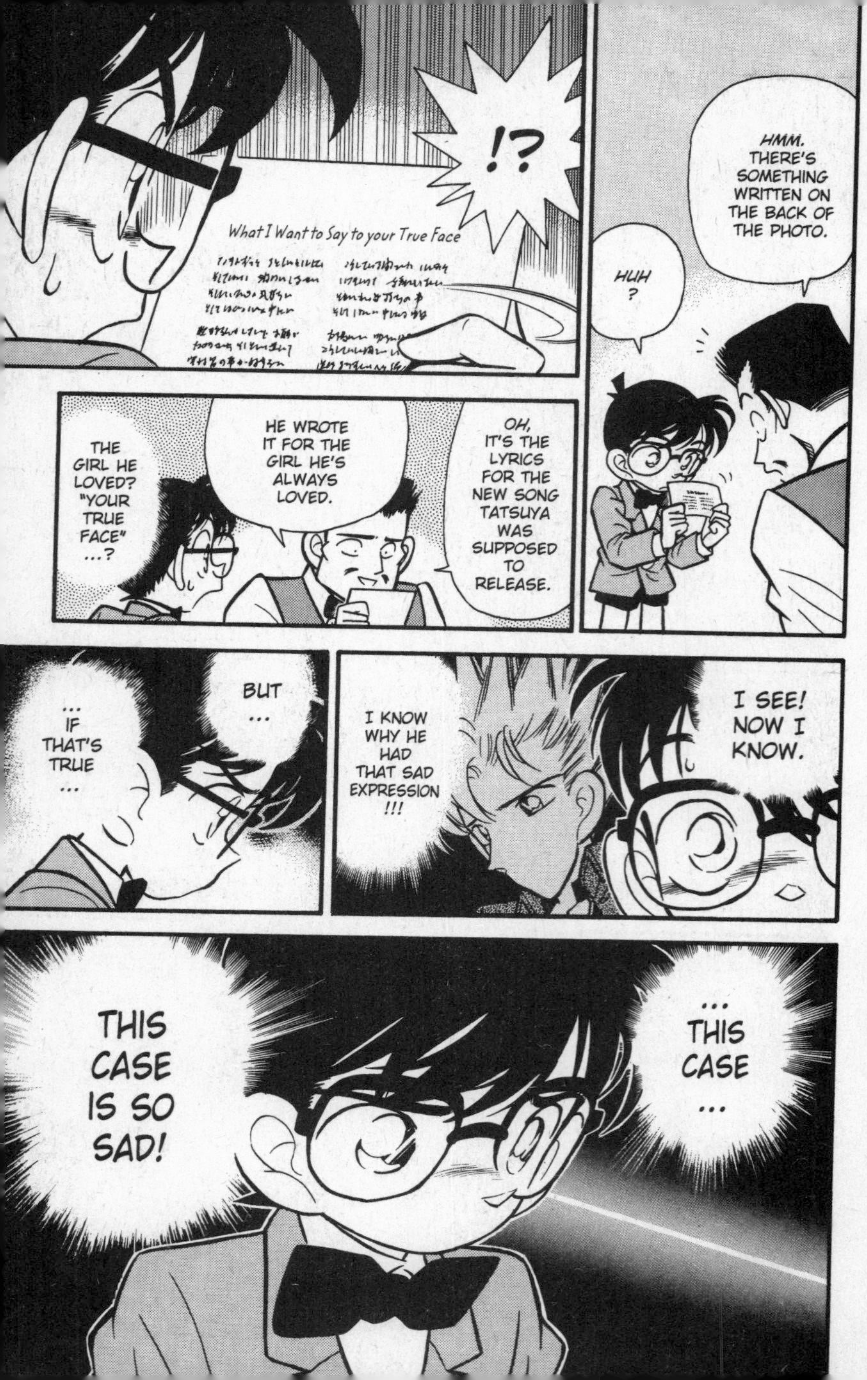
HMM. THERE'S SOMETHING WRITTEN ON THE BACK OF THE PHOTO.
HUH?
!?
What I Want to Say to your True Face
OH, IT'S THE LYRICS FOR THE NEW SONG TATSUYA WAS SUPPOSED TO RELEASE.
HE WROTE IT FOR THE GIRL HE'S ALWAYS LOVED.
THE GIRL HE LOVED? "YOUR TRUE FACE" ...?
I SEE! NOW I KNOW.
I KNOW WHY HE HAD THAT SAD EXPRESSION!!!
BUT...
...IF THAT'S TRUE...
...THIS CASE...
THIS CASE IS SO SAD!

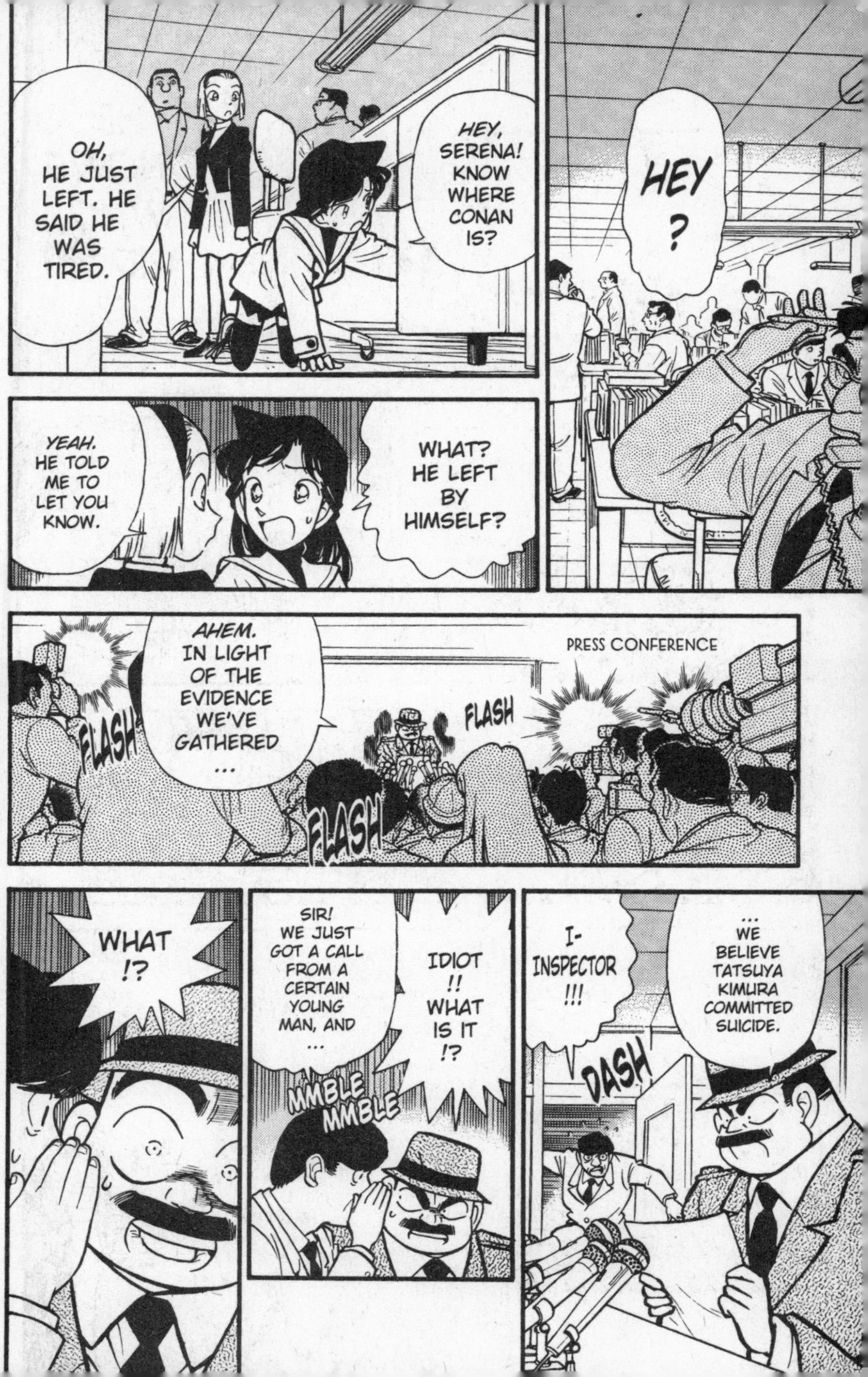
HEY ?
HEY, SERENA! KNOW WHERE CONAN IS?
OH, HE JUST LEFT. HE SAID HE WAS TIRED.
WHAT? HE LEFT BY HIMSELF?
YEAH. HE TOLD ME TO LET YOU KNOW.
PRESS CONFERENCE
FLASH
AHEM. IN LIGHT OF THE EVIDENCE WE'VE GATHERED ...
FLASH
FLASH
... WE BELIEVE TATSUYA KIMURA COMMITTED SUICIDE.
I- INSPECTOR !!!
DASH
IDIOT !! WHAT IS IT !?
SIR! WE JUST GOT A CALL FROM A CERTAIN YOUNG MAN, AND ...
MMBLE MMBLE
WHAT !?

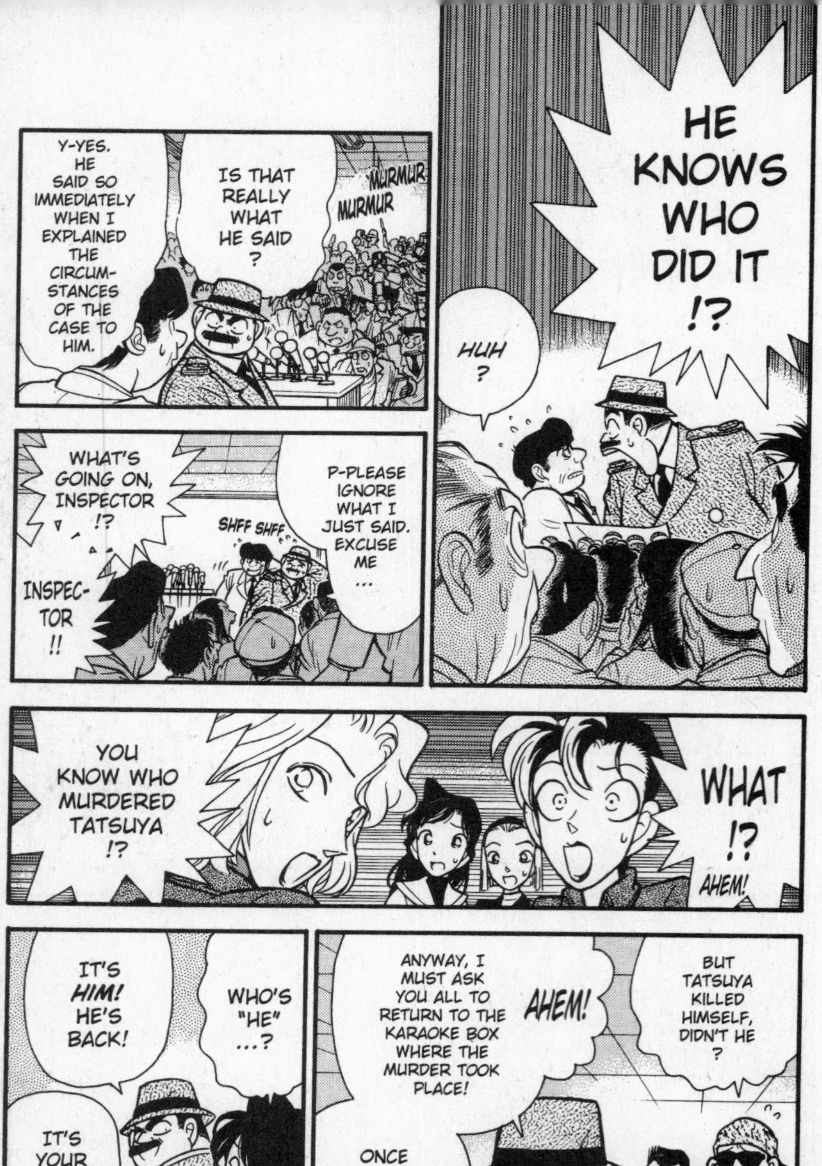
HE KNOWS WHO DID IT !?
HUH ?
MURMUR
MURMUR
IS THAT REALLY WHAT HE SAID ?
Y-YES. HE SAID SO IMMEDIATELY WHEN I EXPLAINED THE CIRCUM-STANCES OF THE CASE TO HIM.
P-PLEASE IGNORE WHAT I JUST SAID. EXCUSE ME ...
SHFF SHFF
WHAT'S GOING ON, INSPECTOR !?
INSPEC-TOR !!
WHAT !?
AHEM!
YOU KNOW WHO MURDERED TATSUYA !?
BUT TATSUYA KILLED HIMSELF, DIDN'T HE ?
AHEM!
ANYWAY, I MUST ASK YOU ALL TO RETURN TO THE KARAOKE BOX WHERE THE MURDER TOOK PLACE!
ONCE WE'RE THERE, *HE'LL* RESOLVE EVERYTHING !!
WHO'S "HE" ...?
IT'S *HIM!* HE'S BACK!
IT'S YOUR DETECTIVE PAL, RACHEL.

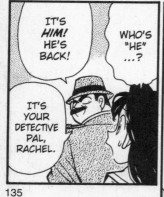

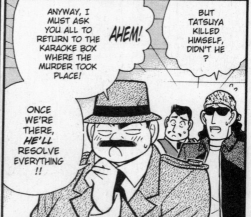

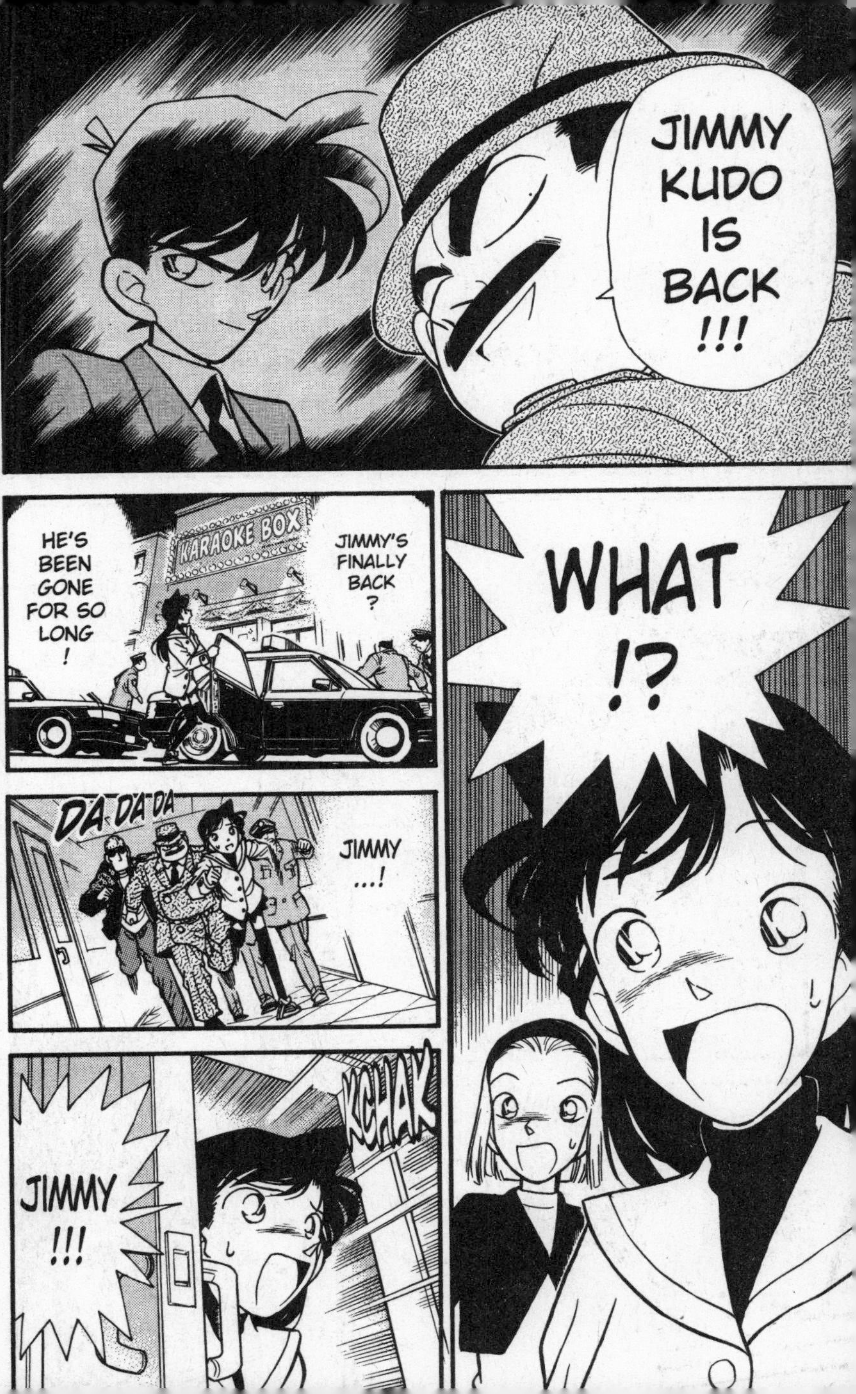
JIMMY KUDO IS BACK!!!
WHAT!?
KARAOKE BOX
JIMMY'S FINALLY BACK?
HE'S BEEN GONE FOR SO LONG!
DA DA DA
JIMMY ...!
KCHAK
JIMMY!!!

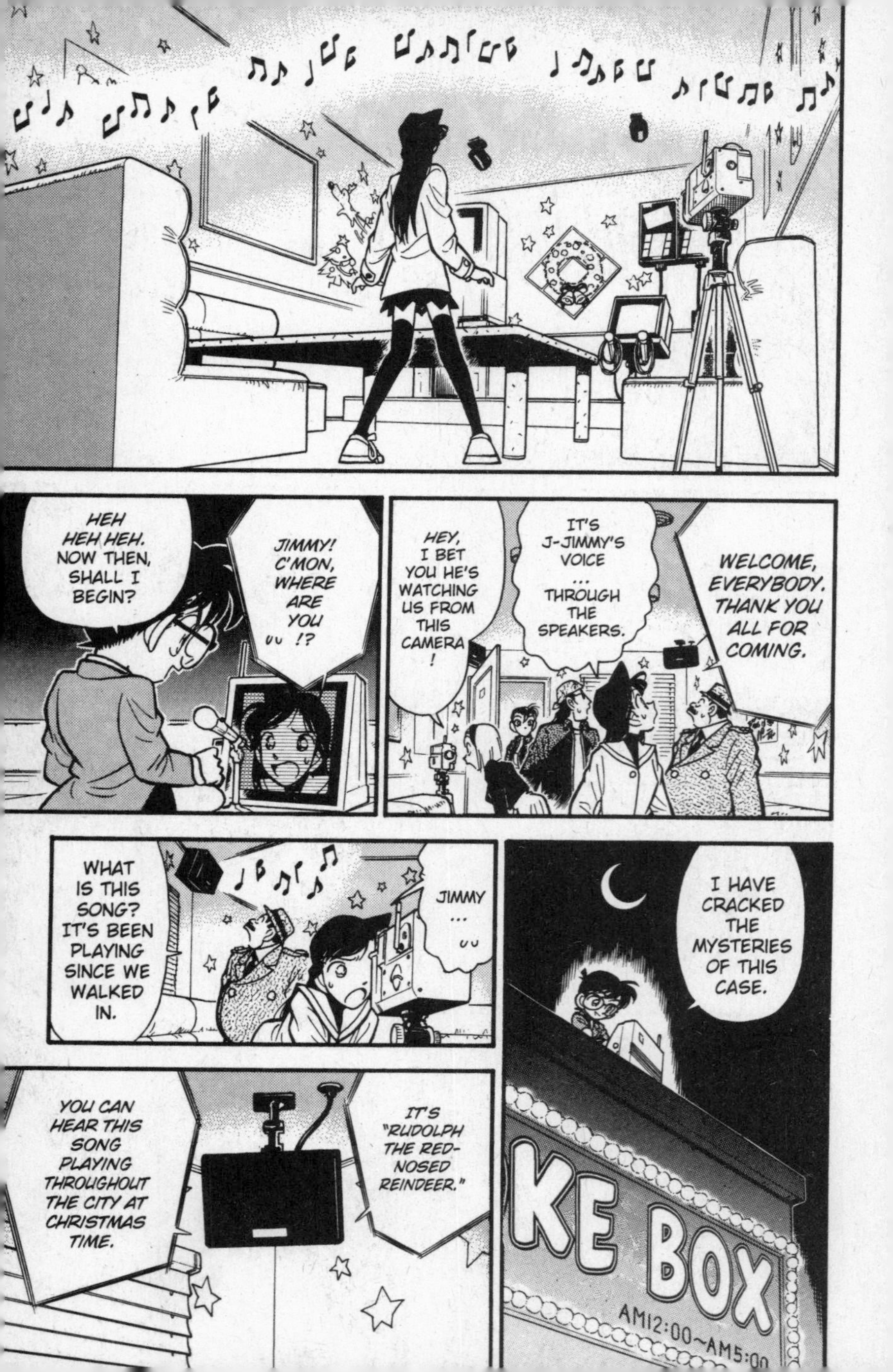
WELCOME, EVERYBODY. THANK YOU ALL FOR COMING.
IT'S J-JIMMY'S VOICE ... THROUGH THE SPEAKERS.
HEY, I BET YOU HE'S WATCHING US FROM THIS CAMERA!
JIMMY! C'MON, WHERE ARE YOU !?
HEH HEH HEH. NOW THEN, SHALL I BEGIN?
I HAVE CRACKED THE MYSTERIES OF THIS CASE.
KE BOX
AM12:00~AM5:00
JIMMY ...
WHAT IS THIS SONG? IT'S BEEN PLAYING SINCE WE WALKED IN.
IT'S "RUDOLPH THE RED-NOSED REINDEER."
YOU CAN HEAR THIS SONG PLAYING THROUGHOUT THE CITY AT CHRISTMAS TIME.

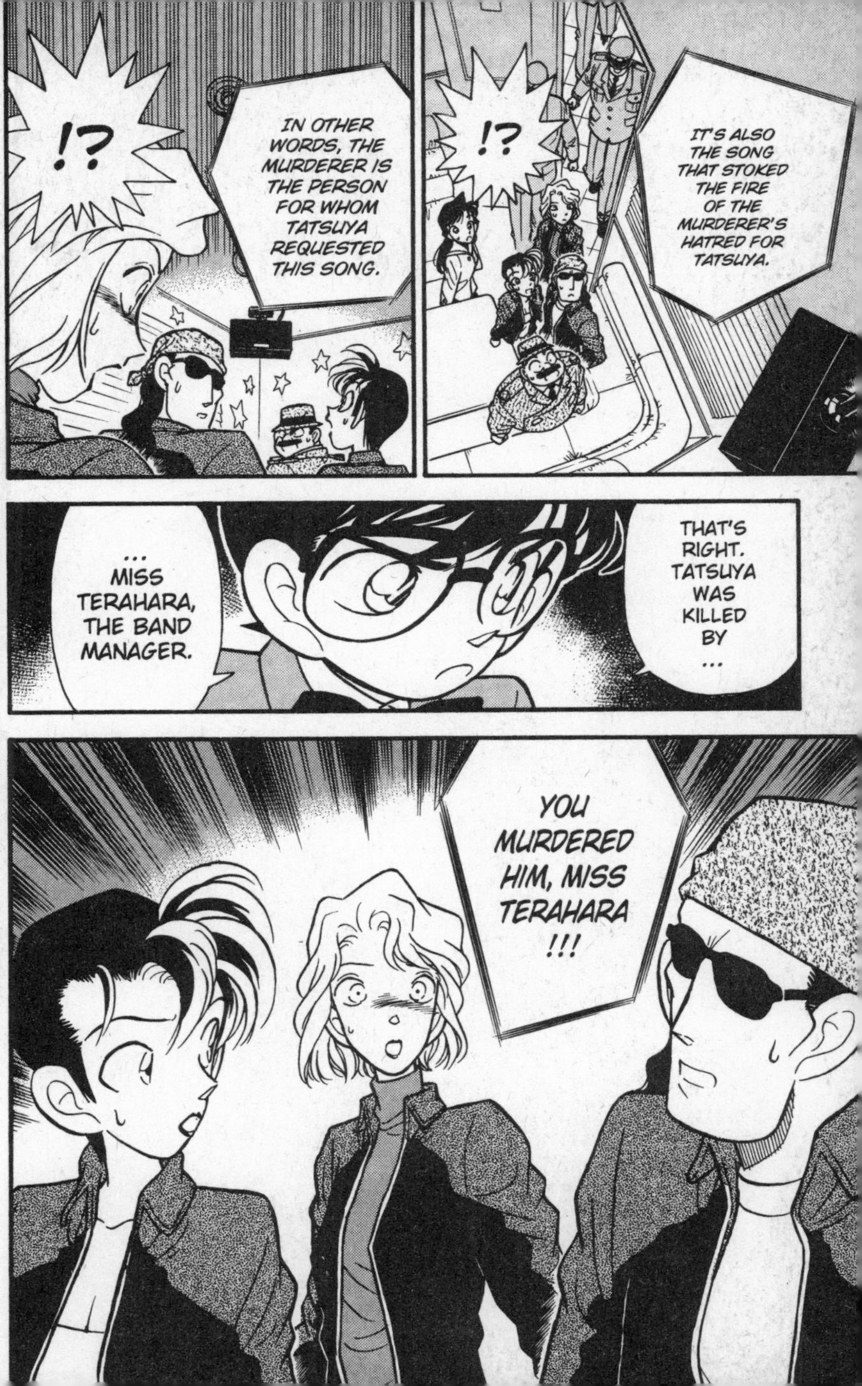
!?
IT'S ALSO THE SONG THAT STOKED THE FIRE OF THE MURDERER'S HATRED FOR TATSUYA.
!?
IN OTHER WORDS, THE MURDERER IS THE PERSON FOR WHOM TATSUYA REQUESTED THIS SONG.
THAT'S RIGHT. TATSUYA WAS KILLED BY ...
... MISS TERAHARA, THE BAND MANAGER.
YOU MURDERED HIM, MISS TERAHARA !!!

FILE 9: A TRAGIC MISUNDERSTANDING

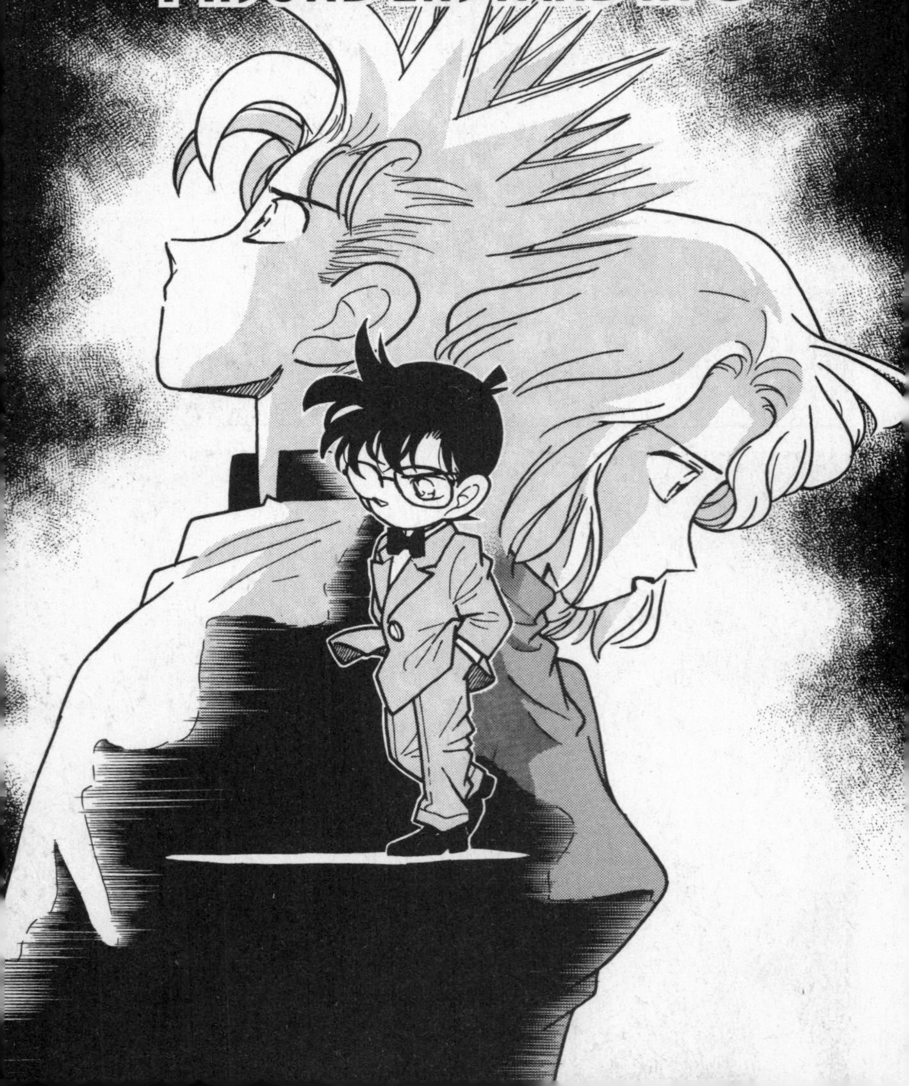

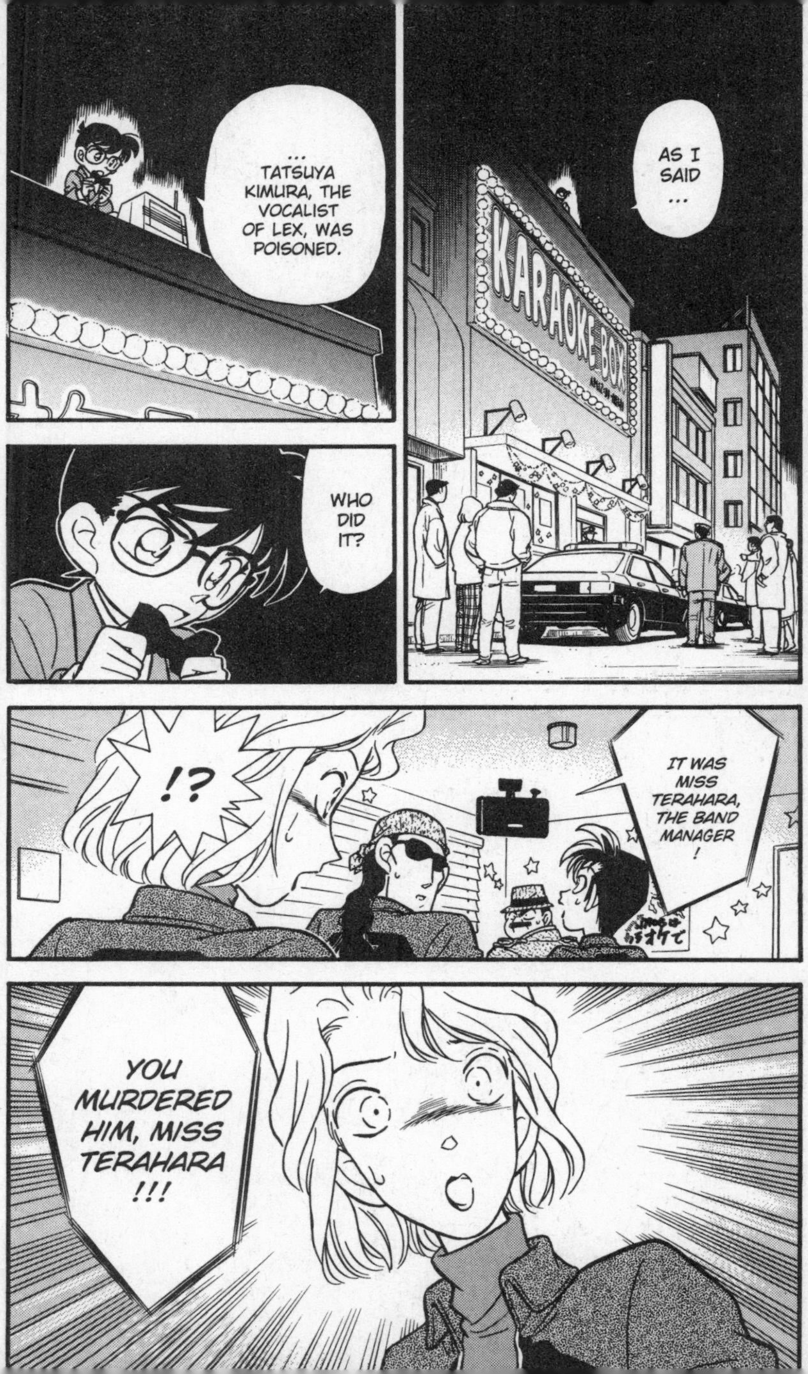
AS I SAID ...
KARAOKE BOX
... TATSUYA KIMURA, THE VOCALIST OF LEX, WAS POISONED.
WHO DID IT?
IT WAS MISS TERAHARA, THE BAND MANAGER !
!?
YOU MURDERED HIM, MISS TERAHARA !!!

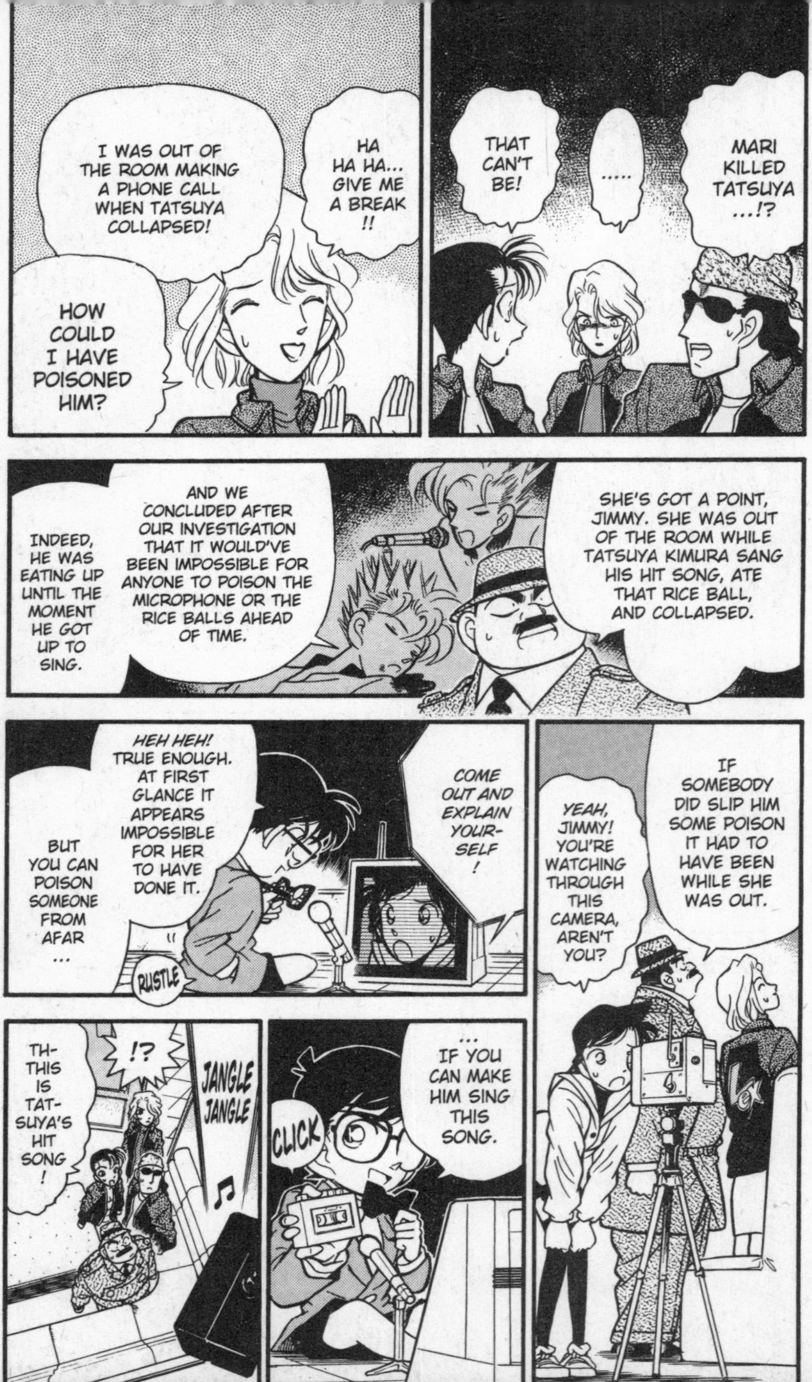
MARI KILLED TATSUYA ...!?
.....
THAT CAN'T BE!
HA HA HA... GIVE ME A BREAK !!
I WAS OUT OF THE ROOM MAKING A PHONE CALL WHEN TATSUYA COLLAPSED!
HOW COULD I HAVE POISONED HIM?
SHE'S GOT A POINT, JIMMY. SHE WAS OUT OF THE ROOM WHILE TATSUYA KIMURA SANG HIS HIT SONG, ATE THAT RICE BALL, AND COLLAPSED.
AND WE CONCLUDED AFTER OUR INVESTIGATION THAT IT WOULD'VE BEEN IMPOSSIBLE FOR ANYONE TO POISON THE MICROPHONE OR THE RICE BALLS AHEAD OF TIME.
INDEED, HE WAS EATING UP UNTIL THE MOMENT HE GOT UP TO SING.
IF SOMEBODY DID SLIP HIM SOME POISON IT HAD TO HAVE BEEN WHILE SHE WAS OUT.
YEAH, JIMMY! YOU'RE WATCHING THROUGH THIS CAMERA, AREN'T YOU?
COME OUT AND EXPLAIN YOURSELF!
HEH HEH! TRUE ENOUGH. AT FIRST GLANCE IT APPEARS IMPOSSIBLE FOR HER TO HAVE DONE IT.
BUT YOU CAN POISON SOMEONE FROM AFAR ...
RUSTLE
... IF YOU CAN MAKE HIM SING THIS SONG.
CLICK
!?
JANGLE JANGLE
TH-THIS IS TATSUYA'S HIT SONG!

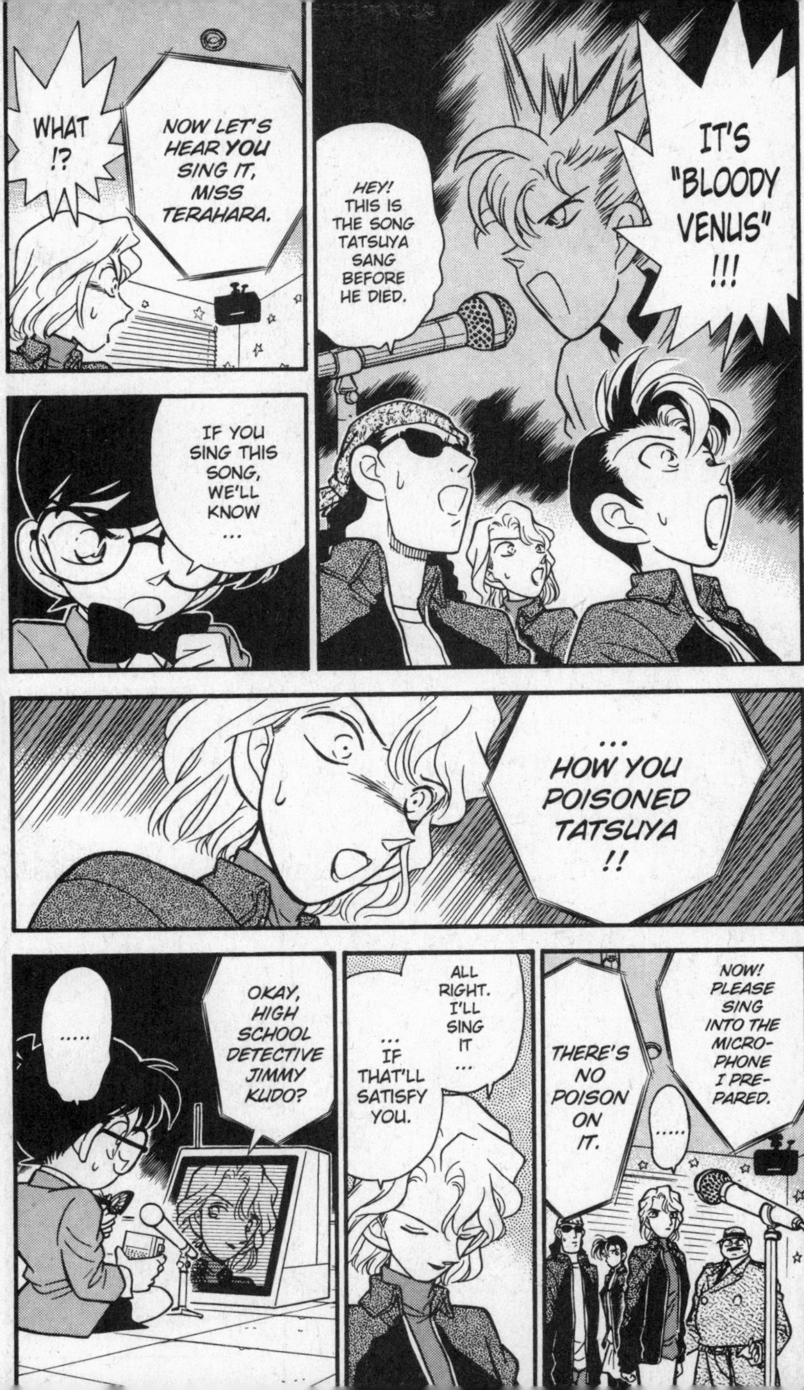
IT'S "BLOODY VENUS" !!!
HEY! THIS IS THE SONG TATSUYA SANG BEFORE HE DIED.
NOW LET'S HEAR YOU SING IT, MISS TERAHARA.
WHAT !?
IF YOU SING THIS SONG, WE'LL KNOW ...
... HOW YOU POISONED TATSUYA !!
NOW! PLEASE SING INTO THE MICRO-PHONE I PRE-PARED.
THERE'S NO POISON ON IT.
.....
ALL RIGHT. I'LL SING IT ...
... IF THAT'LL SATISFY YOU.
OKAY, HIGH SCHOOL DETECTIVE JIMMY KUDO?
.....

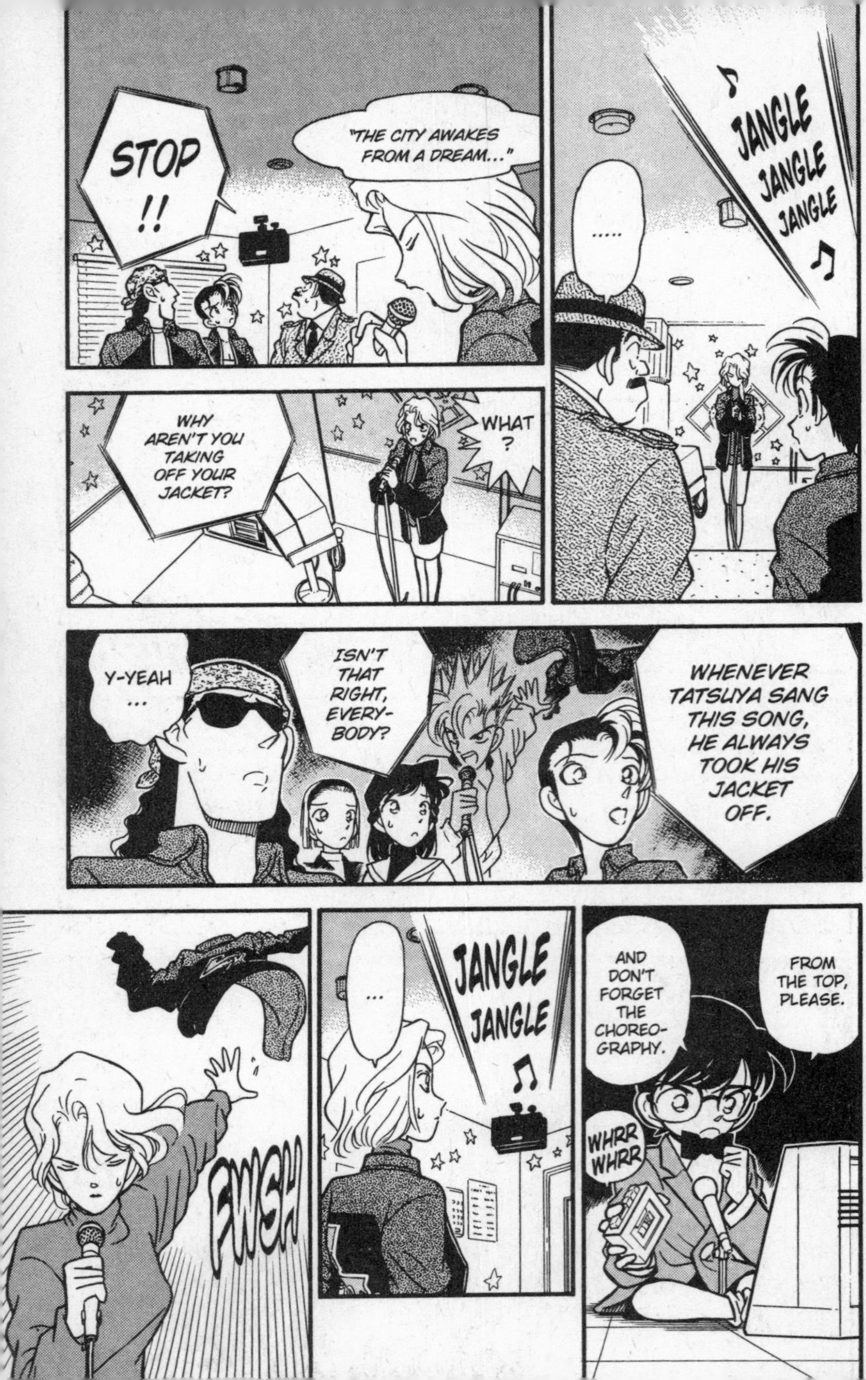

JANGLE JANGLE JANGLE
......
"THE CITY AWAKES FROM A DREAM..."
STOP !!
WHAT ?
WHY AREN'T YOU TAKING OFF YOUR JACKET?
WHENEVER TATSUYA SANG THIS SONG, HE ALWAYS TOOK HIS JACKET OFF.
ISN'T THAT RIGHT, EVERYBODY?
Y-YEAH ...
FROM THE TOP, PLEASE.
AND DON'T FORGET THE CHOREOGRAPHY.
WHRR WHRR
JANGLE JANGLE
...
FWSH

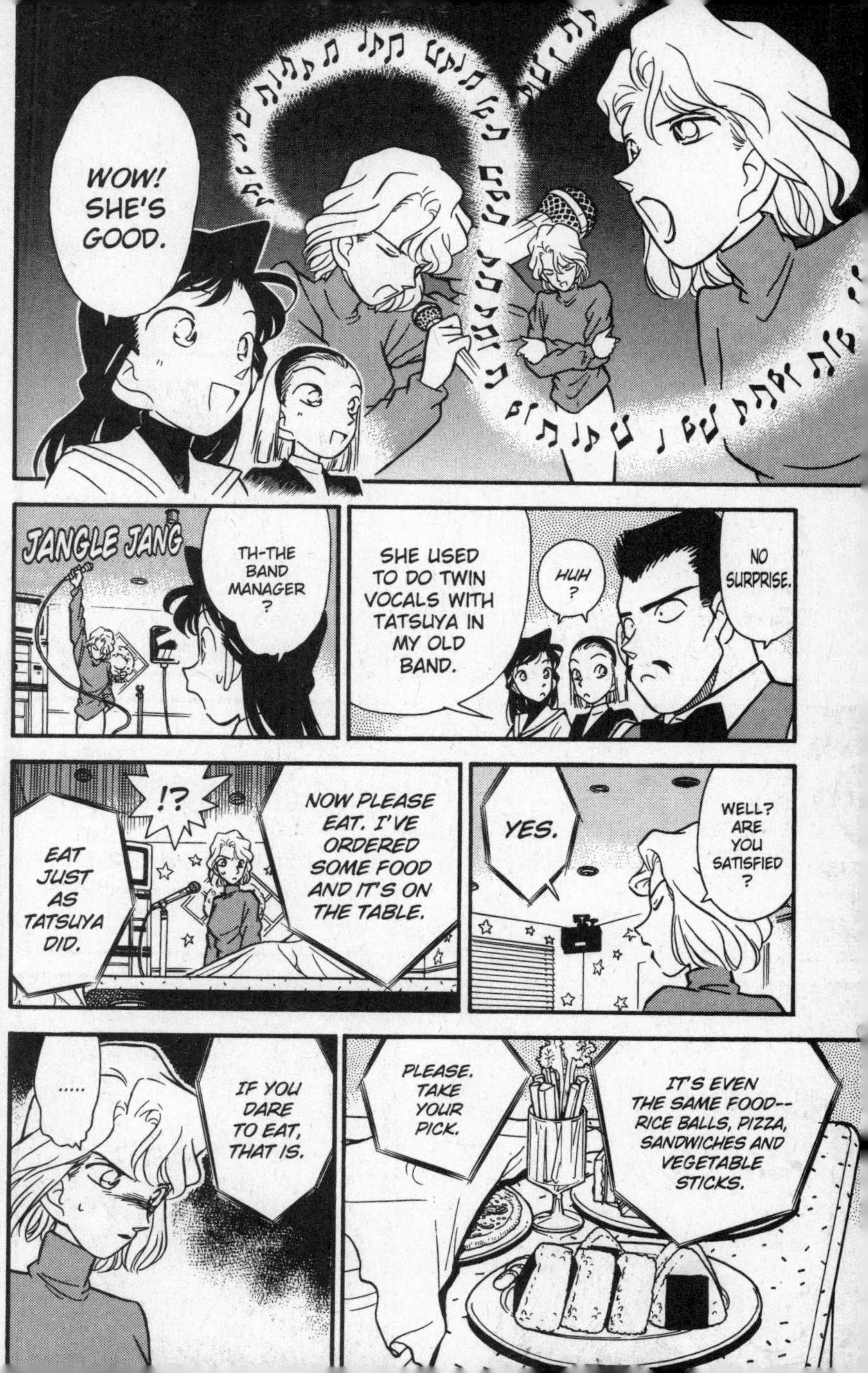
WOW! SHE'S GOOD.
NO SURPRISE.
HUH?
SHE USED TO DO TWIN VOCALS WITH TATSUYA IN MY OLD BAND.
TH-THE BAND MANAGER?
JANGLE JANG
WELL? ARE YOU SATISFIED?
YES.
NOW PLEASE EAT. I'VE ORDERED SOME FOOD AND IT'S ON THE TABLE.
!?
EAT JUST AS TATSUYA DID.
IT'S EVEN THE SAME FOOD-- RICE BALLS, PIZZA, SANDWICHES AND VEGETABLE STICKS.
PLEASE. TAKE YOUR PICK.
IF YOU DARE TO EAT, THAT IS.
.....

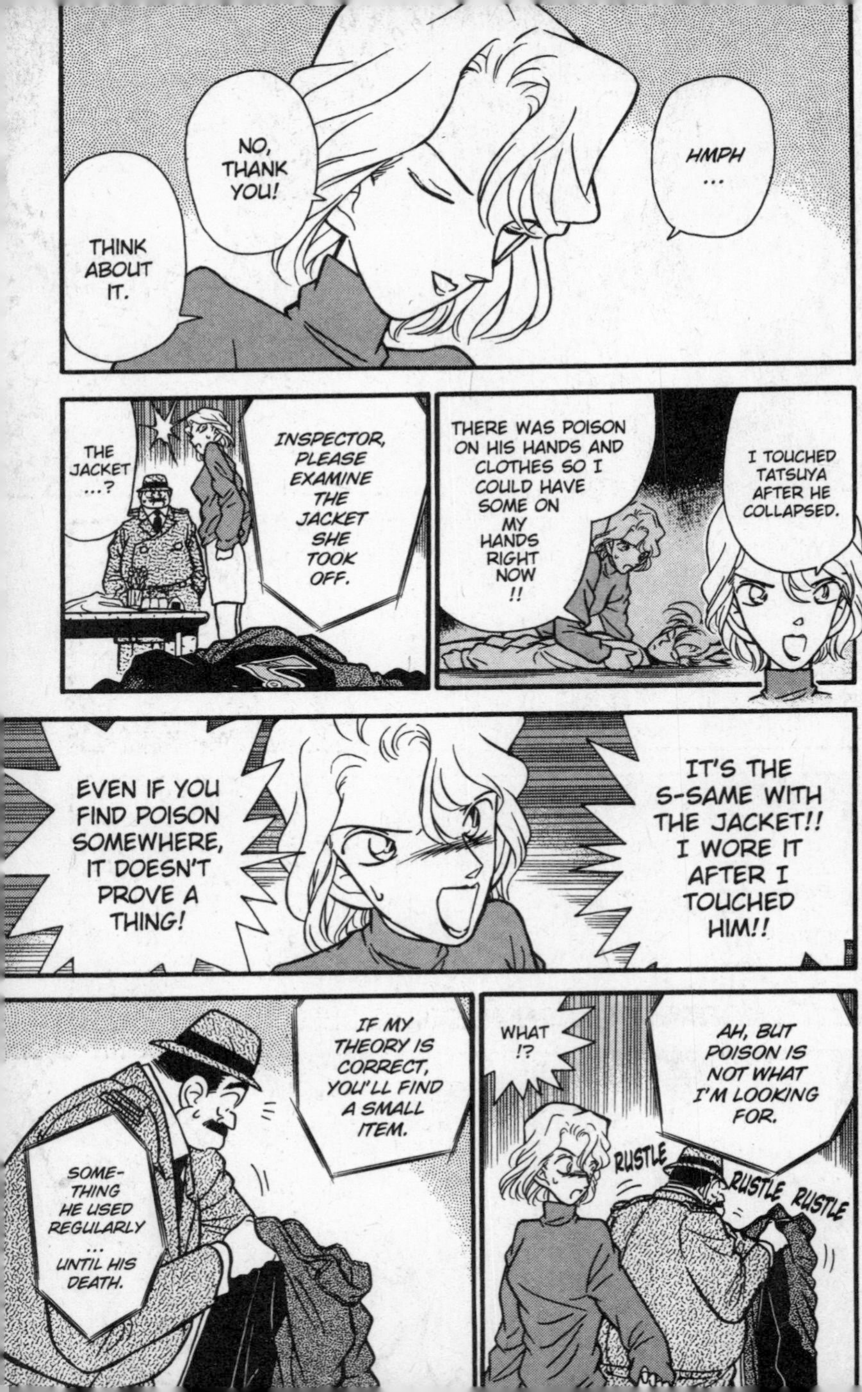
HMPH ...
NO, THANK YOU!
THINK ABOUT IT.
I TOUCHED TATSUYA AFTER HE COLLAPSED.
THERE WAS POISON ON HIS HANDS AND CLOTHES SO I COULD HAVE SOME ON MY HANDS RIGHT NOW!!
INSPECTOR, PLEASE EXAMINE THE JACKET SHE TOOK OFF.
THE JACKET ...?
IT'S THE S-SAME WITH THE JACKET!! I WORE IT AFTER I TOUCHED HIM!!
EVEN IF YOU FIND POISON SOMEWHERE, IT DOESN'T PROVE A THING!
AH, BUT POISON IS NOT WHAT I'M LOOKING FOR.
WHAT!?
RUSTLE
RUSTLE
RUSTLE
IF MY THEORY IS CORRECT, YOU'LL FIND A SMALL ITEM.
SOME-THING HE USED REGULARLY ... UNTIL HIS DEATH.

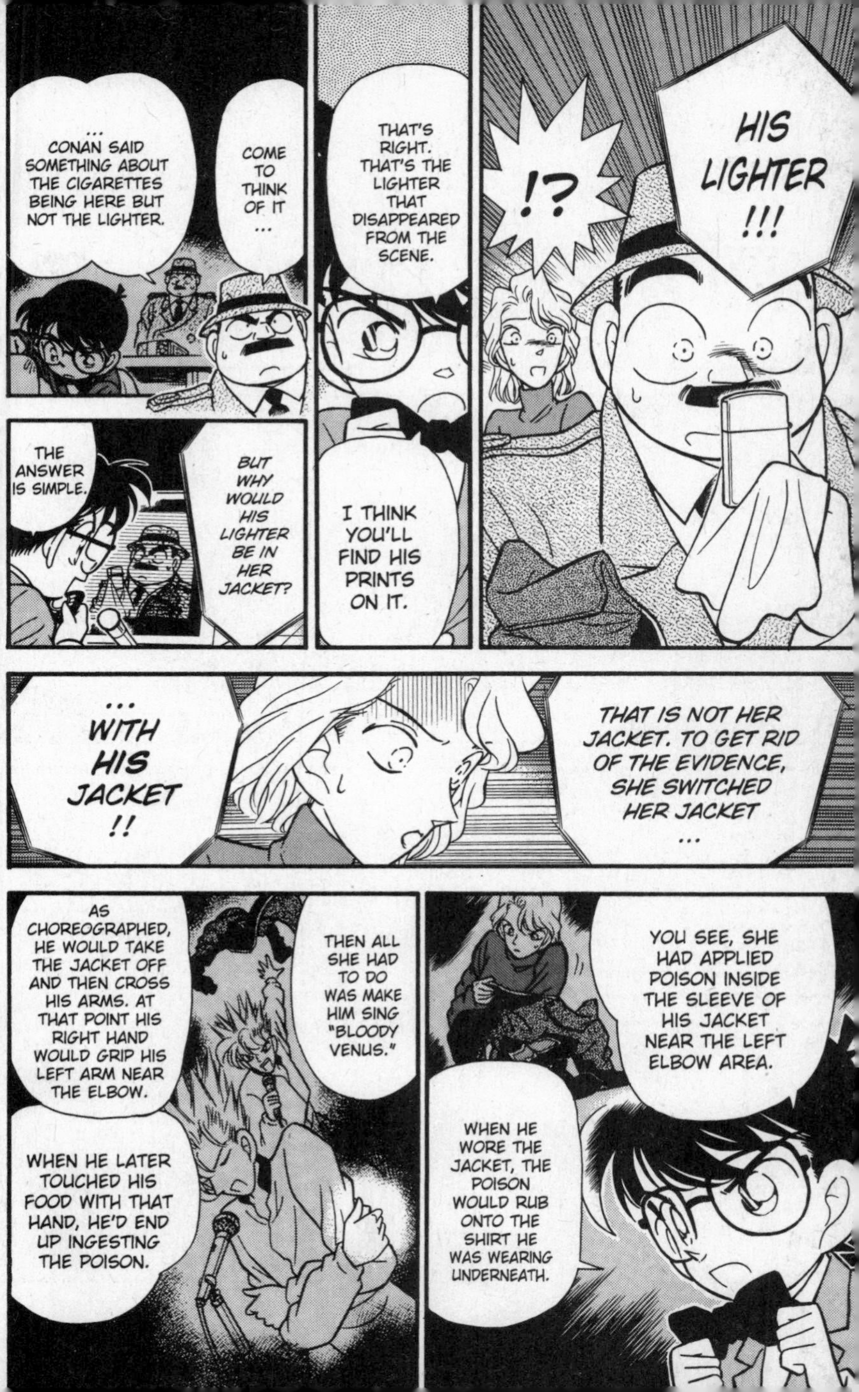
HIS LIGHTER !!!
!?
THAT'S RIGHT. THAT'S THE LIGHTER THAT DISAPPEARED FROM THE SCENE.
I THINK YOU'LL FIND HIS PRINTS ON IT.
COME TO THINK OF IT ...
... CONAN SAID SOMETHING ABOUT THE CIGARETTES BEING HERE BUT NOT THE LIGHTER.
BUT WHY WOULD HIS LIGHTER BE IN HER JACKET?
THE ANSWER IS SIMPLE.
THAT IS NOT HER JACKET. TO GET RID OF THE EVIDENCE, SHE SWITCHED HER JACKET ...
... WITH HIS JACKET !!
YOU SEE, SHE HAD APPLIED POISON INSIDE THE SLEEVE OF HIS JACKET NEAR THE LEFT ELBOW AREA.
WHEN HE WORE THE JACKET, THE POISON WOULD RUB ONTO THE SHIRT HE WAS WEARING UNDERNEATH.
THEN ALL SHE HAD TO DO WAS MAKE HIM SING "BLOODY VENUS."
AS CHOREOGRAPHED, HE WOULD TAKE THE JACKET OFF AND THEN CROSS HIS ARMS. AT THAT POINT HIS RIGHT HAND WOULD GRIP HIS LEFT ARM NEAR THE ELBOW.
WHEN HE LATER TOUCHED HIS FOOD WITH THAT HAND, HE'D END UP INGESTING THE POISON.

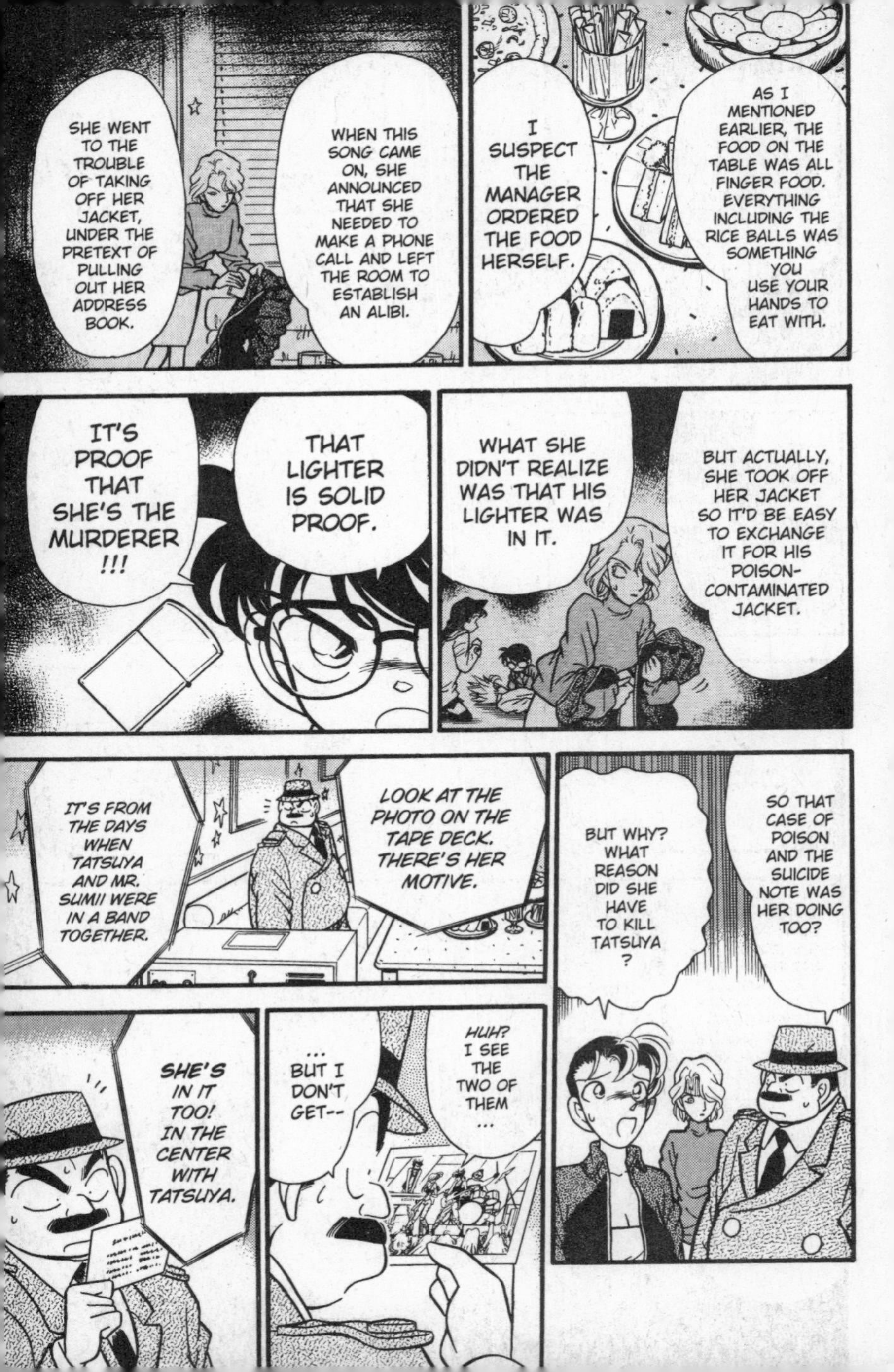

AS I MENTIONED EARLIER, THE FOOD ON THE TABLE WAS ALL FINGER FOOD. EVERYTHING INCLUDING THE RICE BALLS WAS SOMETHING YOU USE YOUR HANDS TO EAT WITH.
I SUSPECT THE MANAGER ORDERED THE FOOD HERSELF.
WHEN THIS SONG CAME ON, SHE ANNOUNCED THAT SHE NEEDED TO MAKE A PHONE CALL AND LEFT THE ROOM TO ESTABLISH AN ALIBI.
SHE WENT TO THE TROUBLE OF TAKING OFF HER JACKET, UNDER THE PRETEXT OF PULLING OUT HER ADDRESS BOOK.
BUT ACTUALLY, SHE TOOK OFF HER JACKET SO IT'D BE EASY TO EXCHANGE IT FOR HIS POISON-CONTAMINATED JACKET.
WHAT SHE DIDN'T REALIZE WAS THAT HIS LIGHTER WAS IN IT.
THAT LIGHTER IS SOLID PROOF.
IT'S PROOF THAT SHE'S THE MURDERER !!!
SO THAT CASE OF POISON AND THE SUICIDE NOTE WAS HER DOING TOO?
BUT WHY? WHAT REASON DID SHE HAVE TO KILL TATSUYA ?
LOOK AT THE PHOTO ON THE TAPE DECK. THERE'S HER MOTIVE.
IT'S FROM THE DAYS WHEN TATSUYA AND MR. SUMII WERE IN A BAND TOGETHER.
HUH? I SEE THE TWO OF THEM ...
... BUT I DON'T GET--
SHE'S IN IT TOO! IN THE CENTER WITH TATSUYA.

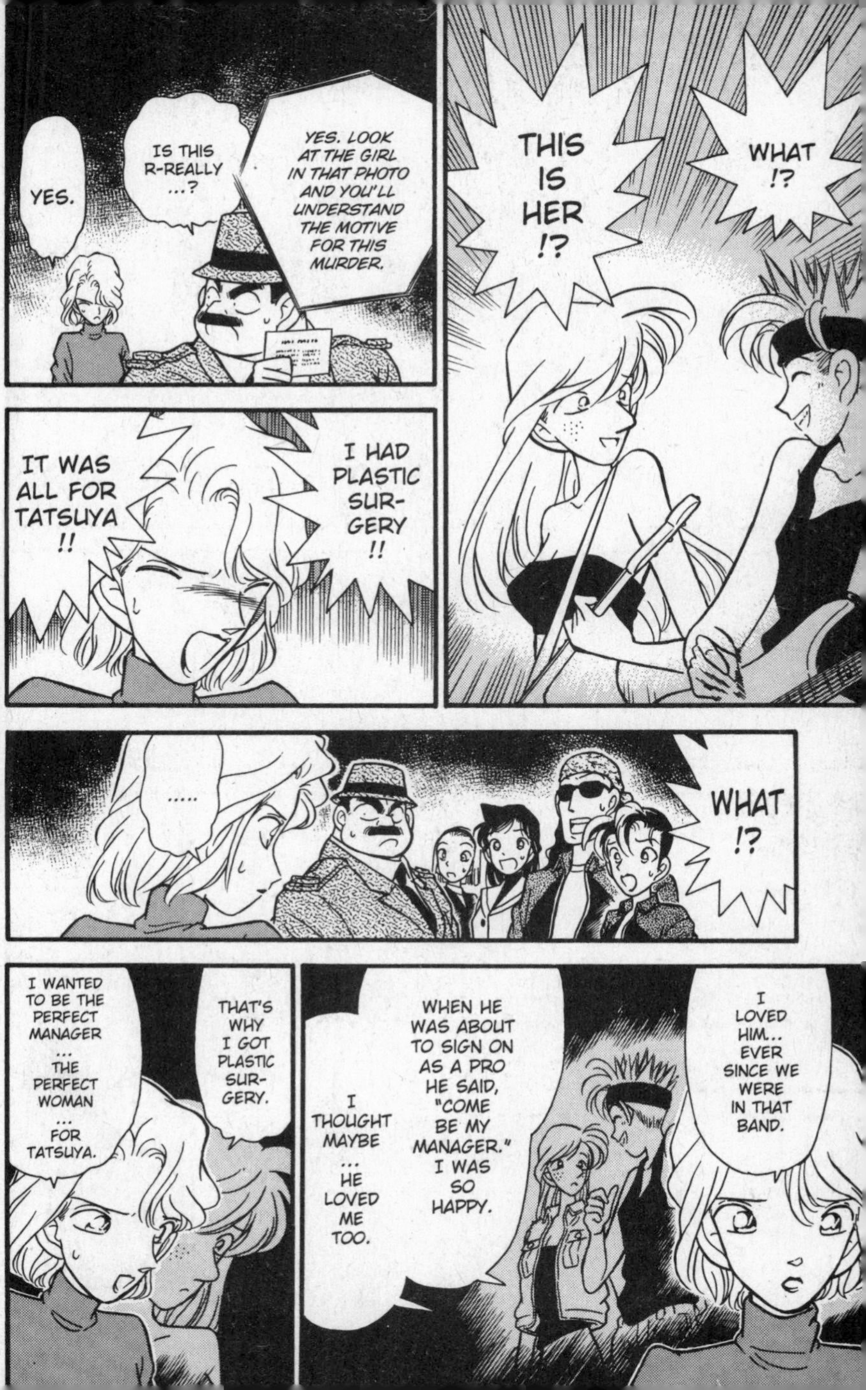
WHAT !?
THIS IS HER !?
YES. LOOK AT THE GIRL IN THAT PHOTO AND YOU'LL UNDERSTAND THE MOTIVE FOR THIS MURDER.
IS THIS R-REALLY ...?
YES.
I HAD PLASTIC SUR-GERY !!
IT WAS ALL FOR TATSUYA !!
WHAT !?
.....
I LOVED HIM.. EVER SINCE WE WERE IN THAT BAND.
WHEN HE WAS ABOUT TO SIGN ON AS A PRO HE SAID, "COME BE MY MANAGER." I WAS SO HAPPY.
I THOUGHT MAYBE ... HE LOVED ME TOO.
THAT'S WHY I GOT PLASTIC SUR-GERY.
I WANTED TO BE THE PERFECT MANAGER ... THE PERFECT WOMAN ... FOR TATSUYA.

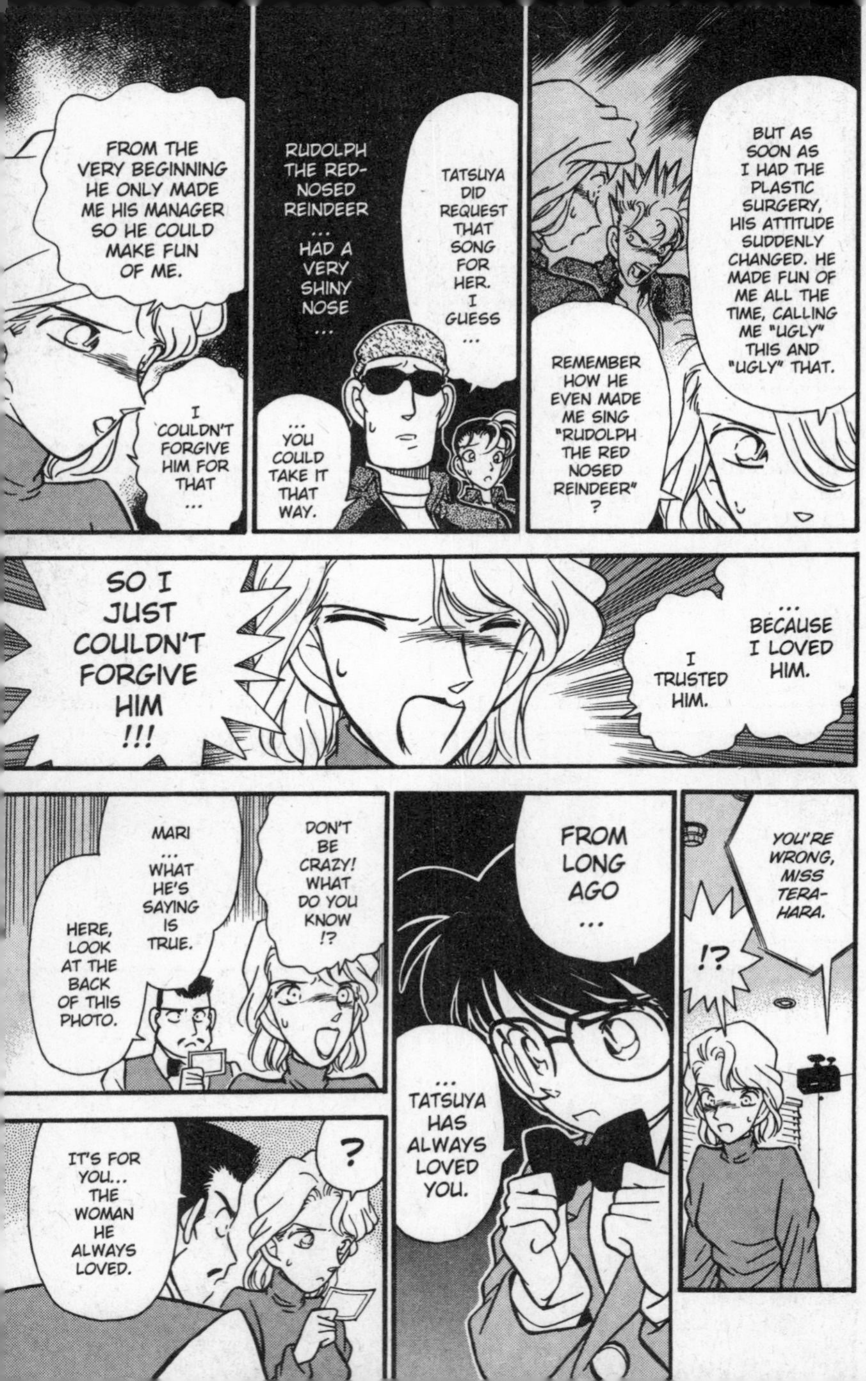
BUT AS SOON AS I HAD THE PLASTIC SURGERY, HIS ATTITUDE SUDDENLY CHANGED. HE MADE FUN OF ME ALL THE TIME, CALLING ME "UGLY" THIS AND "UGLY" THAT.
REMEMBER HOW HE EVEN MADE ME SING "RUDOLPH THE RED NOSED REINDEER"?
TATSUYA DID REQUEST THAT SONG FOR HER. I GUESS...
RUDOLPH THE RED-NOSED REINDEER... HAD A VERY SHINY NOSE...
...YOU COULD TAKE IT THAT WAY.
FROM THE VERY BEGINNING HE ONLY MADE ME HIS MANAGER SO HE COULD MAKE FUN OF ME.
I COULDN'T FORGIVE HIM FOR THAT...
...BECAUSE I LOVED HIM.
I TRUSTED HIM.
SO I JUST COULDN'T FORGIVE HIM!!!
YOU'RE WRONG, MISS TERA-HARA.
!?
FROM LONG AGO...
...TATSUYA HAS ALWAYS LOVED YOU.
DON'T BE CRAZY! WHAT DO YOU KNOW!?
MARI... WHAT HE'S SAYING IS TRUE.
HERE, LOOK AT THE BACK OF THIS PHOTO.
?
IT'S FOR YOU... THE WOMAN HE ALWAYS LOVED.

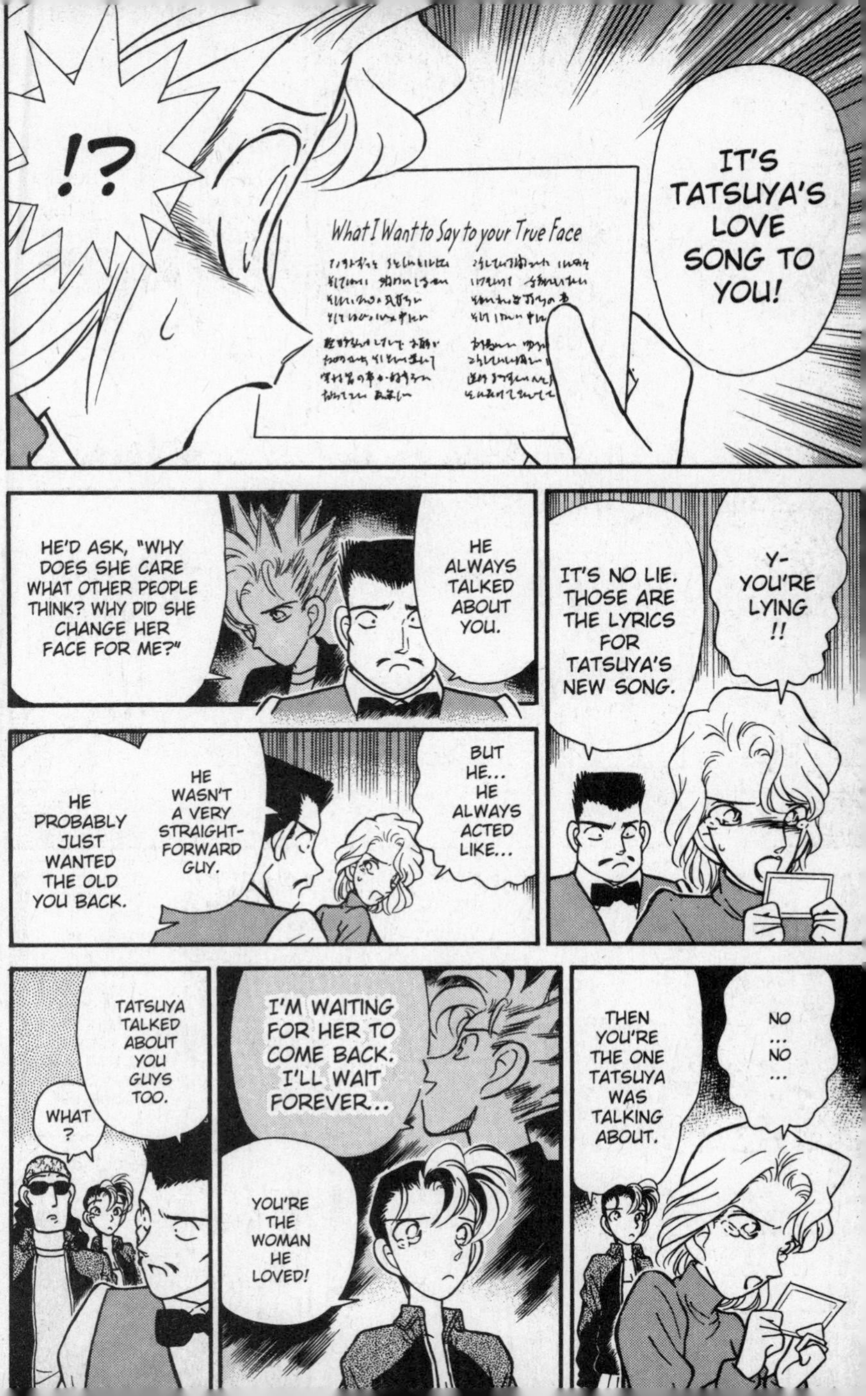
IT'S TATSUYA'S LOVE SONG TO YOU!
What I Want to Say to your True Face
!?
Y-YOU'RE LYING!!
IT'S NO LIE. THOSE ARE THE LYRICS FOR TATSUYA'S NEW SONG.
HE ALWAYS TALKED ABOUT YOU.
HE'D ASK, "WHY DOES SHE CARE WHAT OTHER PEOPLE THINK? WHY DID SHE CHANGE HER FACE FOR ME?"
BUT HE... HE ALWAYS ACTED LIKE...
HE WASN'T A VERY STRAIGHT-FORWARD GUY.
HE PROBABLY JUST WANTED THE OLD YOU BACK.
NO... NO...
THEN YOU'RE THE ONE TATSUYA WAS TALKING ABOUT.
I'M WAITING FOR HER TO COME BACK. I'LL WAIT FOREVER...
YOU'RE THE WOMAN HE LOVED!
TATSUYA TALKED ABOUT YOU GUYS TOO.
WHAT?

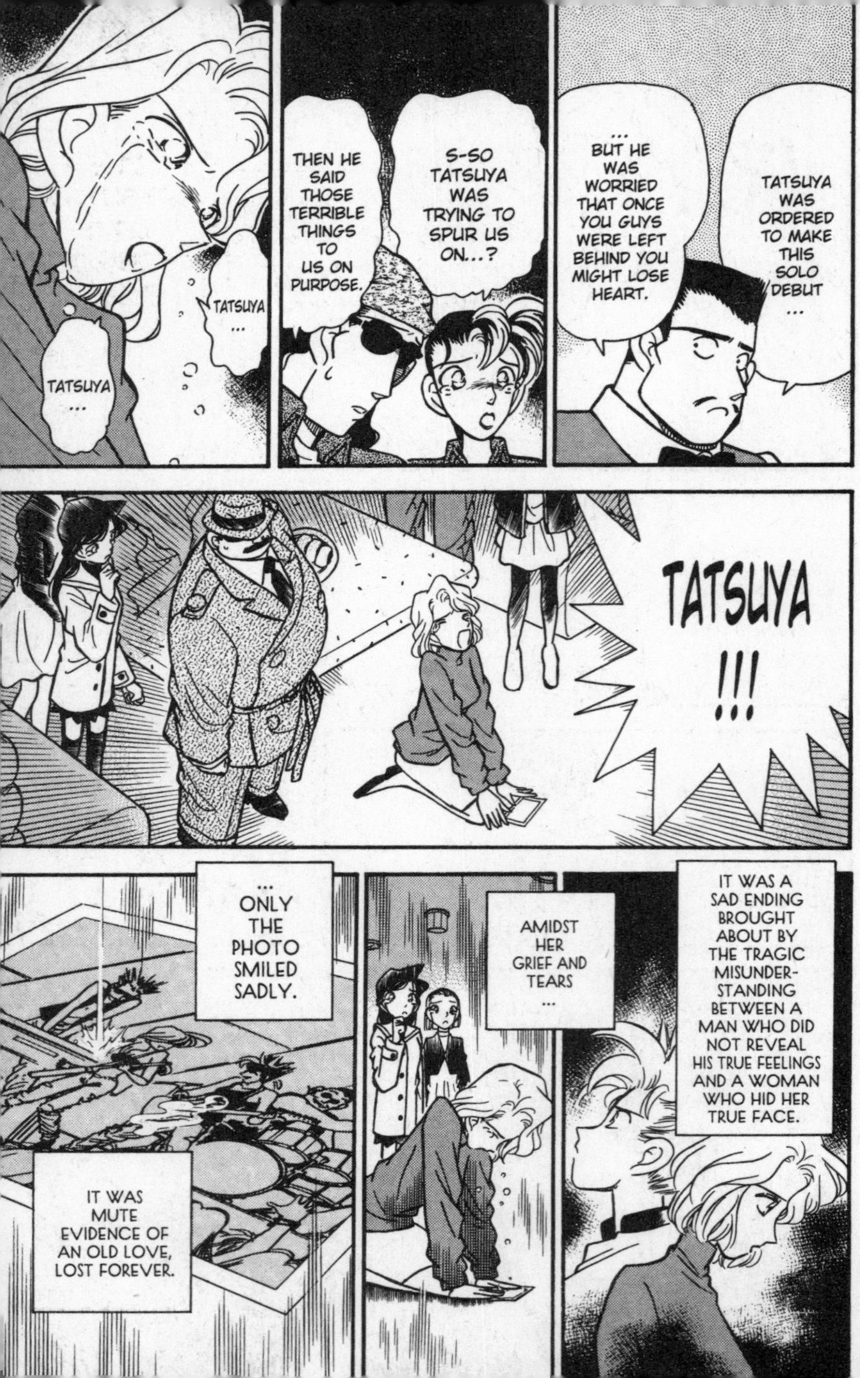
TATSUYA WAS ORDERED TO MAKE THIS SOLO DEBUT ...
... BUT HE WAS WORRIED THAT ONCE YOU GUYS WERE LEFT BEHIND YOU MIGHT LOSE HEART.
S-SO TATSUYA WAS TRYING TO SPUR US ON...?
THEN HE SAID THOSE TERRIBLE THINGS TO US ON PURPOSE.
TATSUYA ...
TATSUYA ...
TATSUYA !!!
IT WAS A SAD ENDING BROUGHT ABOUT BY THE TRAGIC MISUNDER-STANDING BETWEEN A MAN WHO DID NOT REVEAL HIS TRUE FEELINGS AND A WOMAN WHO HID HER TRUE FACE.
AMIDST HER GRIEF AND TEARS ...
... ONLY THE PHOTO SMILED SADLY.
IT WAS MUTE EVIDENCE OF AN OLD LOVE, LOST FOREVER.

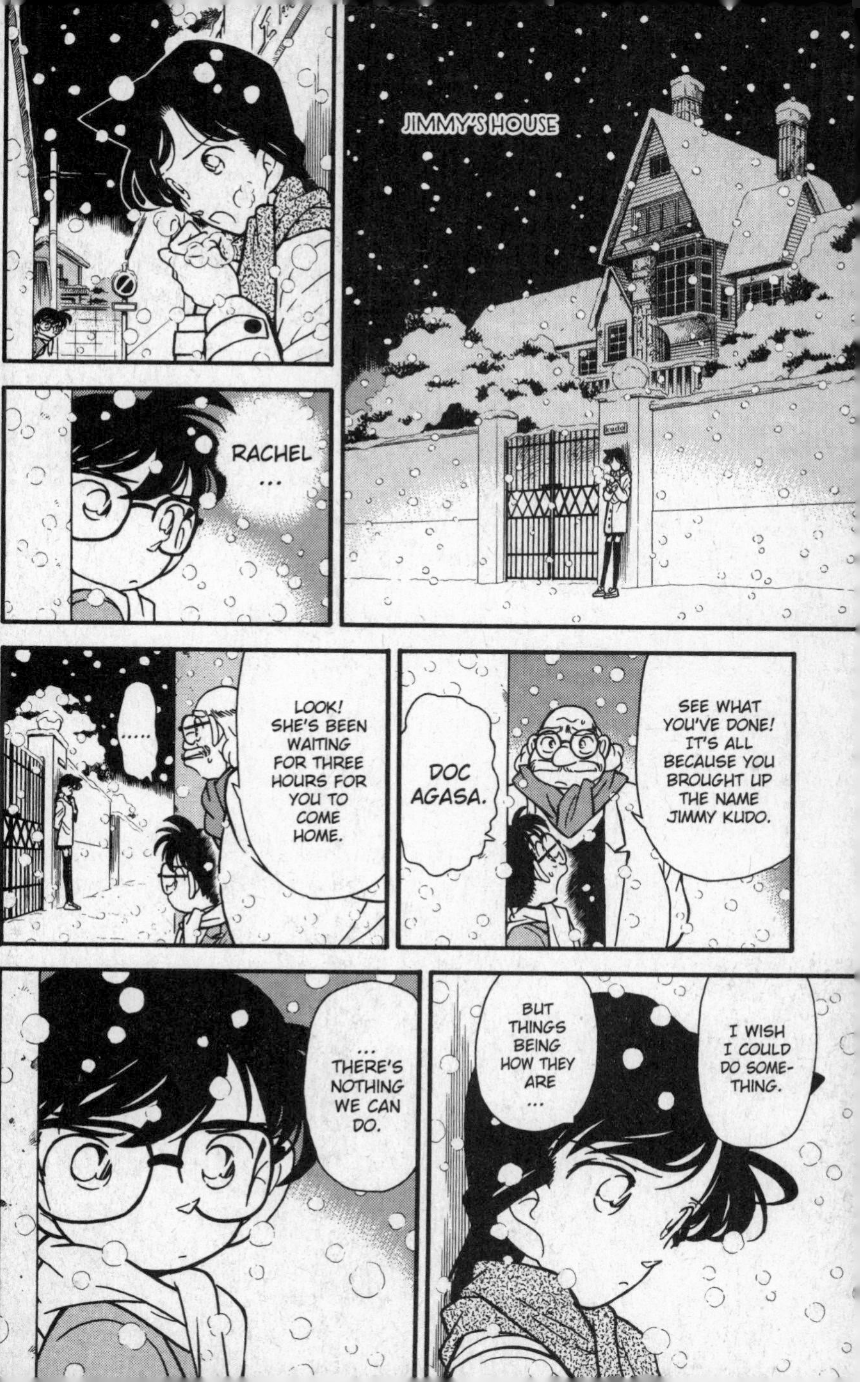
JIMMY'S HOUSE
RACHEL ...
SEE WHAT YOU'VE DONE! IT'S ALL BECAUSE YOU BROUGHT UP THE NAME JIMMY KUDO.
DOC AGASA.
LOOK! SHE'S BEEN WAITING FOR THREE HOURS FOR YOU TO COME HOME.
......
I WISH I COULD DO SOME-THING.
BUT THINGS BEING HOW THEY ARE ...
... THERE'S NOTHING WE CAN DO.

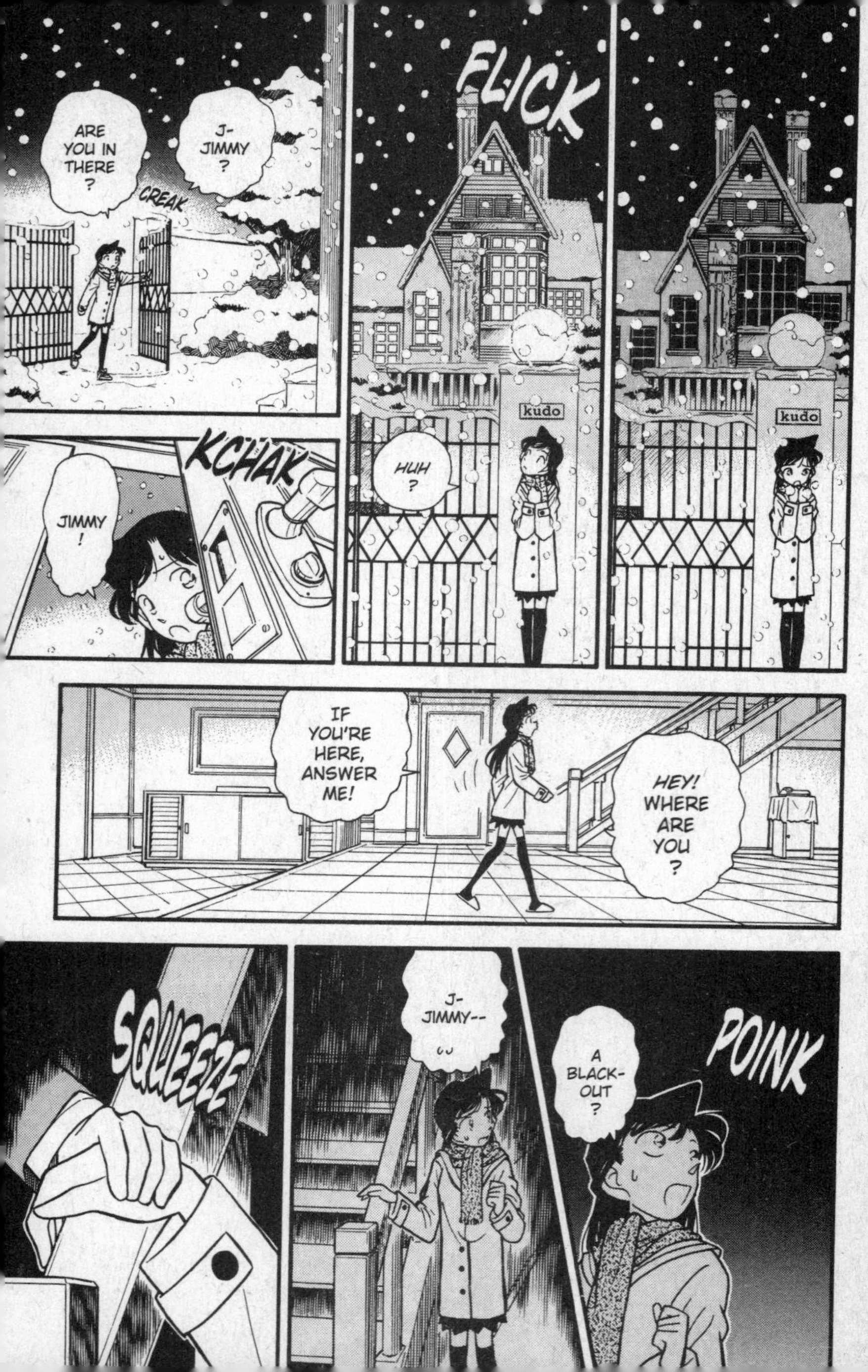
FLICK
HUH?
J-JIMMY?
ARE YOU IN THERE?
CREAK
KCHAK
JIMMY!
HEY! WHERE ARE YOU?
IF YOU'RE HERE, ANSWER ME!
POINK
A BLACK-OUT?
J-JIMMY--
SQUEEZE

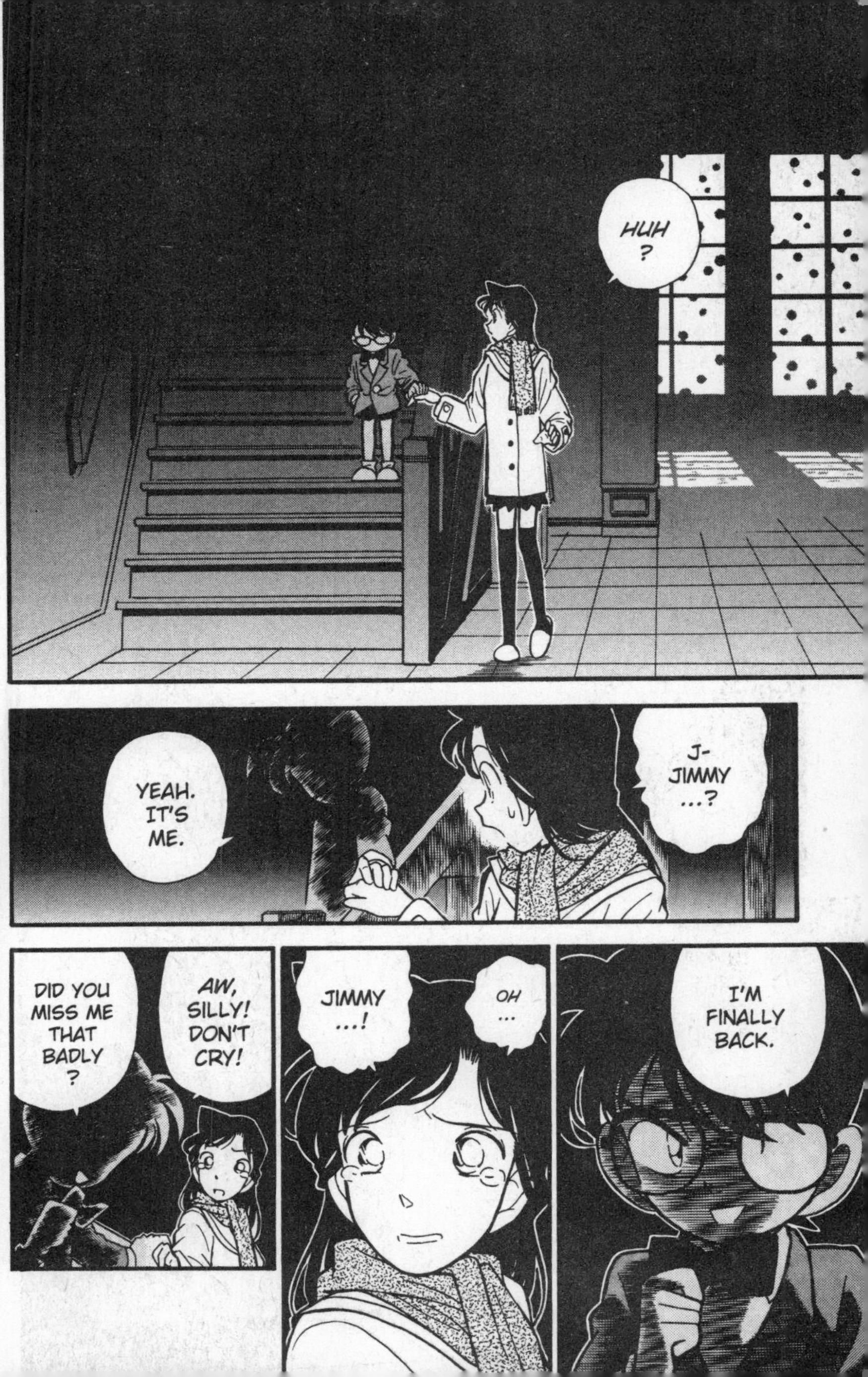
HUH ?
J- JIMMY ...?
YEAH. IT'S ME.
I'M FINALLY BACK.
OH ...
JIMMY ...!
AW, SILLY! DON'T CRY!
DID YOU MISS ME THAT BADLY ?

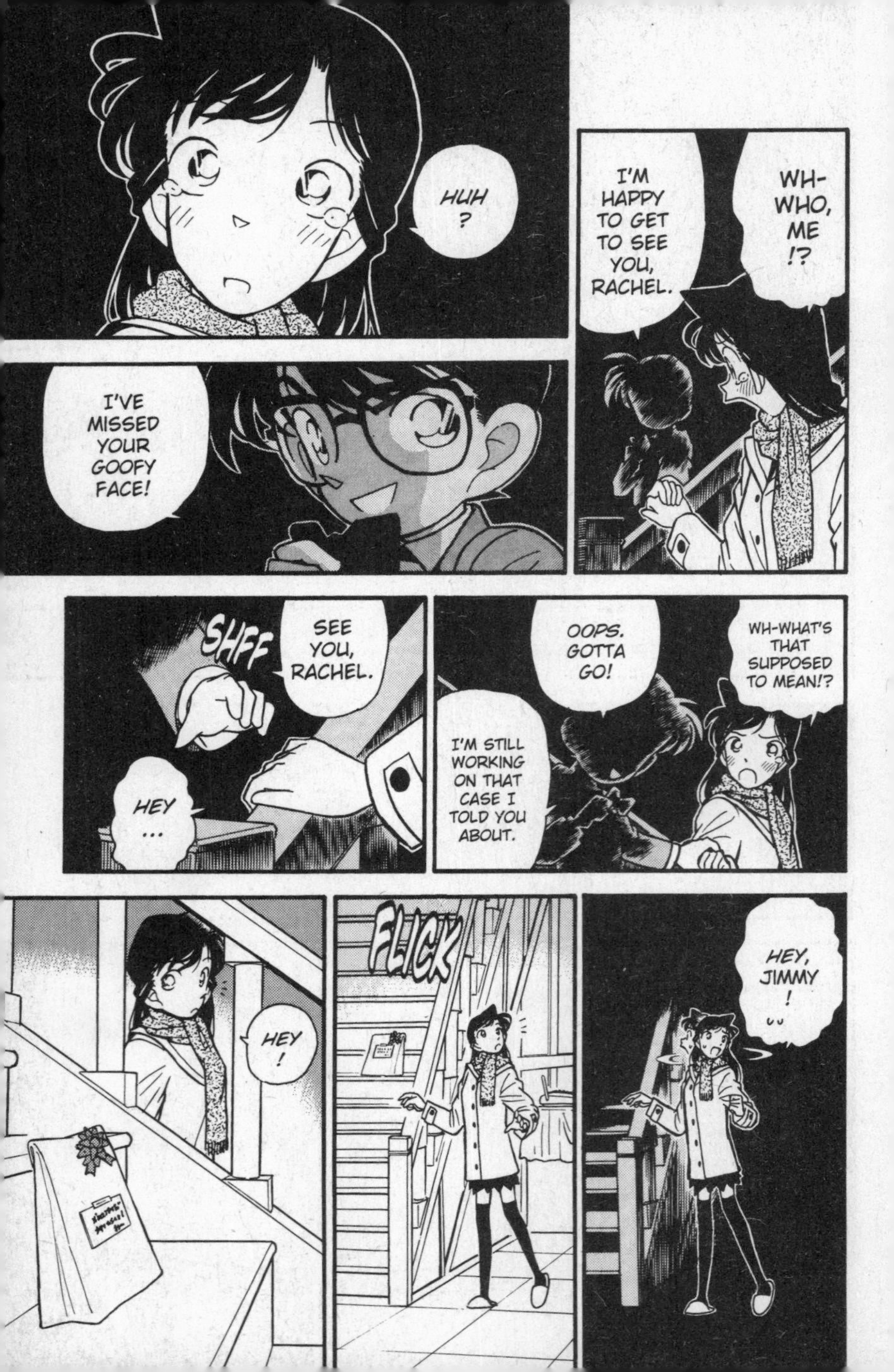
HUH ?
I'M HAPPY TO GET TO SEE YOU, RACHEL.
WH-WHO, ME !?
I'VE MISSED YOUR GOOFY FACE!
WH-WHAT'S THAT SUPPOSED TO MEAN!?
OOPS. GOTTA GO!
I'M STILL WORKING ON THAT CASE I TOLD YOU ABOUT.
SEE YOU, RACHEL.
SHFF
HEY ...
HEY, JIMMY !
FLICK
HEY !

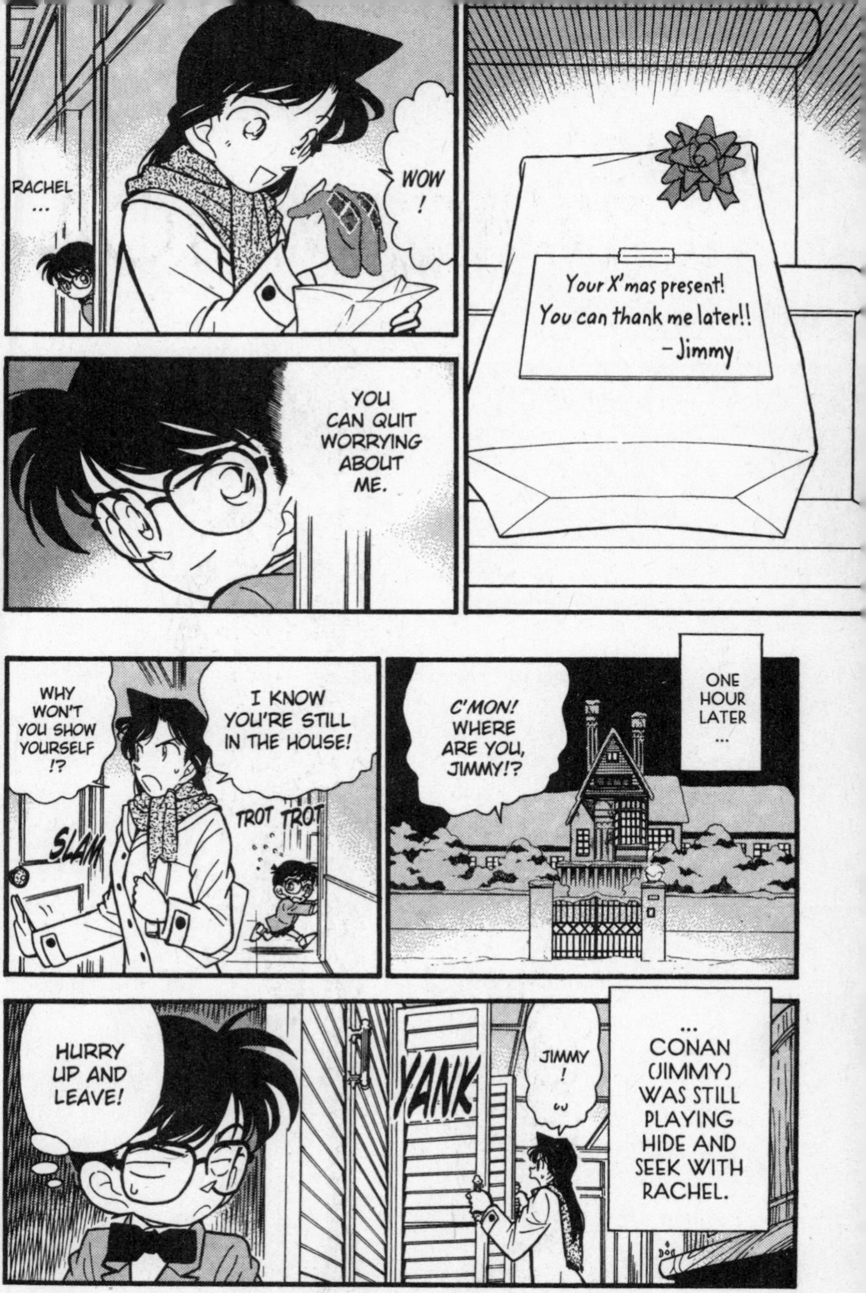
Your X'mas present!
You can thank me later!!
– Jimmy
WOW!
RACHEL ...
YOU CAN QUIT WORRYING ABOUT ME.
ONE HOUR LATER ...
C'MON! WHERE ARE YOU, JIMMY!?
I KNOW YOU'RE STILL IN THE HOUSE!
WHY WON'T YOU SHOW YOURSELF!?
TROT TROT
SLAM
... CONAN (JIMMY) WAS STILL PLAYING HIDE AND SEEK WITH RACHEL.
JIMMY!
YANK
HURRY UP AND LEAVE!

FILE 10:
A STRANGE VISITOR

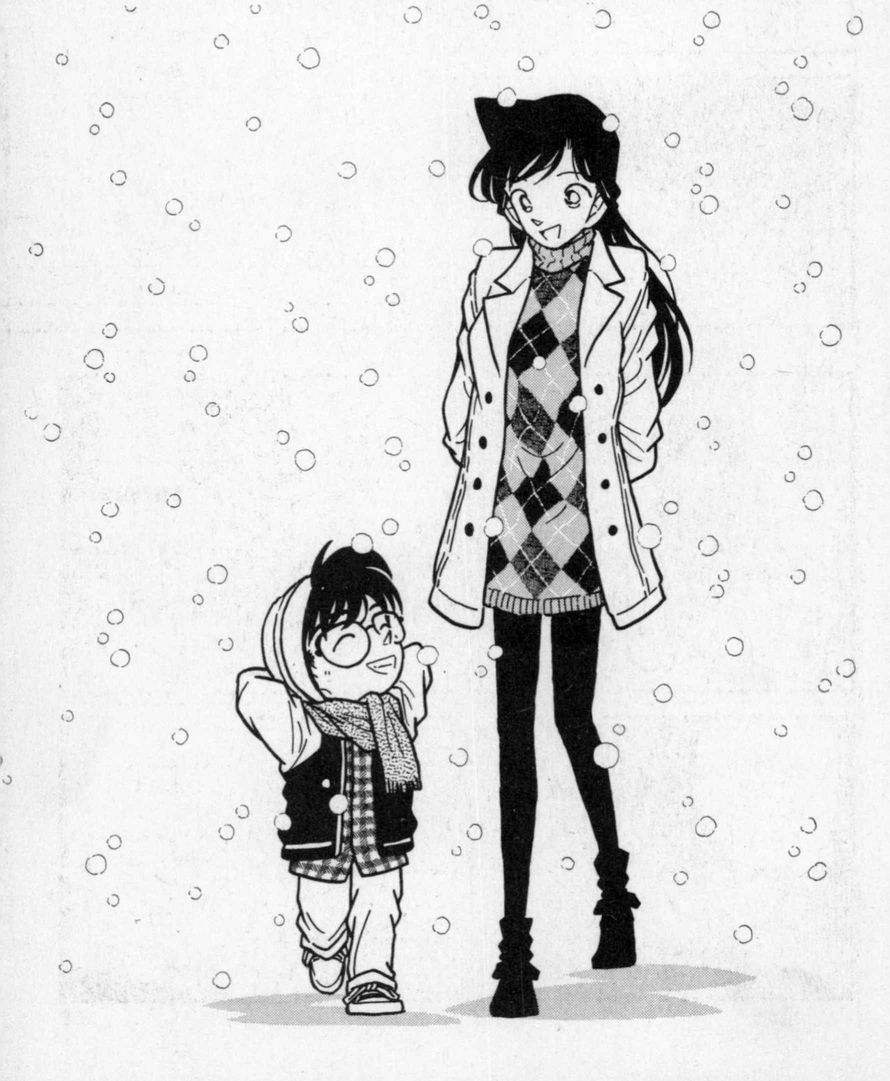

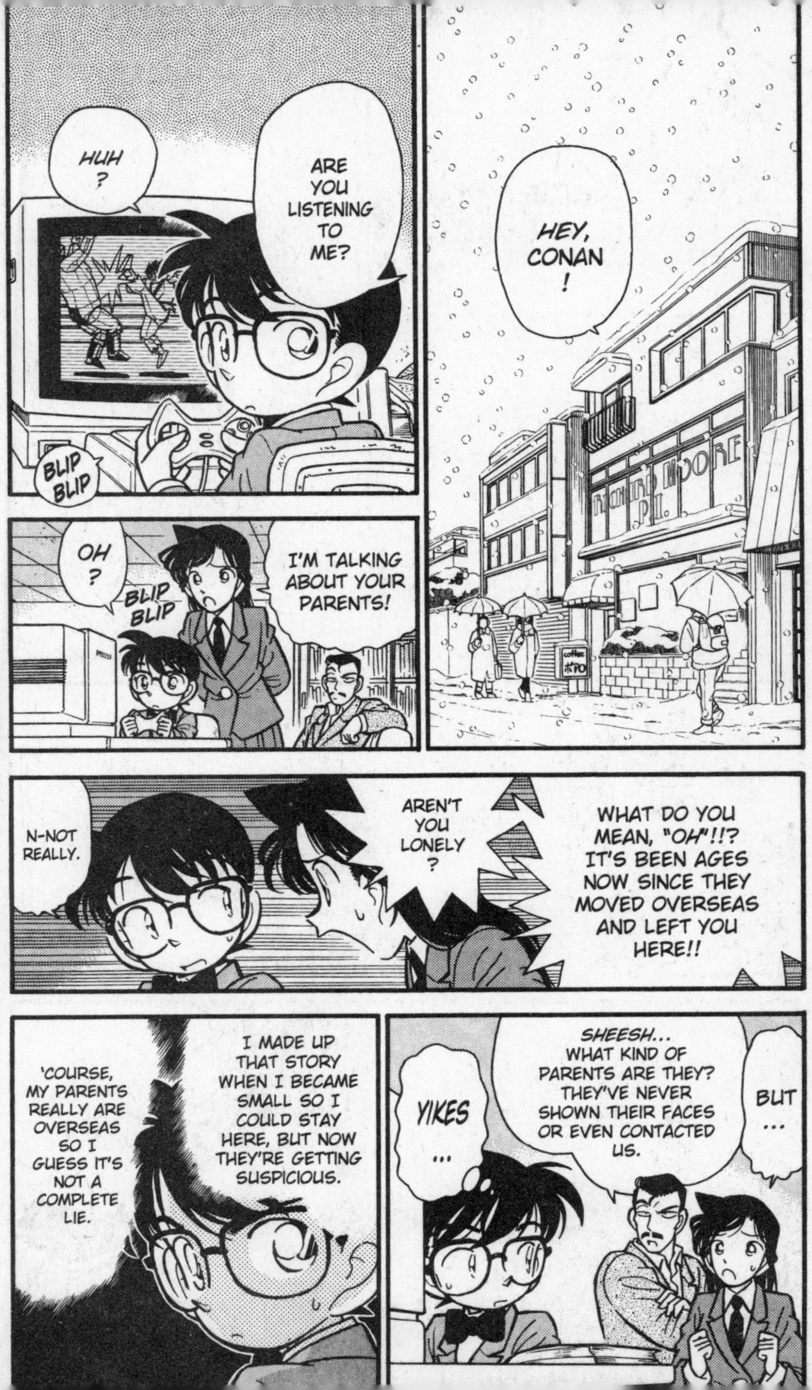
HEY, CONAN!
ARE YOU LISTENING TO ME?
HUH?
BLIP BLIP
I'M TALKING ABOUT YOUR PARENTS!
OH?
BLIP BLIP
WHAT DO YOU MEAN, "OH"!!? IT'S BEEN AGES NOW SINCE THEY MOVED OVERSEAS AND LEFT YOU HERE!!
AREN'T YOU LONELY?
N-NOT REALLY.
BUT...
SHEESH... WHAT KIND OF PARENTS ARE THEY? THEY'VE NEVER SHOWN THEIR FACES OR EVEN CONTACTED US.
YIKES...
I MADE UP THAT STORY WHEN I BECAME SMALL SO I COULD STAY HERE, BUT NOW THEY'RE GETTING SUSPICIOUS.
'COURSE, MY PARENTS REALLY ARE OVERSEAS SO I GUESS IT'S NOT A COMPLETE LIE.

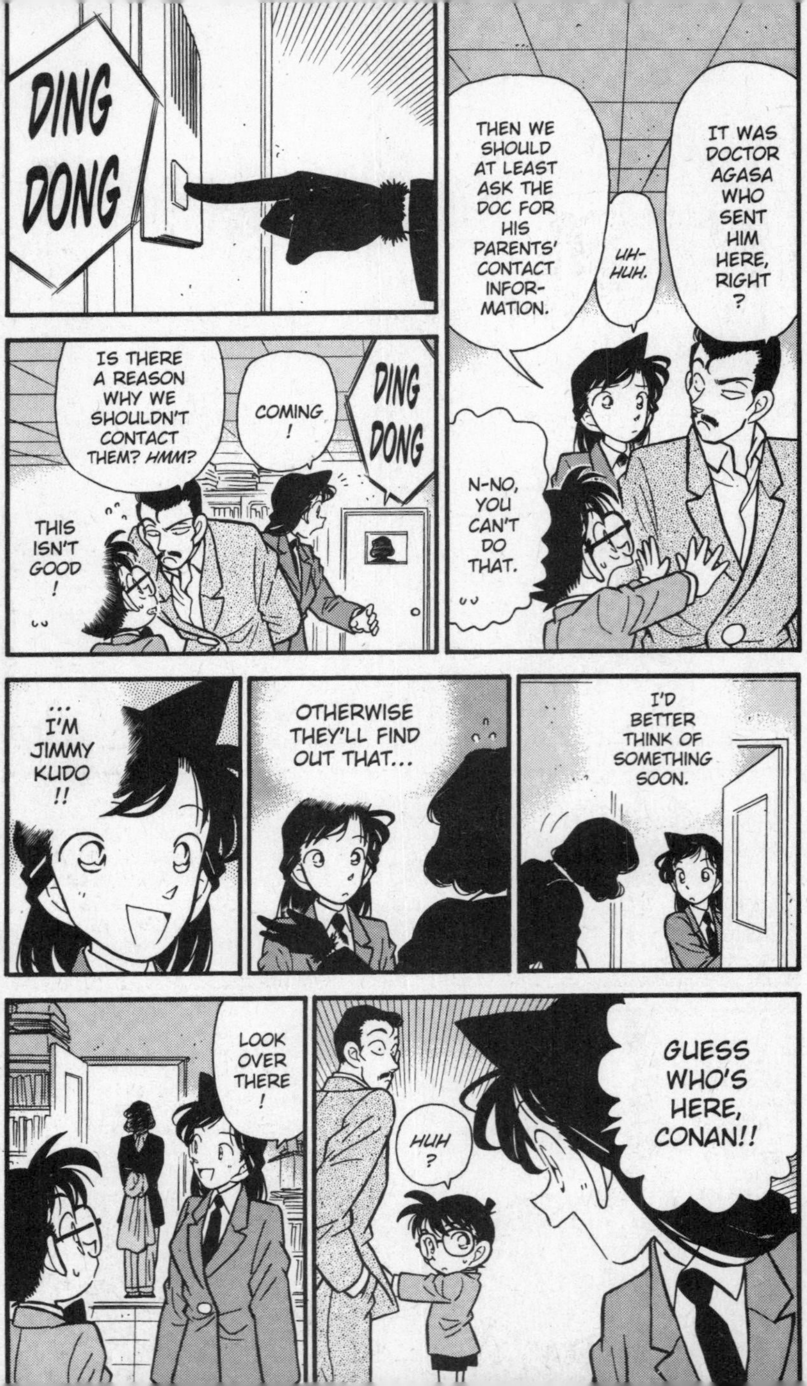
IT WAS DOCTOR AGASA WHO SENT HIM HERE, RIGHT?
UH-HUH.
THEN WE SHOULD AT LEAST ASK THE DOC FOR HIS PARENTS' CONTACT INFORMATION.
N-NO, YOU CAN'T DO THAT.
DING DONG
DING DONG
COMING!
IS THERE A REASON WHY WE SHOULDN'T CONTACT THEM? *HMM?*
THIS ISN'T GOOD!
I'D BETTER THINK OF SOMETHING SOON.
OTHERWISE THEY'LL FIND OUT THAT...
... I'M JIMMY KUDO!!
GUESS WHO'S HERE, CONAN!!
HUH?
LOOK OVER THERE!

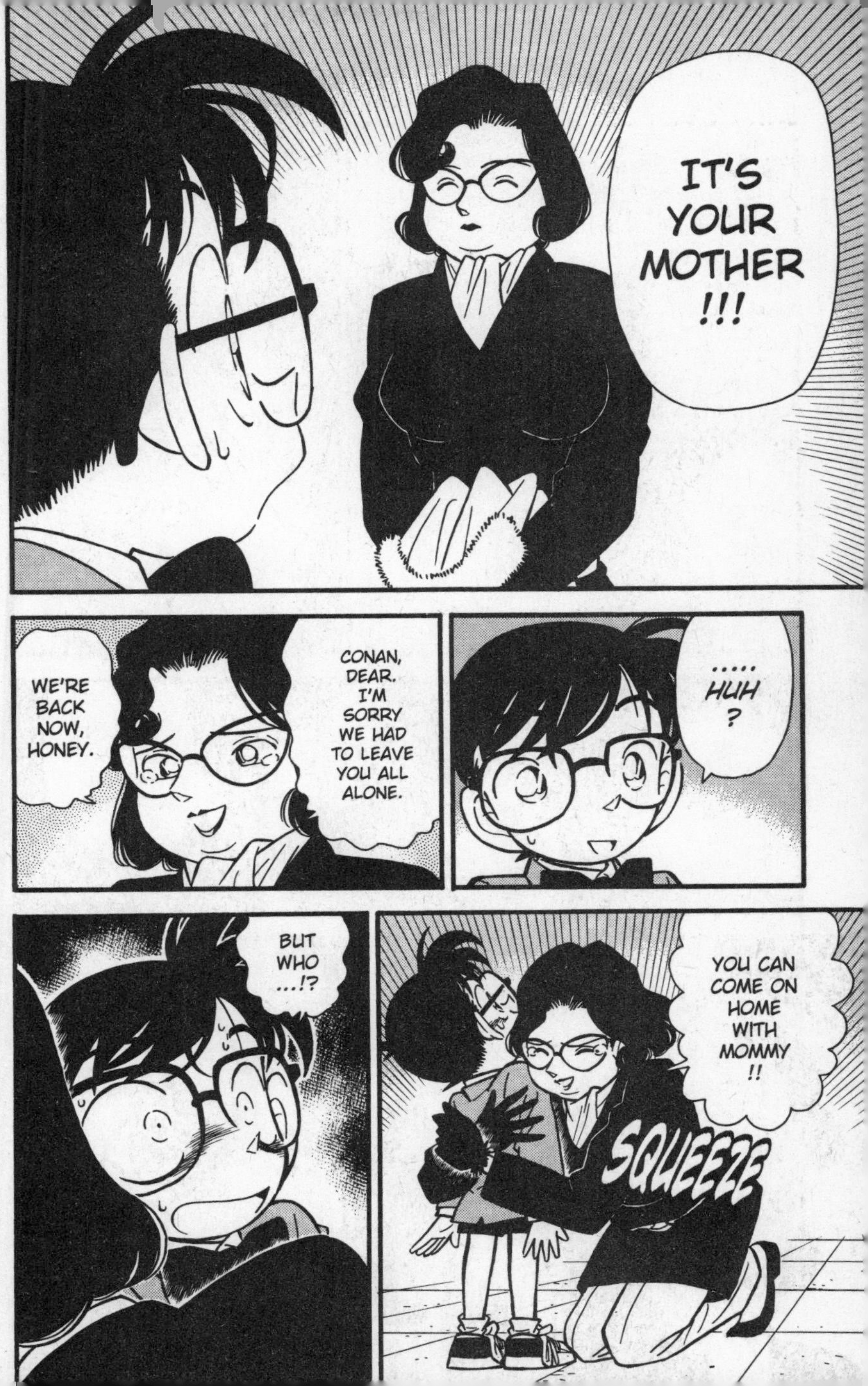
IT'S YOUR MOTHER !!!
.....HUH?
CONAN, DEAR. I'M SORRY WE HAD TO LEAVE YOU ALL ALONE.
WE'RE BACK NOW, HONEY.
YOU CAN COME ON HOME WITH MOMMY !!
SQUEEZE
BUT WHO ...!?

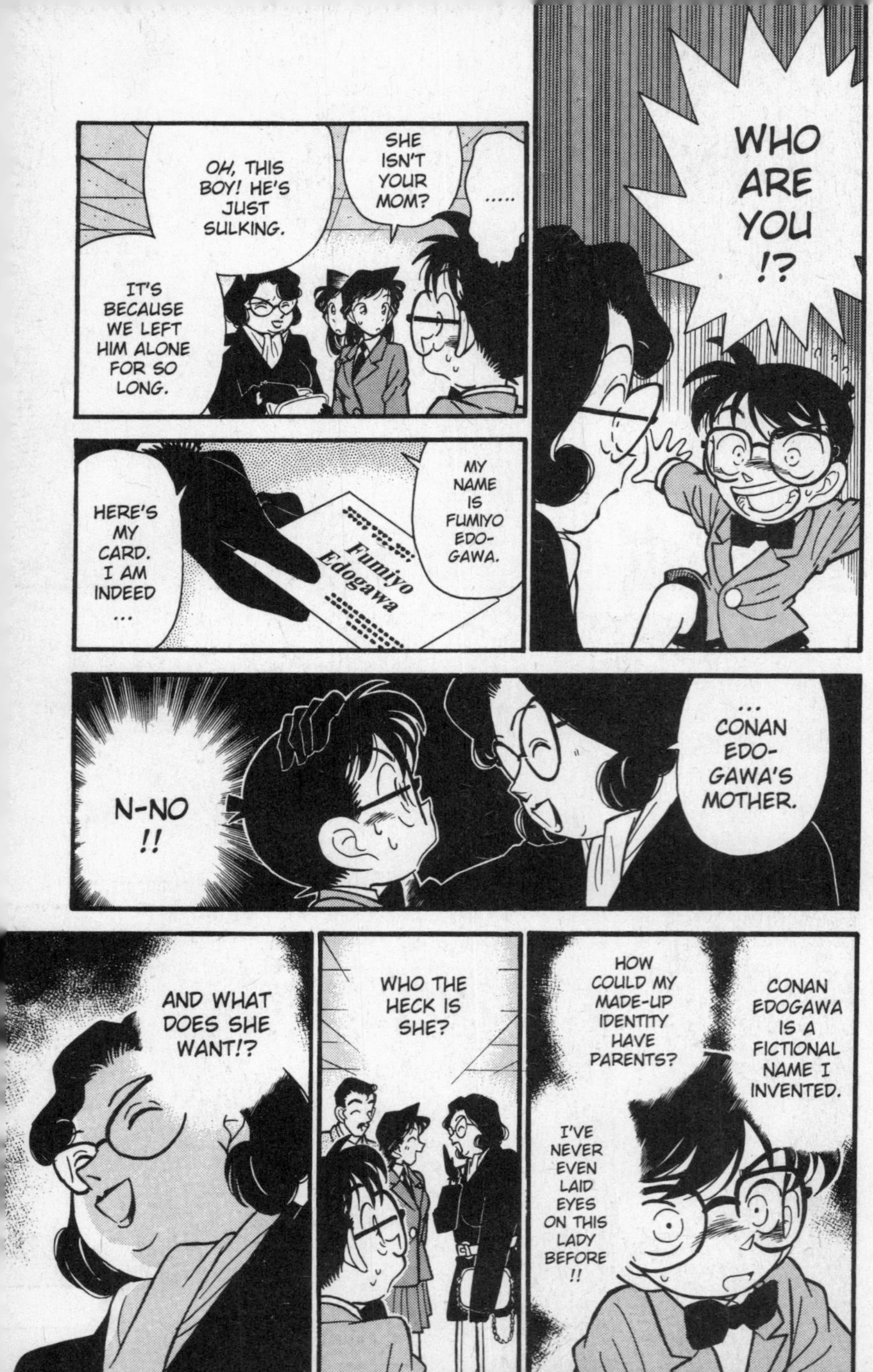
WHO ARE YOU !?
.....
SHE ISN'T YOUR MOM?
OH, THIS BOY! HE'S JUST SULKING.
IT'S BECAUSE WE LEFT HIM ALONE FOR SO LONG.
MY NAME IS FUMIYO EDOGAWA.
Fumiyo Edogawa
HERE'S MY CARD. I AM INDEED ...
... CONAN EDOGAWA'S MOTHER.
N-NO !!
CONAN EDOGAWA IS A FICTIONAL NAME I INVENTED.
HOW COULD MY MADE-UP IDENTITY HAVE PARENTS?
I'VE NEVER EVEN LAID EYES ON THIS LADY BEFORE !!
WHO THE HECK IS SHE?
AND WHAT DOES SHE WANT!?

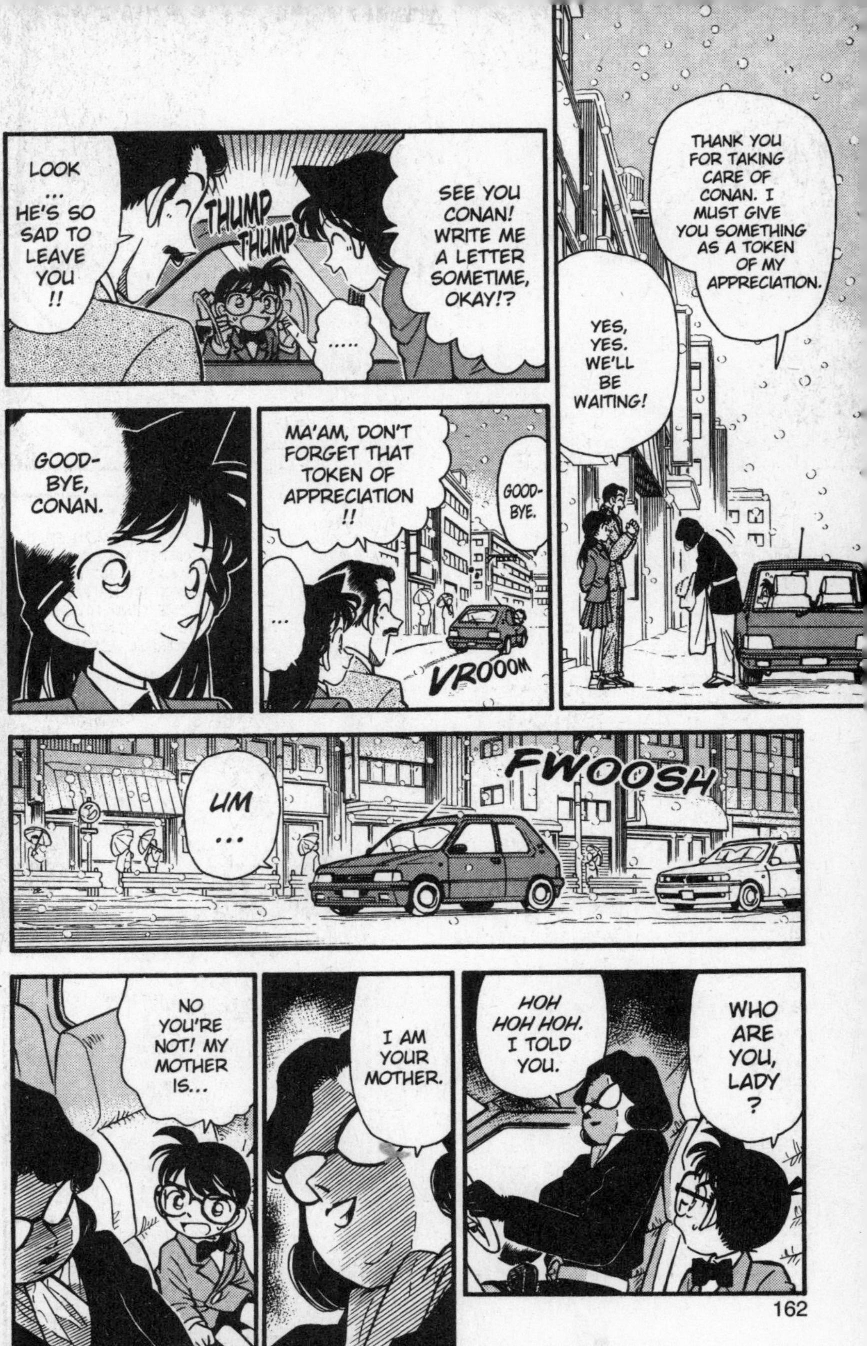
THANK YOU FOR TAKING CARE OF CONAN. I MUST GIVE YOU SOMETHING AS A TOKEN OF MY APPRECIATION.
YES, YES. WE'LL BE WAITING!
SEE YOU CONAN! WRITE ME A LETTER SOMETIME, OKAY!?
THUMP THUMP
LOOK ... HE'S SO SAD TO LEAVE YOU !!
.....
GOOD-BYE.
MA'AM, DON'T FORGET THAT TOKEN OF APPRECIATION !!
...
VROOOM
GOOD-BYE, CONAN.
FWOOSH
UM ...
WHO ARE YOU, LADY ?
HOH HOH HOH. I TOLD YOU.
I AM YOUR MOTHER.
NO YOU'RE NOT! MY MOTHER IS...

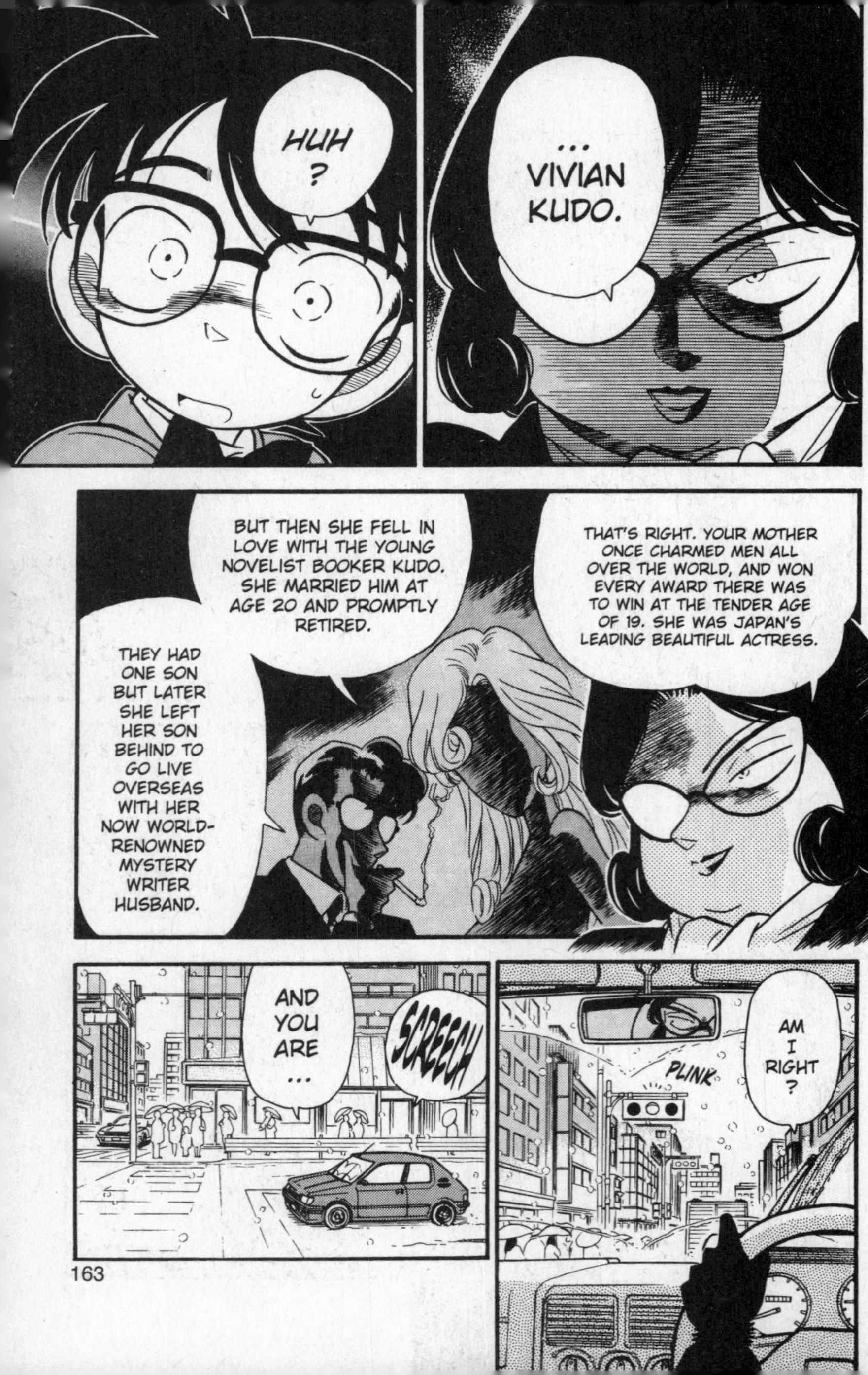
... VIVIAN KUDO.
HUH ?
THAT'S RIGHT. YOUR MOTHER ONCE CHARMED MEN ALL OVER THE WORLD, AND WON EVERY AWARD THERE WAS TO WIN AT THE TENDER AGE OF 19. SHE WAS JAPAN'S LEADING BEAUTIFUL ACTRESS.
BUT THEN SHE FELL IN LOVE WITH THE YOUNG NOVELIST BOOKER KUDO. SHE MARRIED HIM AT AGE 20 AND PROMPTLY RETIRED.
THEY HAD ONE SON BUT LATER SHE LEFT HER SON BEHIND TO GO LIVE OVERSEAS WITH HER NOW WORLD-RENOWNED MYSTERY WRITER HUSBAND.
AM I RIGHT ?
PLINK
SCREECH
AND YOU ARE ...

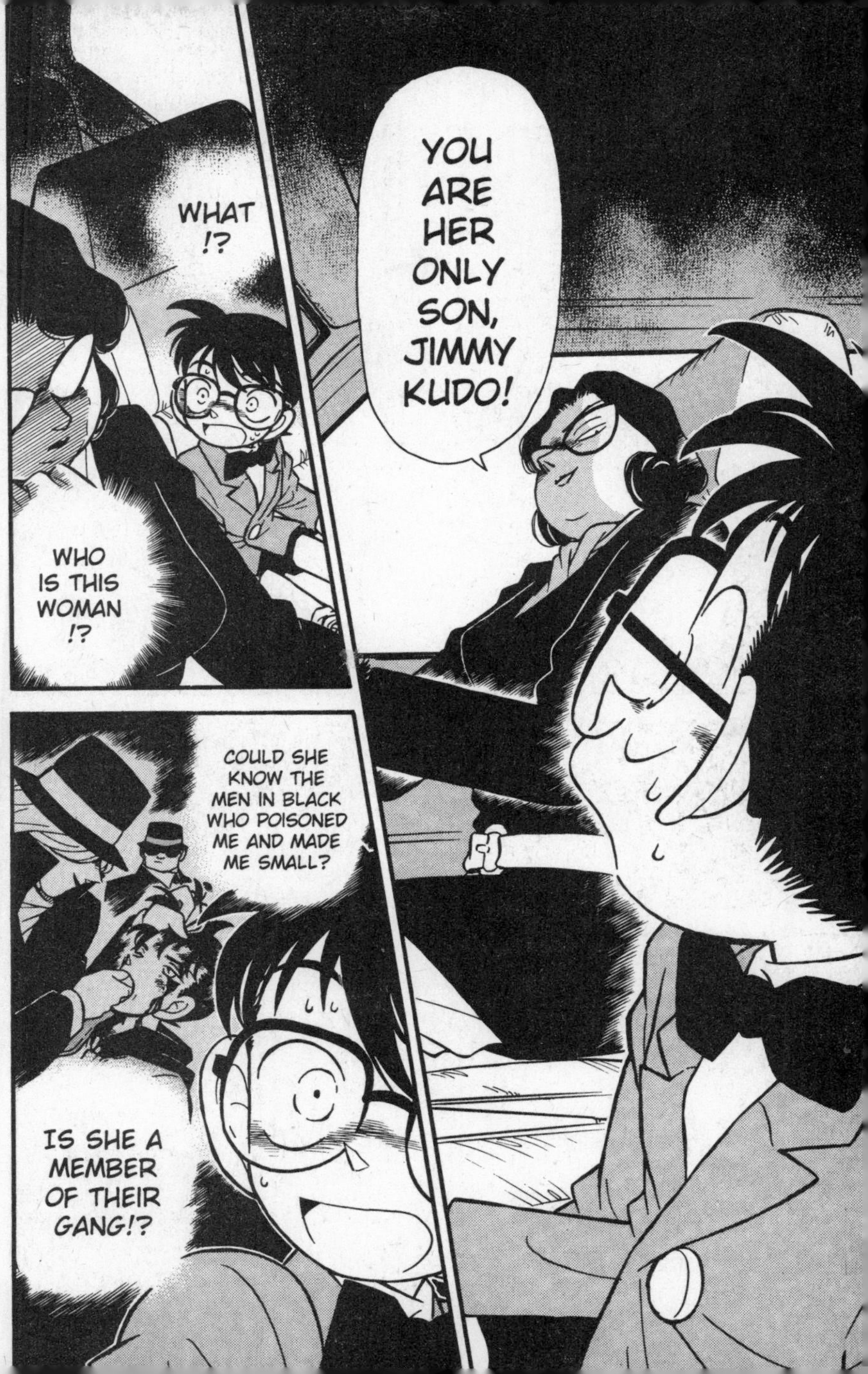
YOU ARE HER ONLY SON, JIMMY KUDO!
WHAT !?
WHO IS THIS WOMAN !?
COULD SHE KNOW THE MEN IN BLACK WHO POISONED ME AND MADE ME SMALL?
IS SHE A MEMBER OF THEIR GANG!?

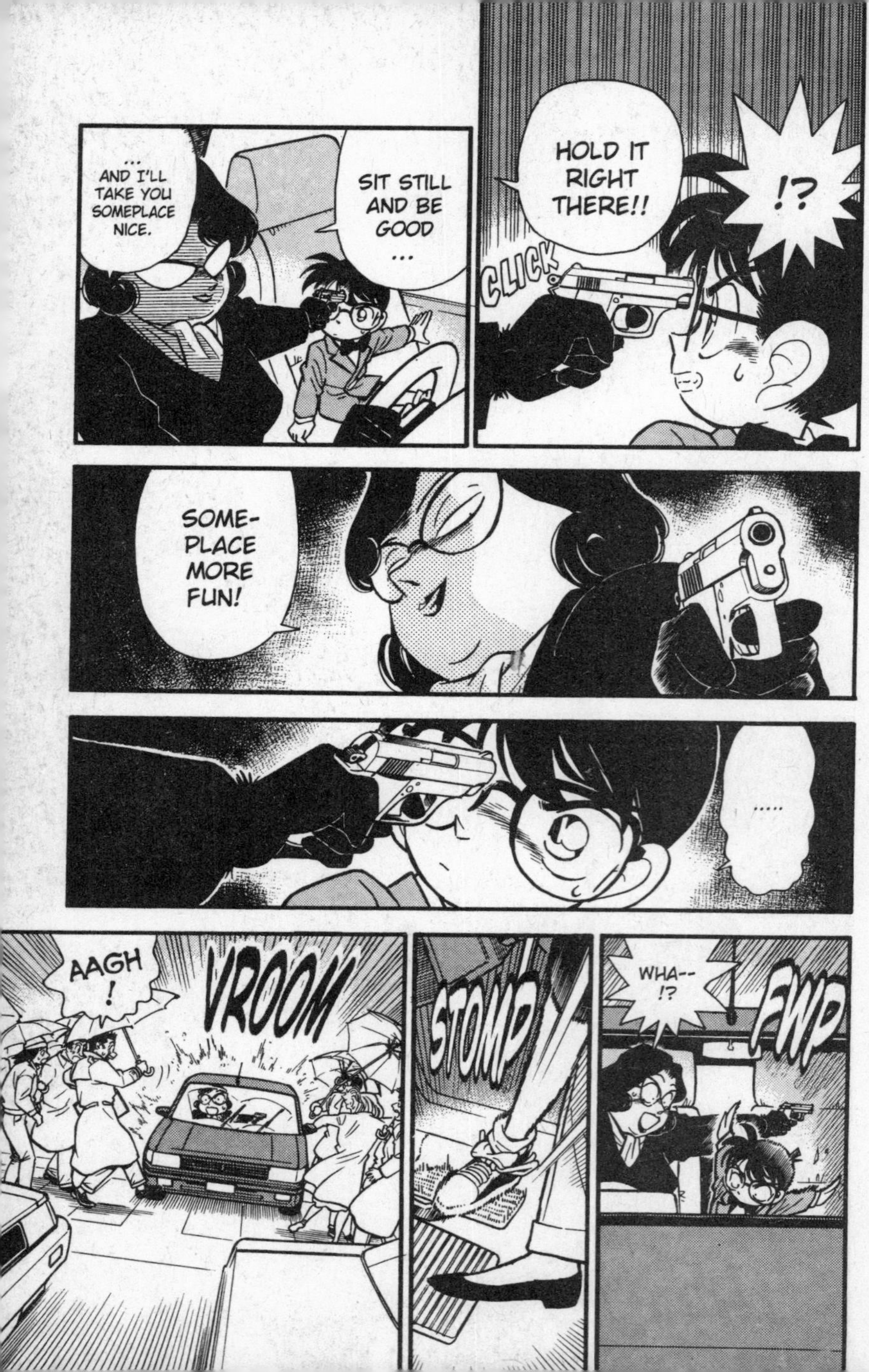
!?
HOLD IT RIGHT THERE!!
CLICK
SIT STILL AND BE GOOD ...
... AND I'LL TAKE YOU SOMEPLACE NICE.
SOME-PLACE MORE FUN!
.....
WHA-- !?
FWP
STOMP
VROOM
AAGH !

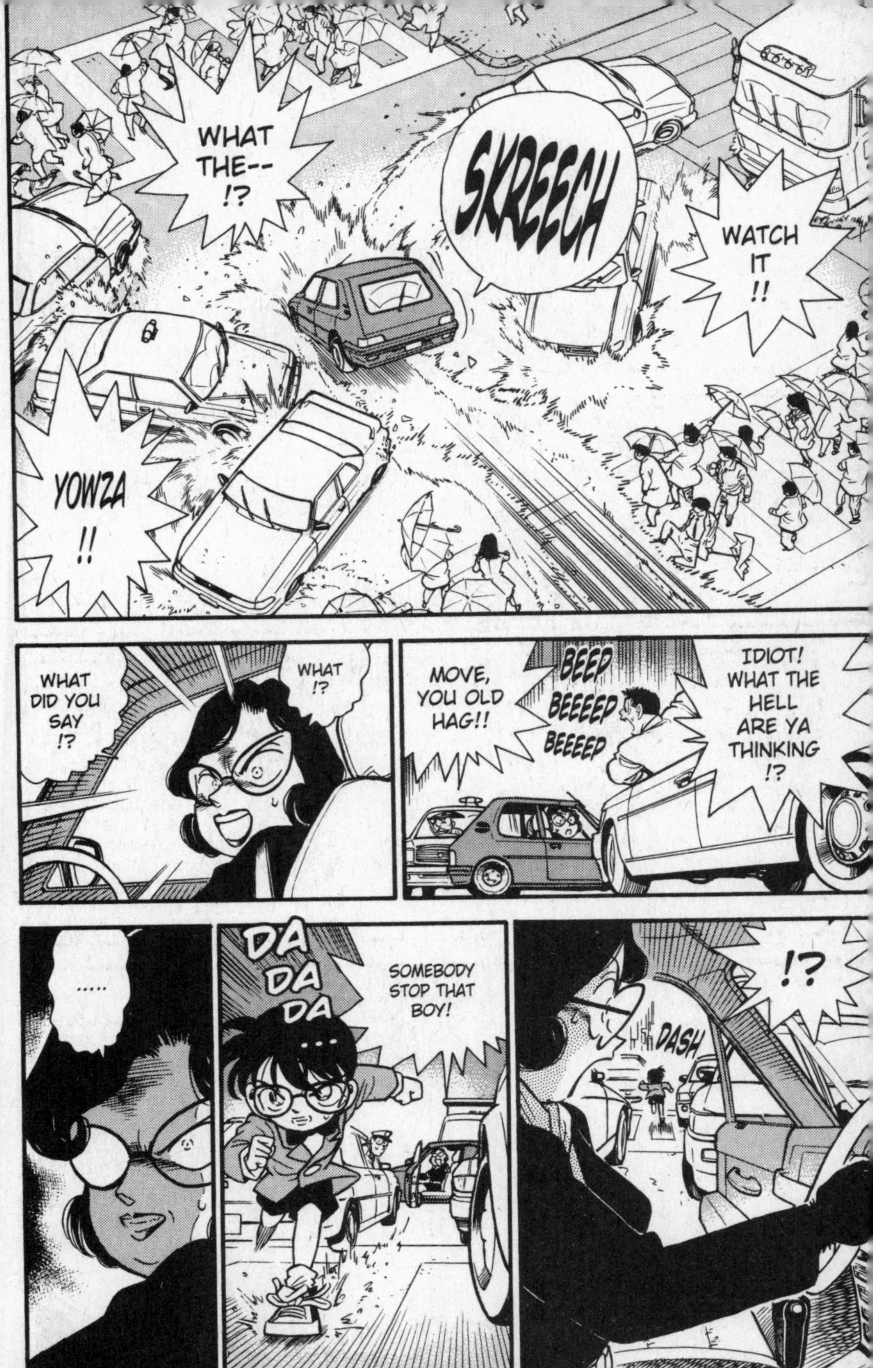
WATCH IT !!
SKREECH
WHAT THE-- !?
YOWZA !!
IDIOT! WHAT THE HELL ARE YA THINKING !?
BEEP BEEEEP BEEEEP
MOVE, YOU OLD HAG!!
WHAT !?
WHAT DID YOU SAY !?
!?
DASH
SOMEBODY STOP THAT BOY!
DA DA DA
.....

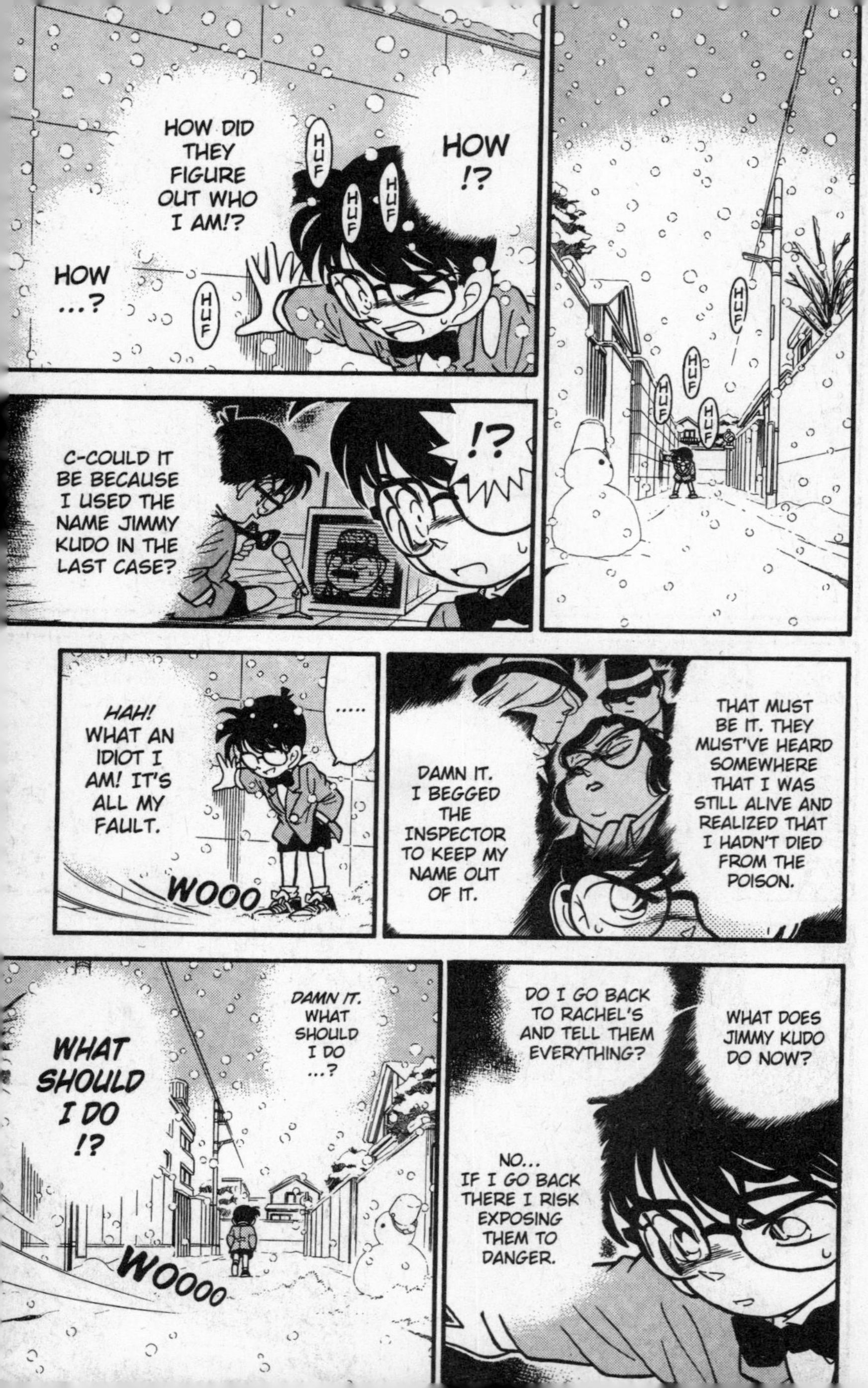
HUF
HUF
HUF
HUF
HOW !?
HUF
HUF
HUF
HOW DID THEY FIGURE OUT WHO I AM!?
HOW ...?
HUF
!?
C-COULD IT BE BECAUSE I USED THE NAME JIMMY KUDO IN THE LAST CASE?
THAT MUST BE IT. THEY MUST'VE HEARD SOMEWHERE THAT I WAS STILL ALIVE AND REALIZED THAT I HADN'T DIED FROM THE POISON.
DAMN IT. I BEGGED THE INSPECTOR TO KEEP MY NAME OUT OF IT.
.....
HAH! WHAT AN IDIOT I AM! IT'S ALL MY FAULT.
WOOO
WHAT DOES JIMMY KUDO DO NOW?
DO I GO BACK TO RACHEL'S AND TELL THEM EVERYTHING?
NO... IF I GO BACK THERE I RISK EXPOSING THEM TO DANGER.
DAMN IT. WHAT SHOULD I DO ...?
WHAT SHOULD I DO !?
WOOOO

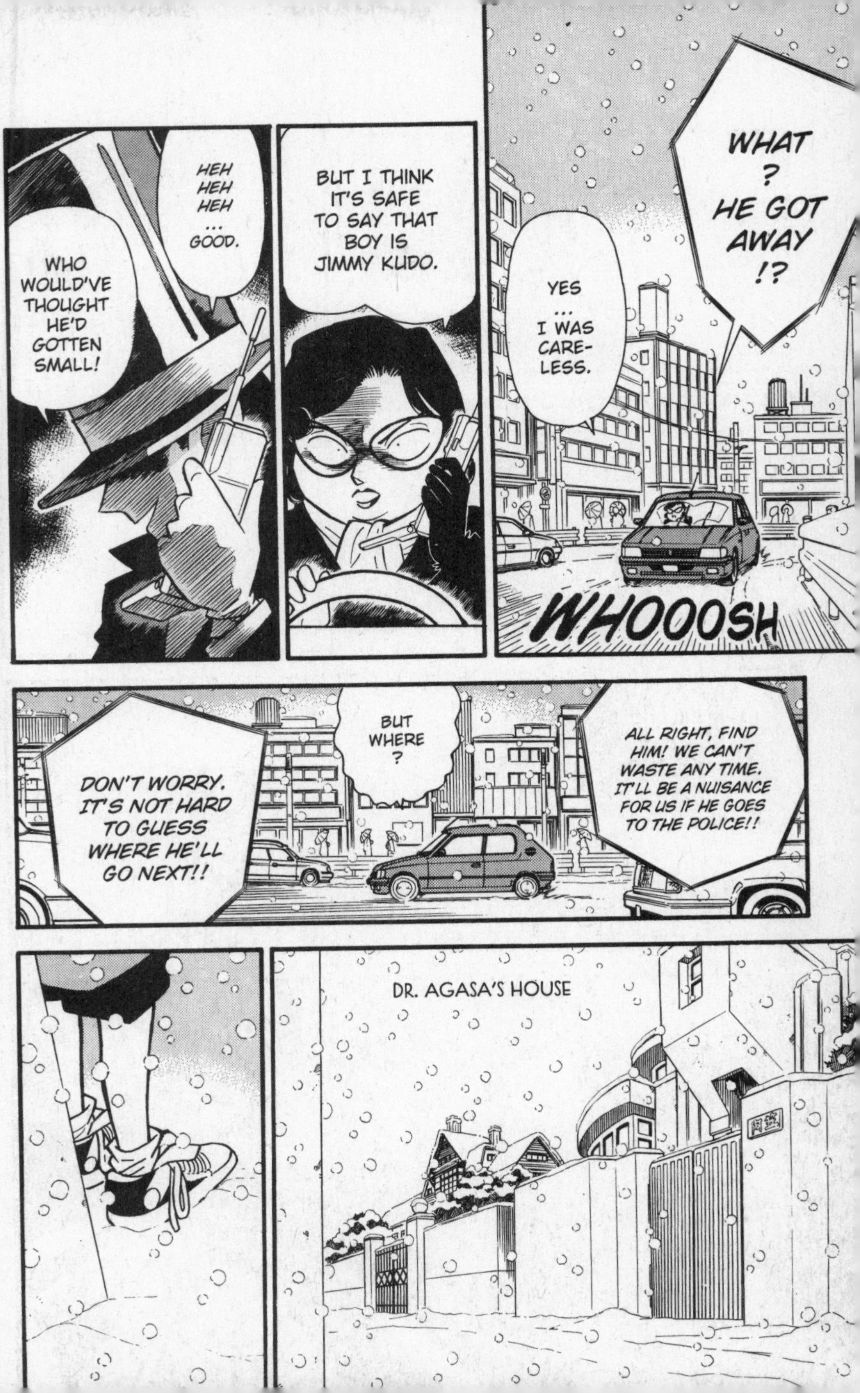
WHAT ? HE GOT AWAY !?
YES ... I WAS CARE-LESS.
WHOOOSH
BUT I THINK IT'S SAFE TO SAY THAT BOY IS JIMMY KUDO.
HEH HEH HEH ... GOOD.
WHO WOULD'VE THOUGHT HE'D GOTTEN SMALL!
ALL RIGHT, FIND HIM! WE CAN'T WASTE ANY TIME. IT'LL BE A NUISANCE FOR US IF HE GOES TO THE POLICE!!
BUT WHERE ?
DON'T WORRY. IT'S NOT HARD TO GUESS WHERE HE'LL GO NEXT!!
DR. AGASA'S HOUSE

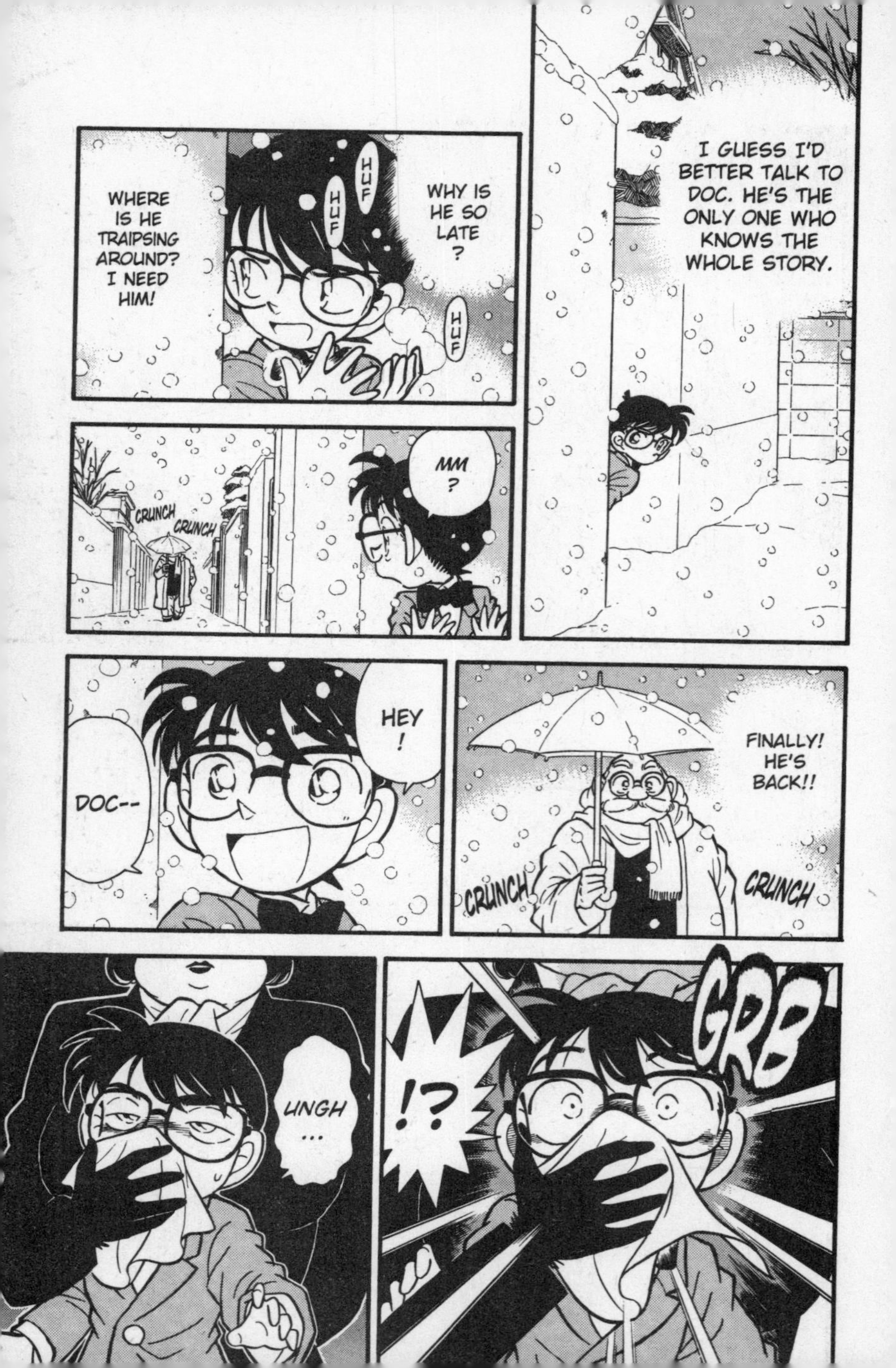
I GUESS I'D BETTER TALK TO DOC. HE'S THE ONLY ONE WHO KNOWS THE WHOLE STORY.
HUF HUF
WHY IS HE SO LATE?
HUF HUF
WHERE IS HE TRAIPSING AROUND? I NEED HIM!
MM?
CRUNCH
CRUNCH
FINALLY! HE'S BACK!!
CRUNCH
CRUNCH
HEY!
DOC--
GRB
!?
UNGH...

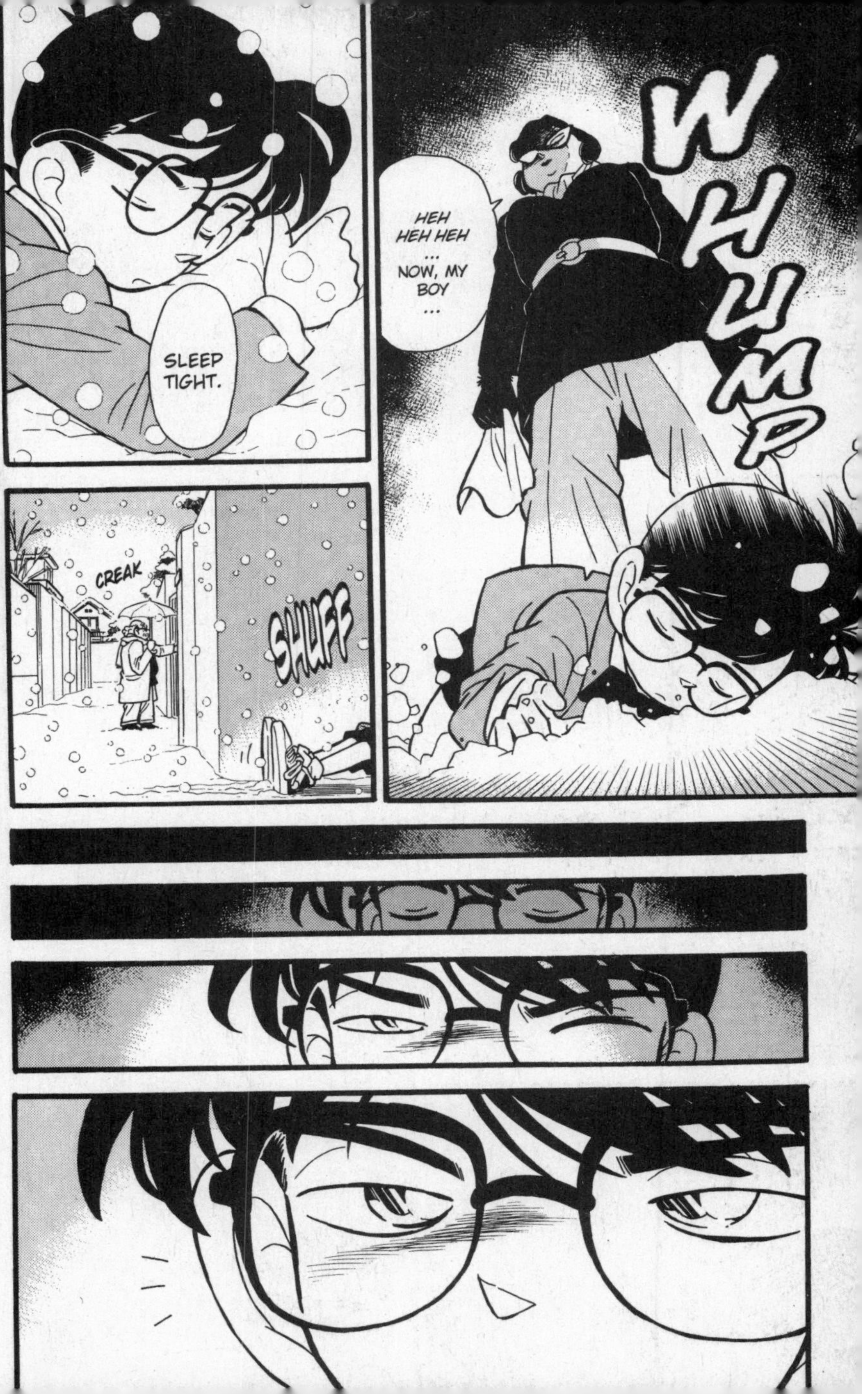
WHUMP
HEH HEH HEH ... NOW, MY BOY ...
SLEEP TIGHT.
CREAK
SHUFF

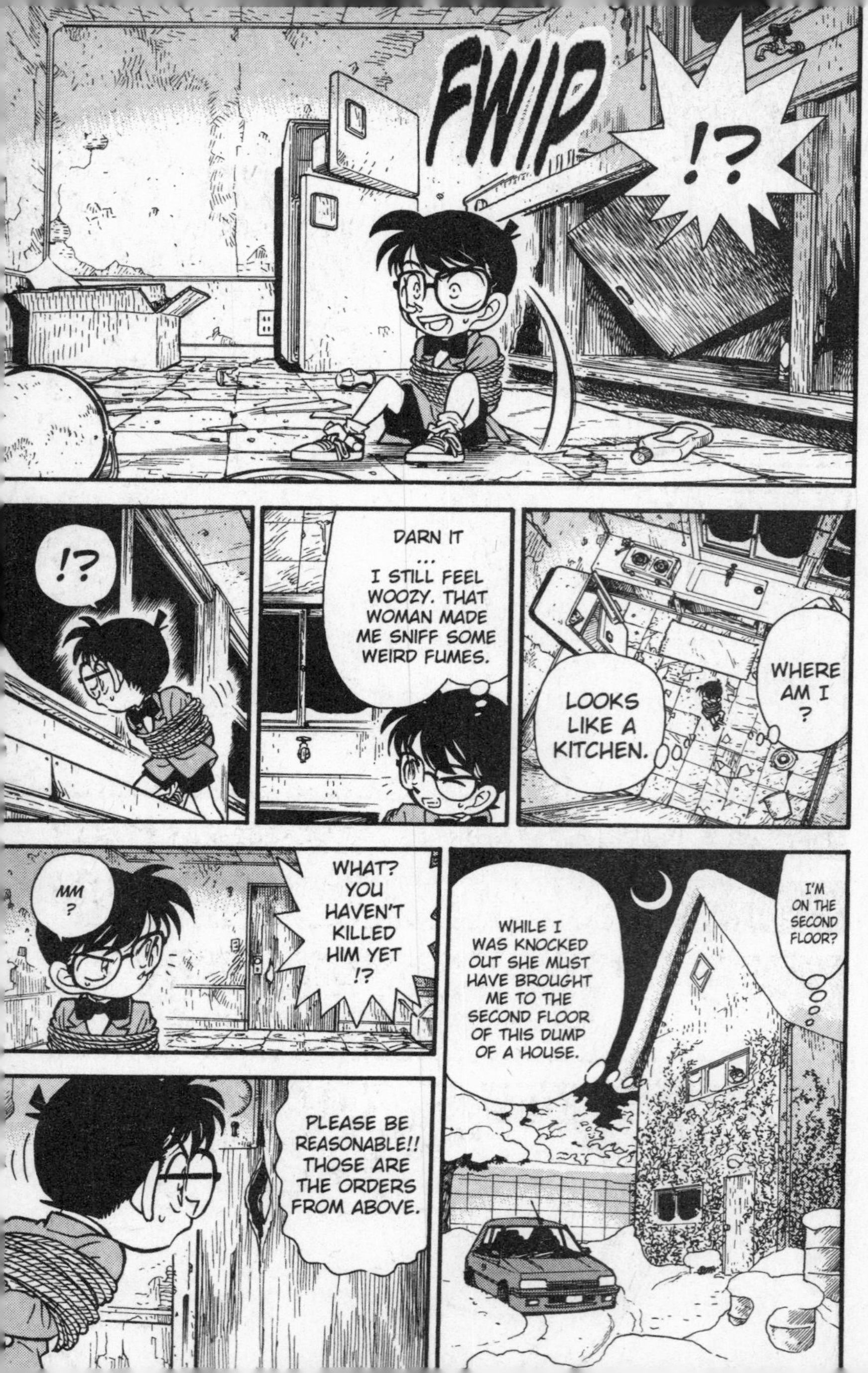
FWIP
!?
WHERE AM I ?
LOOKS LIKE A KITCHEN.
DARN IT ... I STILL FEEL WOOZY. THAT WOMAN MADE ME SNIFF SOME WEIRD FUMES.
!?
I'M ON THE SECOND FLOOR?
WHILE I WAS KNOCKED OUT SHE MUST HAVE BROUGHT ME TO THE SECOND FLOOR OF THIS DUMP OF A HOUSE.
WHAT? YOU HAVEN'T KILLED HIM YET !?
MM ?
PLEASE BE REASONABLE!! THOSE ARE THE ORDERS FROM ABOVE.

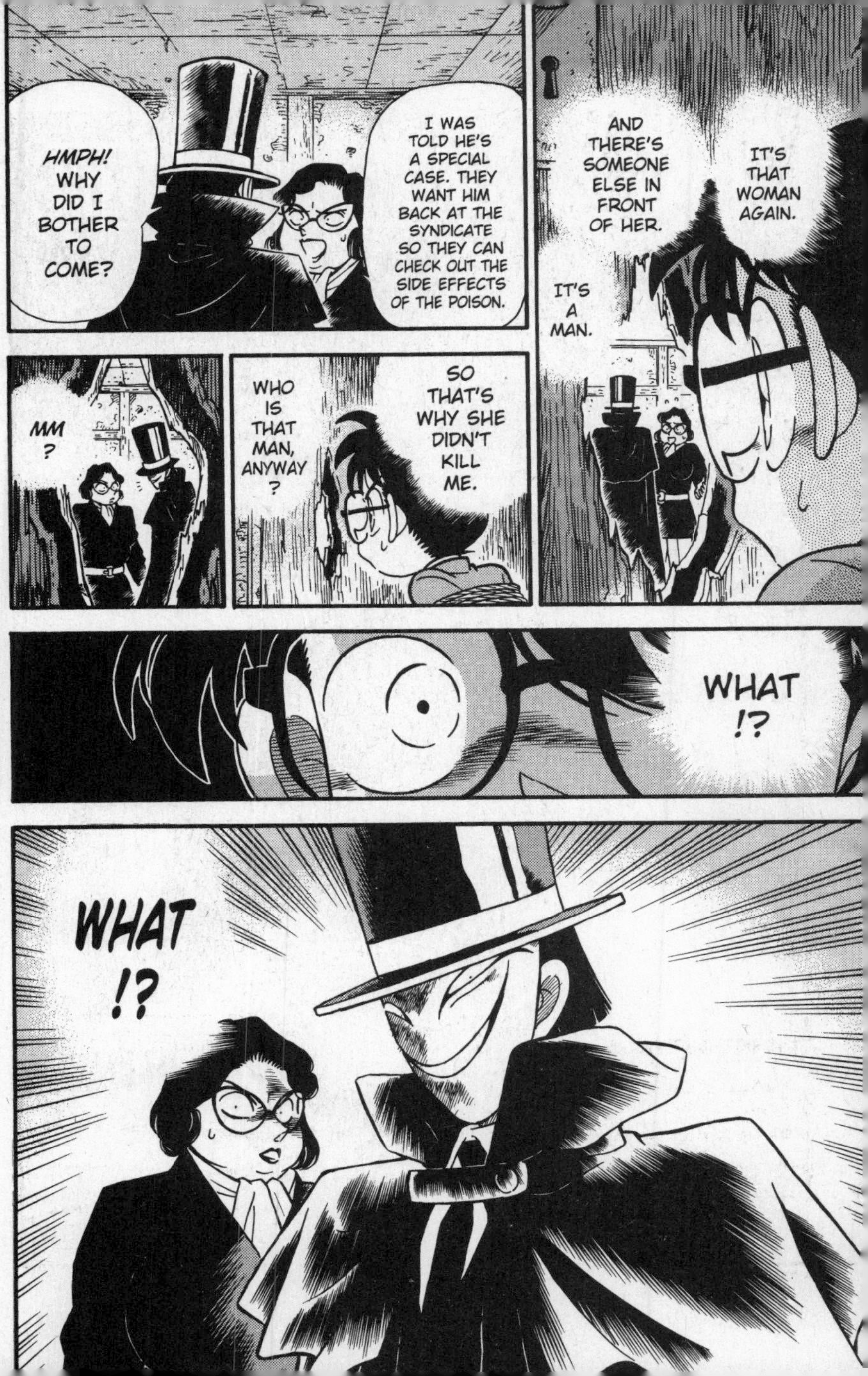
IT'S THAT WOMAN AGAIN.
AND THERE'S SOMEONE ELSE IN FRONT OF HER.
IT'S A MAN.
I WAS TOLD HE'S A SPECIAL CASE. THEY WANT HIM BACK AT THE SYNDICATE SO THEY CAN CHECK OUT THE SIDE EFFECTS OF THE POISON.
HMPH! WHY DID I BOTHER TO COME?
SO THAT'S WHY SHE DIDN'T KILL ME.
WHO IS THAT MAN, ANYWAY?
MM?
WHAT!?
WHAT!?

FILE 11: ESCAPE AND PURSUIT

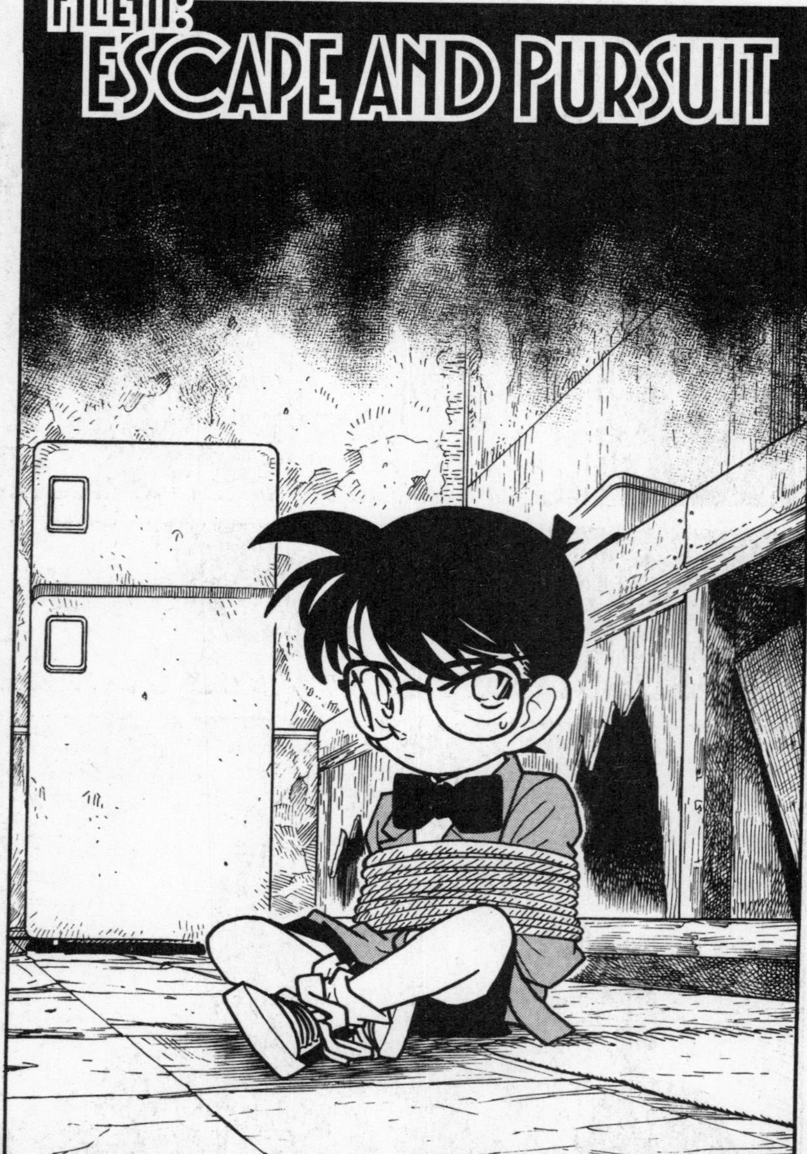

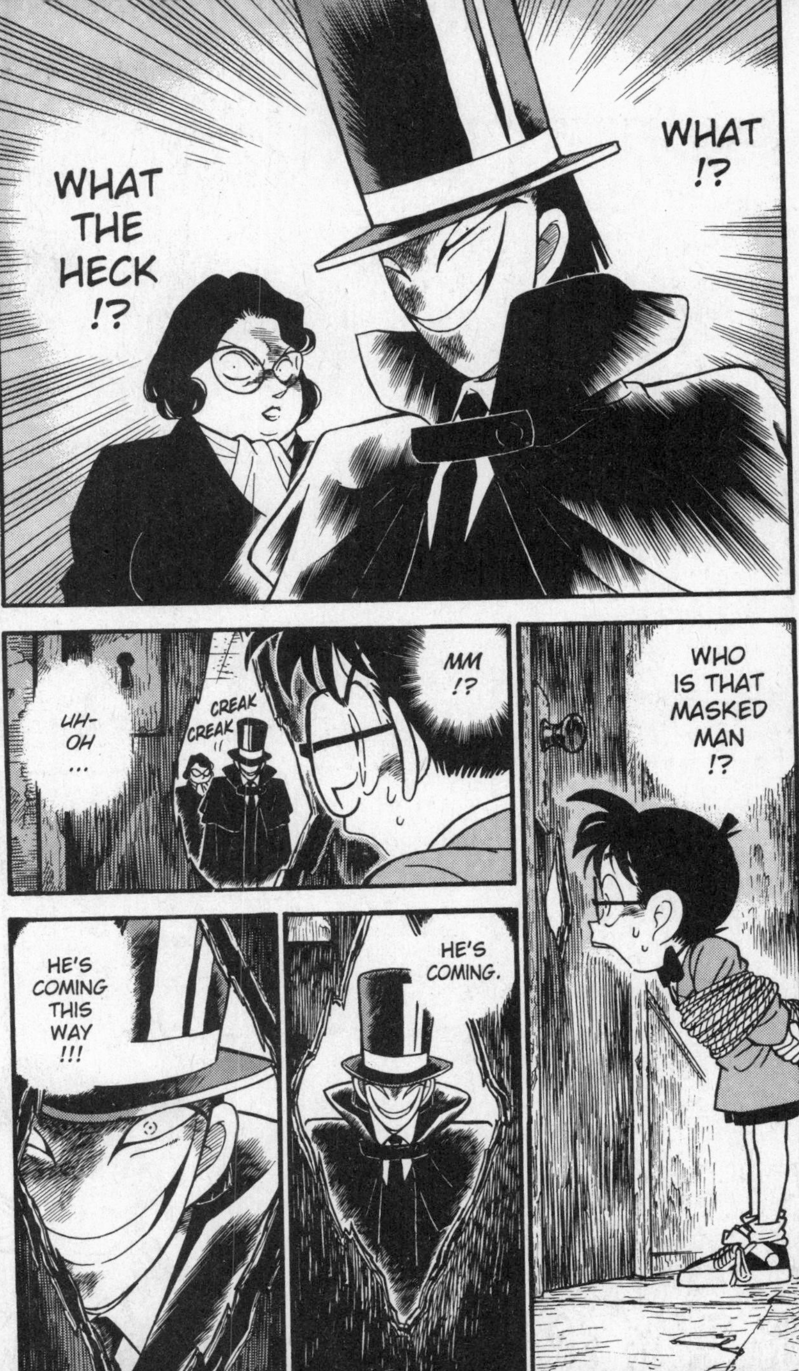
WHAT !?
WHAT THE HECK !?
WHO IS THAT MASKED MAN !?
MM !?
CREAK CREAK
UH-OH ...
HE'S COMING.
HE'S COMING THIS WAY !!!

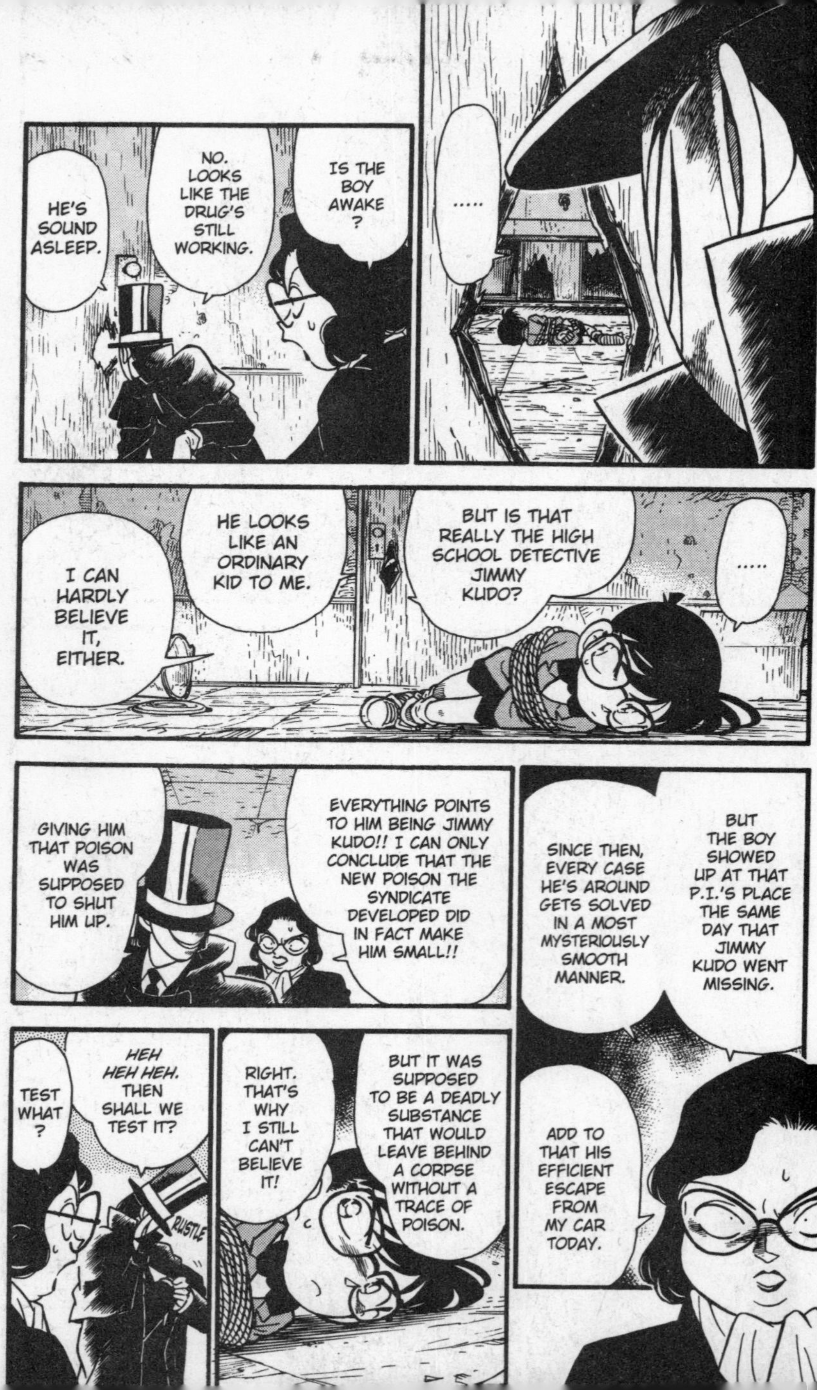
.....
IS THE BOY AWAKE?
NO. LOOKS LIKE THE DRUG'S STILL WORKING.
HE'S SOUND ASLEEP.
.....
BUT IS THAT REALLY THE HIGH SCHOOL DETECTIVE JIMMY KUDO?
HE LOOKS LIKE AN ORDINARY KID TO ME.
I CAN HARDLY BELIEVE IT, EITHER.
BUT THE BOY SHOWED UP AT THAT P.I.'S PLACE THE SAME DAY THAT JIMMY KUDO WENT MISSING.
SINCE THEN, EVERY CASE HE'S AROUND GETS SOLVED IN A MOST MYSTERIOUSLY SMOOTH MANNER.
ADD TO THAT HIS EFFICIENT ESCAPE FROM MY CAR TODAY.
EVERYTHING POINTS TO HIM BEING JIMMY KUDO!! I CAN ONLY CONCLUDE THAT THE NEW POISON THE SYNDICATE DEVELOPED DID IN FACT MAKE HIM SMALL!!
GIVING HIM THAT POISON WAS SUPPOSED TO SHUT HIM UP.
BUT IT WAS SUPPOSED TO BE A DEADLY SUBSTANCE THAT WOULD LEAVE BEHIND A CORPSE WITHOUT A TRACE OF POISON.
RIGHT. THAT'S WHY I STILL CAN'T BELIEVE IT!
HEH HEH HEH. THEN SHALL WE TEST IT?
TEST WHAT?
RUSTLE

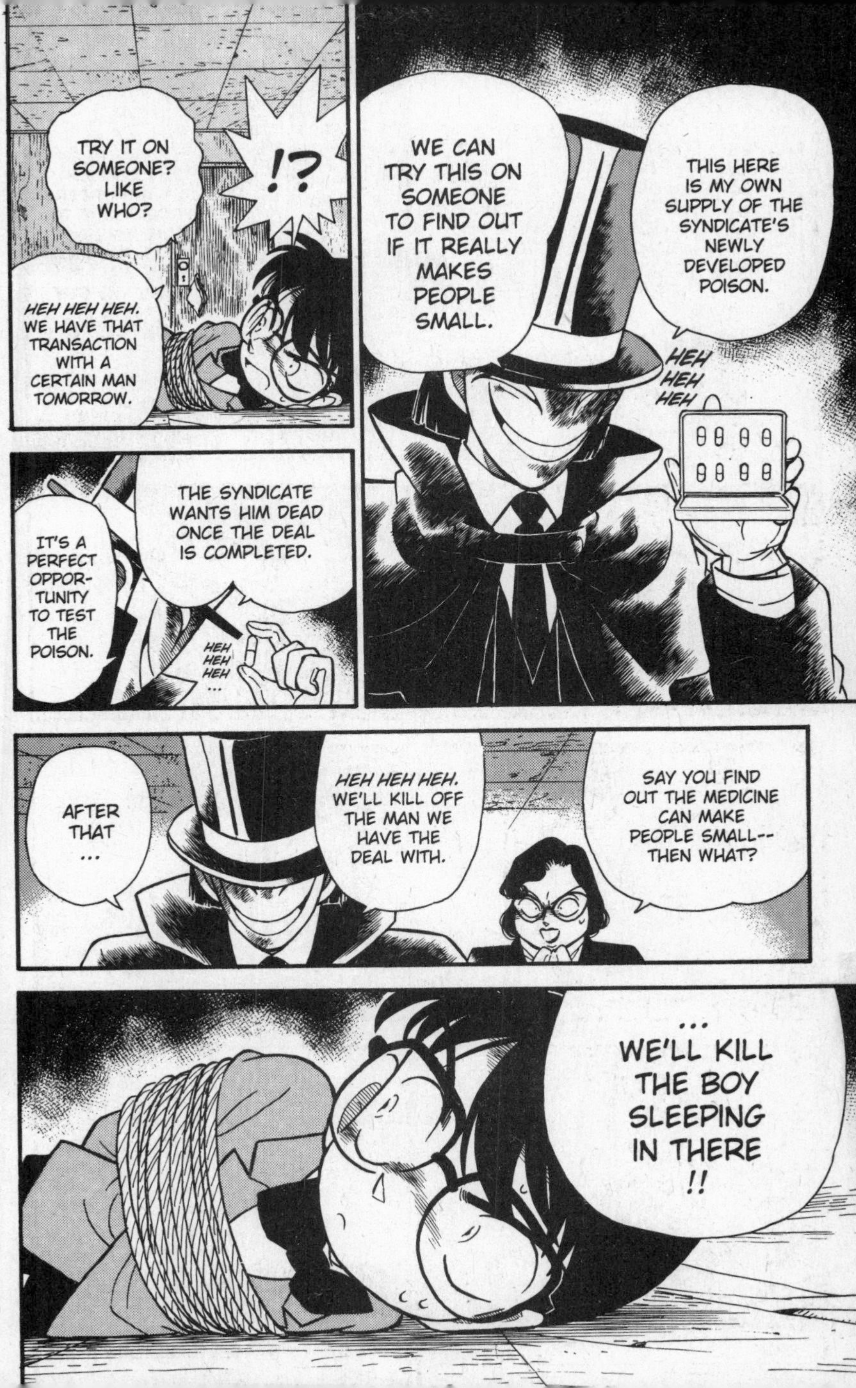
THIS HERE IS MY OWN SUPPLY OF THE SYNDICATE'S NEWLY DEVELOPED POISON.
WE CAN TRY THIS ON SOMEONE TO FIND OUT IF IT REALLY MAKES PEOPLE SMALL.
HEH HEH HEH
TRY IT ON SOMEONE? LIKE WHO?
!?
HEH HEH HEH. WE HAVE THAT TRANSACTION WITH A CERTAIN MAN TOMORROW.
THE SYNDICATE WANTS HIM DEAD ONCE THE DEAL IS COMPLETED.
IT'S A PERFECT OPPOR-TUNITY TO TEST THE POISON.
HEH HEH HEH ...
SAY YOU FIND OUT THE MEDICINE CAN MAKE PEOPLE SMALL-- THEN WHAT?
HEH HEH HEH. WE'LL KILL OFF THE MAN WE HAVE THE DEAL WITH.
AFTER THAT ...
... WE'LL KILL THE BOY SLEEPING IN THERE !!

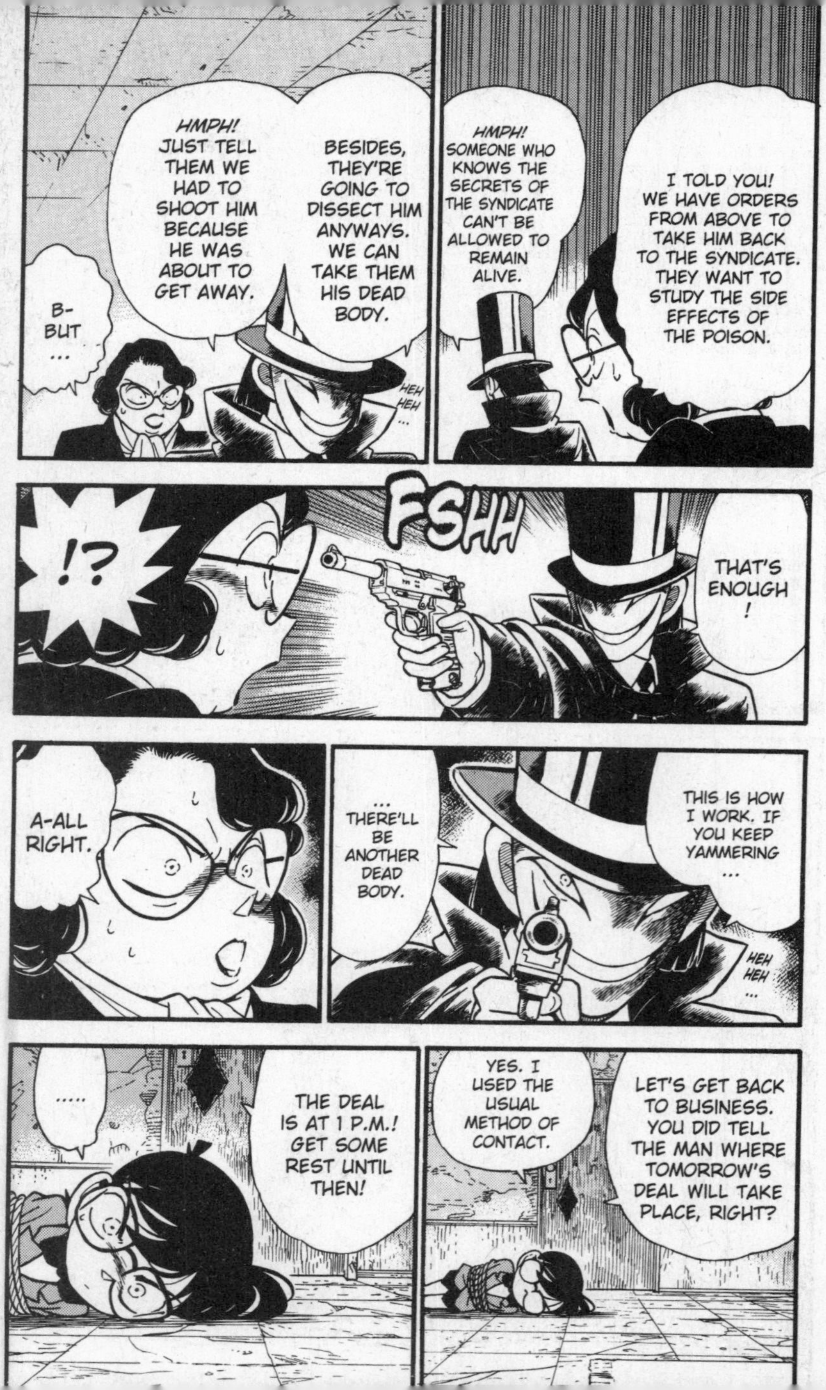
I TOLD YOU! WE HAVE ORDERS FROM ABOVE TO TAKE HIM BACK TO THE SYNDICATE. THEY WANT TO STUDY THE SIDE EFFECTS OF THE POISON.
HMPH! SOMEONE WHO KNOWS THE SECRETS OF THE SYNDICATE CAN'T BE ALLOWED TO REMAIN ALIVE.
HMPH! JUST TELL THEM WE HAD TO SHOOT HIM BECAUSE HE WAS ABOUT TO GET AWAY.
BESIDES, THEY'RE GOING TO DISSECT HIM ANYWAYS. WE CAN TAKE THEM HIS DEAD BODY.
HEH HEH ...
B-BUT ...
THAT'S ENOUGH!
FSHH
!?
THIS IS HOW I WORK. IF YOU KEEP YAMMERING ...
... THERE'LL BE ANOTHER DEAD BODY.
HEH HEH ...
A-ALL RIGHT.
LET'S GET BACK TO BUSINESS. YOU DID TELL THE MAN WHERE TOMORROW'S DEAL WILL TAKE PLACE, RIGHT?
YES. I USED THE USUAL METHOD OF CONTACT.
THE DEAL IS AT 1 P.M.! GET SOME REST UNTIL THEN!
.....

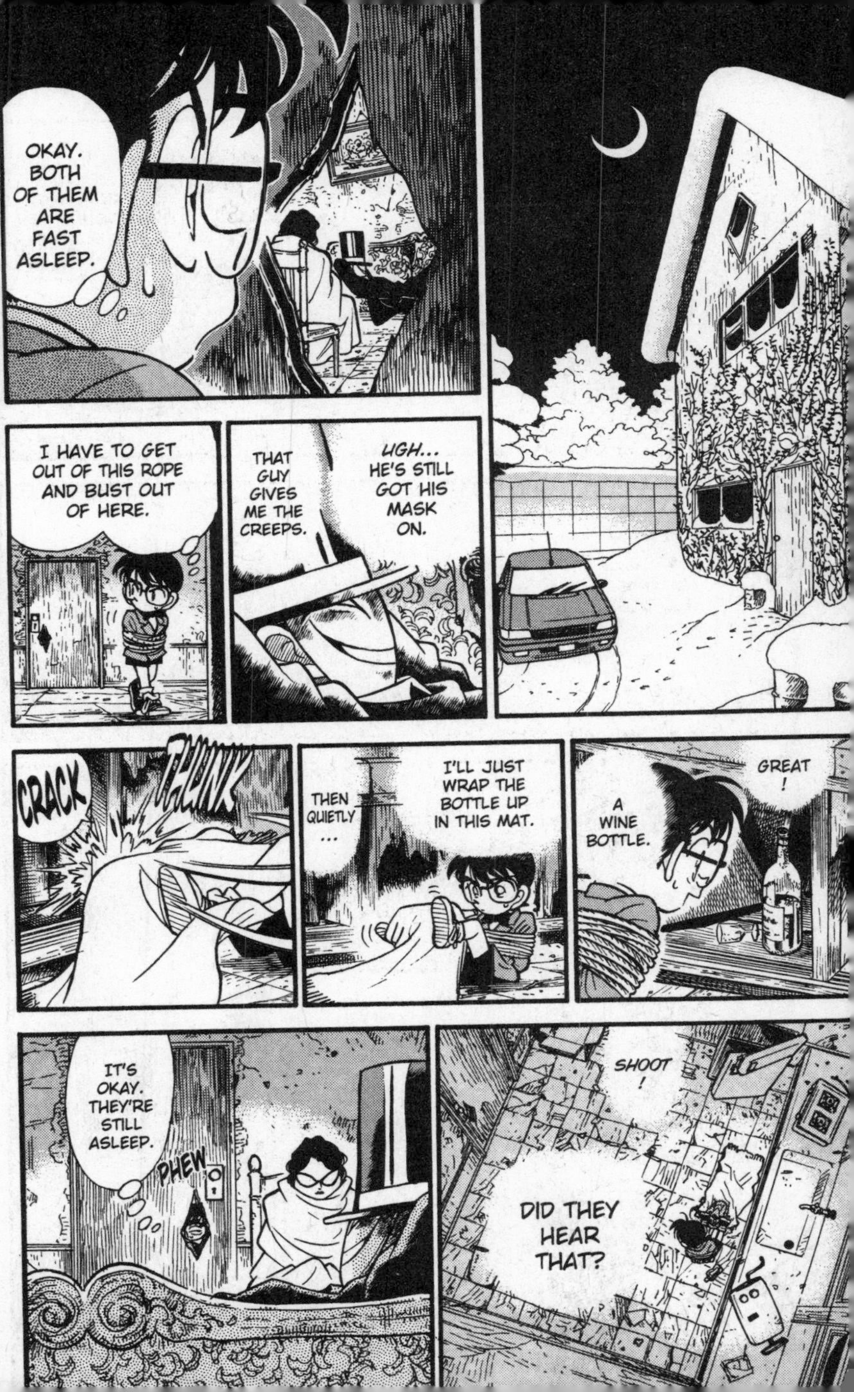
OKAY. BOTH OF THEM ARE FAST ASLEEP.
UGH... HE'S STILL GOT HIS MASK ON.
THAT GUY GIVES ME THE CREEPS.
I HAVE TO GET OUT OF THIS ROPE AND BUST OUT OF HERE.
GREAT!
A WINE BOTTLE.
I'LL JUST WRAP THE BOTTLE UP IN THIS MAT.
THEN QUIETLY ...
THUNK
CRACK
SHOOT!
DID THEY HEAR THAT?
IT'S OKAY. THEY'RE STILL ASLEEP.
PHEW

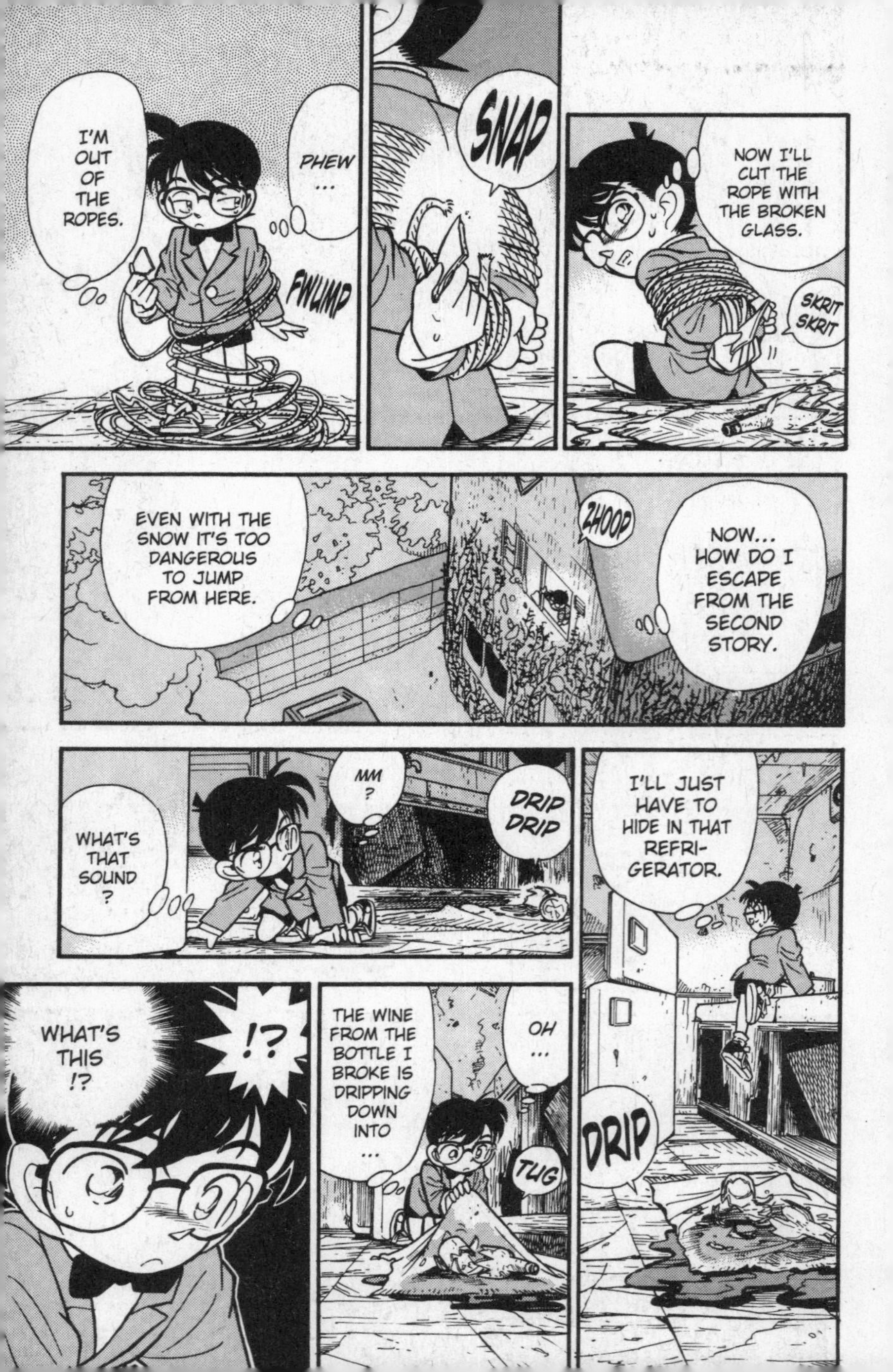
NOW I'LL CUT THE ROPE WITH THE BROKEN GLASS.
SKRIT SKRIT
SNAP
PHEW ...
FWUMP
I'M OUT OF THE ROPES.
NOW... HOW DO I ESCAPE FROM THE SECOND STORY.
ZHOOP
EVEN WITH THE SNOW IT'S TOO DANGEROUS TO JUMP FROM HERE.
I'LL JUST HAVE TO HIDE IN THAT REFRIGERATOR.
DRIP DRIP
MM ?
WHAT'S THAT SOUND ?
DRIP
OH ...
TUG
THE WINE FROM THE BOTTLE I BROKE IS DRIPPING DOWN INTO ...
!?
WHAT'S THIS !?

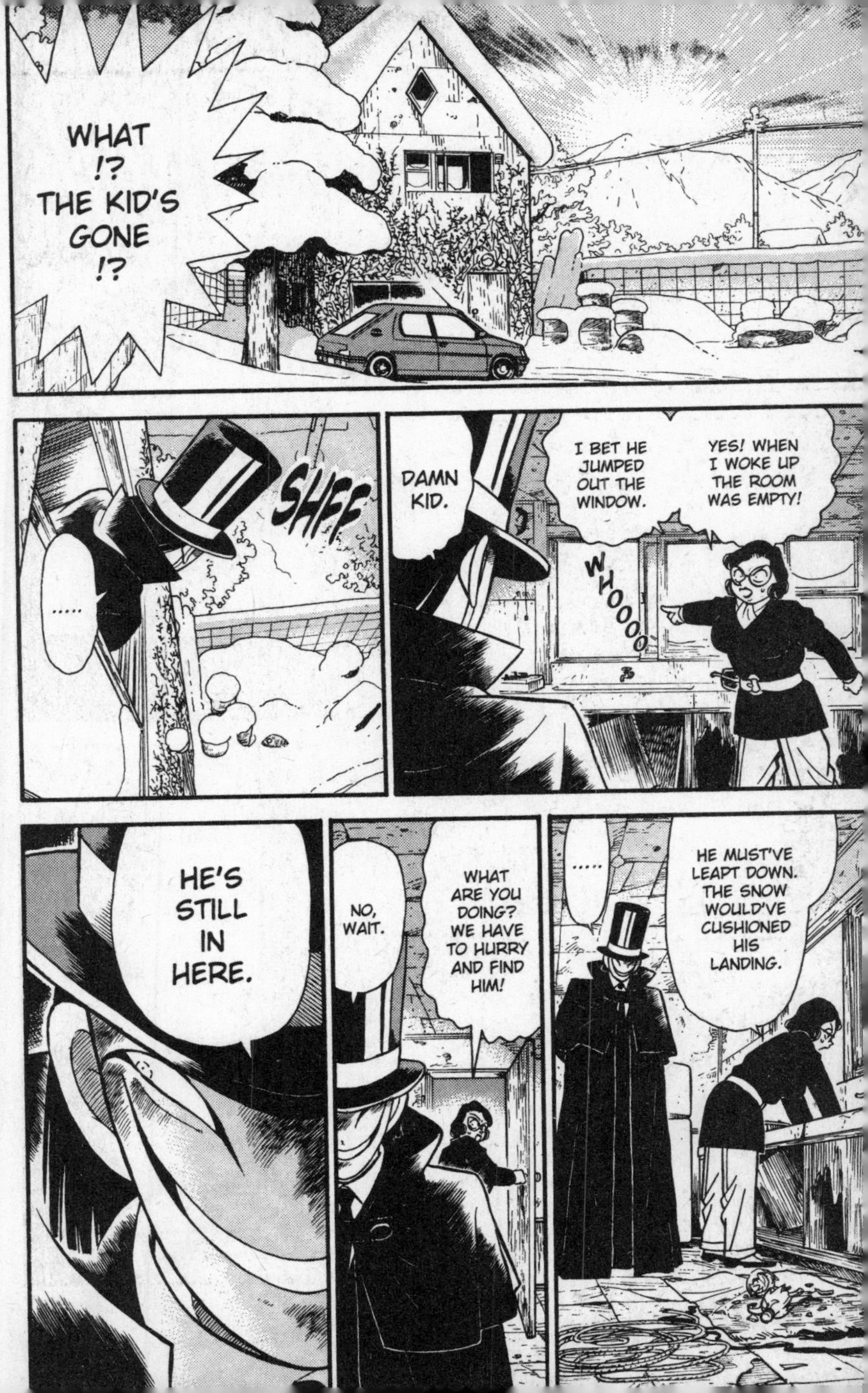
WHAT !? THE KID'S GONE !?
YES! WHEN I WOKE UP THE ROOM WAS EMPTY!
I BET HE JUMPED OUT THE WINDOW.
WHOOOO
DAMN KID.
SHFF
.....
HE MUST'VE LEAPT DOWN. THE SNOW WOULD'VE CUSHIONED HIS LANDING.
.....
WHAT ARE YOU DOING? WE HAVE TO HURRY AND FIND HIM!
NO, WAIT.
HE'S STILL IN HERE.

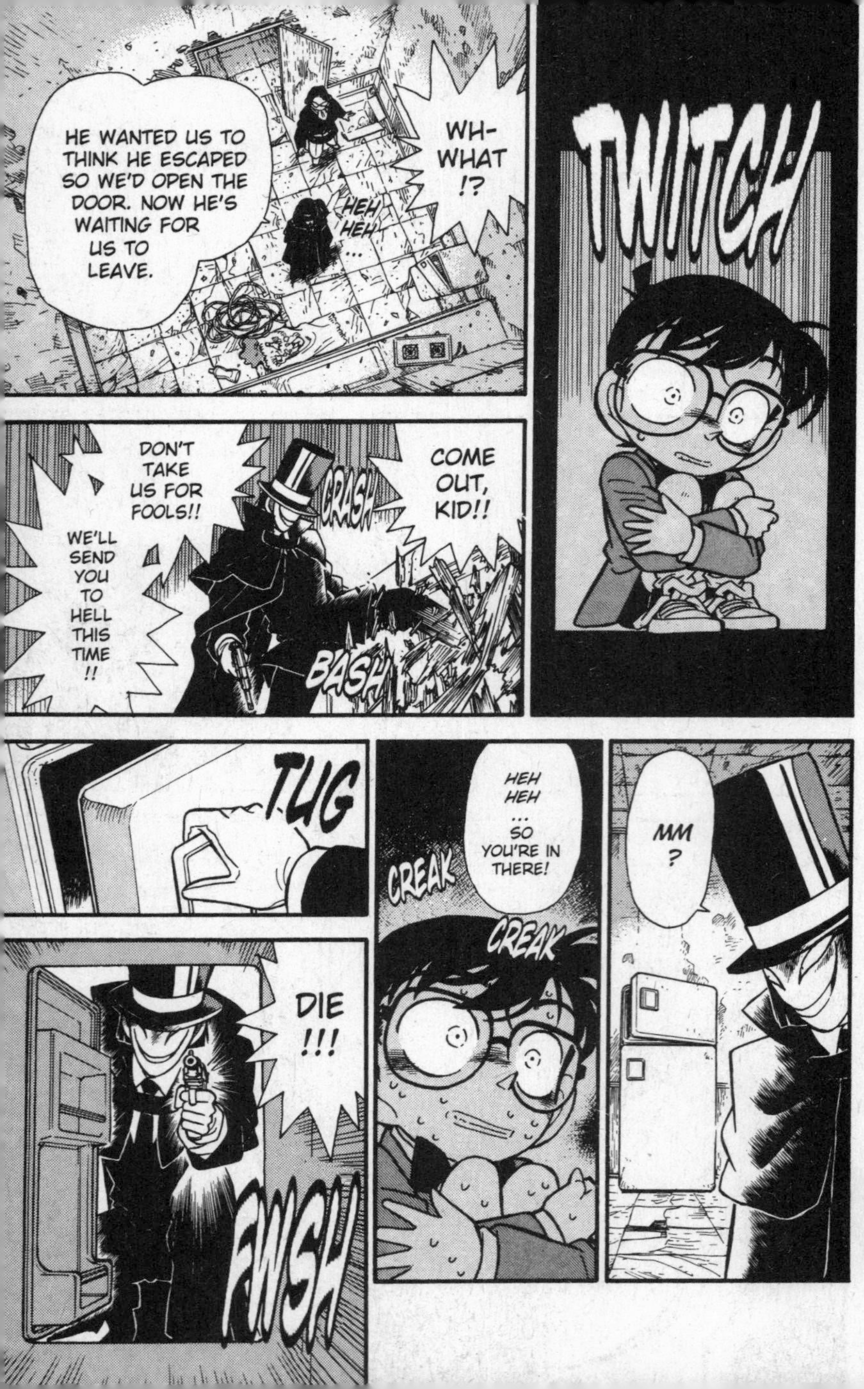
TWITCH
WH- WHAT !?
HEH HEH ...
HE WANTED US TO THINK HE ESCAPED SO WE'D OPEN THE DOOR. NOW HE'S WAITING FOR US TO LEAVE.
COME OUT, KID!!
CRASH
DON'T TAKE US FOR FOOLS!!
WE'LL SEND YOU TO HELL THIS TIME !!
BASH
MM ?
HEH HEH ... SO YOU'RE IN THERE!
CREAK
CREAK
TUG
DIE !!!
FWSH

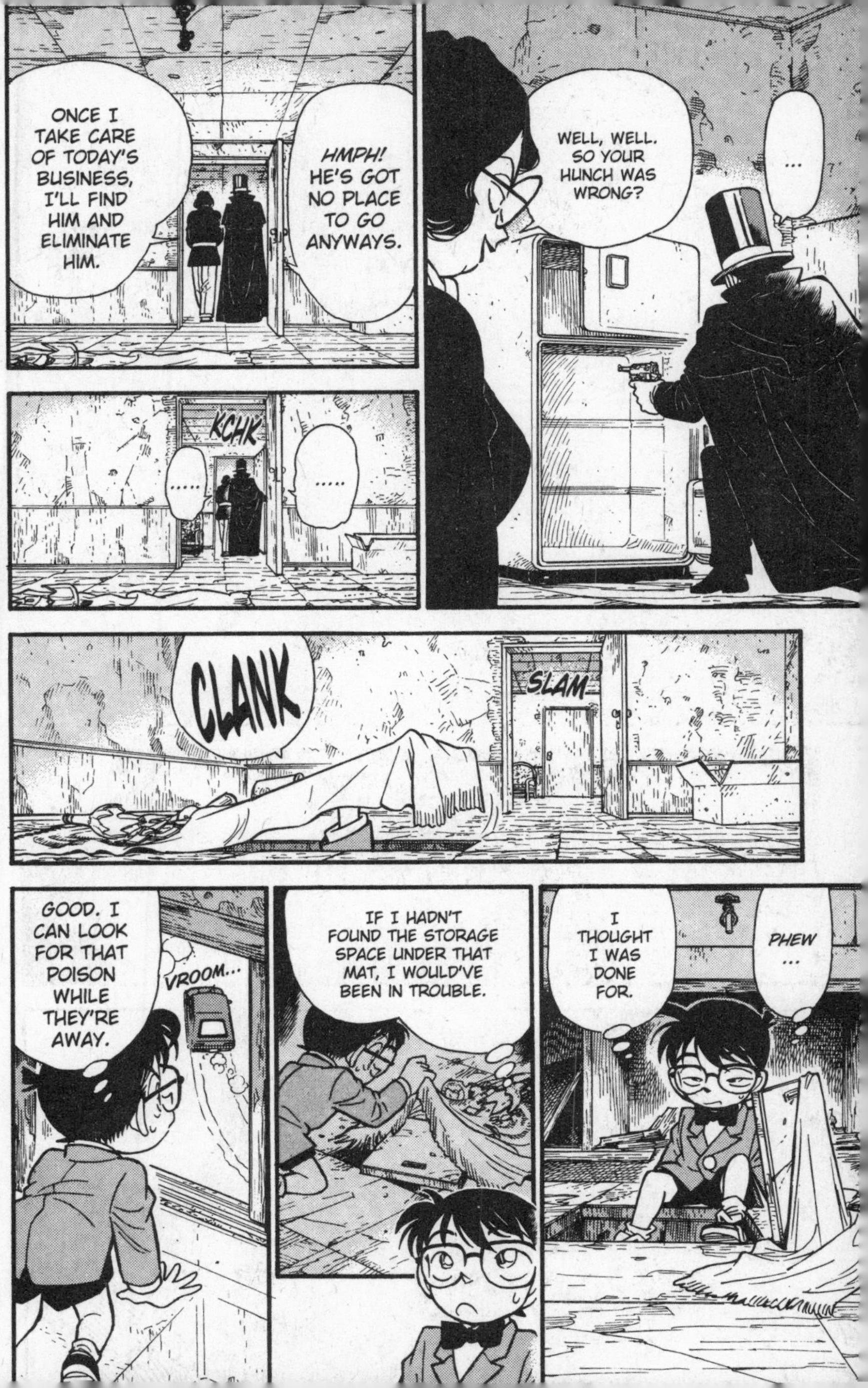
...
WELL, WELL. SO YOUR HUNCH WAS WRONG?
HMPH! HE'S GOT NO PLACE TO GO ANYWAYS.
ONCE I TAKE CARE OF TODAY'S BUSINESS, I'LL FIND HIM AND ELIMINATE HIM.
KCHK
......
......
SLAM
CLANK
PHEW...
I THOUGHT I WAS DONE FOR.
IF I HADN'T FOUND THE STORAGE SPACE UNDER THAT MAT, I WOULD'VE BEEN IN TROUBLE.
VROOM...
GOOD. I CAN LOOK FOR THAT POISON WHILE THEY'RE AWAY.

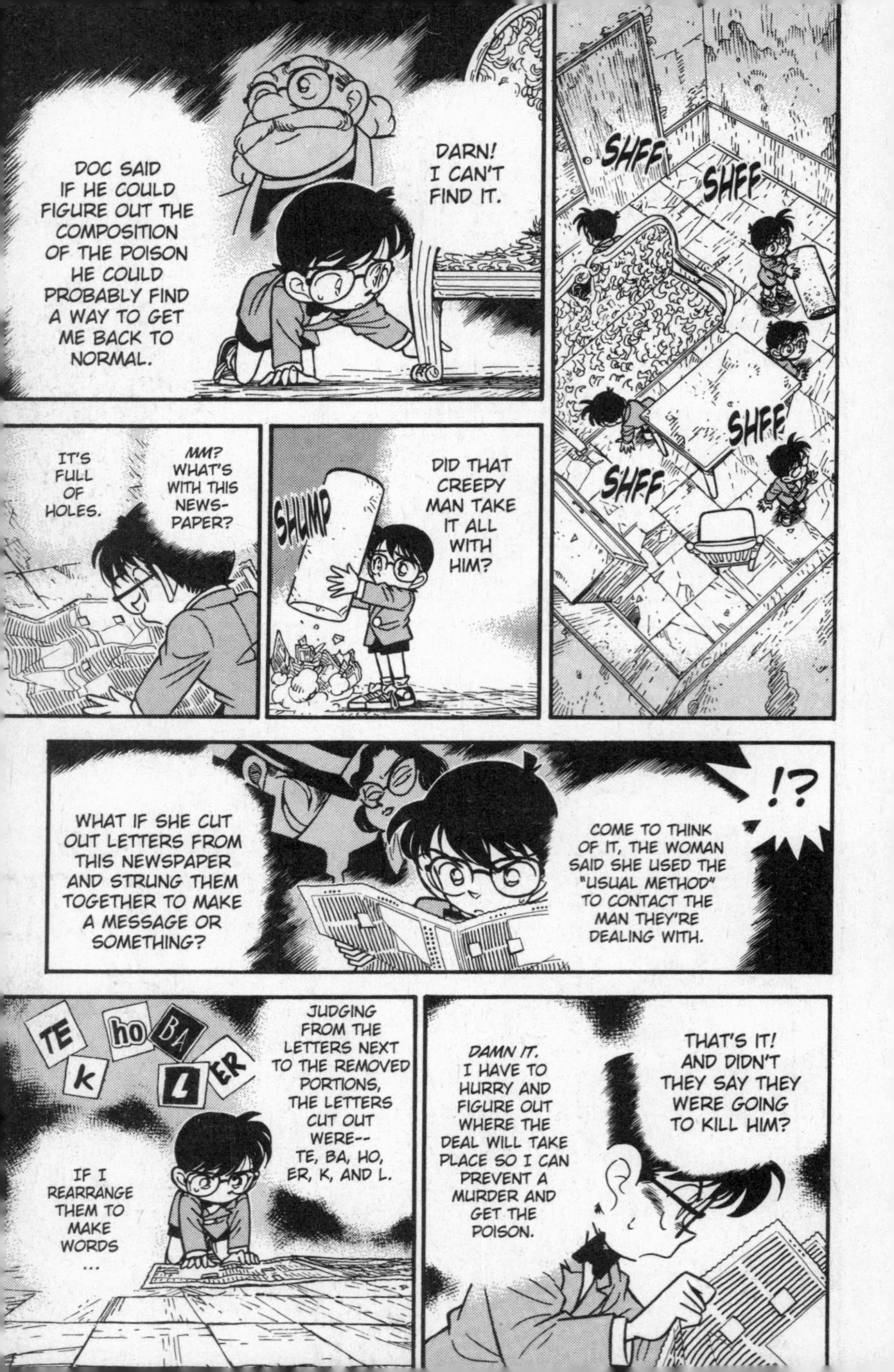
SHFF
SHFF
SHFF
SHFF
DARN! I CAN'T FIND IT.
DOC SAID IF HE COULD FIGURE OUT THE COMPOSITION OF THE POISON HE COULD PROBABLY FIND A WAY TO GET ME BACK TO NORMAL.
DID THAT CREEPY MAN TAKE IT ALL WITH HIM?
SHUMP
MM? WHAT'S WITH THIS NEWS-PAPER?
IT'S FULL OF HOLES.
!?
COME TO THINK OF IT, THE WOMAN SAID SHE USED THE "USUAL METHOD" TO CONTACT THE MAN THEY'RE DEALING WITH.
WHAT IF SHE CUT OUT LETTERS FROM THIS NEWSPAPER AND STRUNG THEM TOGETHER TO MAKE A MESSAGE OR SOMETHING?
THAT'S IT! AND DIDN'T THEY SAY THEY WERE GOING TO KILL HIM?
DAMN IT. I HAVE TO HURRY AND FIGURE OUT WHERE THE DEAL WILL TAKE PLACE SO I CAN PREVENT A MURDER AND GET THE POISON.
JUDGING FROM THE LETTERS NEXT TO THE REMOVED PORTIONS, THE LETTERS CUT OUT WERE-- TE, BA, HO, ER, K, AND L.
TE
ho
BA
K
L
ER
IF I REARRANGE THEM TO MAKE WORDS ...

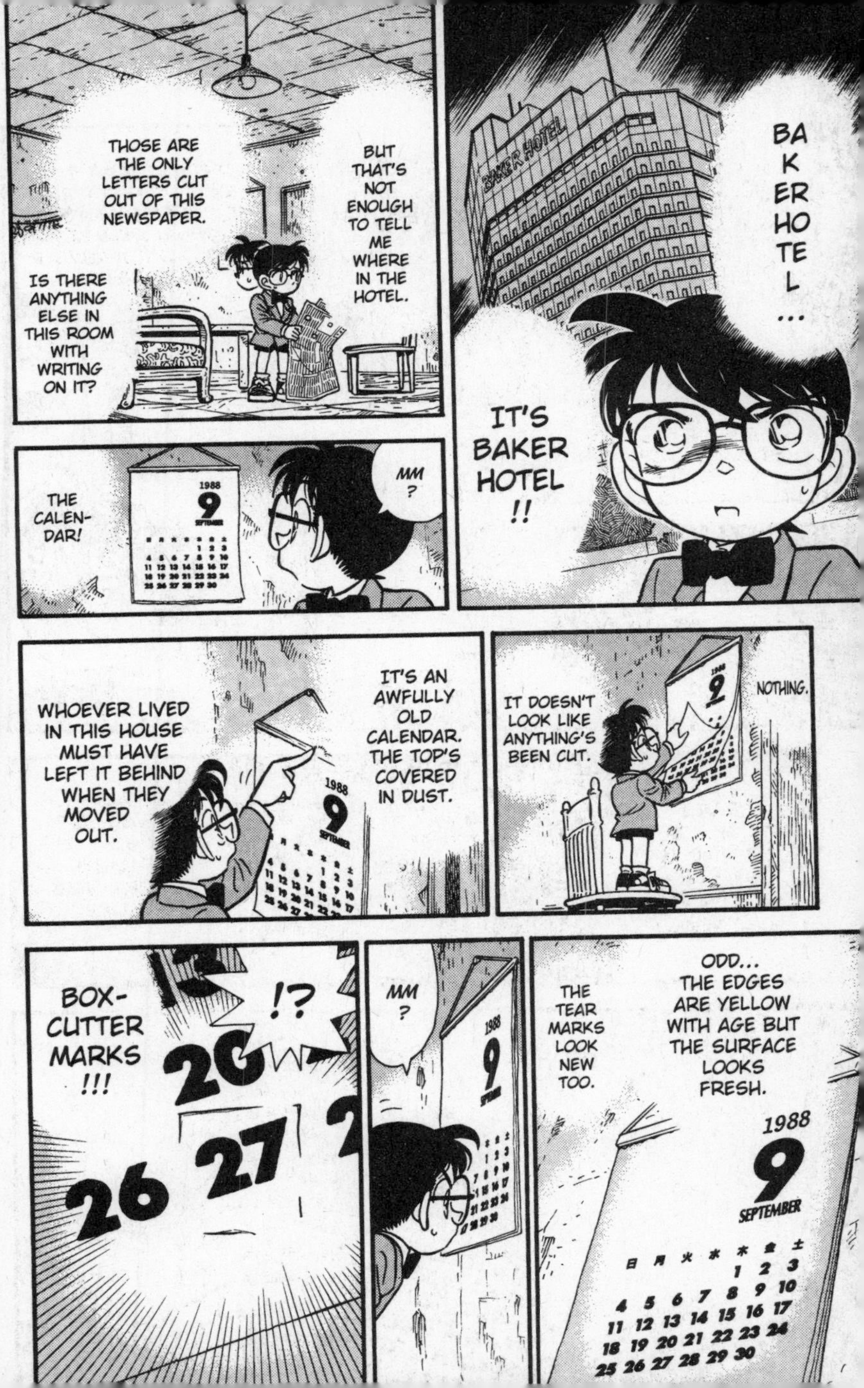
BAKER HOTEL...
IT'S BAKER HOTEL !!
BUT THAT'S NOT ENOUGH TO TELL ME WHERE IN THE HOTEL.
THOSE ARE THE ONLY LETTERS CUT OUT OF THIS NEWSPAPER.
IS THERE ANYTHING ELSE IN THIS ROOM WITH WRITING ON IT?
MM ?
THE CALENDAR!
NOTHING.
IT DOESN'T LOOK LIKE ANYTHING'S BEEN CUT.
IT'S AN AWFULLY OLD CALENDAR. THE TOP'S COVERED IN DUST.
WHOEVER LIVED IN THIS HOUSE MUST HAVE LEFT IT BEHIND WHEN THEY MOVED OUT.
ODD... THE EDGES ARE YELLOW WITH AGE BUT THE SURFACE LOOKS FRESH.
THE TEAR MARKS LOOK NEW TOO.
MM ?
!?
BOX-CUTTER MARKS !!!

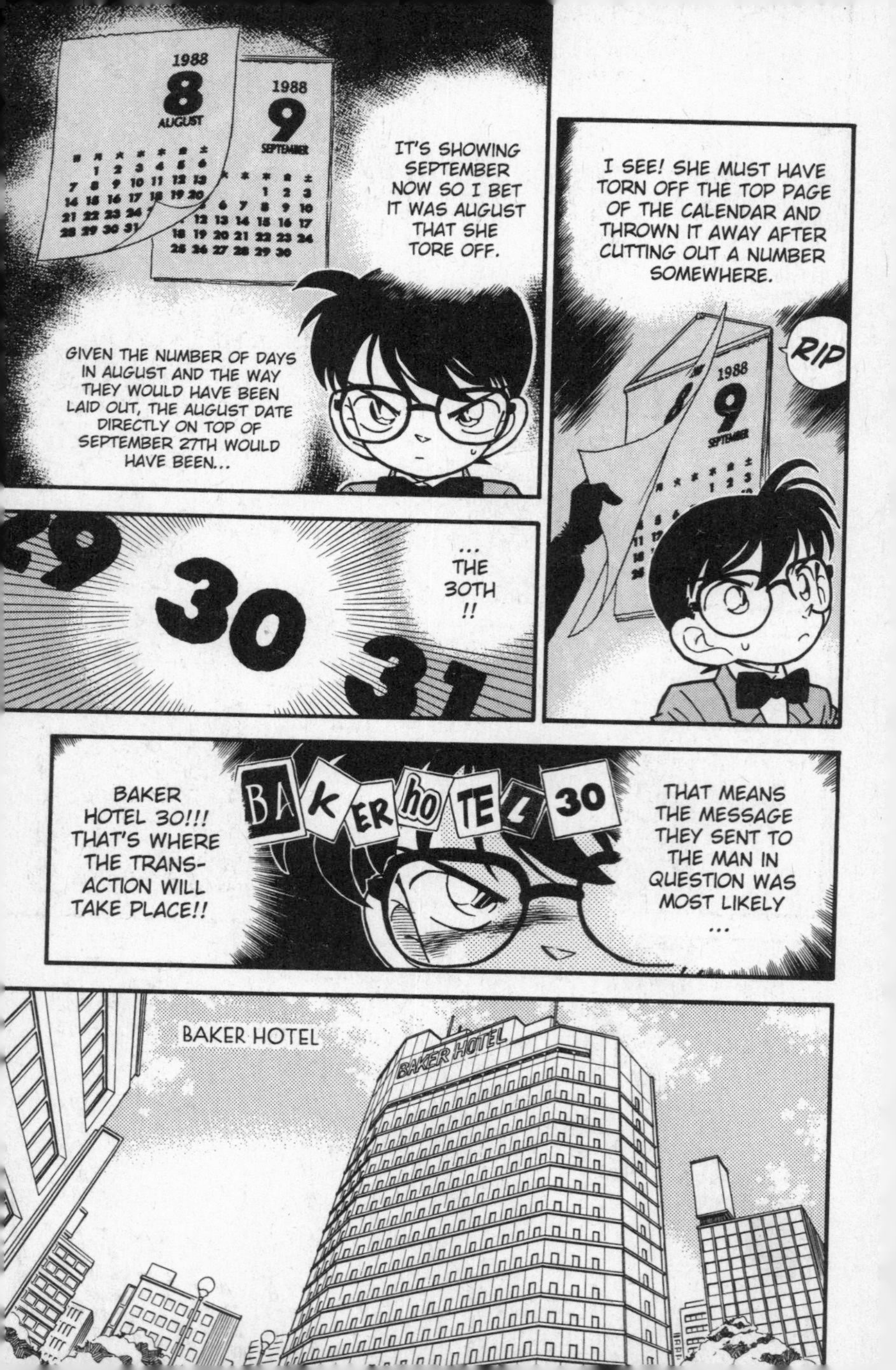
I SEE! SHE MUST HAVE TORN OFF THE TOP PAGE OF THE CALENDAR AND THROWN IT AWAY AFTER CUTTING OUT A NUMBER SOMEWHERE.
RIP
1988
9
SEPTEMBER
1988
8
AUGUST
1988
9
SEPTEMBER
IT'S SHOWING SEPTEMBER NOW SO I BET IT WAS AUGUST THAT SHE TORE OFF.
GIVEN THE NUMBER OF DAYS IN AUGUST AND THE WAY THEY WOULD HAVE BEEN LAID OUT, THE AUGUST DATE DIRECTLY ON TOP OF SEPTEMBER 27TH WOULD HAVE BEEN...
...THE 30TH!!
29
30
31
THAT MEANS THE MESSAGE THEY SENT TO THE MAN IN QUESTION WAS MOST LIKELY...
BAKERhoTEL 30
BAKER HOTEL 30!!! THAT'S WHERE THE TRANS-ACTION WILL TAKE PLACE!!
BAKER HOTEL
BAKER HOTEL

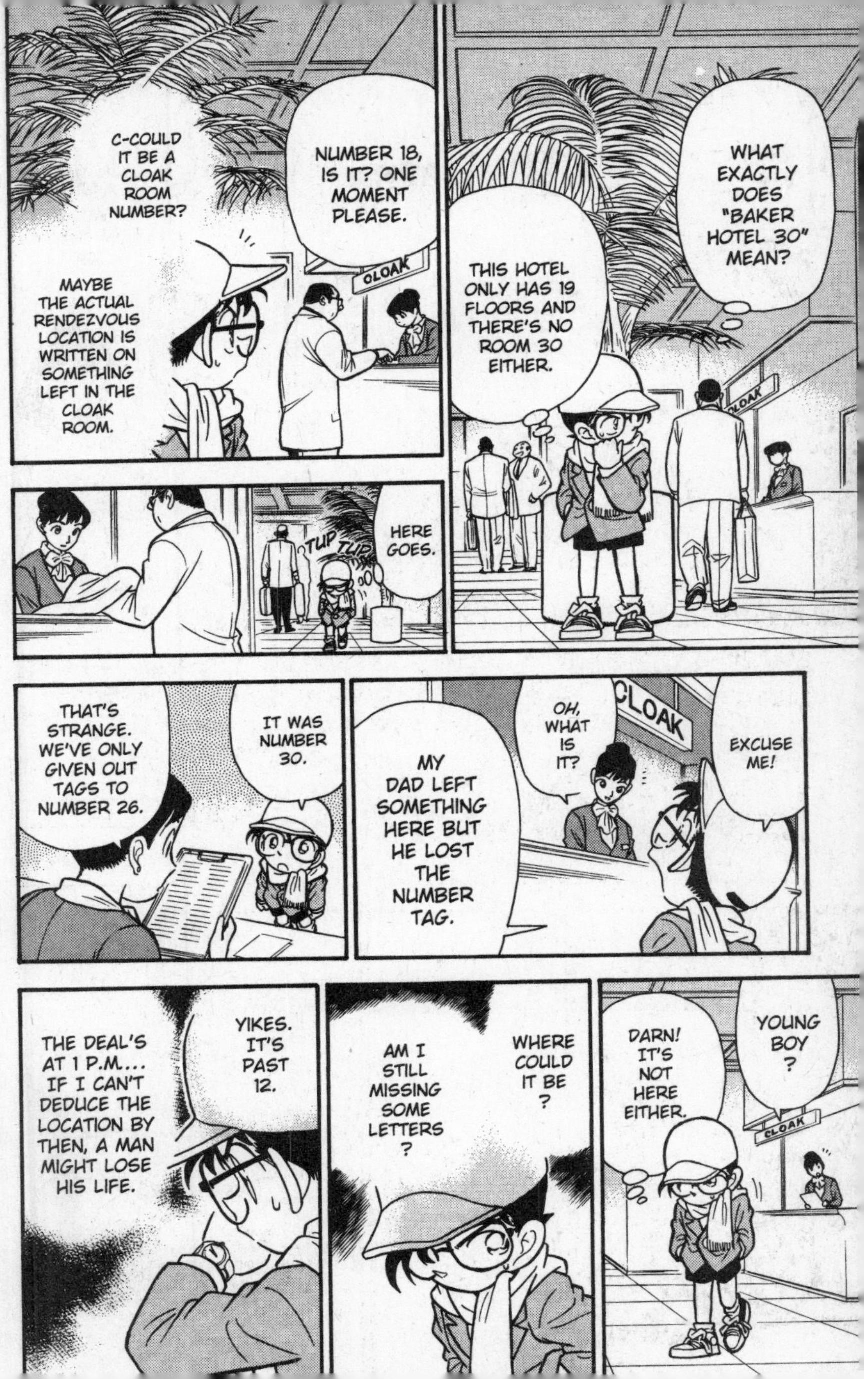
WHAT EXACTLY DOES "BAKER HOTEL 30" MEAN?
THIS HOTEL ONLY HAS 19 FLOORS AND THERE'S NO ROOM 30 EITHER.
CLOAK
CLOAK
NUMBER 18, IS IT? ONE MOMENT PLEASE.
C-COULD IT BE A CLOAK ROOM NUMBER?
MAYBE THE ACTUAL RENDEZVOUS LOCATION IS WRITTEN ON SOMETHING LEFT IN THE CLOAK ROOM.
HERE GOES.
TUP TUP
EXCUSE ME!
CLOAK
OH, WHAT IS IT?
MY DAD LEFT SOMETHING HERE BUT HE LOST THE NUMBER TAG.
IT WAS NUMBER 30.
THAT'S STRANGE. WE'VE ONLY GIVEN OUT TAGS TO NUMBER 26.
YOUNG BOY?
CLOAK
DARN! IT'S NOT HERE EITHER.
WHERE COULD IT BE?
AM I STILL MISSING SOME LETTERS?
YIKES. IT'S PAST 12.
THE DEAL'S AT 1 P.M.... IF I CAN'T DEDUCE THE LOCATION BY THEN, A MAN MIGHT LOSE HIS LIFE.

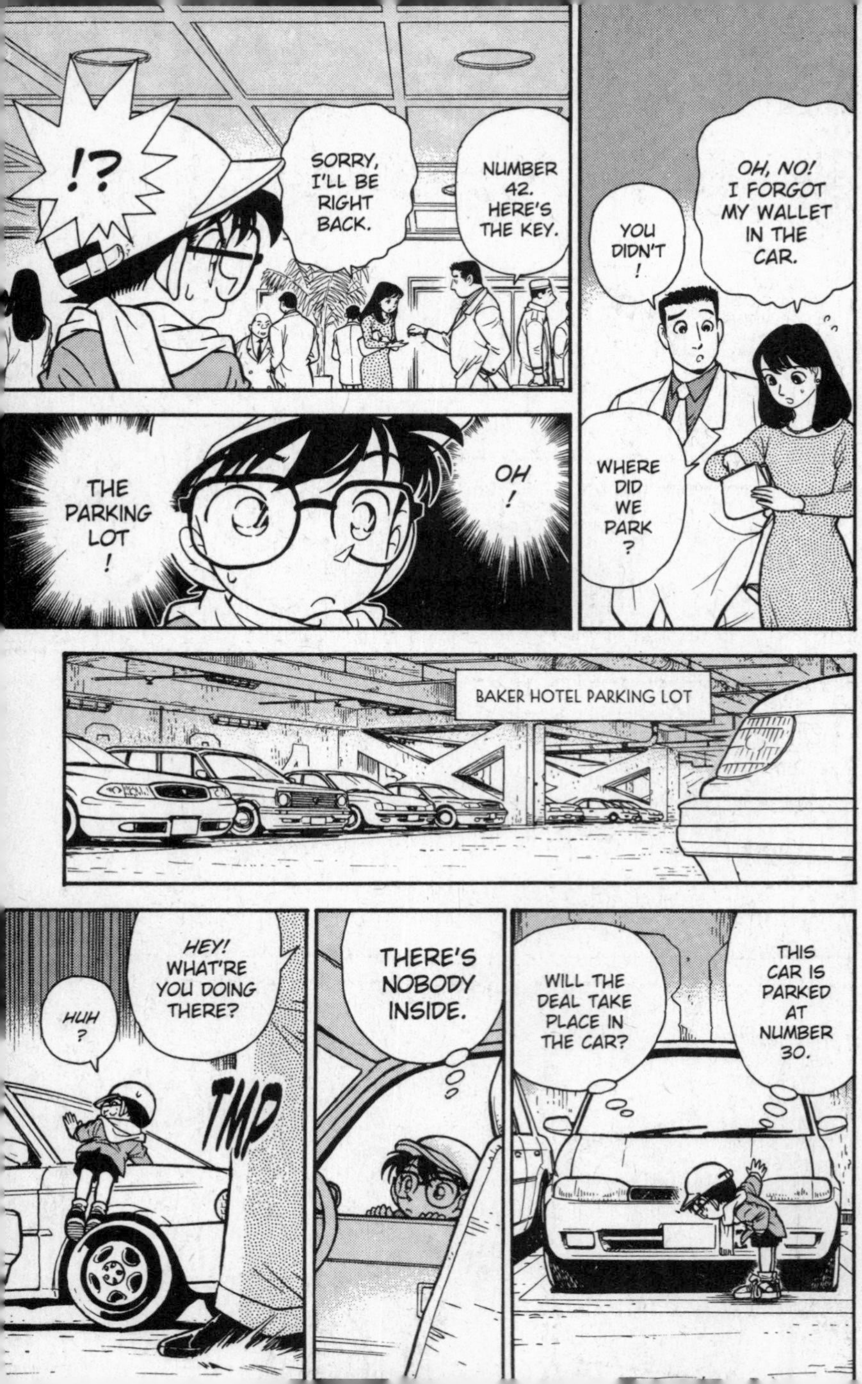

OH, NO! I FORGOT MY WALLET IN THE CAR.
YOU DIDN'T!
WHERE DID WE PARK?
NUMBER 42. HERE'S THE KEY.
SORRY, I'LL BE RIGHT BACK.
!?
OH!
THE PARKING LOT!
BAKER HOTEL PARKING LOT
THIS CAR IS PARKED AT NUMBER 30.
WILL THE DEAL TAKE PLACE IN THE CAR?
THERE'S NOBODY INSIDE.
HEY! WHAT'RE YOU DOING THERE?
TMP
HUH?

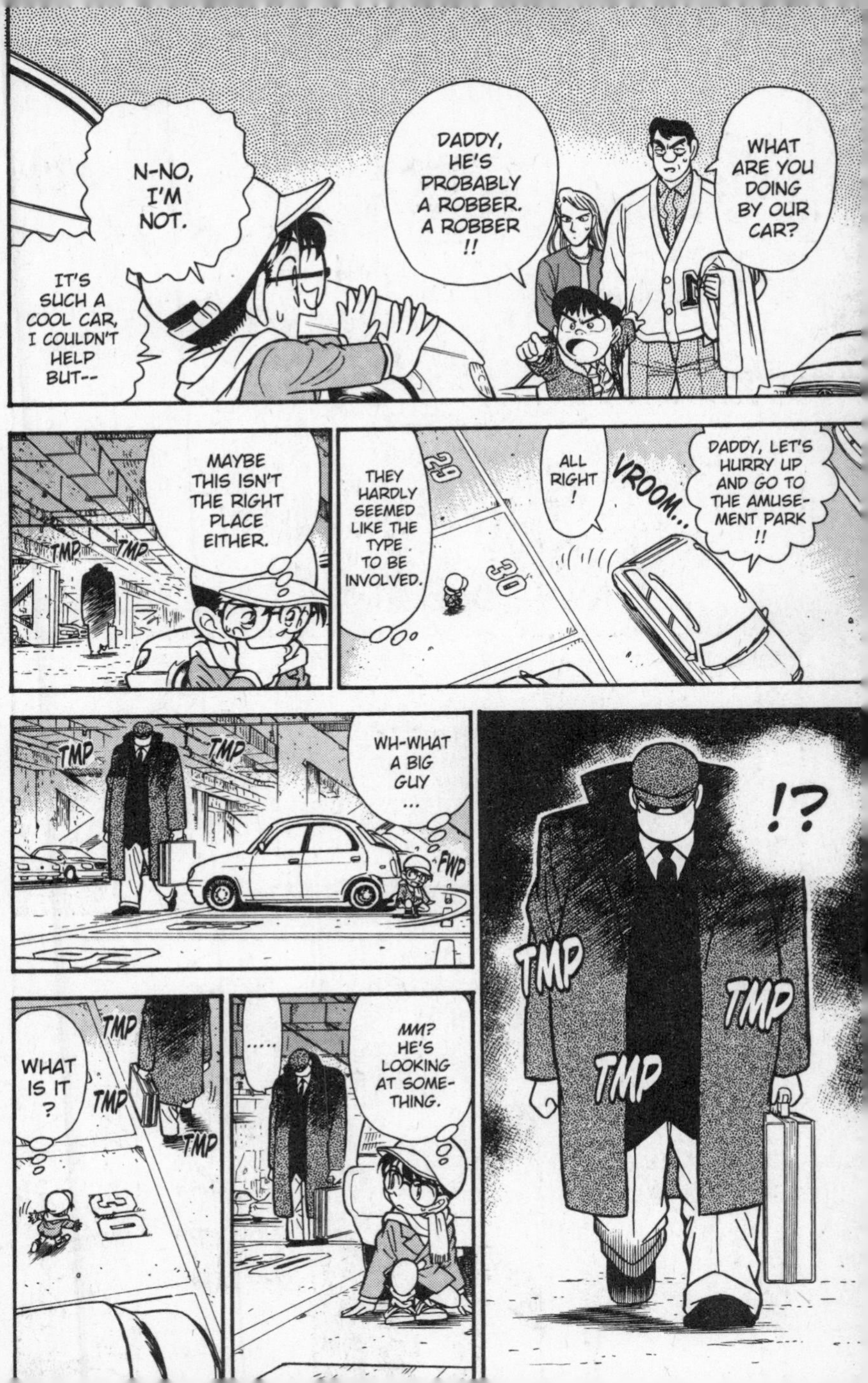
WHAT ARE YOU DOING BY OUR CAR?
DADDY, HE'S PROBABLY A ROBBER. A ROBBER !!
N-NO, I'M NOT.
IT'S SUCH A COOL CAR, I COULDN'T HELP BUT--
DADDY, LET'S HURRY UP AND GO TO THE AMUSE-MENT PARK !!
VROOM...
ALL RIGHT !
THEY HARDLY SEEMED LIKE THE TYPE TO BE INVOLVED.
MAYBE THIS ISN'T THE RIGHT PLACE EITHER.
TMP TMP
!?
TMP
TMP
TMP
TMP TMP
WH-WHAT A BIG GUY ...
FWP
MM? HE'S LOOKING AT SOME-THING.
.....
TMP
TMP
TMP
WHAT IS IT ?

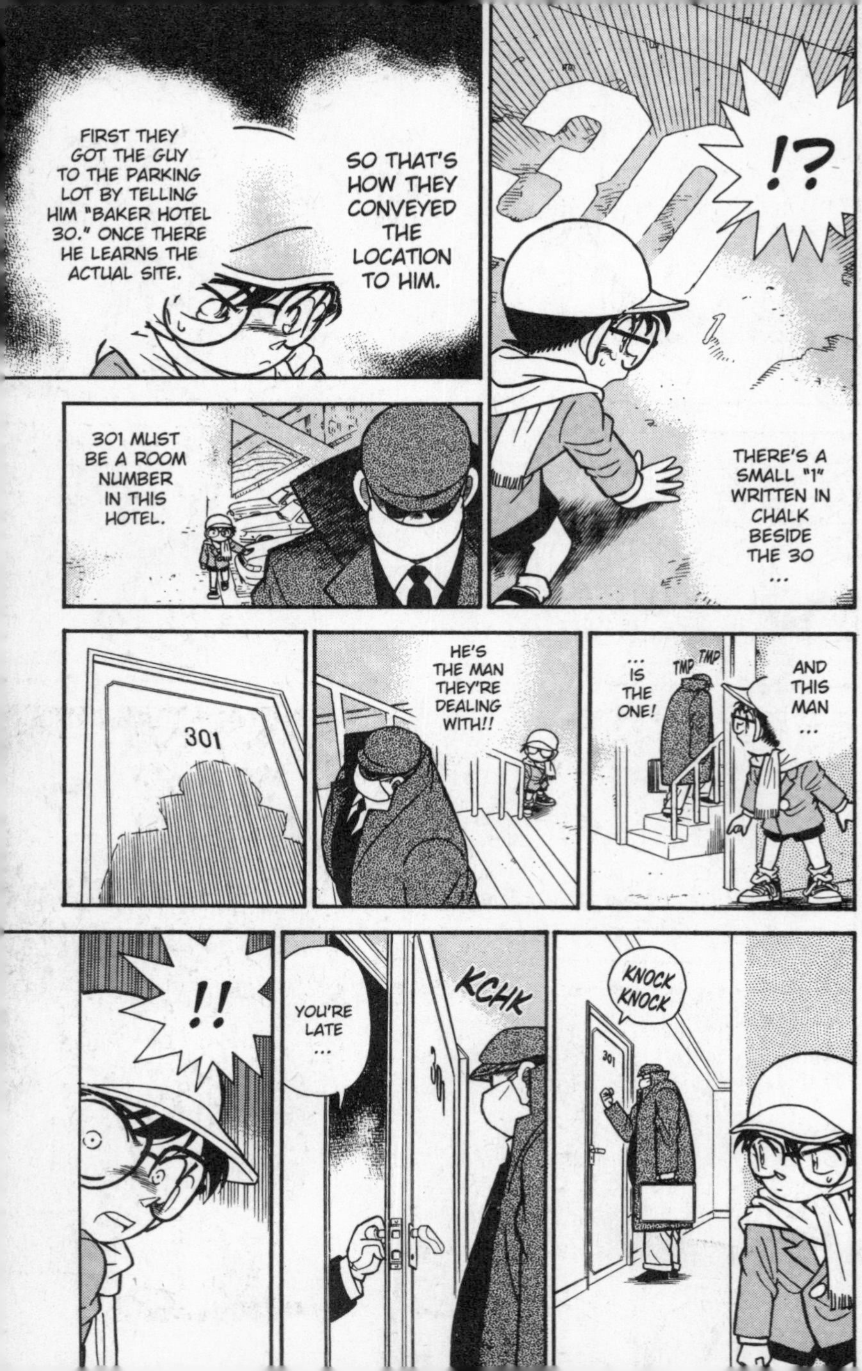

!?
THERE'S A SMALL "1" WRITTEN IN CHALK BESIDE THE 30 ...
SO THAT'S HOW THEY CONVEYED THE LOCATION TO HIM.
FIRST THEY GOT THE GUY TO THE PARKING LOT BY TELLING HIM "BAKER HOTEL 30." ONCE THERE HE LEARNS THE ACTUAL SITE.
301 MUST BE A ROOM NUMBER IN THIS HOTEL.
AND THIS MAN ...
TMP TMP
... IS THE ONE!
HE'S THE MAN THEY'RE DEALING WITH!!
301
KNOCK KNOCK
301
KCHK
YOU'RE LATE ...
!!

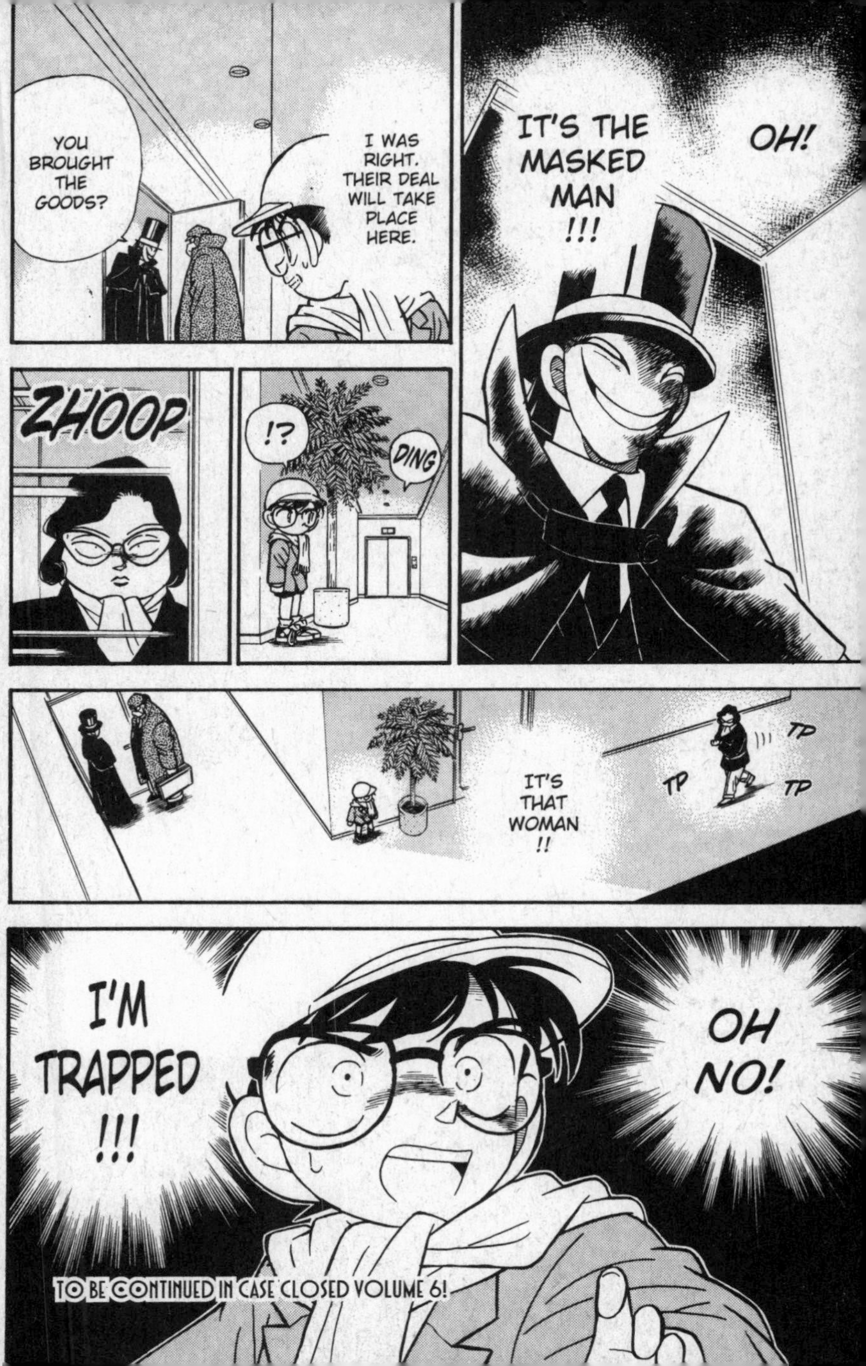
OH!
IT'S THE MASKED MAN !!!
I WAS RIGHT. THEIR DEAL WILL TAKE PLACE HERE.
YOU BROUGHT THE GOODS?
DING
!?
ZHOOP
TP
TP
TP
IT'S THAT WOMAN !!
OH NO!
I'M TRAPPED !!!
TO BE CONTINUED IN CASE CLOSED VOLUME 6!

Hello, Aoyama here.

I'm so busy I don't have time to go watch movies. There aren't any video rental stores nearby so I've no choice but to buy videos. But I don't have time to watch those either so I've got piles of movies I haven't watched. I might as well open up a video store soon. Sob sob!

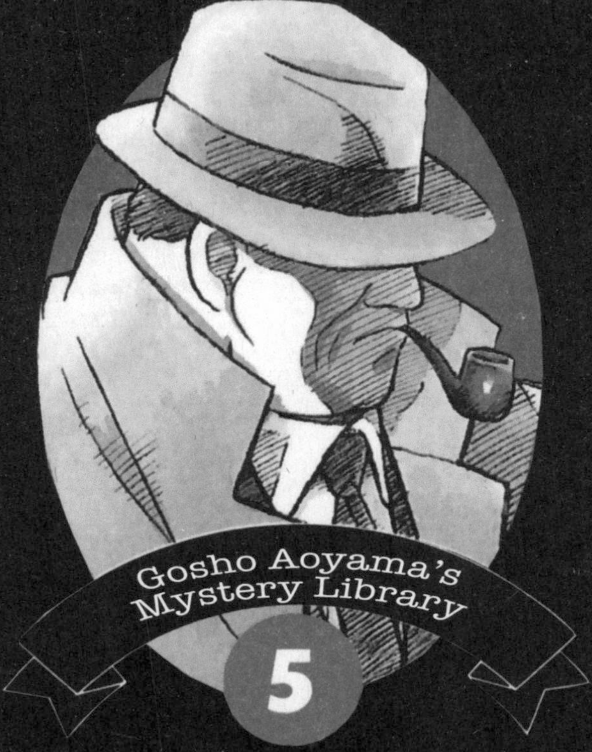
Gosho Aoyama's
Mystery Library
5

JULES MAIGRET

French author Georges Simenon's creation Jules Maigret is the finest devil cop of Paris!! In French, "maigre" means "skinny," but at 180 cm in height and 100 kg, Jules Maigret is a giant. An avid pipe smoker, just about the only time he's not puffing on a pipe is when he's asleep. But when he starts biting away at an unlit pipe, it's a sure sign he is stuck on a case. His method of investigation is to walk around, collect evidence, and utilize his powers of deductive reasoning. Straddling a chair, Maigret will draw out confessions by relentlessly applying psychological pressure in a manner most worthy of his title as a devil cop! If Inspector Meguire had the brains of his namesake Jules Maigret, Conan wouldn't have to work so hard. I recommend **Maigret Sets a Trap**.

Editor's note: Inspector Meguire's name in the original Japanese version of **Case Closed** is Megure Keibu or Inspector Megure. The rendering in the Japanese syllabary for both Megure and Maigret is "me-gu-re."

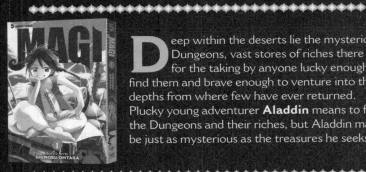

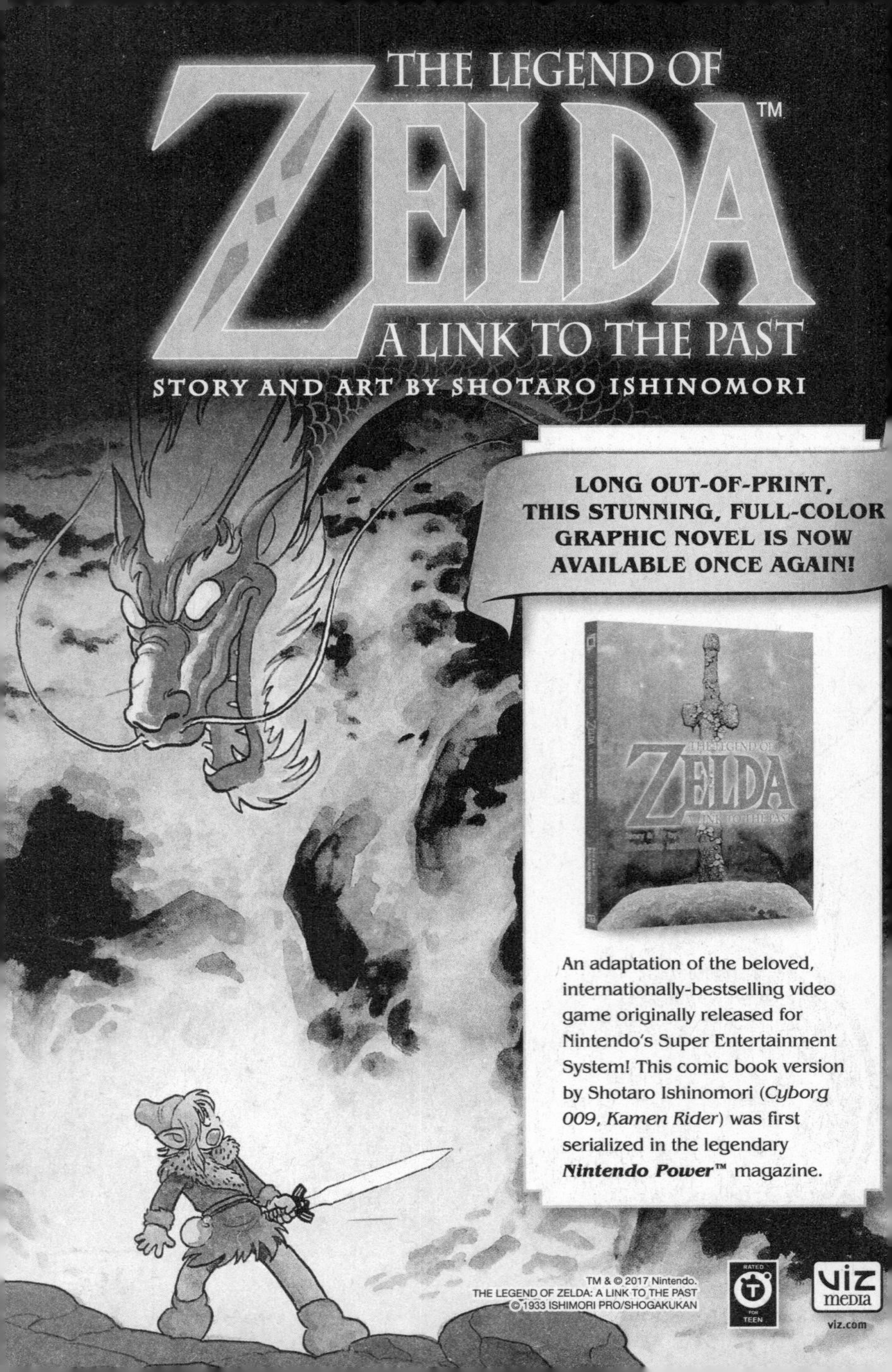

THE LEGEND OF
ZELDA™
A LINK TO THE PAST
STORY AND ART BY SHOTARO ISHINOMORI
LONG OUT-OF-PRINT, THIS STUNNING, FULL-COLOR GRAPHIC NOVEL IS NOW AVAILABLE ONCE AGAIN!
THE LEGEND OF ZELDA A LINK TO THE PAST
An adaptation of the beloved, internationally-bestselling video game originally released for Nintendo's Super Entertainment System! This comic book version by Shotaro Ishinomori (Cyborg 009, Kamen Rider) was first serialized in the legendary Nintendo Power™ magazine.
TM & © 2017 Nintendo.
THE LEGEND OF ZELDA: A LINK TO THE PAST
© 1933 ISHIMORI PRO/SHOGAKUKAN
RATED T FOR TEEN
VIZ MEDIA
viz.com

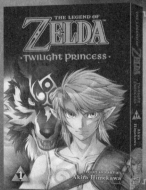

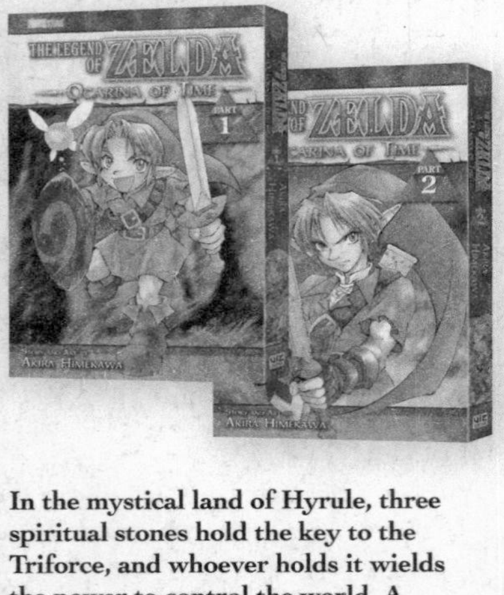
THE LEGEND OF ZELDA
OCARINA OF TIME
PART 1
AKIRA HIMEKAWA
THE LEGEND OF ZELDA
OCARINA OF TIME
PART 2
AKIRA HIMEKAWA

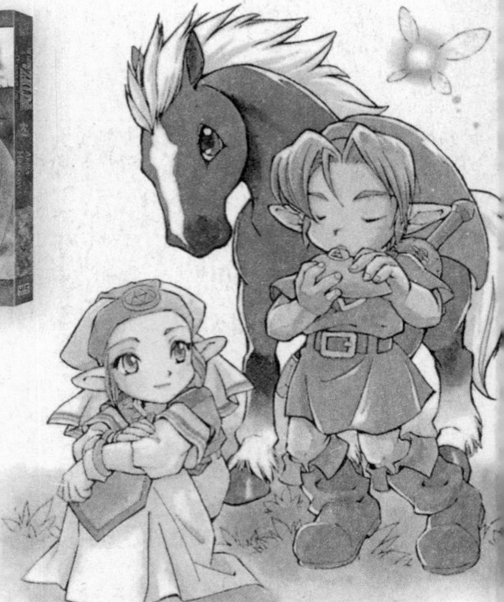

Hey! You're Reading in the Wrong Direction!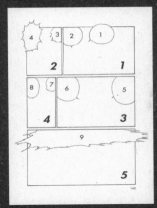

This is the **end** of this graphic novel!

To properly enjoy this VIZ graphic novel, please turn it around and begin reading from **right to left.** Unlike English, Japanese is read right to left, so Japanese comics are read in reverse order from the way English comics are typically read.

Follow the action this way

This book has been printed in the original Japanese format in order to preserve the orientation of the original artwork. Have fun with it!